PRA

Ours Was the

T0277703

"It's a chronicle of almost a century of American economic life,
rich with historical details and resonant narratives. It also makes
a subtle but pointed argument about the present, offering a diagnosis of our current maladies and suggestions about the shape
solutions could take."
      —NICK ROMEO, *The Washington Post*

"Things have changed in America, as *New York Times* writer
David Leonhardt lays out in his important new book. . . . His
take, which I believe is correct, is that democratic capitalism (defined as 'a system in which the government recognizes its crucial
role in guiding the economy') has since the 1970s given way to a
laissez-faire free-for-all in which corporations and short-termism
rule."
      —RANA FOROOHAR, global business columnist, *Financial Times*

"David Leonhardt has chronicled our rampaging economic inequality for a couple decades now in *The New York Times*. His
sweeping history of the collapse of the American dream is an
important contribution to the literature on this topic because,
while some of the material will be familiar to people interested in
this subject, he offers a narrative frame that I found unique and
persuasive. 'Power, culture, and investment' are the three forces
that have warped our priorities, and the three battles we need to
win to reshape them."
      —MICHAEL TOMASKY, editor, Democracy Journal for
      The New Republic

"The economic decline and political migration of the American working class receive the most compelling treatment in *Ours Was the Shining Future: The Story of the American Dream*, by the *New York Times* writer David Leonhardt. . . . Leonhardt has a gift for synthesizing complex trends and data in straightforward language and persuasive arguments whose rationality doesn't fully mute an undertone of indignation. He appreciates the power of stories and weaves obscure but telling events and people into his larger narrative."

—GEORGE PACKER, *The Atlantic*

"An accessible, ultimately bullish profile of the American economy."

—*Chicago Tribune* (top pick for Fall 2023)

"It's a powerful case, and there are good reasons that parts of both right and left, in Trumpism and Bidenomics, have reached for some version of its post-neoliberal vision."

—ROSS DOUTHAT, *The New York Times*

"This insightful, comprehensive, human book provides a perfect jumping-off point to examine the long, imperfect story of our ongoing project as Americans, striving to realize the promises of democracy and capitalism—and all the successes and failures along the way so far."

—KATIE COURIC, "Next Question with Katie Couric"

"A stunning accomplishment . . . It's a luminous narrative of the economic and political history of the modern United States. It's dazzling in its insights into the deeper forces that have shaped the country."

—GEOFFREY KABASERVICE, vice president of political studies, Niskanen Center

"Wonderful . . . I highly recommend it."

—DAVID RUBENSTEIN, co-chairman, the Carlyle Group

Ours Was the Shining Future

THE STORY OF THE AMERICAN DREAM

David Leonhardt

RANDOM HOUSE | NEW YORK

2024 Random House Trade Paperback Edition

Copyright © 2023 by David Leonhardt

Published in the United States by Random House, an imprint and division of
Penguin Random House LLC, New York.

RANDOM HOUSE and the HOUSE colophon are registered trademarks
of Penguin Random House LLC.

Originally published in hardcover in the United States by Random House,
an imprint and division of Penguin Random House LLC, in 2023.

LIBRARY OF CONGRESS CATALOGING-IN-PUBLICATION DATA
Names: Leonhardt, David, author.
Title: Ours was the shining future: the story of the American dream /
David Leonhardt.
Description: New York: Random House, [2023] |
Includes bibliographical references and index.
Identifiers: LCCN 2023008662 (print) | LCCN 2023008663 (ebook) |
ISBN 9780812983333 (paperback) | ISBN 9780679644859 (ebook)
Subjects: LCSH: American Dream. | United States—Economic conditions—
20th century. | United States—Economic conditions—21st century. |
United States—Social conditions—20th century. | United States—
Social conditions—21st century.
Classification: LCC HC103 .L36 2023 (print) | LCC HC103 (ebook) |
DDC 330.973—dc23/eng/20230316
LC record available at https://lccn.loc.gov/2023008662
LC ebook record available at https://lccn.loc.gov/2023008663

Printed in the United States of America on acid-free paper

randomhousebooks.com

2   4   6   8   9   7   5   3   1

For Laura

Alike in mind and together,
Nothing stronger or better than that.

CONTENTS

MY FAMILY'S STORY IS A PARTICULAR ONE, BUT IT IS ALSO A story that millions of families tell about their past. It is a story of progress—the story of the American dream.

My great-grandfather Robert Leonhardt was the first member of the family to try to build a life in this country, and he mostly failed. An Austrian opera singer in the early twentieth century, he had struggled to find work in Europe because he was Jewish. He eventually moved to the United States, while his wife and two children stayed behind in Europe, and he landed a job as a baritone with the Metropolitan Opera. But it did not last long. When World War I began, Americans grew paranoid about the presence of German spies. The Met branded Robert and the nineteen other Austrian and German citizens who worked at the opera as "enemy aliens" and fired them. Not long afterward, Robert became ill and died in New York, alone, at age forty.

His son, René, grew up fatherless in the chaos of interwar Germany, amid hyperinflation and a rising Nazi Party. In his twenties, René left Berlin to work as a photojournalist, moving first to London and then to Paris. He cobbled together enough assignments to earn a living and build a good life for himself in Paris. He made friends with an eclectic mix of locals and foreigners. He wore round-frame eyeglasses, spoke four languages, and—along with his dog, Pit—hung out with his friends at Le Berkeley, a café that was a couple of blocks off the Champs-Elysées.

Yet his new life would not last, either.

In the 1930s, France was growing hostile to immigrants. Many were streaming into the country to flee fascism elsewhere. As the threat of a new European war increased, French authorities became concerned that some of the immigrants inside their country might be part of a fifth-column menace, working as German spies. It was a somewhat strange worry, given how many of the immigrants were Jews or political leftists trying to escape the Nazis, but nationalist hysteria often has irrational qualities. Soon immigrants in France felt like "the hated target of an angry people," one German poet living there wrote. René felt so anxious during this period that a Turkish friend of his said that he looked yellow. He was thirty-one years old.

When the war began, in September 1939, the French government announced that all German and Austrian citizens were to be considered "enemy aliens," a grim echo of Robert's experience in New York two decades earlier. France froze the bank accounts of enemy aliens and ordered men between the ages of seventeen and fifty to report to detention sites across the country. In and around Paris, there were so many detainees that the government used two large sports stadiums to hold them: Stade Olympique Yves-du-Manoir, which had hosted soccer's World Cup the previous year, and Stade Roland-Garros, home to the annual tennis tournament later known as the French Open. René and the other men were told to bring blankets, underwear, eating utensils, and two days' worth of food. It quickly became clear that the detentions would last much longer.

Popular memory of World War II has largely forgotten these camps, partly because their horrors paled in comparison to those run by the Nazis. But the French camps were nasty places where men slept in the open air on cold nights and used large pails to go to the bathroom. The writer Arthur Koestler, who was one of the prisoners, described the conditions as torture through deprivation. As word of the conditions spread, critics inside and outside France pleaded with the government to release the men. Not only were the camps dehumanizing and unjust, the critics said, but they also undercut the liberal image that France was trying to project as its soldiers streamed east to defend the country against Germany. "France is supposed to be fighting this war for democracy," *The New Republic* wrote. "Some people in America would be more willing to accept this point of view if it were not for the shocking treatment the French are now giving to foreign Jews." Jewish relief organizations criticized the camps, as did socialist members of the French Parliament.

In response, the French government began releasing some prisoners in November and December. Among them were men who had visas to leave the country and therefore could not spy on France. René was fortunate to be in this category. In the spring of 1939, with anti-immigrant sentiment rising, he had obtained a visa in Paris to travel to the United States. With that visa, he bought a ticket on the SS *De Grasse* to New York. After a two-week transatlantic journey, the *De Grasse* arrived on February 26, 1940, at Ellis Island.

There, American authorities detained René for three nights, questioning him because his visa gave him permission to be in the country only temporarily. He persuaded them to release him on a $500 bond, with a promise that he would report back by April 18, seven weeks later. He probably obtained at least one visa extension after that, according to immigration experts who have reviewed his records, but his situation was precarious. Whatever the case, he soon met a woman from Brooklyn named Esther Messing. She worked as a secretary at a newspaper and had refused to get married at the age that most of her peers did. She would marry when she chose. In the spring of 1940, René and Esther began an intense romance. Less than three months after his arrival in New York, they got engaged on her thirty-fifth birthday, over lunch at Sardi's, a Times Square restaurant popular among journalists and people in the theater business. The two were married a few weeks later, on June 3, in Warrenton, Virginia, which was known at the time as a marriage mill because the city granted marriage licenses without a waiting period.

René had escaped Europe's war. He had found a more secure place in New York than his father ever had. And although he and Esther could not have realized it, they were creating a family in a society—the United States in 1940—with one of the brightest futures that the world has ever known.

. . .

THE EARLY TWENTY-FIRST century is a cynical time, when the phrase "American dream" is often used ironically or bitterly. People speak of the death of that dream, and politicians run for office promising to restore rather than protect it. The more earnest uses of the phrase today tend to apply to the past and to the uplifting stories that many Americans tell about their family trajectories. They talk gratefully about the material comforts and the opportunities they enjoy that their ancestors could hardly have fathomed. They speak of how proud those ancestors would be to see that their hard work and sacrifice paid off. That hard work eventually made possible the family's first home purchase, the first college graduate or the first doctor. These stories are not only about individual families, either. They are also stories of tribal pride—be it Jewish, Italian, Irish, Mexican, Filipino, Chinese, or Black—that make people feel part of something larger. Ultimately, these narratives of success are miniature versions of the American story.

As best as anyone can tell, people began to use the phrase "American dream" during the Great Depression, thanks to a historian named James Truslow Adams. Adams came from a well-off family and grew up in Brooklyn and Paris during the Gilded Age of the 1880s. He made enough money on Wall Street as a young man to turn to writing full-time. His first book, a history of colonial New England, was published in 1921 and won the Pulitzer Prize. His bestselling book came out a decade later, when the Depression had set in. The book was a short, thematic history of the United States called *The Epic of America*. In the preface, Adams announced that one of his main themes would be

> that American dream of a better, richer, and happier life for all our citizens of every rank which is the greatest contribution we have as yet made to the thought and welfare of the world. That dream or hope has been present from the start. Ever since we became an independent nation, each generation has seen an uprising of the ordinary Americans to save that dream from the forces which appeared to be overwhelming and dispelling it. Possibly the greatest of these struggles lies just ahead of us at this present time—not a struggle of revolutionists against established order,

but of the ordinary man to hold fast to those rights to "life, liberty, and the pursuit of happiness" which were vouchsafed to us in the past in vision and on parchment.

The crux of Adams's American dream was the ability of people to rise above the circumstances of their birth. He did not mean only in terms of material comforts but emphasized that those comforts were a big part of it. Money matters, as anybody who has ever lacked it knows. It can buy food, shelter, transportation, medical care, education, and time to spend with family and friends.

In the decades since Adams's book appeared, the phrase "American dream" has come to have many meanings, some connected to immigration, others to home ownership. Two Broadway plays, one in the 1930s and the other in the 1960s, used the phrase as their titles, helping popularize it. Politicians of both parties promise to defend the dream, and perhaps the most famous protest speech in American history was organized around the concept. "I still have a dream," Martin Luther King, Jr., said at the March on Washington. "It is a dream deeply rooted in the American dream." The idea has proved so alluring that Xi Jinping, the president of a country that seeks to supplant the United States as the world's most powerful in the twenty-first century, has played off of it. Shortly after taking over the Chinese Communist Party in 2012, he began talking about a Chinese dream of common prosperity.

Throughout the decades, Adams's fundamental idea—living a "better, richer, and happier" life than the one into which a person was born—has endured. *Better, richer, and happier:* Progress is embedded in the original definition of the American dream.

Adams was careful to acknowledge the threats to his dream. He wrote about the economic depression the country was experiencing and predicted great struggles ahead. But he ended the book on an uplifting note, quoting another author from the time, an immigrant named Mary Antin. She recalled her feelings as she sat on the steps of the Boston Public Library as a young woman. The library had helped transform her from a Russian girl who had arrived in the United States speaking no English into a writer who published her first book as a teenager. The final words of Adams's book are Antin's: "Mine is the shining future."

It was an audaciously optimistic way to end a book in 1931. It also turned out to be prophetic. In the years to come, the country's motto might as well have been "Ours is the shining future."

Indeed, progress has been the lingua franca of American culture for most of our nation's history. It is a theme that runs through the words of Benjamin Franklin, Thomas Jefferson, Abraham Lincoln, Franklin Roosevelt, Ronald Reagan, and Barack Obama, among many others. In the 1600s, the English philosopher John Locke described "life, liberty, and property" as inalienable rights. Jefferson, when drafting the Declaration of Independence a century later, edited the phrase by dropping property from the list and substituting an idea closely related to progress: "the pursuit of happiness." Progress is embedded in Lincoln's talk of "a new birth of freedom" during the Gettysburg Address and in Reagan's favorite metaphor of a shining city upon a hill. Michelle Obama captured the idea particularly well in a nationally televised speech during her husband's presidency, talking at once about her family, her tribe, and her nation: "That is the story of this country, the story that has brought me to this stage tonight, the story of generations of people who felt the lash of bondage, the shame of servitude, the sting of segregation, but who kept on striving and hoping and doing what needed to be done so that today, I wake up every morning in a house that was built by slaves."

When progress is the norm, it feeds on itself. People are proud of the progress that they and their tribe have made. They have faith in their country and the institutions that surround them—schools, companies, neighborhoods, churches, synagogues, mosques, labor unions, and government agencies. People can trust that their own sacrifices will pay off, not every time but often enough. They can endure hard times without becoming cynical and can be generous toward others. They can look to the future with a can-do optimism. If my family members and I are ever tempted to feel frustrated about any aspect of our lives, we can remind ourselves how much better off we are than Robert or René.

Such optimism has long been a distinctly American trait. International surveys, at least until recently, showed Americans to be more hopeful about the future, with a stronger belief in their ability to influence it, than people elsewhere. No wonder: This nation was born by casting off the world's most powerful empire and later defeated fascism and communism. The United States sent a man to the moon and created the internet, as well as history's largest, most prosperous middle class. Optimism was rational.

Progress begot progress.

Until it didn't.

IF YOU ARE one of the many Americans who, like me, can look back on your family's history with gratitude, I want to ask you to spend a minute considering a different scenario. In it, your family has known scant progress for decades. You are not much richer than your grandparents, and your grandparents were not rich. You are no healthier than your parents, and your kids are less healthy than you. You cannot tell stories of upward mobility, because they would not be true. Instead, you are frustrated about decades of hard work gone unrewarded, and you are anxious, for your future and your children's.

For tens of millions of Americans, this frustration is not a thought experiment. It is their daily life. For almost half a century now, incomes and wealth have grown at a sluggish pace for most Americans, even as they have surged for the wealthy. Measures of public health have also stagnated, and the problems seem to have worsened in the past decade. Consider that average life expectancy in the United States stopped growing about a decade ago, well before the Covid-19 pandemic began, and then declined during it. In very few other countries did life expectancy stop rising before the pandemic. Life expectancy is not supposed to stagnate in an advanced society, absent a crisis like a war or plague. All in all, the United States is suffering through its worst period of stagnation in living standards since the Great Depression. I refer to it as the Great American Stagnation.

To be clear, we have not been living through a depression. The overall quality of life in the United States remains much better than

Life expectancy at birth

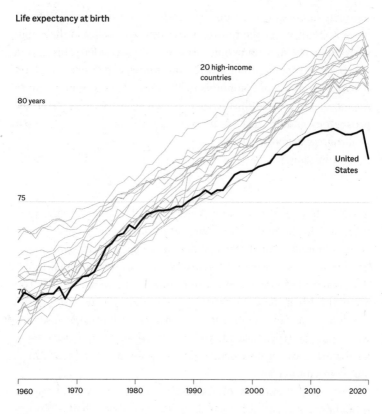

20 high-income
countries

80 years

75

70

United
States

1960   1970   1980   1990   2000   2010   2020

it was throughout most of the country's history. Americans live in larger homes than previous generations did, filled with time-saving appliances. When we leave our homes, we drive safer cars and breathe cleaner air. Living standards here are vastly higher than in much of the world. But this country's identity does not depend on having merely a good standard of living or a better one than many decades ago. It depends on progress in our time.

HOW CAN WE measure the American dream? Many people have a general sense that our economy once delivered more rapid progress than it has in recent decades. I have spent most of my career chronicling this stagnation. Like my grandmother Esther and grandfather René, I have worked in the newspaper business, in the same neighborhood where they worked: Times Square. Since 1999, I have been a reporter and editor at *The New York Times,* and I have spent much of that time writing about the American economy. I have traveled around the country interviewing workers, business executives, politicians, and unemployed people. I have done reporting in cities, suburbs, and rural areas, in factories, warehouses, schools, hospitals, and a prison. I have spent many hours talking with experts, reading academic studies, and digging through statistics.

While doing so, I often felt disappointed about a particular problem with the economic data: It did a poor job of describing the paths that people's lives followed over time. As a result, the data could not tell us how many people achieved a core part of the American dream—enjoying higher living standards than their parents did.

I realize that some readers may be surprised to hear this data did not exist, given the vast amount of economic information available on unemployment, income, wealth, and much more. But the best-known statistics share a major limitation in that each tends to be a snapshot of a single moment: How many people were out of work last month? How much money did people earn? These economic indicators generally come from surveys that do not track individuals from year to year. The surveys instead gather information on one group of people this year and a different group the next, which means that they cannot say much about the course that individual lives take. The surveys cannot shed light on the chances that a poor child will grow up to escape poverty or that an immigrant will build a good life. They cannot distinguish between a society in which the rich stay rich while the poor stay poor and one in which large numbers of middle-class and lower-income people climb the economic ladder. The surveys cannot tell us how well the United States is living up to its ideals as a society with opportunity for all.

To understand those issues, researchers need something known as a longitudinal survey, which does follow the same people over time. Longitudinal surveys can tell a story. If you have ever watched the *Up* series of documentaries from Britain, you know what I

mean. The first *Up* film, *Seven Up!,* was released in 1964, and it
profiled a group of seven-year-olds from different economic classes
around England. Every seven years, the filmmakers returned to see
how the subjects' lives had changed. The latest installment, *63 Up,*
came out in 2019. The series is not social science, but it is enlight-
ening. By following people over their lives, it helps viewers understand economic opportunity and mobility, as well as the barriers
to advancement.

Until recently, the few American surveys that tracked specific
people tended to be small. They started off decades ago with only
a couple of thousand families, some of whom later dropped out.
And the ones who dropped out were not a random selection. They
were often those who led troubled lives, frequently moving from
one home to another. As a result, the remaining respondents offered an artificially sunny version of reality. Academic researchers
still relied on these surveys because nothing better was available,
and the researchers tried to adjust their numbers to take into account the survey dropouts. But the smallness of the data sets was a
problem. Different researchers could come to different conclusions
analyzing the same data.

In 2009, though, a few officials in Washington realized something important: The federal government already had the data that
academic researchers needed to conduct a longitudinal study. It
was tax data, containing families' work and income history, year
after year. At the time, Barack Obama had recently become president and had promised to use the federal government to improve
people's lives. He wanted to do so not only in grand ways, like
universal healthcare, but also in smaller, less political ways. He
wanted to make government more user-friendly. The term that
Obama used to describe this idea to me in an interview at the time
sounds dated now, but it captured the goal: "iPod government."
He believed that Washington should take common-sense steps to
help policy makers and citizens understand how the economy
functioned and, by extension, how they could improve it.

As part of Obama's push, the Internal Revenue Service announced that it would release decades of tax data, with all identifying personal information removed, to a small number of

researchers. Although the records were anonymous, researchers would be able to link an individual's data from one year to the next. The tax data could be turned into a gigantic longitudinal survey, with tens of millions of respondents. It would be more accurate than most surveys because it did not rely on faulty human memory to record how much money somebody made the prior year. The tax database offered the kind of breakthrough that is rare in the social sciences, even if most academic researchers did not yet realize it.

ONE RESEARCHER WHO did see the data's potential was a twenty-nine-year-old economist at Harvard University named Raj Chetty. He and a few colleagues applied for access to the data, and they were one of four research teams that the federal government selected. Building on research techniques developed by social scientists who analyzed the smaller longitudinal studies of earlier years, Chetty and his colleagues have used the tax data to publish papers about the odds of escaping poverty in every neighborhood across the country and the unique inequities faced by Black men, among other subjects. The research helped Chetty win the John Bates Clark Medal, nicknamed the Baby Nobel, which goes to the nation's top research economist under forty. Chetty was thirty-three when he won it.

After writing about his work in the *Times* and getting to know him, I told Chetty that I thought he and his colleagues had a chance to do something that no researchers had done before: They could use the IRS data to figure out what percentage of Americans made more money than their parents had and how the percentage had changed over time. That comparison—enjoying better material living standards than one's parents—is the most basic definition of the American dream. Chetty and his colleagues could create an index of it.

He seemed intrigued, but he also explained that the task was harder than I thought. It would require decades of data, and the IRS data went back only to the early 1990s—not nearly far enough to make historical comparisons across generations. Still, Chetty said he and his colleagues would see what they could do. After several weeks of work on the idea, they emailed me to say that they had solved the methodological issues. They had found census data, going back decades, that could be matched with later IRS data. They could use the census data to estimate the income of a household in which a child grew up and compare it with that child's household income as an adult. To make the comparisons meaningful, they would adjust for inflation and compare children with their parents at the same adult age.

The data started with people born in 1940—the same year, by coincidence, that René arrived in the United States and that he and Esther married. It was also a year when many Americans were deeply worried about both the possibility of war and their economic futures. From today's vantage point, it can be difficult to grasp how much economic anxiety existed in the 1940s. When the decade began, the unemployment rate was 15 percent, a level it has not reached since. War mobilization would soon return the economy to health, but many Americans worried that the eventual demobilization—and the return of job-seeking soldiers after the war—would send the economy back into a slump. At that point, the country had not enjoyed both peace and prosperity in more than a decade. Even the Roaring Twenties came with an asterisk; they had been a lot better for the affluent than for most people. To many Americans, war alone seemed able to create a truly vibrant economy.

In retrospect, we know what happened after World War II. The American economy experienced a remarkable boom. Chetty had expected to find that most children born in 1940 grew up to have higher household incomes than their parents, but he hadn't expected how many did: 92 percent.

Achieving the American dream was a virtual guarantee for this generation. It was true whether they graduated from college or never enrolled. It was true in every region and for Americans of every race. Even most people who had to overcome a hardship, like a divorce, an illness, or a layoff, earned more money than their parents had. As for the relatively few 1940 babies who ended up earning less, many still did just fine. Some were earning less than their parents because they had grown up affluent; think of a child of a corporate executive who became a teacher or an artist.

This pattern did not mean that life in America was free from trouble or injustice. Racism remained horrific during these postwar decades. Government programs, like subsidized housing for veterans, deliberately excluded Black Americans. Violence against Black and Latino Americans, and against women, was common and often went unpunished. Most women had few professional opportunities, while gay and lesbian Americans faced daily oppression. Other forms of discrimination—including religious bigotry and discrimination against people with disabilities—were also prevalent.

Moreover, daily life in postwar America was filled with tragedies that have become less common over time. Even with the declines in life expectancy over the past decade, people live longer now than in the past. Heart disease treatments are much more effective. Cancers that once were death sentences, including some that afflict children, are now frequently cured.

My own family endured one of the tragedies that today probably could have been prevented. In 1950, a decade after arriving in New York, René was running a small photography studio in Times Square, and he and Esther were raising a six-year-old boy, Robert, named in honor of the father René had hardly known. That summer, René began having stomach problems, and his health deteriorated quickly. He died, evidently of cancer, on August 28, at the age of forty-two. Like René, my dad—Robert—grew up hardly knowing his father. Esther, tough as ever, took over the photography studio, called Camera Clix. "At first I was in a state of shock," she said in a *New York Times* feature about widows who were running their late husbands' businesses. "I was working mechanically—purely by instinct." Camera Clix thrived under Esther, and it allowed her and my father to enjoy a good middle-class life in New York during the long postwar economic boom. But René's death nonetheless cast a shadow over the rest of their lives. Modern medicine probably would have saved his life or at least extended it.

The greatest attribute of the postwar United States was not the quality of life but its rapid progress. The economy grew swiftly, and inequality declined, with incomes of poor and middle-class workers rising even faster than those of the rich. Well before the great victories of the civil rights movement, racial inequality began to decline, with wages of Black workers rising faster than those of White workers. Black life expectancy also rose faster than White life expectancy. Inequality and discrimination obviously did not come anywhere close to disappearing during these decades, but the declines in inequity were substantial. The large gains for less advantaged groups made possible the remarkable statistic that 92 percent of Americans who were born in 1940 grew up to earn more money than their parents.

For the generation known as the baby boomers (those born between 1946 and 1964), the chances of outearning their parents remained extremely high. About 80 percent of them would do so. Many of their parents had come of age during the Great Depression and World War II. The boomers, by contrast, would spend their working lives in a growing economy where the benefits were widely shared. Many of these boomers would also be able to buy homes before prices soared in the late twentieth century, and some would be able to buy stocks when the market was relatively cheap, between the late 1960s and early 1980s.

The situation for the next generation—my own, Generation X—would not be so good. Slightly more than 60 percent of us would make more early in our careers than our parents had. For millennials (generally considered to have been born between 1981 and 1996), the chances became worse yet. Babies born in 1980 were about as likely to earn less than their parents as to earn more. For them, as Chetty says, "achieving the American dream is a 50-50 proposition." There is not yet solid data on the youngest generation of adults today, known as Generation Z, but they are unlikely to fare much better. They have had to launch their working lives in the aftermath of the worst financial crisis in almost a century and the worst pandemic in a century.

Chetty and five colleagues eventually published their findings in the academic journal *Science,* and the data has received national attention. Politicians continue to cite the findings, as do journalists and other academics. The researchers had succeeded in producing a rigorous measure of the American dream. Though it is only one study, it is consistent with a large amount of other data, and all of it suggests that the United States entered a dark new economic era starting around the mid-1970s.

TWO BASIC PROBLEMS explain the phenomenon. First, the economy has grown more slowly than it did in the postwar decades, producing less bounty for the population to share. Second, the economy has become more unequal, with a declining share of that bounty available to most Americans because so much of it is flowing to a relatively small percentage of affluent households. The result is stagnation in nearly every reliable measure of well-being.

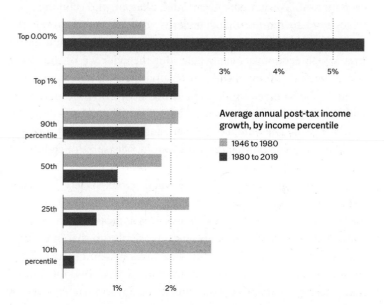

Average annual post-tax income growth, by income percentile
- 1946 to 1980
- 1980 to 2019

Household income—whether measured before tax or after, with government benefits or without—has grown only weakly for most economic groups over this period, even as incomes for the affluent have soared. The situation has been a bit brighter over the past several years, as a tight labor market has lifted wages for lower-income workers, but the overall picture is unchanged. In the twenty-first century, after-tax pay for the poor and middle class has grown more slowly than the economy. The toll has been especially harsh on Black Americans. The White-Black wage gap began widening in the 1980s and in recent years has been almost as large as it was when Harry Truman was president.

The trends in wealth are worse than the income trends. The standard measure of wealth is net worth, which adds up a household's home value, cash, stocks, and all other assets and then subtracts its mortgage, college loans, and other debts. A typical family in 2019 had a net worth slightly lower than the typical family in 2001. There has not been such a long period of wealth stagnation since the Great Depression.

As alarming as these numbers are, the noneconomic data is even more so. Money isn't everything, after all, and economic statistics tend to require many underlying assumptions (about the true rate of inflation, the changing size of households, and more) over which economists can argue. But the evidence of the Great American Stagnation extends far beyond the data on incomes and wealth. The number of children living with only one parent or with neither has doubled since the 1970s. The obesity rate has nearly tripled. The number of Americans who have spent time behind bars at some point has risen five-fold. Measures of childhood mental health have deteriorated.

If there is any question about whether our society has stagnated, the statistics on life and death answer it. In 1980, average life expectancy in the United States was typical for an affluent country. It was longer than in Germany, similar to that in Britain, and not much shorter than in Canada, Australia, and France. Then things began to change. For almost forty years now, the United States has been doing a worse job than any similar country of keeping its citizens healthy and alive. One reason is a phenomenon that the economists Anne Case and Angus Deaton have described as "deaths of despair"—those from drug overdoses, alcohol-related liver disease, and suicides. Progress against heart disease and strokes has also slowed, which is partly a reflection of rising obesity.

These trends have hit working-class Americans—defined as

those without a four-year college degree—much harder than white-collar professionals. Among Americans without a bachelor's degree, life expectancy began to decline in the early 2010s and then fell sharply during the Covid pandemic. By 2021, working-class adult life expectancy fell to its lowest level since at least the 1980s. For Americans with a bachelor's degree, the data looks much better. Their lifespans continued to rise before Covid and fell much less during the pandemic. As Covid recedes, life expectancy for both groups will surely rebound, but the larger problems will persist.

JUST AS THE progress of earlier eras created a virtuous cycle, the stagnation of our era is creating a vicious one. We Americans are losing our can-do attitude. We are losing some of our generosity toward fellow citizens and our willingness to sacrifice for future generations. We are growing angry and exasperated. We shout at one another on social media and consider people with different political views to be our enemies. At no point since 2005 have a majority of Americans said the country was on the right track, according to Gallup. Whether the economy is growing or shrinking, whether the president is a Democrat or Republican, most Americans believe that we have lost our way.

The Great American Stagnation is the problem that makes every other problem harder to solve. It makes us less willing to combat the gargantuan risks of climate change, though the costs of doing so are manageable, because so many people are anxious about their daily lives. The stagnation has fueled an alarming anti-democratic movement in this country, one that is disdainful of truth and unwilling to accept election defeat. This movement comprises a powerful segment of the Republican Party. The country's economic troubles are certainly not the only cause of it. Racial and religious fears about a country that is becoming more diverse and secular play an important role, as does the growth of a right-wing media ecosystem that peddles falsehoods. But the long stagnation in living standards feeds the anger that weakens democracy. After all, many of the Americans who have fared the worst in recent decades—members of the working class, often living outside of major metropolitan areas—are the ones who have drifted toward a radicalized, angry political agenda.

This book is for anybody trying to understand how our economy—and, with it, our society—has been hobbled. It is a biography of the American dream over the near century since Adams popularized the term. In telling this story, I will explain the creation of the most prosperous mass economy in recorded history during the decades after the Depression and the slow unraveling of that economy in the half century since the 1970s. Along the way, I will introduce you to people who helped cause both the rise and the fall of this economy. Some are familiar names—like Frances Perkins, Dwight Eisenhower, A. Philip Randolph, Betty Friedan, Cesar Chavez, and Robert Bork—but their full significance is not always so familiar. Other people you will meet in this book—like Carl Skoglund, Paul Hoffman, Grace Hopper, and Anne Gorsuch— are less well known. All of them played important roles in shaping the American economy, and all of them are symbolic of broader changes that have occurred over the past century among politicians, activists, business executives, and workers.

I have written this book partly because I have heard too many people say that they know the economy is a crucial subject but find it hard to understand. I think that confusion is unnecessary. The economy is not as complicated as it sometimes seems or as experts often make it appear. When you cannot understand what the experts or journalists are saying, it is usually our fault, not yours. We use too many technical terms and obscure statistics and offer too few clear, logical explanations. Yes, the economy is complex, and I will not shy away from nuance and numbers. You will find charts scattered throughout this book. But I also believe that the biggest forces guiding the economy are accessible to people who do not have any formal training in the subject.

My central argument is that capitalism remains the best system for delivering rising living standards to the greatest number of people—but only a certain type of capitalism. The evidence for both halves of that statement is voluminous. No economic system other than capitalism has demonstrated that it can produce sustained improvement in material comfort, health, knowledge, and incomes. The Soviet Union, the world's first grand experiment with Marxism, spent decades mired in poverty and finally collapsed, while the United States, Japan, and western Europe prospered. Communist North Korea remains impoverished, while capitalist South Korea has achieved affluence. China's communist economy descended into chaos in the 1960s and began its own rise only after the country introduced capitalism in the late 1970s. In the Western Hemisphere, life in communist Cuba is sufficiently unpleasant that the government restricts its citizens from leaving, knowing many would if they could, and conditions in socialist Venezuela have turned miserable.

Yet not all forms of capitalism are equally effective. Rough-and-tumble capitalism—in which taxes are low, corporations behave largely as they want, and a laissez-faire government allows market forces to dominate—has a demonstrably worse record than a different form of capitalism. Some people refer to this other form as "managed capitalism" or "moral capitalism." My preferred term is "democratic capitalism." It describes a system in which the government recognizes its crucial role in guiding the economy. The free market does many things well, mostly thanks to the price system, an efficient method for incorporating vast amounts of information and for allowing businesses and consumers to respond to that information when making everyday decisions. The price system explains why Soviet workers were waiting in breadlines while American workers were buying new cars. Yet the free market also tends to lapse into a predictable set of excesses.

It allows the rich to become richer and more powerful over time, able eventually to distort society's rules to benefit themselves at others' expense and further increase inequality. The free market is also vulnerable to a problem known as the tragedy of the commons, in which self-interested behavior can leave everybody worse off in the end. The canonical example is a town green ruined by overgrazing sheep because individual farmers have no incentive to limit their own flock's grazing. A contemporary example is the pollution that dirties the air and causes climate change. For similar reasons, the free market typically devotes scant resources to areas that are vital to human flourishing but that do not produce reliable profits. Left to its own devices, a market economy underinvests in education, medical care, and a decent retirement for the elderly. Under rough-and-tumble capitalism, all these problems can undermine the benefits of capitalism and damage the quality of life for millions of people.

Under democratic capitalism, a society respects both the power as well as the weaknesses of the market. The government uses taxes to prevent the formation of an economic aristocracy and to pay for activities that the market neglects. The government regulates businesses to protect consumers and workers. The term "democratic capitalism" is particularly apt because it reflects the symbiotic relationship between democracy and capitalism under the best of circumstances. Democratic governance prevents the excesses of free market capitalism, while the material gains produced by capitalism foster the faith in society on which democracy depends. Democracy strengthens capitalism, and capitalism strengthens democracy.

Much as capitalism has a superior record to socialism, democratic capitalism has a superior record to rough-and-tumble capitalism. The laissez-faire economy that prevailed in the United States during the late nineteenth and early twentieth centuries produced the soaring inequality of the Gilded Age and led eventually to the Great Depression. The democratic capitalism that emerged from the 1930s led to much larger gains in living standards for most Americans than in any previous period. Over the past half century, the shift back toward rough-and-tumble capitalism has led to stagnation. One way to see the differing results is to compare the American economy's performance over the past century under Democratic presidents and Republican presidents. Although there are subtleties to the pattern, as I will explain, Democratic presidents tend to push the economy toward democratic capitalism, and they have also presided over faster economic growth and more job growth than Republican presidents. The conclusion holds under a wide array of different assumptions and calculations.

A final advantage of the term democratic capitalism is that it helps point the way out of our current morass. Large parts of the story I tell in this book are tragic. They explain the decline of the American dream. Nonetheless, there is a heartening strand that runs through the story: For both good and ill, the levers of democracy have shaped American capitalism over the past century. It was a grassroots movement in the 1930s that organized workers into the labor unions that improved their lives after the Great Depression, and it was a grassroots movement that expanded those benefits to Black Americans in later years. The great surge in living standards during the middle of the twentieth century was in large measure a triumph of democracy. The opposite is also true. There is no longer a mass movement focused on improving economic outcomes for most Americans. The country's largest activist groups, on both the left and the right, are focused on other subjects.

American democracy certainly has its problems, and I realize that some people have come to believe that the system is inevitably rigged in favor of the rich and powerful. But history offers a more optimistic lesson. Democracy created a broadly prosperous economy in the middle of the twentieth century, and democracy dismantled that economy in the late twentieth century. The story does not need to end there.

IN THE PAGES ahead, you will hear about how three forces have driven the rise and fall of democratic capitalism in the United States: power, culture, and investment.

Power, as I use it here, is chiefly political power. It is any tool that allows one group of citizens to influence the behavior of others. The passage of new laws is a form of power, as is the ability to shape public opinion. Power, whether used for good or ill, is an inescapable part of life. In a democracy, different groups are constantly competing for it. Those who have it will often be able to get their way. The great economist John Maynard Keynes understood this dynamic. Keynes, as one of his biographers noted, saw "economic history as a fundamentally political story."

In the middle of the 1900s, ordinary Americans built power through political movements, especially labor unions. These movements succeeded to a remarkable degree. In the past half century, the power dynamic changed. The American left, whose most important institution is the Democratic Party, increasingly came to reflect and represent the views of relatively well-off college graduates and professionals. The contemporary economist Thomas Piketty uses the term "Brahmin left" to describe this development, which has also occurred in Europe. (The Brahmins were originally the highest caste in India, and during the nineteenth century the word came to describe New England's Protestant elites, often as "Boston Brahmins.") Democrats still push for government programs that benefit middle- and lower-income people, often paid for with taxes on the wealthy. But in recent decades Democrats have put little emphasis on building political movements that include large numbers of working-class people—or on helping working people win higher wages and better working conditions at their jobs. Instead, the Brahmin left has alienated many voters with increasingly liberal views on social and cultural issues, including religion, guns, immigration, abortion, gender, climate change, and the use of language.

I recognize that this part of my argument will be challenging to some readers. In the interest of disclosure, I will tell you that I hold many of these socially liberal views myself. But blue-collar Americans, across races, have long been more moderate on social issues. In recent years, large parts of the Brahmin left have given up on finding compromises that could build a coalition that includes more working-class voters. Today's left has struggled to distinguish between issues on which compromise is impossible (basic civil rights) and those on which compromise is a necessary if uncomfortable part of democracy and progress (most issues). The left has instead defined many positions held by working-class Americans as ignorant if not hateful, and a significant number of working-class voters have responded by abandoning the Democratic Party. From World War II until the end of the twentieth century, Democrats fared better among voters without a bachelor's degree than the population as a whole, and every Democratic president from Franklin Roosevelt to Obama won Americans without a four-year degree. In the current century, the politics of class have inverted. Democrats now fare considerably worse with blue-collar voters than professionals and lose the non-college vote in most elections.

The working-class drift to the right, which was initially concentrated among White voters, has spread over the past several years to voters of color. Most Latino and Asian Americans still vote Democratic, but they shifted toward the Republican Party in the 2020 and 2022 elections. Black voters, who are overwhelmingly Democratic, appear to have moved slightly to the right as well. The flip side of these trends is that the most liberal Americans are disproportionately White, polls show; Black and Latino voters are most likely to identify as moderate Democrats. Given that more than 60 percent of American adults do not have a four-year college degree—and that the Senate has a built-in advantage for rural areas, which tend to be less affluent —the Democrats' struggles among working-class voters have made it difficult for the party to attain enough power to pass its agenda.

The Republican Party to which these voters have fled better reflects some of their views on social issues, but it has shown little interest in policies that would lift their living standards. Rhetoric aside, Republicans remain the party of small government, big business, and rough-and-tumble capitalism. Party leaders favor tax cuts for the wealthy, reductions in benefit programs that serve the middle class and poor, and a relatively free hand for businesses to maximize profits at the expense of wages. A few right-leaning intellectuals have called for a different approach—a true conservative populism—but their ideas have so far had scant effect on the elected officials and judges who set policy. The combined result is that neither of the country's dominant political parties reflects the views of working-class Americans and fights for their economic interests.

This shift in political power since the 1970s has had direct effects on the American economy, through tax rates, workers' bargaining power, and more. It also has had indirect effects, especially on the prevailing culture in corporate America and the rest of the economy.

Culture—the second of these forces I will emphasize—is more

amorphous than many economic factors, and often overlooked as a result, but it is vital. It molds the beliefs and behaviors of executives, politicians, and others whose actions shape society. In recent decades, many of the country's leaders have drifted away from a communitarian, patriotic vision of the economy and toward a more self-interested one. They have justified this vision, sometimes cynically, but often with genuine belief, by talking about the invisible hand of capitalism and its ability to create prosperity for everyone. Unfortunately, this invisible hand has failed to do so for most of the past half century.

The last of the three big forces—investment—is the one on which consensus across the country's polarized political blocs should be most natural. Investment is a society's willingness to devote resources to improving the life of future generations by sacrificing today. It involves diverting money that might otherwise be spent on consumption and instead spending it on education, scientific research, emerging technology, or transportation.

Nothing has a better track record of expanding the size of the economic pie than investment. The country's massive investments during the 1940s and 1950s—under both Democratic and Republican presidents, supported by CEOs and labor leaders alike—transformed American society. They educated millions of people, revolutionized travel, led to the invention of lifesaving treatments, created high-paying jobs, and made the United States the scientific envy of the world. In the last few decades, government has retreated from this approach. The private sector has not filled the void because many basic investments are not profitable for any individual company, even though they are hugely beneficial to the private sector and society. The private sector did not build the internet. Only after the Defense Department created a network of computers were Microsoft, Apple, Google, Amazon, and Facebook able to develop the innovative products that turned them into multibillion-dollar companies.

Power, culture, and investment are obviously not the only factors shaping the American economy. I have focused on them because of their importance and their historical variation. Some other important economic factors have been relatively constant over the past century. The United States continues to have a strong legal system that protects property rights, for example. This country also continues to benefit from an ethos that celebrates individual freedom and risk-taking. But power, culture, and investment have all changed in crucial ways over the past century. In doing so, they have shaped government policy, the private sector, and the living conditions of the American people.

A FINAL REASON that I have written this book is the gratitude that I feel for this country. I know that it has not always treated my family well. Americans, as you will recall, unjustly classified my great-grandfather as an enemy alien. He was fired from his job as a result, and he died in New York, far away from his family. I am also aware that millions of other people in this country have endured much worse than my family has over the centuries. But while America is a flawed embodiment of its founding ideals of equality, liberty, opportunity, and democracy, those ideals matter. Across history, they have inspired Americans—founders and abolitionists, suffragettes and civil rights activists, union organizers and entrepreneurs, Democrats and Republicans—to create a more just society, one that comes closer to embodying those original promises. For nearly fifty years after the Depression, American ideals helped drive progress.

In the fifty years since, we have drifted from our ideals. Progress has slowed in many areas of life and stopped altogether in others. This stagnation is tearing at the fabric of our society, undermining democratic values, and weakening our country in world affairs. The United States cannot simply return to the economy of the mid-twentieth century, nor should we want to. That economy depended in part on a lack of competition from the rest of the world, as Japan and western Europe coped with wartime destruction, the Southern Hemisphere was hobbled by colonialism, and China and the Soviet Union endured communism. The United States was effectively benefiting from others' misfortune, and once the rest of the world became more competitive, American economic growth was bound to slow. But that previous period of rapid progress, when the future seemed to shine, can help us find a path out of our current predicament. Some of the forces that produced rapidly rising living standards in the past can be re-created, in an updated form appropriate for this century.

The defining challenge of our era is figuring out how to make American progress feel as normal as it once did. I recognize how difficult a challenge that is, and I do not know whether we will surmount it. There is abundant reason for pessimism. History, however, does offer reason for hope. The stirring victories of the middle of the twentieth century—the recovery from the Depression, the victory in World War II, the rapid rise in mass living standards, and the creation of a new American economy—were hardly assured. In the moment, they often seemed unlikely. Yet they happened.

PART ONE

The Rise

CHAPTER 1

A Union Town

ON THE EDGE OF A TYPICAL MINNEAPOLIS COAL YARD IN THE 1930s was a wooden shack known as a doghouse. It was where the coal yard's truck drivers spent time while they waited for local families and businesses to phone in orders for coal to fill their furnaces. Once an order arrived, a driver would load his truck with coal and deliver it. The drivers spent a lot of time in the doghouse, because the coal companies insisted that one of them be available whenever an order came in. Six-day workweeks, with ten-hour shifts, were common.

But the drivers were not paid for many of those hours. The coal companies instead paid them by the delivery, which meant that the drivers earned nothing while they waited. It was just one of the ways that the economic risks of the business fell on the drivers rather than the companies. A driver was responsible for paying for his own gasoline and truck—typically a Ford with an extra transmission to generate enough power to haul the coal. In many cases, a driver hired a helper, a strong young man who could carry the coal into houses. Coal work was also seasonal, falling off during the spring and summer, when drivers had to find other work.

In today's terms, the drivers could be considered gig economy workers. They lived on the edge of poverty, with constant uncertainty. They had little control over their working lives. Across Minnesota at the time, the same was true of most workers.

Minneapolis had sprung up as a frontier city, the capital of the vast stretch of resource-rich land beyond the Great Lakes known as the northwest empire. Lumber, wheat, and ore would flow into Minneapolis via the Mississippi River and then be sent out into the world. The region's frontier history had contributed to an individualist culture, dominated by aggressive, savvy businessmen. These executives understood that their success did not depend only on economic forces like supply and demand. It also depended on political power. Minneapolis embodied the power imbalance in the American economy of the early twentieth century and the highly unequal economy that resulted from that imbalance.

Political power explained why the city's truck drivers spent so much time sitting in a coal yard doghouse without being paid. They had little alternative. The city's business executives had amassed tremendous power. Leading politicians, from both parties, were their allies. Daily newspapers were reliably deferential to business, publishing press releases almost verbatim. Most important, the executives had prevented workers from forming labor unions that could have counterbalanced the influence of business.

The executives had formalized their hold on power by creating a group called the Citizens Alliance of Minneapolis. It had grown out of the business community's united effort to defeat a 1901 strike by local machinists. The executives had portrayed the machinists' would-be union as an illegitimate representative of the workers and had recruited replacement workers to keep their factories running. The effort was a total success: The strikers went back to work without accomplishing any of their goals—no wage increase, no nine-hour workday, no extra pay for overtime work. Emboldened, the executives created the Citizens Alliance with the goal of keeping unions out of other local industries. By the early 1930s, it was able to boast that every local strike since World War I had "failed utterly due to the assistance rendered by the Citizens Alliance."

The workers of Minneapolis remained scattered, unable to exercise power. The city's business leaders were united.

The disparity shaped the local economy. In many industries, wages were about one-third lower than in other Midwestern cities, like Chicago, Cleveland, and St. Louis. In the federal government's statistical tables of economic data for different cities, Minneapolis almost seemed to be an extension of the American South. It resembled cities like Birmingham, Little Rock, Memphis, and New

Orleans, where wages were low and profits were high. In Minneapolis, rough-and-tumble capitalism dominated, and the American dream was out of reach for many families.

In the winter of 1933–34, however, dissent began to build in the doghouse of one Minneapolis coal yard. A Swedish immigrant named Carl Skoglund told his fellow drivers that they did not need to meekly accept low wages and unfair working conditions. Skoglund, then in his late forties, had a broad build that his friends teasingly compared to an outhouse—or, as one said, "a little brick shit-house." He walked with a limp, the result of a tree that had crushed his foot when he was working for a logging company in northern Minnesota years earlier. As he spoke, in a Swedish accent, he sometimes twirled one of the bushy eyebrows that hung over his blue eyes. The other drivers called him Skogie or the Old Swede, and he kept repeating the same message to them: Only a labor union could give them the power to change life in the coal yard. Secretly—"on the Q.T.," a then popular code word for quiet—Skoglund and a small group of other activists began holding nighttime meetings at his home to explain the benefits of a union to their colleagues.

Carl Skoglund, third from left, meeting with the other leaders of Teamsters Local 544, 1937.

Skoglund had spent much of his life trying to organize unions, and he had repeatedly failed. In 1922, while working as a railroad mechanic, he participated in the Great Railroad Strike, which ended in defeat for the workers after President Warren Harding intervened on behalf of employers. It was a common story in the early twentieth century. Business owners were gaining power, and workers were losing it. Judges invalidated workplace regulations, allowing companies to operate as they wished. Presidents and governors halted strikes. Union membership declined in the 1920s. A visiting Australian journalist, trying to explain the United States to his readers, wrote, "America is an employer's paradise." Inequality, as a result, was growing. The share of income flowing to the richest 1 percent of households nearly doubled between the 1870s and 1920s. Most Americans were not receiving their fair share of the country's economic bounty.

This chapter tells the story of how workers in Minneapolis gained enough political power to reverse that trend and how they contributed to a larger shift across the rest of the country. Their success eventually helped to create an economy in which living standards rose rapidly for the rich, middle class, and poor.

ECONOMIC THEORY MIGHT seem to suggest that political power should not have such a big effect on the economy. According to the laws of supply and demand, market forces dictate economic outcomes. Companies pay workers what they are worth, based on a combination of a worker's productivity, the number of available workers, the strength of the business, and the health of the overall economy. A company that underpays its workers will lose them to rival businesses that do pay market wages. A company that overpays its workers will lose money and go out of business.

Yet the world does not operate as elegantly as some economic theories suggest. It is messier. One reason is that few workers know the exact worth of their contributions to their employers. Employers themselves are often unsure. A mid-twentieth-century economist named Richard Lester coined a phrase for this uncertainty: the "range of indeterminacy."

To understand the concept, it can help to look at other areas of economic life. A wage is a kind of price—the price that workers can charge for their labor—and prices often vary for reasons unconnected to an item's true value. Hospitals charge wildly different prices for the same procedure. Gas stations, sometimes on the same street, charge different amounts for a gallon of gas. Home sellers obsess over the list price of their house, rather than trusting that an efficient market will dictate the ultimate value. The sale price of these items and many others can vary widely, depending on a host of factors, including the relative knowledge, patience, and leverage of the buyer and seller.

In the case of wages, the range of indeterminacy helps employers more often than employees because employers have some natural advantages. They have more knowledge—about how much money different workers make and how productive each is. Employers also have more leverage. Companies employ many workers, and losing one of them is usually manageable. For most workers, by contrast, quitting over a pay dispute can create financial hardship.

These dynamics can cause a worker's pay to settle on the low end of the range of indeterminacy. In the relationship between an employer and an individual employee, the employer has more power. But there is an important adjective in that previous sentence: *individual*. When employees band together, they can reduce the power imbalance. They can share information with one another and can exert some of their own leverage. A business that can afford to lose one worker over a pay dispute may not be able to lose dozens of workers.

There is a name for a group of workers who come together to increase their bargaining power. It is a labor union.

Two leading philosophers of capitalism, Adam Smith and John Stuart Mill, understood this reality and wrote positively about unions. "Masters are always and everywhere in a sort of tacit, but constant and uniform combination, not to raise the wages of labour above their actual rate," Smith wrote in *The Wealth of Nations*. Employers had the advantage over workers in almost any negotiation, Smith explained, and workers' best hope for matching the sway of employers was to form a "combination." Mill, similarly, wrote, "The labourer in an isolated condition, unable to hold out even against a single employer, much more against the tacit combination of employers, will, as a rule, find his wages kept down at the lower limit."

I know that many Americans have mixed feelings about labor unions. I have mixed feelings myself. I was in a union for more than a decade, as a reporter at *The New York Times,* and I was both grateful for the pay and benefits it had negotiated on my behalf and frustrated by some aspects of the union. On the desk of my union representative was a digital clock, facing outward, that counted down until her retirement, in days, hours, minutes, and seconds. The clock conveyed her lack of interest in the job, and it was a fitting symbol of the union's problems. When my infant son had a medical emergency and the union's health plan lacked any pediatric specialist to treat it, union officials were maddeningly uninterested in helping my family find a doctor we could afford. They seemed more interested in getting their own paychecks and reaching retirement than helping their members. Later, after I joined management at the *Times,* I had new frustrations with the union, mostly involving its resistance to change at a company that needed to evolve in order to thrive in the digital era.

Many other Americans have had their own disappointments with unions. In some situations, unions have overreached, demanding cumbersome work restrictions or wages that are too high for a company to pay sustainably. Both the "range" and the "indeterminacy" parts of Lester's idea are important, after all. The more successful a company is—the more attractive its products and the more efficient its operations are—the higher the wage range can rise.

For all their imperfections, though, it is worth remembering what an economy without strong labor unions looks like. It is an economy in which employees, left to act as individuals, have far less power than employers, and wages tend to settle at the low end of the range of indeterminacy. It is an economy that resembles the Minneapolis economy of the early 1900s (or the American economy of the early 2000s, but that is a story for the second half of this book).

Looking back over history, many Americans rightly glorify the civil rights, women's, and gay rights movements for creating an America that comes closer to fulfilling its founding ideals. None of those movements were perfect. All of them were necessary. The labor movement deserves a similar place in our memories, as a central cause of social progress. Unions allowed ordinary people to acquire political and economic power that they had never previously had. That power allowed them to enjoy better, healthier, longer lives.

The labor unions of the mid-twentieth century cannot be recreated in today's globalized economy, and some aspects of them do not deserve to be. Different times call for different solutions. But there is an enduring principle across the past century: The attainment of the American dream—or the failure to attain it—has depended on the balance of political power.

FOR MUCH OF American history, the country's workers, or at least its White workers, had not needed power in order to enjoy better living standards than their counterparts in other countries. The United States economy was naturally less unequal than Europe's.

"The average American colonist ate better, was taller, and lived longer than did the average Englishman," the economic historians Peter Lindert and Jeffrey Williamson have noted. Colonists benefited from the fact that America lacked the inherited wealth and economic institutions that Europe had at the time. People from ordinary backgrounds were able to acquire land and start businesses more easily than the working classes back home. When Benjamin Franklin arrived in Philadelphia as a seventeen-year-old in 1723, the city was home to only ten thousand people. Franklin invested in real estate and opened a printing press, a publishing house, and a newspaper, all of which would have been difficult back in England. The amount of economic opportunity was clear even to colonists who were unhappy about it. "Fellows who would have cleaned my shoes five years ago," groused one *Mayflower* descendant in the 1770s, "have amassed fortunes, and are riding in chariots."

While the American colonies were not necessarily richer overall than western Europe, the affluent in America took home a smaller share of income, leaving more for everyone else. On the eve of the Revolutionary War, the richest 1 percent of American households earned 8.6 percent of the national income. Across western Europe at the same time, the share was almost twice as high—about 15 percent. The gap is especially striking given that the American colonies had the brutal institution of slavery, which allowed wealthy White plantation owners to capture the economic value created by Black workers.

The main explanation for the gap between the United States and Europe is that inequality in a society tends to increase over time, as the economist Thomas Piketty has documented. (An old saying makes a similar point, albeit less rigorously than Piketty: It takes money to make money.) Many promising investments require a significant amount of capital. People who have that capital can earn higher returns than people who do not. Wealthy farmers can buy equipment that makes their farms more productive than small farms. A wealthy individual can invest in a new company and earn a gigantic return. The stock market is one place to see this idea in action: Stocks usually rise at a faster rate than a country's economy grows, and the wealthy own a disproportionate share of stocks.

Over time, this dynamic caused inequality to rise in the United States. The affluent expanded their fortunes, and companies grew. By the late 1800s, corporations spanned multiple industries and employed tens of thousands of workers. Their size allowed them to charge higher prices and pay lower wages, because consumers and workers had limited alternatives. Political institutions also played a role in increasing inequality. In 1886, the Supreme Court ruled that the Fourteenth Amendment—originally intended to give equal protection under the law to formerly enslaved people—applied to corporations as well as individual citizens. In the decades after the ruling, most Fourteenth Amendment cases to come before the Supreme Court involved the protection of corporate rights, often at the expense of workers. Together, these forces helped to create the extreme inequality that came to be known as the Gilded Age.

As Piketty has explained, there are a few exceptions to the tendency of inequality to increase over time. They typically involve war, depression, or a natural disaster, all of which destroy wealth or create a political reaction that redistributes wealth through government policies. The Gilded Age inspired one of those reactions, known as the Progressive movement, around the turn of the twentieth century. But the Progressive Era had a mixed legacy for workers. For the most part, Progressivism was a middle-class movement, rather than a workers' movement. Many of the era's reformers defined themselves in opposition to both the tycoons above them and the toiling masses below. "Middle-class progressive thought centered on an abiding faith that individualism and class harmony would flourish if more avenues were opened to hard work, education, initiative, and upward mobility," the historian Jefferson Cowie has written. Many Progressives believed in expertise and efficiency and distrusted the working class, especially immigrants who had recently arrived in the United States. This distrust helped to fuel the temperance movement, which led to Prohibition, as well as the eugenics movement, which argued for immigration restrictions on racist grounds.

Even Progressives who opposed eugenics and Prohibition were often influenced by their movement's middle-class, paternalistic outlook. They pushed for government regulations to protect workers—like minimum wages, maximum workweeks, bans on child labor, and, most significantly, a federal income tax—rather than emphasizing the creation of a workers' political movement. Progressives preferred top-down protections over bottom-up organizations that would have empowered workers. Some activists, particularly at the state level, did try to strengthen the labor movement, and unions grew during the Progressive Era, but major strikes repeatedly failed.

In the end, the Progressive movement reduced economic inequality only modestly and fleetingly. Too tame to alter the balance of political power, it was nonetheless sufficiently ambitious to cause a counterreaction from the business sector. By the 1910s, many executives were rebelling against the rules restricting their behavior. Public opinion was also shifting to the political right. The horrors of World War I had made many people cynical about government's ability to do good, and the Bolshevik revolution in Russia raised suspicions about any workers' movement.

The economic boom that followed the war—the Roaring Twenties—reinforced such conservative beliefs by lifting living standards. They did not rise as rapidly as the economy was growing because an outsize share of the gains went to the wealthy. Still, the economy was strong enough to make many Americans satisfied with the status quo, and they elected three business-friendly Republican presidents starting in 1920. The middle of those three, Calvin Coolidge, summarized the national mood in a 1925 speech in which he defended the accumulation of wealth as being in society's interest. Specifically, he told an annual newspaper convention, Americans should not distrust press coverage merely because wealthy publishers owned the newspapers providing that coverage. "After all, the chief business of the American people is business," Coolidge said, in the speech's best-known line. "They are profoundly concerned with producing, buying, selling, investing and prospering in the world."

In this atmosphere, the business community was able to reassert itself politically. It pushed to overturn Progressive laws on minimum wages and child labor, and the Supreme Court complied. And corporate America's biggest priority remained the undermining of labor unions. Even if Progressive reformers minimized the importance of labor unions, business executives recognized it. The vanguard of the counterreaction was the National Association of Manufacturers, an industry group based in Manhattan. In 1921, the NAM developed an economic vision that it came to call the American Plan. To implement the plan, the NAM worked with local business groups, several of which used the same name— Citizens Alliance—as the Minneapolis organization. The effort to shape public opinion began with the very name of these groups. It was not the Business Alliance or the Employers Alliance. It was the

Citizens Alliance. Who could object to that? In its public materials, the Minneapolis chapter explained that it was "composed of the People who are interested in the welfare of Minneapolis." Its abiding message was freedom. The American Plan promised to allow "every man to work out his own salvation" and specifically revolved around the idea of an "open shop."

In an open-shop company, individual workers could choose whether they wanted to belong to a union. In a closed shop, all workers were required to join the union. The open shop was an effective rhetorical tool because it seemed to offer workers a choice. Otis Briggs, the owner of a machine company and a founder of the Minneapolis Citizens Alliance, invoked "life, liberty, and the pursuit of happiness" when explaining the virtues of the open shop. Yet Citizens Alliance leaders understood that the open shop was in fact a way to weaken and eventually eliminate unions. In an open shop, an employer could replace union members with more docile employees. The American Plan was a clever bit of political marketing. It sounded a lot better than "the low-wage plan" while accomplishing the same result.

The Minneapolis Citizens Alliance also employed harsher methods. To keep tabs on workers, it operated a private detective agency, with spies who joined unions and armed guards who broke strikes. To keep the business community in line, it encouraged local companies not to buy goods from companies that had signed union contracts. When encouragement was not enough, banks in the Alliance would threaten to withhold credit. The organization was "a union against unions," as the title of a book about the Alliance described it. Its most important lever of power was government. Alliance members cultivated politicians with financial gifts and job offers for relatives and friends. Many politicians were already sympathetic, given that Minnesota was a conservative state in a conservative era. At one point, Alliance members persuaded a pro-business Democratic candidate for Minneapolis mayor to drop out of the race so that he would not risk splitting the vote with a pro-business Republican and allow a pro-labor third-party candidate to win. The Democrat did so, and the Republican candidate, a Citizens Alliance member, won. After taking office, the new mayor devoted a quarter of the city police force to breaking a single local strike.

American business, to be sure, has never been a monolith. It has always included aggressive figures like the Citizens Alliance members as well as moderates open to accommodating workers and regulators. Both the relative hard-liners and the moderates have tended to be influenced by the political atmosphere at any given time. Hard-liners could become moderates, and vice versa, depending on the zeitgeist.

During the Progressive Era, moderates had been ascendant. They pushed an idea that became known as "welfare capitalism," which tried to smooth the rough edges of capitalism. Dozens of companies established pension and employee stock ownership plans. General Electric offered paid vacations and medical care. Henry Ford provided an instructive case study. His famous pay increase—he more than doubled his company's minimum wage, to $5 a day, and established a profit-sharing plan for adult male employees—occurred in 1914, when the country was still in the later stages of the Progressive Era. Ford justified the pay increase with rhetoric that reflected Progressive values. "Our men have been efficient and faithful, and we believe they should share in what this means to us," he said. The move turned Ford into a lasting symbol of corporate enlightenment. But Ford was not actually a corporate moderate who favored paying more than he had to, at least not most of the time. He sent inspectors to employees' homes to check on their behavior. He worked vigorously to keep labor unions out of his company, and he changed his approach to compensation during the business backlash that followed the Progressive Era. As vehicle sales and company profits skyrocketed between 1919 and 1929, he never raised his workers' pay scale. The 1920s was a decade when businesses found more room to exercise power and became more comfortable doing so.

The shrinking of labor unions was a major consequence of the backlash by the business community. At the start of the 1920s, more than 16 percent of nonagricultural workers in the United States belonged to a union. When the decade ended, that share had fallen to 11 percent. National magazines ran headlines like "The Collapse of Organized Labor." After William Howard Taft, the former president, became chief justice of the United States in 1921, he wrote a letter to his brother explaining the tough stance that his court would take toward organized labor. "That faction," Taft wrote, "we have to hit every little while." Union leaders contributed to their own problems by refusing to recruit workers they viewed as inferior, such as Black Americans, immigrants, and unskilled workers. These groups instead became recruiting targets when companies went looking for replacement workers during a strike.

Together, these forces led to a remarkable turnabout. The share of income flowing to the top 1 percent of households reached 18 percent in the late 1920s, up from 10 percent in the 1870s. The United States had become more unequal than western Europe, even though European countries were centuries older.

It was not clear what might possibly change the situation—until the global economy collapsed.

AT FIRST, THE Great Depression made everything much worse. Stock prices fell by more than one-third in the last three months of 1929, and unemployment began climbing. Those fortunate enough to have jobs often had their wages reduced. Yet the Depression would ultimately cause a reaction that upended the power dynamic in the American economy. Workers, both white-collar and blue-collar, skilled and unskilled, would no longer have to accept a shrinking share of the nation's economic output. They would ask for more—higher wages, more leisure time, greater physical safety—and often get it. The Great Depression would end a Darwinian economic era and lead to an era of democratic capitalism, featuring both more economic equality and faster growth. The historian Alexander Field has described the 1930s, counterintuitively, as the Great Leap Forward.

In Minnesota, one of the first signs of change was the 1930 midterm elections, halfway through Republican Herbert Hoover's four-year term as president. A young Minneapolis politician named

Floyd Bjørnstjerne Olson ran for governor, and Olson did not resemble most politicians, in appearance or agenda. Six-foot-two with swept-back hair, he was sometimes described as a modern Viking. He exuded self-confidence and charisma, and his political views were unlike those of any governor in the state's history.

Olson had worked blue-collar jobs as a young man, handling riverboat freight and installing telegraph poles, and he had joined the Industrial Workers of the World, the radical labor union known as the Wobblies. "I knew what it was to never have enough of anything," he said, "and I guess I've never gotten over it." He had gone to the University of Minnesota but dropped out rather than take part in military exercises that were mandatory on many campuses at the time. Eventually, he went to law school, despite not having a college degree, and while in his late twenties, he rose to become the top prosecutor for Hennepin County, the county where Minneapolis was located. Olson was a one-man melting pot, with a personal connection to several of the big ethnic voting blocs in the Twin Cities. His wife, Ada Ann Krejci Olson, was the daughter of Czech immigrants. Olson's mother was born in Sweden and his father in Norway. Olson even spoke Yiddish, having grown up in a heavily Jewish neighborhood in Minneapolis.

As county prosecutor, Olson considered it his mission to use the law on behalf of ordinary workers. He exposed railroads that were fixing prices and sued milk companies that required job applicants to promise they would not join a union. During the 1920s, he was one of the few Minnesota politicians willing to take on the Citizens Alliance: He accused Briggs, a top Alliance official, of trying to hire private detectives to plant a bomb that could be blamed on union members. In 1924, Olson ran for governor, not as a Democrat or a Republican, because he did not think either party was doing enough for workers, but as a member of a new party, the Farmer-Labor Party. He finished ahead of the Democratic nominee yet lost by 5 percentage points to a Republican who promised low taxes and painted Olson and his party as too extreme for Minnesota. A governor's term lasted only two years at the time, and Olson decided not to run in 1926 or 1928, thinking he would lose again. He remained county attorney.

In 1930, though, Olson believed that the Depression had created an opening for his brand of populism. To appeal to more voters, he moderated the Farmer-Labor Party's positions on agriculture and other issues, and he accused Republicans of aligning with "special privilege." This time he won comfortably, with 59 percent of the vote. As the Depression deepened, he pushed for unemployment relief and public works. He did not succeed initially, because the legislature remained controlled by conservatives. But another election was coming soon.

That 1932 election transformed the political landscape, in Minnesota and nationwide. Olson won reelection, and his liberal allies won control of the state's House of Representatives. Franklin Delano Roosevelt became the first Democratic presidential candidate to win Minnesota in the state's seventy-four-year history. He took office along with large Democratic majorities in Congress. Roosevelt grasped that the Depression had its roots in the unequal economy of the 1920s and castigated the combination of low wages and high profits during his presidential campaign. Still, it remained unclear what exactly he would do about the problem. His campaign agenda had been vague, promising above all to get the economy working again. He did not enter the White House with a clear theory of how to change the country's economic distribution. His early policies focused more on halting the panic than altering the structure of the economy. The administration's first bill tried to resuscitate the banking system, and officials in Herbert Hoover's Treasury Department had written the bill's original draft.

If anything, Roosevelt's initial policies were more timid than Progressive Era policies had been. Roosevelt did not want to risk exacerbating the downturn by weakening business through tough new regulations. And like many Progressives, he did not see labor unions as the best counterbalance to the power of the corporate sector. Organized labor seemed feckless. It was so weak that Roosevelt had mostly ignored it during his presidential campaign. Some of the biggest unions had backed Hoover, which meant that the new president owed them little. After the election, as Roosevelt planned his new administration, he decided to abandon bipartisan precedent and did not name any of the major union leaders as his secretary of labor.

Instead, he chose an ally from his years in New York State government who was steeped in the Progressive movement. Union leaders were aghast. "Labor," the head of the American Federation of Labor announced, "can never become reconciled to the selection made."

FANNIE PERKINS HAD a privileged upbringing. Her parents owned a stationery store in the then-booming industrial city of Worcester, Massachusetts, and sent her to nearby Mount Holyoke College, where she was elected president of her class. She often wore a three-pointed aristocratic hat known as a tricorne, which her mother said complemented the shape of her face, and she spoke with a soft Massachusetts accent, elongating her *a*'s and dropping her *r*'s.

But if Perkins was influenced by her upper-middle-class childhood, she was not captive to it. She rejected the life her parents wanted for her: returning to Worcester after college and raising a family in their Congregationalist community. At Mount Holyoke, Perkins heard visiting speakers describe the excitement of politics and social reform, and she wanted to be part of that world. After graduating, she moved to Chicago for a job teaching at a private school. She reinvented herself in her new city, changing her name to the less playful Frances and joining the Episcopal Church, whose formal rituals appealed to her. When not teaching, she spent time at Hull House, the community center for immigrants that was a hive of political activity. There, she met people struggling with poverty as well as activists trying to help them. Perkins had found her path. She later moved to Philadelphia, where she worked with recently arrived immigrant women to help them avoid being pressured into prostitution, and then to New York for graduate school at Columbia University.

By happenstance, Perkins was having lunch with a friend in Greenwich Village one day in 1911 when a fire broke out in the neighborhood, and Perkins ran to see it. It had consumed the top floors of the Asch Building, home to the Triangle Shirtwaist Factory, and Perkins watched in horror as factory workers, many of them young women and girls, jumped to their deaths. They could not escape down the stairs because management locked the workers inside the factory during their shifts, in the name of preventing theft. At this stage of her life, Perkins had made enough political connections that she was able to secure a job on a state commission created to investigate the fire. That work launched her career in New York politics. Governor Al Smith became her mentor, and in 1928 Smith's successor—Franklin Roosevelt—appointed her to run the state's industrial commission, making her one of the most senior female officials in any state government.

Perkins was a quintessential Progressive: She devoted her life to improving the living conditions of the less fortunate, and she believed that government regulations, overseen by experts like herself, offered the best route to progress. She considered labor unions to be useful but secondary. "I'd much rather get a law than organize a union," she said. Unions seemed too weak to be effective, constantly losing strikes and court cases. In New York, Perkins had worked with labor leaders and was often unimpressed. Some, like Rose Schneiderman, who galvanized public anger after the Triangle fire, were brave and inspiring. Others were narrow-minded and selfish: When Perkins pushed for a new law in New York State to require compensation for injured workers, one union refused to support the effort because its workers already had such a benefit. Perkins was also turned off by the disdain that many union leaders showed for immigrants and women—the groups she had dedicated her early career to helping—and by union corruption. She described the leaders of one textile union as "lunatics and grafters." She was more enthusiastic about the idea of unions than the reality of them.

After Roosevelt won the presidency in 1932, word began to circulate in New York political circles that he planned to select Perkins as his secretary of labor. The rumors gave Perkins time to think about what her agenda would be if the job offer came. When Roosevelt summoned her to his townhouse on East Sixty-fifth Street in Manhattan one night, Perkins arrived with a list. She told him that she would not accept the position unless he supported the policies that she wanted to pursue. Her agenda included public works, a minimum wage, disability payments, an eight-hour workday, workplace safety, unemployment insurance, and a benefit program that would allow older workers to retire. Roosevelt was encouraging, objecting to only two of her ideas, unemployment insurance and the old-age benefit program. Both reminded him of the "dole" in England and might encourage laziness, he told Perkins. He later changed his mind, and the two programs made up much of the Social Security Act, a defining part of his legacy.

Frances Perkins greets President Franklin D. Roosevelt, 1943.

In retrospect, Perkins's list was notable both for its ambition and for its absence of policies to help workers form labor unions. Perkins wanted to finish the uncompleted agenda of the Progressive Era—an agenda that would impose new rules on pay, benefits, hours, and safety, rather than help workers negotiate for advances on their own.

Roosevelt tended to be less interested in economic theory than his advisers and to think first in terms of politics. As his administration looked for ways to restart the economy during his early months in office, Roosevelt emphasized policies that could win wide approval, among members of Congress, business executives, farmers, workers, and other groups. Doing so, he believed, would inspire confidence, which in turn would help revive the economy. In exchange for their support, business executives had one clear request for the new administration: They hoped to be freed from antitrust laws preventing them from cooperating with their rivals.

Many of them blamed the Depression on ruinous competition among firms, which they believed had led to overproduction, price cuts, and job losses. The executives wanted salvation from their own worst impulses by cooperating with one another, and they were willing for government to have a role in the cooperation. Together, industry and government would engage in voluntary economic planning and devise codes of fair competition, covering production levels, prices, and wages. When companies disagreed about what should be in the codes, the White House would settle the matter. These codes would involve more government intervention than the country was accustomed to, but they stopped well short of the authoritarian economic planning that Germany, Italy, and Russia were implementing. The approach was a distinctly American response to the Depression, Roosevelt and his aides believed.

It fell to Perkins to learn what organized labor wanted as part of this recovery bill. Weak as labor was, Roosevelt still hoped it would sign off to increase the bill's popularity. Perkins started with William Green, the head of the AFL, the country's largest labor organization, even though he was the same person who only months earlier said he would never be reconciled to her selection as labor secretary. She had waved away his criticism, viewing it as standard political bluster, and quietly sought his advice after she became labor secretary. Green told Perkins that he and other labor leaders wanted the undisputed right to organize nonunionized workers into new unions. Federal law was vague on the issue, and the previous decade had been so tough on unions that this right barely existed anymore.

As Perkins thought about the recovery bill, she saw a practical problem with it, and she came to believe that strengthening unions could solve it. Her preferred way to write each industry's code of fair competition was to form something called a tripartite board, made up of representatives from the three key groups: employers, workers, and the federal government. The flaw, she realized, was that there would often be nobody to represent workers on the tripartite boards. In most industries, workers were unorganized, without any obvious way to choose negotiators who could act on their behalf. For the boards to succeed, and not simply be a sop to business, the administration would need to give workers the right to elect their own representatives. And an elected representative of a company's workers was just another way to describe a labor union. The crisis of the Depression had awakened Perkins to the importance of empowering workers to negotiate for themselves, rather than trusting government officials to do so on their behalf. The government could instead act as a mediator between management and labor.

Perkins became the administration's primary advocate for adding a provision to the recovery bill giving workers the right to organize unions without interference from management. A few moderate business leaders, including the heads of General Electric and Filene's department store, agreed with this approach. But most executives strongly opposed it, fearing a fundamental shift that would lead to higher wages. The National Association of Manufacturers and the Chamber of Commerce made the removal of the provision their top priority during negotiations over the recovery bill, with NAM officials telling members of Congress that unions would deprive Americans of their liberty. Henry Ford lobbied against the idea, as did members of the Minneapolis Citizens Alliance. Some of Roosevelt's advisers, wary of alienating business and feeling little allegiance to organized labor, urged him not to add the provision.

Perkins pushed back. She asked Green to come to the White House and explain the provision's importance to Roosevelt, and he did. Perkins also worked closely with an old colleague of hers from New York State government, Robert Wagner, a German immigrant who by this point had been elected senator. He was organized labor's strongest advocate in Washington and drafted the union provision—Section 7(a) of the National Industrial Recovery Act. It stated that "employees shall have the right to organize and bargain collectively through representatives of their own choosing, and shall be free from the interference, restraint, or coercion of employers."

"No 7(a), no bill," Wagner said during the negotiations.

Roosevelt sided with Wagner and Perkins, and the provision remained. "No business which depends for existence on paying less than living wages to its workers has any right to continue in this country," Roosevelt declared during the bill's signing ceremony, on the 105th day of his presidency.

Perkins, a traditional Progressive by training and philosophy, had helped redefine what it meant to be a small-*p* progressive on economic policy. It would still involve the writing of government rules to govern pay, hours, and working conditions, but progressives would also make it a top priority to empower workers to bargain for themselves. Perkins, Wagner, and Roosevelt had made economic progressivism less paternalistic and more democratic.

SECTION 7(A) ROUSED American labor. It did not take months or weeks. It happened within days.

Once the Senate passed its version of the bill in June 1933 and before Roosevelt had even signed it, national labor leaders directed their local affiliates to begin recruiting campaigns. The United Mine Workers devoted all its available funds to the effort. The union's public message was shrewd and only somewhat exaggerated. When organizers arrived in a new town, they carried placards announcing, "The President wants you to join the union." Technically, the signs were referring to the union's president, John L. Lewis, but the organizers did not mind if people thought they meant Roosevelt.

As union organizers fanned out across the country, they found a workforce suddenly eager for a fight. The Great Depression had initially made people desperate—desperate to hold on to their job if they still had one and wary of doing anything that might jeopardize it. The number of strikes across the country, already low in 1929, plummeted at the start of the 1930s. But Roosevelt's election and the flurry of legislation in his first few months in office had created enough hope to transform the desperation into energy.

On June 17, a day when newspapers across the country carried front-page stories about Roosevelt signing the National Industrial Recovery Act, a United Mine Workers organizer in Ohio wrote to the union's national leaders to say that he had already signed up 80 percent of the miners he was trying to recruit. On June 23, a Mine Workers organizer in Kentucky reported to headquarters that he had formed nine new local chapters. By the end of the following week, the union had enlisted 128,000 new members nationwide.

On June 30 in Hollywood, a group of actors founded a new union called the Screen Actors Guild, with early members including James Cagney, Ann Harding, Groucho Marx, and Spencer Tracy. In the garment district of Los Angeles, Latina dressmakers organized a union, as did Jewish and Italian garment workers in New York. In Detroit, autoworkers went on strike, seeking to organize and to end the industry's notorious hostility to unions. Workers at rubber companies, oil companies, hotels, restaurants, and newspapers began forming unions, too. The mere formation of a union was not enough to lift wages and improve working conditions. An employer would still need to recognize the union and agree to make changes. But by banding together and increasing their leverage, workers were taking the first crucial step.

The publicity that the recovery act was receiving helped their efforts. Businesses hung signs with the recovery program's blue eagle logo and the motto "We do our part" in their windows to announce their participation in the codes of fair competition. To rally support for the law, New York City threw a ticker-tape parade in mid-September, featuring workers marching in industry groups. More than 250,000 people participated, and 1.5 million attendees lined the Fifth Avenue parade route. Perkins, Wagner,

Eleanor Roosevelt, and other dignitaries watched from a reviewing stand in front of the New York Public Library. The parade
lasted from one-thirty in the afternoon until almost midnight.

By late 1933, the recovery effort had captured the country's attention. When workers signed up for a union, they seemed to be
signing up for the recovery. They also seemed to be asserting their
Americanness. Enormous American flags became a staple of labor
rallies, including those led by socialists. Many of the workers attending the rallies were immigrants or their children, for whom
joining a union was an expression of their family's newfound democratic rights. "All of America's great reform movements, from the
crusade against slavery onward," the labor historian Nelson Lichtenstein has written, "have defined themselves as champions of a
moral and patriotic nationalism, which they counterpoised to the
parochial and selfish elites who stood athwart their vision of a
virtuous society."

Even conservative Minnesota was swept up in the new mood.
In his second inaugural address, in 1933, Floyd Olson declared,
"The United States has created the greatest industrial system in the
history of the world, but that system has concerned itself almost
entirely with profit, and has been blind or selfish insofar as the
welfare of the mass of the people is concerned." In rural parts of
the state, farmers banded together to help neighbors facing fore-
closure. When a bank announced that a foreclosed farm was going
to be auctioned off, local farmers spread the word that nobody
should bid more than $1 for the property. Sure enough, when auc-
tion day arrived, nobody did. The winning $1 bidder then returned
the farm to its original owner, who could try to rebuild the family
business. It was a bailout for farmers rather than banks. These bits
of collective action eventually led to the formation of the Farmers
Holiday Association, which organized the equivalent of strikes—
"farm holidays"—to demand better payment for crops, meat, and
dairy products.

In Minneapolis's coal yards, this political spirit helped Carl
Skoglund persuade other drivers to join his fledgling, still-secret
union. At almost any other point in the drivers' working lives, the

notion of taking on an employer might have seemed reckless. The odds had been so dire that the national union representing truck drivers, the Teamsters, had previously shown little interest in confronting the coal companies. A few years earlier, the Teamsters president had urged a Minneapolis union official not "to enter into trouble of any kind." By late 1933, Skoglund and a handful of other local organizers decided that they were willing to defy the Teamsters' national organization and take on the coal companies.

After weeks of quiet meetings with drivers, the organizers decided they had enough support to form a Teamsters local and approach the coal companies to demand higher wages, shorter hours, overtime pay, and a union election. When the companies said no to every request, the leaders prepared to call a strike. They sent a letter to the Teamsters' headquarters asking for approval but, knowing they would not get it, did not wait for an answer. They paused only long enough for a rare January warm spell to pass, and when the temperatures dropped again, they called a strike for February 7, 1934. No coal would move in Minneapolis, the strikers announced.

To make good on that vow, they organized "flying squads" of vehicles to stop coal trucks, operated by replacement drivers, from making deliveries. A flying squad would surround the truck, forcing it to stop. Then strikers would jump out of their vehicles, climb onto the back of the coal truck, and dump its load in the street. It was a confrontational tactic, but Skoglund implored the strikers not to treat the replacement drivers as the enemy during these incidents. The strikers should instead explain the rationale behind the strike and their need to prevent coal deliveries in order to win better wages. "They're uninformed," Skoglund said, describing the replacement drivers to one young striker. "So you shouldn't call them scabs. Give them a chance."

Skoglund understood that a strike was not simply an internal dispute between a company and its workers. A strike was also a political campaign, in which public opinion could determine the outcome. Everywhere Skoglund looked, he saw people—even replacement drivers—who might be won over to the workers' side.

. . .

SKOGLUND AND SEVERAL of the other organizers had something in common: They were political radicals, either socialists or communists. Several organizers, including Skoglund, considered themselves Trotskyists because they opposed Josef Stalin's rule of the Soviet Union and had split with the American Communist Party over the issue. Political radicalism was a frequent trait among labor organizers during this period, including in two other high-profile strikes in 1934, by auto parts workers in Toledo, Ohio, and dockworkers in San Francisco.

Since its inception in the nineteenth century, the American labor movement had been somewhat elitist. It consisted mostly of skilled workers, who joined what were known as craft unions. Unskilled workers were not always welcome. Generations of cautious, exclusionary labor leaders had argued that unskilled workers were too easily replaced to be able to form strong unions. William Green, the AFL president, came from this tradition, as did the Teamsters' leadership. A new group of labor organizers, led by John L. Lewis of the mineworkers' union, believed this approach was wrong. They formed a committee inside the AFL that favored something called industrial unionism, based on organizing all workers in an industry, across different job categories. Unskilled workers might have less bargaining power than craftsmen or machinists, but they could still acquire power if they banded together. The alternative was to condemn these workers to non-union jobs and low wages. In 1938, Lewis's reformist committee split from the AFL and formed its own umbrella group for unions, the Congress of Industrial Organizations.

To be sure, many industrial unionists were not radicals. Some were avowedly anti-communist, and Lewis considered himself a Republican. Still, communists and socialists often played crucial roles in the campaigns to organize new workers. The radicals were less tolerant of the unwillingness of traditional unions to organize immigrant, Black, and female workers. From the beginning, many CIO organizers favored racially integrated unions. The radicals, believing in a higher cause of societal transformation, were also often willing to take tremendous personal risks, including jail time, injury, and death, to organize workers.

Skoglund's politics had been forged in Sweden, where his parents had essentially been serfs, paying for their small plot of land in a forest by felling trees in the winter and floating them down the local river to a sawmill in the summer. As a teenager, he joined a new political party, the Swedish Social Democratic Workers' Party, one of several leftist parties that had sprung up in Europe during the late nineteenth century. These parties shared a belief that workers could improve their lives through democratic means, by forming unions, winning national elections, and implementing socialist policies, rather than by armed revolution. The closest American equivalent, the Socialist Party led by Eugene V. Debs, was never as successful as the versions in Sweden, Germany, and some other parts of Europe. The United States had a more individualist culture, and the American political left was riven by internecine disputes among socialists, communists, Trotskyists, Stalinists, and other factions. Nonetheless, the ideals of social democracy guided many union organizers and economic reformers in the United States.

Skoglund's devotion to radical politics allowed him to endure one defeat after another without giving up. After he became known as a union organizer in Sweden, mills refused to hire him, and in 1911 he immigrated to the United States, where he suffered the permanent foot injury in a logging camp. He then found work as a mechanic for the Pullman Company, leading to his participation in the failed Great Railroad Strike of 1922. Eventually, he got a low-paying job driving coal around Minneapolis.

Skoglund absorbed important lessons from these defeats. He saw how employers operated the levers of political power to achieve their goals. They shaped public opinion through sympathetic newspaper and radio coverage, which often cast employers as defenders of freedom and union activists as some mixture of thuggish, corrupt, and communist. This press coverage damaged morale among strikers and swayed the opinion of people who were not involved in strikes. Employers also conducted grassroots campaigns to persuade workers to return to work during a strike, offering financial incentives if they did and threatening financial ruin if they refused. These campaigns included alliances of convenience with potential replacement workers, like low-wage immigrants or the unemployed. During the 1922 railroad strike, for example, employers had used replacement workers to great effect.

The Citizens Alliance had perfected this approach. If the coal drivers were to have any chance at winning their strike, Skoglund believed, they would need to create a mirror image of the Alliance's political network. The strikers would have to outorganize their employers.

To do so, Skoglund and a handful of other organizers devised a masterful and intricate strategy. They started a daily newspaper, called *The Northwest Organizer,* to create an alternative to the city's pro-management press. The organizers agreed to an informal pact with local unemployed workers: The strikers promised to add expanded public relief to their list of demands if unemployed workers agreed to become de facto members of the union. As union members, the unemployed workers would refuse to serve as replacement drivers and instead join the flying squads trying to halt coal deliveries.

The strikers, who were by then calling themselves members of Local 574 of the Teamsters, also opened a headquarters in a large garage just outside of downtown Minneapolis that doubled as a community center for the drivers and their families. It included a dispatchers' room, with four telephones, to receive reports about coal trucks making deliveries and to dispatch flying squads to stop those trucks. The headquarters housed a kitchen to serve ten thousand meals a day, often with food donated by sympathetic farmers or shopkeepers, and a medical clinic, staffed by volunteer nurses and doctors. In the main area of the garage was a twenty-foot-wide platform, where strike leaders gave speeches and musicians performed for evening dances.

As part of their planning, Skoglund and his colleagues made the then unusual decision to include women formally in the strike. Minneapolis truckers were virtually all men, and Skoglund believed that previous labor leaders had made a mistake by ignoring women, especially workers' wives, who often made a family's most important decisions—including when a striker should give up and return to work. "Strikes were lost in the homes of the strikers as desperate wives saw the last of the grocery money go down the drain or the landlord had served a dispossess notice," Skoglund said to Marvel Scholl Dobbs, who was married to one of his fellow Local 574 leaders. To avoid that outcome, Dobbs and Clara Dunne, the wife of another union leader, organized the Ladies' Auxiliary. The two women first tried to convince striking drivers of the wisdom of the idea, and Marvel Dobbs later recalled that the men responded to their pitch with smirks and sneers. But then they went home and told their wives about it. "Much to their surprise, the women liked the idea," Dobbs said. The Auxiliary eventually grew to about seventy-five core members, with another few hundred women involved at times. The group helped run the strike headquarters and daily newspaper, and some members worked on the flying squads.

EVEN WITH THE infrastructure that the drivers had built, they lacked an obvious path to victory. The coal companies held firm. They refused to acknowledge that the drivers had voted to form a union and refused to negotiate with Local 574. In response, the union persuaded other truck drivers to join the strike and expanded the work stoppage beyond coal, shutting down major parts of the Minneapolis economy. Their rallying cry became "Make Minneapolis a union town." The employers responded with their own slogan: "Keep Minneapolis an open-shop city." The companies portrayed the union organizers as radicals trying to bring socialism to Minneapolis (and were not entirely wrong about that). "How Do You Like Having Our Minneapolis Streets in the Control of Communists?" asked an advertisement that ran in local newspapers.

Business executives may have lost the battle over whether Section 7(a) would be included in Roosevelt's recovery act, but they still believed they could prevent unions from forming. And if they could keep out unions, they could maintain the northwest empire's highly unequal economy through the Depression and into the future.

This intransigence was common across the country in 1933 and 1934. The National Association of Manufacturers, as usual, led the way. Its legal department sent a bulletin to its members with advice for subverting Section 7(a). The bulletin claimed that employers could still refuse to hire union members, could still tell workers not to join unions, and could still refuse to negotiate after workers had voted for a union, as Minneapolis's coal companies were doing. In Pennsylvania, steel mills ignored a union vote by their workers and announced they would negotiate with only a company-controlled union. At the Labor Department in Washington, steel executives attending a meeting in Perkins's office refused to talk or shake hands with Green, the AFL president, lest they seem to be legitimizing unions. In Michigan, automakers fired workers who attended organizing meetings. "The motor manufacturers have a good system," a writer for *The New Yorker* magazine wryly explained. "They keep the A.F. of L. unions out of the plants and then denounce them for being outsiders."

Executives were unyielding because they expected to win. They believed they continued to hold two crucial advantages that they had long enjoyed: time and government support.

Time tended to be on an employer's side because businesses had more resources with which to endure a strike than a union did. A company had cash reserves and lines of bank credit. By contrast, workers often lived paycheck to paycheck, and few unions could underwrite a long strike. When a strike ground on, many workers decided that a low wage was better than no wage.

The second advantage—government support for companies—was even more important. For decades, when a company and its workers became locked in unresolvable disputes, the government typically backed the company. Employers, with all their resources, had more to offer politicians, be it a campaign donation, a well-paying job in the future, help winning election to a higher office, or, in some cases, outright bribes. Many elected officials and judges during the late 1800s and early 1900s also agreed philosophically with employers. Political leaders and business executives were members of society's elite, with an interest in preserving the status quo. Again and again, mayors, governors, and presidents sided with employers during extended strikes and, when necessary, called on armed troops or police officers to stop the strikes.

In a 1919 essay, Max Weber, the German philosopher, noted that a defining characteristic of government was its monopoly on the legitimate use of violence. Over the course of American labor history, government officials had repeatedly chosen to use this monopoly on behalf of employers, rather than serve as a neutral arbiter during workplace disputes. National Guard troops and police officers worked closely with private agents hired by employers, like the Pinkerton agency. Some states removed the distinction entirely, allowing employers to pay the salaries of special sheriff deputies appointed to quell labor strife. In Pennsylvania, the Coal and Iron Police Act, which lasted from the Civil War until the Depression, permitted railroads, coal mines, and steel mills to appoint and arm their own police, with the power to arrest.

Rather than minimizing violence, this system stoked it. "The United States has had the bloodiest and most violent labor history of any industrial nation in the world," wrote two scholars in a history of labor conflict that the federal government commissioned in the 1960s. The most common scenario leading to violence, the scholars explained, occurred when a company simply refused to recognize a union. In some instances, the company tried to suppress unions violently, including through the lynching of labor organizers, like Frank Little in Montana in 1917 and E. C. McGregor in Arkansas in 1923. On dozens of occasions, troops and company agents killed workers. The victims included Pennsylvania railroad workers in 1877; Pennsylvania coal workers in 1897; textile workers in Ipswich, Massachusetts, in 1913; coal miners in Ludlow, Colorado, in 1914; and lumber workers in Everett, Washington, in 1916.

Other times, unions responded to the lack of recognition by initiating the violence. Many union tactics depended on physical force, or at least the threat of it, to prevent companies from operating normally during a strike. The flying squads that prevented coal deliveries in Minneapolis were an example. So were the sit-down strikes that idled factories or the picket lines that tried to keep replacement workers from entering a workplace.

Adjudicating these situations was tricky. But elected officials rarely tried to achieve a balance during the 1800s and early 1900s. They acted as an extension of company management. "Employers and unions were both guilty of violence," the 1960s federal commission concluded. The difference was that "employer violence had the cover of law." Decades earlier, William Howard Taft, the future president and chief justice, captured the prevailing attitude in a letter to his wife, when he was a judge and had just heard a report that federal troops had killed thirty striking railroad workers. "Though it is a bloody business," Taft wrote, "everybody hopes that it is true." In the highly unequal American economy, the forceful suppression of unions was the ultimate expression of political power.

IN THE SPRING of 1934, the Minneapolis strike became yet another labor dispute that descended into violence. The employers, with help from the police, attacked first. One night in May, a double agent posing as a union supporter used the loudspeaker inside strike headquarters to dispatch three truckloads of workers to an alley in downtown Minneapolis, supposedly to stop a delivery. When they arrived, private agents working for the employers and police officers trapped the workers in the alley and began beating them with saps and nightsticks. A few workers were left unconscious. Others had broken bones.

The union responded by escalating the violence. Two days after the alley attack, people on both sides of the strike gathered near the city's market area, expecting a fight over trucks attempting to deliver market goods. Photographs that ran in newspapers around the country the next day showed men in workmen's clothes and business attire slugging one another. Some carried wooden bats and iron pipes. During the brawl, workers beat two Citizens Alliance supporters so viciously that they died.

Teamsters and police clash in the streets of Minneapolis, 1934.

The employers and police then went even further. "You have shotguns and you know how to use them," the city's police chief told his officers. When a group of union supporters tried to block a truck from making a delivery one Friday afternoon that summer, officers fired on the group. The police continued firing as the workers fled, hitting sixty-seven of them and killing two. The day became known as Bloody Friday. Many of the victims had been shot in the back, according to Eric Sevareid, a young local journalist who would later become a national television correspondent. The initial stories in the city's major newspapers covered the attack accurately, Sevareid noted, but later editions switched to a false retelling, claiming that the strikers had attacked the police and the officers fired in self-defense. *The Northwest Organizer,* the union newspaper, covered the event more accurately and urged readers to attend a funeral march. Forty thousand people did so.

A major American city was throbbing with open violence between management and workers.

Governor Olson now found himself in an almost impossible position. His sympathies lay with the strikers. When the union first attempted to organize drivers, Olson wrote a public letter supporting the effort. Unions had their roots in the ancient human need to cooperate for survival, he argued. Roosevelt's recovery act gave workers the right to organize, he explained, and workers should seize it. "You should follow the sensible course and band together for your own protection and welfare," he wrote. Doing so could end the "reign of exploitation of the working man and woman." Once the violence began, however, Olson needed to restore order. He declared martial law in Minneapolis, even though the move seemed likely to help the employers by allowing replacement drivers to restart deliveries under the protection of the National Guard. Carl Skoglund and the other union leaders, knowing that Olson's move could doom the strike, announced that they would defy martial law. If need be, strikers would battle the National Guard to continue blocking deliveries.

"You're crazy," Olson told the union leaders during a negotiating session. "I won't even argue with you."

The strike appeared to be following a familiar trajectory. Workers went on strike for better pay and working conditions. Employers refused to recognize the union or negotiate. Conflict erupted. The government intervened. The workers seemed destined to lose.

Yet this strike ended up being different. It was different because of how the political atmosphere had changed by 1934 and because of who held power. While previous governors and presidents had used the government's authority to resolve strikes on behalf of employers, Olson and Roosevelt chose to use their authority on behalf of workers. Their approach was audacious and new, but less because of their tactics than because of the beneficiaries of those tactics.

Olson's first step was to get rid of the local union leaders defying martial law. One August morning before dawn, the National Guard burst into the strike headquarters on Olson's order and arrested the leaders. (Skoglund, traveling that night in Illinois to

raise money for the union, avoided arrest.) Olson had tired of the
leaders' politics. They sometimes seemed to care more about building a socialist movement than winning a raise for the city's drivers,
and their radicalism was alienating Minneapolis residents who
might otherwise support the workers' cause. Privately, Olson referred to the union leaders as "ritualists." Skoglund and others
returned the scorn, describing Olson as a capitalist tool.

Olson's next step belied that description. He told the National
Guard to raid the headquarters of the Citizens Alliance, and he
released embarrassing Alliance records that demonstrated its history of underhanded tactics, including an effort to portray Eleanor
Roosevelt as belonging to a "red network." Olson had exposed
the Alliance as the self-interested, anti-democratic organization
that it was. With the raids having weakened both sides, he announced that he would impose a settlement that included pay increases for the drivers. It was the same settlement that federal
mediators had suggested weeks earlier and that the employers had
rejected. Olson said that only those employers accepting the settlement terms would be allowed to operate in Minneapolis. He had
chosen to follow a path that virtually no previous governor, in
Minnesota or any other state, had: He used his authority to resolve
a strike in favor of higher pay, better working conditions, and
union recognition.

Senate campaign poster for Floyd Olson, 1936.

His final step was to involve the federal government. Roosevelt happened to be on a cross-country train trip that would take him through Minnesota days after Olson's imposed settlement. White House officials were careful to keep the president out of the Twin Cities, except for a brief nighttime stop, so that he would not be tainted by the chaos of the strike. Roosevelt instead stopped in the smaller city of Rochester and attended a celebration honoring the Mayo brothers, two doctors who had built their father's medical practice into a renowned clinic.

The major players in the strike—top business executives, leading union officials, and Olson—all traveled from the Twin Cities to Rochester to lobby Roosevelt and his aides. But the aides granted a one-on-one meeting with Roosevelt only to Olson. The two men had become fond of each other while they were fellow governors fighting the Depression in 1931 and 1932. They exchanged public praise and private letters. Some liberal Democrats viewed Olson as a potential successor to Roosevelt in 1940, after the president finished his presumed two terms. (Instead, Olson died of stomach cancer in 1936, at age forty-four, while he was governor and running for a seat in the United States Senate. He almost certainly would have won the Senate election.)

Roosevelt and Olson left no record of their conversation in Rochester, but subsequent events were clear enough. Almost immediately, the federal government intervened to help the workers win the strike.

The Roosevelt administration had leverage over Minneapolis businesses because many relied on loans from a federal agency, the Reconstruction Finance Corporation, to stay afloat during the Depression. The day after Roosevelt and Olson met, officials from the agency summoned Minneapolis business executives to a meeting in the city. These executives had spent months refusing to negotiate with Local 574 and doing everything possible to keep unions from gaining a foothold in Minneapolis. Their resolve suddenly disintegrated after the meeting with the Reconstruction Finance Corporation officials. The companies announced that they would negotiate with the union and made an initial settlement offer. Hundreds of previous strikes had failed when workers faced the prospect of running out of money. Now that Minneapolis's employers faced the same prospect, they too yielded to the realities of political power.

Over the next two weeks, their settlement offer became steadily more generous to the drivers. Finally, A. W. Strong, a longtime Citizens Alliance leader, told the trucking companies that it was time to accept reality and end the fight. The employers did. They agreed to establish a minimum wage, rehire striking drivers, hold union elections, and submit to collective bargaining in the future.

The head of the Reconstruction Finance Corporation, Jesse Jones, sent a telegram to Roosevelt with the news. "Glad to report Minneapolis strike settled," Jones wrote. "Employers have made substantial concessions in the general interest."

A banner headline in the next edition of the strikers' newspaper was more succinct: "VICTORY!"

Workers at about five hundred local companies voted to join Local 574 in the next two years, and the average weekly wage in the region's transportation sector roughly doubled. Workers in many other industries around Minnesota also formed unions. The low-wage northwest empire was crumbling.

Around the country, workers at thousands of companies would stage strikes during the mid-1930s. Some failed, including a textile strike up and down the East Coast that was happening at the same time as the truckers' strike in Minnesota. But many succeeded, often with support from elected politicians.

Perhaps the most famous strike of the era took place at a General Motors factory in Flint, Michigan, in 1937, by the United Auto Workers, which was part of the CIO. Trying to overcome the automobile industry's longtime hostility to unions, workers staged a sit-down strike, refusing to leave their workstations and shutting down the factory. Historically, politicians had responded to such tactics by sending in armed law enforcement to remove the workers, and John Nance Garner, Roosevelt's conservative vice president, advocated this approach in Flint. But Michigan's governor, Frank Murphy, rejected it. Murphy instead ordered the National Guard to keep the peace by preventing company agents and local police officers from attacking the strikers. He then helped negotiate a settlement favorable to workers. In doing so, Murphy was following a path that Olson had pioneered three years earlier in neighboring Minnesota. Murphy was using government power on behalf of workers. He was enforcing democratic capitalism.

On Capitol Hill, labor-friendly lawmakers also took steps to protect unions. Early in Roosevelt's presidency, the Supreme Court had continued its long history of siding with business and overturned major parts of the New Deal, including Roosevelt's recovery act and, with it, Section 7(a). In response, Wagner, the New York senator, helped pass a law in 1935 that codified workers' right to collective bargaining. Many observers expected the Supreme Court to throw out the Wagner Act, officially called the National Labor Relations Act. But by the time the justices heard the case in 1937, Roosevelt had been reelected by a record margin, and they upheld the law, evidently wary of confronting a popular president who had begun to criticize the court as undemocratic. The Wagner Act almost immediately caused labor-related violence to decline, never again to reach its earlier levels. The federal government had created a bureaucratic process through which management and workers could resolve disputes peacefully, rather than with fists, bats, and guns.

Together, Washington's new friendliness to labor unions and the successful Flint strike led to a surge of labor activity. Flint legitimized the United Auto Workers, and other parts of the automobile workforce soon unionized. The strike also legitimized the CIO and its inclusive strategy of industrial unionism. Union membership grew more rapidly in 1937 than in any other year in American history. It grew in part because the CIO abandoned the AFL's longtime support of segregated unions and welcomed Black workers. "He who hates Negroes and wishes to curtail their rights also hates labor and wishes to curtail its rights," read a CIO pamphlet aimed at Black workers. "Your enemies are our enemies: and your friends are our friends." An article in the NAACP's main publication advised, "Negro workers ought to flock to the CIO, unhesitatingly," because CIO organizers are known "far and wide for their absolute equality, regardless of color."

The start of World War II provided the final big push toward unionization. Roosevelt's desire for domestic tranquility during the war made him an even more aggressive advocate for union formation. When awarding defense contracts, the government often insisted that employers accept collective bargaining. More than 30 percent of American workers were union members by the mid-1940s, up from just over 10 percent in the mid-1930s. Even nonunionized workers benefited from the change because many companies without unions raised wages and improved working conditions to attract workers. In the span of a single decade, the power dynamic in the economy had changed.

IN TODAY'S PESSIMISTIC political climate, Americans distrust many of society's institutions, be they labor unions, large corporations, the government, the news media, or organized religion. This broader pessimism has fed a specific skepticism, still aggressively promoted by business groups, about whether unions have a record of delivering on their central promise: to raise wages. Mistakes and misconduct by unions contribute to the skepticism. When you first saw the word "Teamsters" in this chapter, I imagine your initial reaction may have been negative, with thoughts of Jimmy Hoffa and corruption.

Over the course of their history, however, the legacy of unions is not a cause for cynicism. Unions have a clear record of increasing workers' pay and improving working conditions. Business executives have understood as much, which is why they have often fought so hard to keep their workers from forming unions. Adam Smith and John Stuart Mill, as mentioned earlier, also recognized the power of unions. So have some of the most celebrated American civil rights activists. Susan B. Anthony advised: "Join the union, girls, and together say, 'Equal pay for equal work.'" Martin Luther King, Jr., who was assassinated while participating in a sanitation workers' strike in Memphis, described the labor movement as "the principal force that transformed misery and despair into hope and progress."

Academic researchers who have analyzed the economic effects of unions have reached similar conclusions. In recent years, the digital revolution has allowed economists to refine these conclusions by examining a much larger pool of data than they could before. With help from computers, the economists can scan thousands of old records, such as tax returns and polling responses, analyzing information that had languished in file cabinets. This change is part of the "big data" revolution in social science, and this book will describe several such studies. Raj Chetty's analysis of upward mobility, which I discussed in the introduction, is one such study. Another, conducted by a different team of economists, examines how unions have affected workers' pay since the 1930s.

That project began when the researchers discovered a set of records that allowed for a more complete answer than previous studies provided. Since 1936, the Gallup poll has asked Americans about both their pay and their union status; many other data sets have only one of those two pieces of information. The Gallup surveys allowed the researchers to build a database that ultimately included almost a million observations, which made it possible to answer all kinds of fascinating questions: Which types of workers belonged to a union? How has this changed over the years? How does the pay of a union member compare with that of a nonunionized worker of the same education level, age, experience, race, and gender?

Going back to the 1930s—whether the economy was booming or busting, whether unions were growing or shrinking—the typical member of a labor union earned roughly 10 percent to 20 percent more on average than an otherwise similar worker. The finding confirms that the range of indeterminacy for wages is large and that unions lift wages out of the low end of that range. As a result, unions have had a profound impact on economic inequality in the United States. At the beginning of the study's timeline, unions had not fully left behind their history as elite guilds, made up disproportionately of White men with higher skill levels. During the Depression and World War II, however, the rise of industrial unionism led to a more egalitarian approach. The Minneapolis strike was part of this trend, as was the organization of Black and White autoworkers in Michigan, Latino cannery workers in California, and immigrant workers in many industries in the Northeast. By the 1950s, the makeup of unions had flipped. Non-White workers and relatively unskilled workers were more likely to be in unions than other workers.

This change, together with the large wage premium for union members, played a vital role in lifting the pay of the poor and middle class. Scholars refer to the mid-twentieth century as a time of economic compression because lower-income workers enjoyed even larger raises, in percentage terms, than the rich. Median family income more than doubled between the mid-1940s and mid-1970s, after accounting for inflation. The White-Black pay gap shrank (the focus of an upcoming chapter). The world's largest middle class was forged.

The economists analyzing the Gallup data—Henry Farber, Daniel Herbst, Ilyana Kuziemko, and Suresh Naidu—asked one other vital question as part of their research: When union members received raises, where did the money come from? That is, did the raises prevent employers from hiring as many workers as they needed, thereby raising unemployment, or did the raises mostly reduce company profits? Economists who believe in a smoothly functioning market have long argued that union pay increases must come at the expense of overall employment and the economy's health. The market sets a worker's pay at the efficient level, according to this view; any higher wage will necessarily increase unemployment and reduce economic growth. The theory sounds plausible, but the experience of the past century suggests that it is wrong. The evidence indicates that the raises won by unions most often reduced profits without damaging the economy.

The researchers found that when unions have grown, unemployment has not tended to rise. One period when the pattern

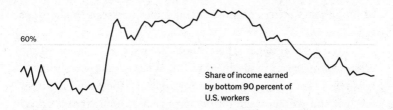

Share of income earned
by bottom 90 percent of
U.S. workers

Share of U.S.
workers in unions

stood out was the 1950s, when unions were at their apex and the United States economy was booming. Another way to see the phenomenon is to look at regional data: Areas with a higher share of unionization have not suffered from lower economic growth or more joblessness than regions with fewer unions. True, some places with a big union presence, like Michigan, have struggled in recent decades, and both unions and corporations, along with forces beyond the control of either, deserve some blame. Unions can indeed win raises, benefits, and work rules that damage a company's well-being. But these pyrrhic victories are not the norm. If anything, some of the country's fastest-growing, dynamic economies are in places with a large union workforce, like California, Massachusetts, New York, and Minnesota, the heart of the old northwest empire. In 2021, Minnesota had the ninth-highest share of unionized workers of any state and the fourteenth-highest per capita income.

This evidence suggests that unions alter the distribution of the economic pie more than the size of it. When workers are weak—when they lack political and economic power—their wages settle at the low end of the range of indeterminacy. Money that workers could be earning instead flows to corporate profits and executive salaries, increasing inequality. When workers gain power, they earn more money and enjoy better living standards. These gains do not usually come at the expense of the national economy, but they are not a free lunch, either. They come at the expense of the affluent.

No wonder, then, that the struggles over unions in the 1930s and 1940s were so bitter. The stakes were extremely high.

THE SUCCESSFUL ORGANIZING of American workers during these decades was a triumph of democratic politics. And it depended on two forces that came together and strengthened each other.

One was a mass movement that included millions of Americans. Workers signed union cards when it was risky to do so, and they participated in thousands of strikes during the 1930s. They attended rallies and public events like the flag-waving parade up Fifth Avenue in New York. They benefited from creative grass-roots organizing like the Ladies' Auxiliary and alliance with the unemployed in Minneapolis. This mass movement created public pressure for change. It focused attention on low pay, long hours, and dangerous working conditions.

Ultimately, though, the movement could not have succeeded on its own. It depended on the backing of political leaders like Roosevelt, Perkins, and Olson. In almost every major labor battle of the Depression, elected politicians and their appointees had the power to shape the outcome. Without support from Roosevelt and Perkins, Section 7(a) would not have made it into the 1933 recovery act, and the surge of union organizing that followed probably would not have happened. Without Olson's decision to break with history and use the National Guard to enforce a settlement favorable to workers—and then Roosevelt's financial squeezing of Minneapolis's employers—the truck drivers' strike probably would have failed. "For the first time in peacetime history," two labor scholars wrote about this period, "union organizations had the attention and approval of the Federal Government." The government wielded its power on behalf of workers.

The Progressive Era is a useful point of reference. It too included a mass movement of workers who responded to high levels of economic inequality by taking great personal risks to form unions. Often, unions did form during these years, and the number of strikes surged. The Progressive Era also included an elite effort to reduce inequality, led by activists and elected officials. This effort had major accomplishments, creating the federal income tax to reduce inequality, the Federal Reserve System to reduce the influence of private banks, and the Food and Drug Administration to monitor product safety. But the mass movement and the elite campaign never quite came together during the Progressive years. Many labor leaders, scarred by government's support for employers, failed to conceive of federal officials as potential allies. Samuel Gompers, the AFL's founder, once said that the "best thing the State can do for Labor is to leave labor alone." Progressive reformers, for their part, focused on regulating wages, hours, and working conditions rather than helping workers form unions. In the end, this disjointed approach led to only a modest, fleeting decline in inequality.

The New Deal alliance between workers and political elites had a more enduring impact, both economically and politically. It reshaped the economy and created its own feedback loop. As the political system became more responsive to workers, they became more invested in that system. They came to see government as a force that could improve their lives. "It is very possible that the New Deal's impact should be measured less by the lasting accomplishments of its reforms and more by the attitudinal changes it produced in a generation of working-class Americans who now looked to Washington to deliver the American dream," the historian Lizabeth Cohen wrote. American workers—urban and rural, Black and White, immigrant and native-born—formed the core of a political coalition that elected Democratic presidents to serve five consecutive terms, usually with strong Democratic majorities in Congress. The New Deal, as one pollster said, drew a class line across American politics. That said, the workers' coalition contained a contradiction that would eventually help break it apart: It depended for its majority on southern White supremacists and tolerated shameful racism for decades. But its accomplishments were nonetheless profound. It raised wages and living conditions for workers across races and regions. It forged the world's most prosperous working class and its largest middle class.

It even did a more effective job of creating top-down government regulations to protect workers than the Progressive Era itself had done. The earlier Progressives had only limited success passing minimum wages and eight-hour workday laws, and the Supreme Court struck down several of those measures. The Progressives had not built a strong enough democratic coalition. The New Deal Democrats and their labor allies managed to build such a coalition. As a result, much of the ambitious agenda that Perkins presented to Roosevelt when he offered her the job of labor secretary became reality: a forty-hour workweek, a minimum wage, a ban on child labor, unemployment insurance, welfare benefits, and Social Security. These laws played a major role in lifting incomes and reducing inequality, including for low-wage workers who often were not members of unions.

Labor unions are not sufficient to create democratic capitalism and ensure the ideals of the American dream. Government regulations and benefits are necessary, as well. But the existence of those regulations and benefits often depends on the political support that comes from a workers' movement.

Perhaps the most surprising legacy of that movement was its effect on corporate leaders. For decades, employers had resorted to extreme measures to keep wages as low as possible. They had formed groups like the Citizens Alliance and insisted that businesses could not possibly pay more without risking their survival. But once wages rose, a growing number of executives began to shift their position. They realized that it was still possible to make a good profit in a high-wage capitalist economy. They became accustomed to sharing power.

CHAPTER 2

Trustees of the Common Welfare

PAUL HOFFMAN KNEW THAT HE WAS FLOUNDERING DURING his freshman year at the University of Chicago. He had failed an English class and began to wonder whether college was right for him. He was also aware that his parents, struggling to find steady work during the economic slump that followed the Panic of 1907, could not easily afford his tuition payments.

Looking for advice, Hoffman went to see a family friend who was a businessman in Chicago. Hoffman admired the man and asked how he too could have a successful business career, perhaps without finishing college. "The surest way that I know for you, or any other young man, to get ahead," the friend told Hoffman, "is to find yourself a job in a growing business—in a growing town."

Hoffman liked that idea. He had grown up reading Benjamin Franklin's autobiography and Horatio Alger novels. He bought into their glorification of hardworking young men from ordinary backgrounds who achieved success. Following the first part of the advice—finding a growing business—seemed simple enough. The fastest-growing American business at the time was the automobile business. Cars had been a novelty only a few years before. By 1909, when Hoffman dropped out of college, they were everywhere. Hoffman's middle-class family had joined the craze, having bought a used car that resembled an old-fashioned open buggy with a motor attached to the front. Hoffman was enthralled. He had seen a glimpse of the future.

He soon managed to get hired by a car dealership in downtown Chicago, initially as a janitor, before being promoted to "grease boy" (as mechanics were known) and then salesman. He turned out to be a natural. He had a sunny personality, and he found it easy to talk to people. He was boyishly nice-looking without being intimidating. His selling strategy involved driving a new car around Chicago's West Side and waiting for a passerby to ask him about it. He would then invite the person to take it for a drive with him. Frequently, the drive ended with a sale.

As well as Hoffman was doing in Chicago, he never forgot the second part of the businessman's advice: Find a growing town. Chicago's great growth was already behind it. But Los Angeles, where Hoffman happened to have relatives, was just getting started. He moved there in 1911, at the age of twenty, with visions of Alger-like success, and his plan worked beautifully. Hoffman was soon selling seven or eight Studebakers a month. He met a young woman from New England named Dorothy Brown when her parents came into his showroom to look at cars, and the two of them married. He would later open his own dealership, the Paul G. Hoffman Company.

The business did so well by 1925 that executives from Studebaker's corporate headquarters, in South Bend, Indiana, asked Hoffman to move east and become a vice president. The promotion "upset all tradition in the executive fields of motor-car manufacture," the *Los Angeles Times* reported, because salesmen did not usually ascend to executive jobs. And Hoffman kept rising at the Studebaker headquarters. In 1931, when he was forty, the board of directors promoted him to president, second only to the company's chairman.

In his outlook on the world, Hoffman was a typical businessman. At work and in his and Dorothy's social life, he was surrounded by other businessmen. He did not drink or smoke, but he did like to eat steak and to play golf and bridge. He had established himself professionally during the conservative 1920s, when business was rolling back Progressive Era regulations and squeezing labor unions. Businessmen like him believed in individual initiative. They viewed America as prosperous and fair. They generally abhorred government action—or "collectivism," the term Hoffman used to deride the New Deal and especially the National Recovery Administration, the federal agency implementing Roosevelt's recovery act. "The N.R.A. was a thoroughly vicious experiment in the fascist control of business," he said publicly, more than once.

Hoffman voted Republican, first for Warren Harding, Calvin Coolidge, and Herbert Hoover and then for every challenger to Franklin Roosevelt. Sometimes, Hoffman did volunteer work for Republican campaigns. He and his friends would lament the criticisms—"scathing attacks," Hoffman called them—that Roosevelt leveled against business leaders. When Roosevelt said that the country's business and financial profiteers were "unanimous in their hate for me—and I welcome their hatred," Roosevelt was thinking of men like Hoffman. He seemed precisely the sort of executive who could have led a counterattack against the federal government and labor unions, modeled after the past successes of the Citizens Alliance in Minneapolis or the National Association of Manufacturers.

Yet Hoffman chose another path.

He would spend much of his career leading a campaign to reform the culture of American business. Hoffman became an evangelist for a corporate America that was less self-interested and more concerned with the national interest. He argued that good wages were crucial to prosperity for businesses and workers alike. He figured out how to work with labor unions and government regulators, at least most of the time. He tried to persuade other executives to adopt a similar approach—and many of them did. In the 1940s and 1950s, Hoffman's vision of corporate America triumphed.

The hard-liners in corporate America never disappeared, but they did become a minority. Many executives did not try to maximize their own personal compensation and instead raised their employees' wages higher than strict economic forces dictated was necessary. When the Republican Party, the party of big business, finally returned to the White House in the early 1950s under Dwight Eisenhower, the administration did not try to eliminate the New Deal bureaucracy or reduce the top marginal income tax rate, the rate that applied to the highest incomes and that was then a staggering 92 percent.

Paul Hoffman inspects potato production on a French
farm as part of his work administering the Marshall Plan,
1950.

Hoffman, many of his fellow executives, and the Republican
leaders of their era were part of an extraordinary shift in the
American economy. Political power played a vital role in that shift.
But something else was also happening. Business executives themselves changed their minds about what was the ideal economic
system. They changed their behavior, too.

CAPITALISM DEPENDS ON the assumption that people want to improve their material well-being. When entrepreneurs see an opportunity for a profitable new business, they start it. Investors then
back the company, and talented workers join it. This pursuit of
profit creates investment returns, good jobs, and useful products.
It is the invisible hand that Adam Smith described as subtly guiding human behavior. But the sharpest observers of capitalism have
always understood that materialism is not the only guiding force

in a market economy. Smith, whose academic field was moral philosophy, wrote eloquently on this subject. In *The Wealth of Nations*, his 1776 masterwork, he used the phrase "invisible hand" only once. He spent more time describing the emotional and moral influences on behavior, including pride, envy, and respect.

For the most part, people do not make independent judgments about these moral issues. Trying to do so would be overwhelming. We are instead influenced by customs that guide our interactions with friends, relatives, colleagues, and strangers. Together, these customs constitute a society's culture. "Culture is a set of beliefs, values, and preferences, capable of affecting behavior, that are socially (not genetically) transmitted and that are shared by some subset of society," the economic historian Joel Mokyr has written. A society's culture is distinct from its institutions and laws, although the two shape each other. Institutions and laws tend to revolve around rules that dictate how people must behave. Culture involves more judgment. The law says that a customer must pay a restaurant bill and that an employer must pay at least minimum wage. Culture affects how much of a tip the customer leaves and how much more than minimum wage an employer pays an entry-level worker.

An animating question of social science has been how culture changes over time. Cultures certainly do change, but it is less obvious why and when they do—or do not. In the 1980s, a sociologist named Ann Swidler published an influential academic article, "Culture in Action," that offered a framework for thinking about cultural change. Swidler distinguished between two different periods in a society: settled and unsettled. In a settled period, patterns of behavior take on an undisputed authority. People do not think about their actions as involving a choice. They behave as others do. They dress in certain ways. They shake hands to say hello, or they kiss on the cheek. They hold shared beliefs about how society should operate, especially if they come from the same social group. In an unsettled period, however, people start to question many of their core assumptions. They analyze their actions and ask whether different behavior might make more sense.

The early twentieth century was a settled period for corporate executives in the United States. They did not each independently try to develop a worldview. The culture of American business provided them with their views. The men running the largest companies in Minneapolis during the 1920s did not spend time agonizing over whether to fight labor unions, and Hoffman did not try to figure out his attitudes toward government intervention in the economy. The answers were clear to them. The country ran best on a laissez-faire, free-enterprise economic system, in which companies tried to earn big profits, hardworking people rose to the top, and government mostly stayed out of the way. The alternative, as these executives saw it, was not a gentler version of capitalism. No other country was trying that. The alternative was a slide toward Bolshevism.

Sometimes, though, events can bring an end to a settled period. This is most likely to happen when people have reason to believe that society has stopped working in some important way. In that situation, people can abandon old habits and behaviors quickly. The English upper classes spent centuries with a settled view of poverty, arguing that the poor would always be dependent on charity and largely incapable of work. When the Industrial Revolution forced craftsmen and artisans out of work—people who were clearly capable of holding a job—the upper classes changed their view. They rewrote England's poor laws and encouraged members of the lower classes to find factory work. The English aristocracy's view of the work ethic had become unsettled. Similarly, the Chinese Communist Party spent decades treating market capitalism as a treasonous idea, only to begin adopting it under Premier Deng Xiaoping in the late 1970s. The chaos of the Cultural Revolution, the death of Mao Zedong, and the evident breakdown of his economic model unsettled China's political culture. More recently, in the United States, white-collar workers had long gone into the office five days a week, mostly without fathoming an alternative. After the Covid pandemic disrupted this practice, many companies signaled that they would never return to the previous model.

Swidler pointed out that unsettled periods typically do not involve people renouncing their old views as wrong. Instead, they use culture as a "tool kit," as she put it. They abandon old habits and adopt new ones while justifying the changes with some of the same language that they previously used. They insist, and believe, that they are pursuing the same ends that they always have. Take China, for example. The ruling party that oversaw the shift to capitalism continues to call itself the Communist Party, to celebrate Marxism, and to venerate Mao. China's leaders have used these symbols as a tool kit, helping them justify their embrace of capitalism.

Two of the prime disruptions to a settled culture have been depression and war, and in the late 1930s the world was coping with both. Together, they unsettled the culture of the American economy. The business executives ascending the ranks—those in Hoffman's generation—began to question some of the beliefs that they had once unthinkingly accepted.

They had witnessed the economy of the 1920s self-destruct and watched Roosevelt halt the worst of the crisis. They also knew that other countries were turning to fascism or communism in response to the crisis. A managed version of capitalism, with a greater role for the government and workers' organizations, no longer seemed like the worst scenario imaginable. To some business executives, it increasingly looked like the least bad option. When the pollster Elmo Roper surveyed executives in 1939, he captured the changing mood. Roper asked their view of two laws that business had strenuously tried to prevent from passing: the Wagner Act, the labor relations law that established a right to collective bargaining, and the Social Security Act, which many executives had once described as socialism (and Roosevelt himself had initially considered too radical). By 1939, however, most executives were accommodating themselves to a new reality. Only 41 percent of the executives favored the repeal of the Wagner Act, and only 17 percent favored ending Social Security. Many executives said that they wanted the laws modified, not scrapped. The executives were starting to accept the idea of a different kind of capitalism, even if they did not know exactly what it should be.

World War II further scrambled people's beliefs. Although wartime mobilization finally restored the economy to health, the boom did not seem sustainable. It was based on the production of tanks, ships, planes, guns, and artillery that would no longer be needed after the war. Adding to the problem, millions of soldiers would eventually return home looking for work. Both economists and the general public were deeply anxious about the possibility of a post-war crisis.

An article in *The American Economic Review,* an academic journal, warned that a "severe depression" was "highly probable" without huge government spending. *The New Republic* predicted that whenever peace arrived, "more people might be thrown out of work than were unemployed at the bottom of the Great Depression." A poll by *Fortune* magazine found that nearly half of American civilians were so worried about future unemployment that they wanted the federal government to prevent troops from leaving the military when the war ended, until jobs became available for them. When *Stars and Stripes,* the military newspaper distributed on the fronts in Europe and Asia, reprinted the poll's findings, so many soldiers wrote angry letters to *Fortune* that its editors printed a groveling apology.

Even soldiers, who obviously had bigger and more immediate threats to worry about, spent a lot of time talking about the uncertain postwar economy. They wondered if they would win the war only to come home to unemployment. A cartoon that ran in *Stars and Stripes* late in the war showed thousands of soldiers pouring off ships onto American shores, as if landing for a D-Day–style invasion, this time of their homeland. Amid the throng, one soldier held a huge white flag aloft, announcing, "We Want Jobs." There was a straightforward explanation for the worries: By the 1940s, more than a decade had passed since the country had enjoyed both peace and prosperity. The economy seemed very fragile.

By this point, Hoffman had become a public figure, as the president of Studebaker. He received invitations to give speeches around the country, and he enjoyed giving them. He was able to offer his views on how the United States could solve its problems. In these speeches, he continued to warn that too much government control of business threatened free enterprise and personal liberty. But he added new warnings in the late 1930s. He argued that

American business also needed to change. If it didn't, it too could jeopardize free enterprise and personal liberty. "Business men who believe in free enterprise," Hoffman declared, "must recognize that free enterprise is in greater danger from business reactionaries than it is from communists." At one point, he explained, "The best way I can serve Studebaker, my family, and myself is to help fortify capitalism against all attacks, to help keep it strong and dynamic."

At the 1940 graduation ceremony of his alma mater, Lyons Township High School, outside Chicago, he contrasted the optimism at his own 1907 graduation with the fear that had replaced it. Democracy, he told the students, was fighting a losing battle with dictatorship because democracy had not been working well for the previous two decades. The economy in many countries was growing slowly and inequitably, leading to "a spirit of futility and frustration which provided the ideal opportunity" for demagogues. Unity had been replaced by strife; people had stopped fighting for the common good and started fighting one another. The only way to save democracy, Hoffman argued, was for society's leaders—in business, labor, farming, and politics—to stop looking out only for their narrow interests and start caring about America as a whole. These leaders needed to become "zealots for democracy."

BY THE LATE 1930S, Robert Maynard Hutchins was at the peak of his powers as the president of the University of Chicago. The son and grandson of ministers, Hutchins had become Chicago's president a decade earlier, at age thirty. He was an audacious leader who had shocked alumni by eliminating the football team, calling it a trivialization of higher education. He championed the study of great books. He defended academic freedom, getting into a public spat with Charles Walgreen after the drugstore founder accused the university's professors of brainwashing his niece with leftist thoughts. Hutchins would also help create a secret research project in 1940 and recruit top atomic scientists to Chicago to work on it. The work, initially known as the Metallurgical Project, would become part of the Manhattan Project.

Hutchins believed that higher education was a means toward

building a better society through rational inquiry and argument. In Hoffman—a civic-minded businessman whose South Bend office was not far from Chicago—Hutchins saw a potential ally. Although Hoffman had dropped out of the University of Chicago, he had become successful enough that the university was happy to claim him as an alumnus and gave him a spot on its board of trustees.

After a trustee meeting in the spring of 1940, Hoffman pulled aside both Hutchins and a university vice president, William Benton, to pitch an idea. "I think the time is here when the university must try to do something about the state of the nation," Hoffman told them. "The University of Chicago has the economists and other scholars. These men have the knowledge, but their knowledge isn't being applied for the good of the country. What can be done about it?"

Hoffman went on for almost twenty minutes, laying out his proposal. As a car salesman, he had believed that the art of persuasion depended on emotion, and he felt genuinely emotional about this topic. Free enterprise was in danger. Fascism was on the march. Yet many businessmen were responding with bromides recounting past glories of the American economy. Hoffman disdained it as "flag-waving." He wanted business to take concrete action. The task, Hoffman said, was to create an economy that provided "real jobs"—well-paying jobs—to anyone willing and able to work. "The system which best raises wages will win out," he said. Americans needed to see that democracy and capitalism could deliver better than Nazi Germany, Fascist Italy, imperial Japan, or Soviet Russia. Hoffman told Hutchins and Benton that the University of Chicago could help, consistent with Hutchins's ambitious vision for higher education. The university could create a small organization that spanned academia and the business world and would develop a plan for allowing America to meet the rising challenge from totalitarianism.

Hoffman had a specific model for the group in mind. Several years earlier, his own industry had undergone a crisis. There had been a national panic about car crashes. The automobile revolution had unleashed a new form of transportation on a country that was not ready for it. Roads had not been designed to keep vehicles away from pedestrians, cyclists, or trolleys, and cars had not been designed to keep their riders safe. Newspapers began to print gruesome photographs of accidents: cars hanging from bridges, embedded in houses, crumpled by trees, and more. Crashes were killing almost forty thousand Americans annually, nearly four times the toll from homicide at the time and ten times the toll from lung cancer.

The initial response to the crisis from auto executives, including Hoffman, was denial. He and other executives minimized the problem, through dubious statistics purporting to show that driving was safe, and blamed others, like a small minority of bad drivers and government officials who were not spending enough money on new roads. As deaths kept climbing, however, more executives recognized that fear of accidents threatened the growth of their business. The industry created a safety commission and named Hoffman its president. He asked for help from university professors who were creating a new academic field, called traffic analysis, and he took their conclusions seriously. He prided himself on being a person who could be swayed by empirical evidence.

"I have changed my mind," he said. "I might better have said that it has been changed for me." The experts, he added, "have succeeded in blasting my mind open."

He embarked on a barnstorming tour, giving speeches around the country, appearing on radio shows, and writing for *The Saturday Evening Post*. He urged widespread changes. The government should build safer roads, Americans should drive more cautiously, and the industry should do its part by redesigning its vehicles. He told audiences that he and other automobile executives were not acting merely out of altruism. "Our selfish interests in these respects coincide with public interest," he said. The industry had flipped from a shortsighted emphasis on holding down manufacturing costs while pretending there was no safety problem to an attempt to solve the problem.

The auto safety campaign took on a classically American form. It combined a national group—the one Hoffman ran—with local chapters that had the autonomy to make their own decisions. It was the same model that civic organizations had been using since the country's founding, including the Freemasons, farmers' alliances, the American Red Cross, and groups advocating temperance, women's suffrage, and the abolition of slavery. This approach has been important in the United States, as the scholar Theda Skocpol has explained, because the central government is relatively weak and the federalist system requires different solutions in different places. These hybrid efforts, part national and part local, have altered American life by influencing people's attitudes and, by extension, their behavior. They have been exercises in cultural change.

Hoffman's auto safety campaign created enduring features of American life. It persuaded high schools to teach a new class, initially called Driver Training and later known as Driver's Ed. Car companies began building cars with all-steel bodies, hydraulic brakes, and shatterproof windshields. Local governments began to keep track of drivers' safety records and suspended the licenses of repeat offenders. Governments also started building many more divided highways—modeled after roads along the Hudson River in New York City and Lake Michigan in Chicago—to replace what Hoffman called "suicide traps," in which oncoming traffic was separated by only a white line. There was no single revolutionary change, no sweeping new federal law, and no technological breakthrough. And not all of Hoffman's efforts succeeded. (He urged Americans not to drive if they had consumed even one alcoholic drink.) Yet his larger effort did succeed. The death rate per mile would never again reach its 1934 peak. It fell by almost one-third from 1934 to 1940. The difference amounted to more than ten thousand lives saved each year. The campaign confirmed Hoffman's optimistic vision of what Americans could do when they put their minds to a big task. He had helped change the culture of automobile safety.

In 1940, he wanted to do the same for the American economy. When he explained his idea to Hutchins and Benton at the University of Chicago board meeting, they immediately liked it. Benton, a former businessman himself—he had cofounded the Benton &

Bowles advertising agency before retiring to work for the university—agreed to run the effort with Hoffman.

Together, they recruited some of the biggest names in corporate America, including the magazine publisher Henry Luce and top executives at Eastman Kodak, General Foods, and Lehman Brothers. Hoffman and Benton sought advice from intellectuals outside Chicago, like the theologian Reinhold Niebuhr and Peter Drucker, a young economics writer who would become an influential management guru. Drucker told Hoffman and Benton that their group was precisely what the country needed. The world's democracies had to win both the war and the peace that followed, and winning the peace meant building a stronger economy, Drucker believed.

The group was in its early planning stages when Japan attacked Pearl Harbor, pulling the United States into the war. Hoffman and Benton soon paid a visit to Roosevelt's secretary of commerce, Jesse Jones. Jones was another example of the changing norms among the corporate elite. A former banker, real estate developer, and newspaper publisher from Texas whom Hoover had brought into the federal government, Jones was among the most conservative members of Roosevelt's administration. He was appointed partly to assuage Democrats concerned about the liberalism of the vice president Roosevelt chose in 1940, Henry Wallace. But Jones was also the same official who had helped resolve the Minneapolis trucking strike in favor of the workers in 1934, when he was running the Reconstruction Finance Corporation. The fact that he represented the conservative corporate voice in the cabinet demonstrated how much the mainstream had moved to the left.

Jones, Hoffman, and Benton agreed that the federal government was too busy with war planning to do a good job with postwar economic planning. The University of Chicago group would handle that task, with a little help from the federal government. Jones offered the new organization office space at the Commerce Department—no small thing during wartime mobilization—and the imprimatur of the Roosevelt administration in exchange for influence over the group's membership. He rejected Luce, a critic of Roosevelt, and several others on the initial list. To take their place, Jones helped recruit an even more impressive roster of executives. It included the chairmen of Coca-Cola and Quaker Oats; the presidents of General Electric and Scott Paper; the lead partner at Goldman Sachs; and the president of Kansas State University, Milton Eisenhower, whose brother was an obscure but rising army general.

The group called itself the Committee for Economic Development and got to work. In the span of a year, Hoffman's idea had turned into something grander than he envisioned. It was part of the country's all-out war effort. The Roosevelt administration and the leaders of corporate America were working together on a vision for a new economy.

HOFFMAN ALWAYS DISPLAYED a bit of a salesman's panache. His hair was perfectly parted and gently slicked back. Whatever he was selling, he laid out a vision of a sunny future to his listeners and told them it could be theirs. In the 1910s, his audience had been people who had never owned a car, and his product had been the Studebaker. During World War II, his audience was other business executives, and his product was a prosperous America. He set out to convince them they could usher in the greatest boom that the country had known.

The Committee for Economic Development adopted the hybrid structure that the auto-safety effort had used, combining a national umbrella group with local chapters. It soon had about two thousand chapters, each run by local businesspeople. The national group provided the local groups with worksheets to help them plan their postwar economies and with expert advice from academic economists and Federal Reserve officials. Hoffman and other national officials traveled around the country, giving speeches at regional gatherings, where local leaders could hear how their work was part of the country's war effort.

Hoffman described the challenge as "a dual date with destiny." He began each speech by saying that the country's first priority was defeating Germany and Japan. But that would not be enough. "We must win the war," he said, "and this time we must also win the peace." Left unsaid, but clear to many listeners, was that the world had failed to do so after World War I. Desperation in Germany had enabled the Nazis' rise. In the United States, people remembered the army's Bonus March of 1932, when thousands of struggling veterans came to Washington, only to be fired on by federal troops. This recent history contributed to the anxieties about a postwar economic slump.

Working with the economists who were advising the CED, Hoffman was persuaded that the solution involved a consumer economy built on abundant jobs paying high wages. Thanks to the wartime boom, many families were already enjoying higher incomes, but they could not buy cars and appliances because factories were instead making military equipment. After the war, the CED argued, pent-up consumer demand would be unleashed and defy the predictions of a depression. Executives should make decisions about their future employment and product investments based on an assumption of prosperity, Hoffman argued. As he and other CED officials traveled around the country, they delivered a message infused with an "evangelistic fervor rivaling the late Billy Sunday's," *Business Week* magazine wrote. Billy Sunday had been a professional baseball player who became a successful Christian evangelist in the early 1900s.

In part, Hoffman was conducting a national exercise in building confidence. If everyone acted as if prosperity were coming, it would be more likely to arrive. When the CED's worksheets showed that the companies in a metropolitan area were not planning on hiring enough workers after the war to keep unemployment low, CED officials went back to individual companies and urged them to be more optimistic. If each company took a chance on hiring more workers, the local economy would be healthy enough to justify the higher employment levels. A virtuous cycle would begin.

This campaign was about more than confidence, however. It was also an ideological project to persuade thousands of executives that cost control was not their only route to profitability. Yes, they could make money as they had in the past, by keeping out labor unions, holding down wages, lobbying for minimal taxes, and beating back government regulations. But they could also earn a profit—potentially a larger, more sustainable profit—by doing their part to create an economy in which American families had enough income to buy all kinds of new products. The group's founding documents, distributed around the country, proclaimed that workers had the right to combine into labor organizations for collective bargaining and that there was no inherent conflict between government and business.

The CED became the highest-profile part of a larger shift in corporate America. The twin crises of depression and war had increased the appeal of a less rapacious version of capitalism. In the 1920s, the number of corporate moderates was small. By the 1940s, the notion of paying high wages and working cooperatively with labor unions and government regulators had entered the mainstream.

A major reason was fear—fear not only of the totalitarianism rising in other countries but of the possibility of quasi socialism in the United States. The wartime boom, many executives understood, involved substantially more government spending than the New Deal. If the country were going to return to a less statist economy after the war, as corporate leaders desperately wanted, they would need to ensure that it provided rising living standards. As Robert Henry Brand, a top executive at the investment firm Lazard Frères, said in a 1943 speech to his fellow bankers, the war had created millions of jobs and high wages for Americans. "After it," Brand predicted, "they will not be content with less without a very great struggle." Brand told his fellow bankers that he and they were the "upholders of the present system"—capitalism, that is—and they must find a version of it that benefited "the ordinary man and woman."

Messages like this were common. "The challenge is coming," Charles Wilson, the president of General Electric and a CED board member, told executives in another speech. "It is not merely a threat. It is an opportunity for the free enterprise system to repair its mistakes, do a better job than ever before and regain the confidence of the people." Near the end of a widely circulated CED manifesto summarizing the group's beliefs, Benton included this sentence: "THERE'S STILL AN AMERICAN DREAM."

Throughout these pleas, the new generation of corporate moderates made sure to use many of the same phrases—especially "free enterprise"—that hard-line executives had used in the 1920s and 1930s to defend a laissez-faire economy. The moderates edited their public materials to remove the word "collective," which smacked of Soviet collectivism, even as Benton and Hoffman talked privately about the need for collective action to win the war. By doing this, the reformers were using the culture of American business as a tool kit, to use the term from Ann Swidler's later research, and repurposing old symbols for new ends. They were arguing that their approach was in fact more consistent with a healthy capitalist system than the old approach. In private, CED officials were often blunter and more disdainful. They described the remaining corporate hard-liners as "intellectual Neanderthals" who believed in "self, self, self" and who were undermining the capitalist system they claimed to venerate.

One CED board member was particularly careful about the group's message because he knew how hard it would be to win over some executives. His name was Jay Hormel, and he ran Geo. A. Hormel & Co., the Minnesota food company that his father had established in 1891. Although Jay Hormel had grown up in the deeply conservative business community of the northwest empire, he was part of Hoffman's generation, open to new ways of doing things. He had instituted one of the nation's first systems for paying workers a set amount each week, rather than wages that fluctuated with business conditions. In 1938, he added a profit-sharing plan to create a sense of shared mission among the company's workers. As the CED planned a meeting to launch the Minneapolis chapter in March 1943, Hormel urged Benton to take care in dealing with the "old guard."

"I had forgotten about the Old Guard in Minnesota," Benton replied in a letter, "which is perhaps older and more guarded than most."

To win them over, Hormel had some suggestions. The CED

should stop using the word "equality" by itself and replace it with "equality of opportunity." The group should also make clear that opportunity did not conflict with the principles of security that many Americans were seeking during a war that had followed a depression. Hormel was trying to scrub the CED's material of language from the political left and replace it with terms from the pro-business right—all without changing any substantive recommendations. He believed that the choice of words could be more persuasive than intricate statistical arguments. "You are too much concerned with economics and not enough concerned with psychology," Hormel wrote another CED board member. Finally, Hormel said, the launch for the local CED chapter should involve a "whoop-de-do" meeting that included prominent members of the old guard who were open to the reform message. Their presence would signal that the new ideas deserved a hearing.

Meetings like Hormel's spread the gospel of a high-wage economy and made the CED the symbol of it. In September 1943, Hoffman appeared on *Time* magazine's cover, which called him "Businessman Hoffman" and included the tagline "America's frontiers are still beyond the horizon." In the cover's background—behind Hoffman's smiling face and his immaculately parted, graying hair—was a collection of sketches depicting a prosperous postwar country. There were industrial blueprints, a graph with rising lines, and a futuristic car. A helicopter, a type of aircraft that only the military was using at the time, hovered over an office building in a leafy suburb. All of this can be ours, Hoffman seemed to be saying, if only we are willing to make some changes.

BIG BUSINESS HAD fought for so long against government intervention and labor unions that some Americans understandably wondered whether the new moderation was merely a ploy. These concerns were especially common among political progressives. One of the harshest critics was Robert Brady, an economics professor at the University of California, Berkeley. Brady viewed the CED's postwar planning as public relations—an attempt to repackage the self-interest of big business in softer language and thus to make palatable a return to a 1920s-style economy. When Hoffman and his fellow executives claimed to be promoting the common welfare, Americans should not believe them, Brady argued. "There are few lovable 'trustees of the common welfare,'" he wrote. As evidence, Brady pointed to the "cross-fertilization" between the membership of the CED and that of hard-line business groups like the National Association of Manufacturers and the Chamber of Commerce.

Other progressives made similar arguments. *The New Republic* described the CED proposal for a postwar tax code as "a rich man's tax program" because it called for imposing some taxes on the bottom half of the income distribution. The top half, the article argued, should pay all taxes. *The New Republic* also mocked the CED's postwar employment worksheets with the headline "Look Who's Planning!" Historically, political conservatives and business executives had equated economic planning with socialism.

A specific concern of the critics was that Hoffman and his colleagues were using false pretenses to prevent Washington from planning a major government jobs program for the war's aftermath. Instead, Hoffman was traveling the country arguing that unemployment could remain low so long as business voluntarily embraced the idea of a prosperous consumer economy. Many experts thought this hopeful vision was delusional. They predicted that the unemployment rate would reach 15 percent when the war ended. Beneath Hoffman's flowery language about democracy and patriotism, he and the CED were just another lobbying group trying to undermine the rationale for another New Deal, critics said.

In later decades, progressive historians and other commentators would expand this skeptical argument and question the entire notion that postwar corporate America ever moderated its approach to workers. According to this view, big business simply lacked the political power during the 1930s and 1940s to assert itself. Executives remained as aggressive as ever, according to this argument; they were simply less able to get what they wanted.

The argument makes some valid points. The CED was always, in part, an interest group. Its tax plan, for example, called for lower corporate tax rates than disinterested economists advised.

Big business also remained at least somewhat antagonistic toward labor unions. The key plank in this effort was the Taft-Hartley Act, which became law in 1947 after a bipartisan, pro-business coalition overrode the veto of President Harry Truman, a Democrat. The act allowed states to pass right-to-work laws that helped employers keep unions out of their workplaces. More than twenty-five states eventually did so, including most of the rapidly expanding Sun Belt states. Taft-Hartley prevented organized labor from extending its gains into the South and helped hold down wages in the region.

But the notion that the culture of American business remained unchanged—that executives behaved with the same naked self-interest in the 1940s and 1950s as in the 1920s—is more wrong than right. It mistakenly treats corporate executives as monolithic, rather than recognizing that there have always been both moderates and hard-liners, with the relative size and influence of the two groups shifting over time. During World War II and the years that followed, the hard-line approach of the National Association of Manufacturers waned, while the moderate CED approach grew. "By the end of World War II, a moderate, pragmatic corporate elite had emerged, based primarily in the largest American corporations," the sociologist Mark Mizruchi has written. The hard-liners never went away, and they won some victories. Even so, the dominant culture in corporate America shifted substantially.

There are several ways to see that the more cynical argument is mistaken. For one thing, the skeptics were incorrect about the postwar economy, and Hoffman's optimism was borne out. The unemployment rate did not spike to 15 percent or anywhere close to it. It hovered around 4 percent in the late 1940s. The CED vision of a prosperous economy had not merely been a way to prevent a government jobs program. A vibrant economy had come to fruition. High employment and wages led to household spending, which led to industrial production—and, in turn, to more jobs at good wages. The country's corporate executives had imagined a prosperous economy and created it.

Once their factories wound down wartime production, executives quickly retooled them to make consumer goods. Studebaker,

under Hoffman, became the first automobile company to introduce a new car model after the war. The new Studebaker was a
two-door sedan that pioneered the flat trunk that other cars would
feature for decades. The company marketed the new model with
the slogan "First by far with a postwar car!" and it became a top
seller.

It was one of many new products in the second half of the
1940s. Some were mindless if fun: Wartime production led to the
invention of new toys like Silly Putty and the Slinky. Others had a
bigger effect on living standards. The defense contractor Raytheon
began selling an item called the Radarange, the first commercially
available microwave oven. A chemical engineer in Cincinnati invented a medicine to relieve allergy symptoms and called it Bena-
dryl. The Oster Manufacturing Company made a new kitchen tool
called a blender and branded it the Osterizer. Procter & Gamble
introduced a new laundry detergent, Tide.

Many of the jobs in the burgeoning economy paid well, too.
The economy did not return to the inequality of the pre-Depression
years. The share of income flowing to the top 1 percent of earners
soon fell to its lowest level since the mid-nineteenth century, before the Gilded Age, partly because many high wartime tax rates
remained in place. In labor negotiations, companies adopted a
more accommodating approach than they had in previous decades.
U.S. Steel, Westinghouse Electric, and others finally agreed to bargain collectively with their workers. In 1950, General Motors and
the United Automobile Workers signed the so-called Treaty of Detroit, which gave workers large pay increases tied to GM's productivity, a model that other companies also used. The linking of
wages and productivity was important. It aligned the incentives of
workers and management. So long as a company's sales rose and
it continued to find new ways to produce goods efficiently, wages
and profits could climb without prices having to rise much. At
some companies, unions helped increase profits by creating a
mechanism through which workers could share their ideas with
management.

Even the Taft-Hartley Act contained evidence of corporate
America's new attitude. Its Senate sponsor was the leading conser-

vative Republican of the day, Robert Taft of Ohio, who was known simply as "Mr. Republican." Like his father—William Howard Taft, the former president and chief justice who had once exulted when hearing about the death of striking workers—the younger Taft loathed unions. He and his congressional allies originally proposed a bill that would have all but ended federally sanctioned collective bargaining and "put the labor movement back to where it had been in 1929," as the journalist John Judis has written in his history of corporate attitudes. But many executives, including the leaders of the CED, and members of Congress believed that Taft's approach went too far. They favored measures to constrain the growth of unions, but they did not want to eliminate them. To pass his bill, Taft had to weaken it. Into the 1960s, more than 30 percent of American workers would be unionized.

The younger Taft's successes and setbacks made clear that hard-liners remained relevant but were no longer dominant. When the 1952 presidential campaign began, he was the favorite to win the Republican nomination. He was Mr. Republican. But the party chose another candidate in the end. It chose the candidate whom big business liked better than Taft.

DWIGHT EISENHOWER DID not come from corporate America. He had spent almost his entire adult life in the military. But after World War II turned him into an international celebrity, the men who ran large corporations began to seek Eisenhower's friendship. And he was happy to oblige them.

Eisenhower had never owned a home of his own, yet he was suddenly welcome at lavish estates and country clubs. When he finished writing his memoirs in 1948, one of his new friends, the publishing executive William Robinson, gave Eisenhower a celebratory gift: a two-week trip to Augusta National, the Georgia golf club that business executives had founded as a retreat for themselves in the 1930s and that hosted the annual Masters Tournament. Eisenhower felt comfortable with these men. Like him, they spent their lives exercising authority.

They were also coming to understand how Eisenhower could

Paul Hoffman talks with President Dwight D. Eisenhower, 1952.

help them. In the late 1940s, many corporate executives felt demoralized about politics. They had expected the Republican Party
to win the White House in 1948, only to watch the incumbent
Truman somehow come from behind to defeat Thomas Dewey,
the governor of New York. Truman did so with a populist campaign that described Republicans as the party of greed that represented "the privileged few and not the common everyday man."
Many executives had grown tired of Democratic presidents who
could be hostile to business. Yet Republicans could not win the
White House because they could not overcome their image as the
party that had caused the Great Depression and seemed not to care
about American workers. "For more than twenty years," Eisenhower would say, "economic depression had been the skeleton in
the Republican closet."

Eisenhower appeared to present a unique solution. As soon as
the war had ended, people began speculating about him as a candidate. Both parties courted him, and Eisenhower chose the Republican Party. Like other Republicans, he too was worried
about the growth of the federal government and Truman's handling of the Korean War. By 1951, Eisenhower's new social circle
of corporate executives made a passionate case that he needed to

run for president. They saw him as the only conservative who could win.

One of these corporate executives was Hoffman. He and Eisenhower had met through Eisenhower's brother Milton, a CED board member. In 1951 and 1952, while Dwight Eisenhower was overseeing the new North Atlantic Treaty Organization in Europe, Hoffman traveled there to lobby him to come home and run for president. At first, Eisenhower playfully turned the question around, telling Hoffman to run. "If *you* would only get into this particular ring, you can be sure of at least one man in the front row cheering you on—I would even carry the water bottle," Eisenhower wrote him at one point. Hoffman recognized this flattery as deflection. He replied to Eisenhower: "Whether you like it or not, you have to face the fact that you are the one man today who can . . . redeem the Republican party."

Eisenhower soon entered the race, wrested the Republican nomination from Taft, and used his status as a war hero to win the presidency easily in 1952 over Adlai Stevenson, the Democratic nominee. As soon as he did, Eisenhower made clear that he had been the candidate of big business and would govern as such. The morning after his victory, he boarded a plane in New York with a small group—his wife, a top aide, and two of his top corporate backers—for a trip to Augusta National. They spent the next ten days at the club, with Eisenhower playing golf, writing thank-you notes, and making decisions about who would fill his administration. For nearly every cabinet post, he selected a corporate executive. The cabinet became known as "nine millionaires and a plumber," the latter a reference to Eisenhower's labor secretary, who had run the plumbers' union. The new defense secretary was Charles Wilson, previously the chief executive of General Motors. During his confirmation hearing, when a senator asked whether Wilson's ownership of GM stock presented a conflict of interest, Wilson famously replied, "I thought what was good for the country was good for General Motors and vice versa."

With Eisenhower's ascension, American business finally had a chance to undo two decades of New Deal policies. The Depression and World War II had ended, bolstering the argument for a return to an economy without high tax rates, heavy regulation, and government support for labor unions. But by the time Eisenhower took office, another threat had arisen: the Cold War. The Soviet Union, and Marxism more generally, had become frightening to American leaders. In the few years before Eisenhower's election, the Soviets had developed an atomic bomb and taken over much of eastern Europe; Chinese Communists had won their civil war; North Korea had invaded South Korea; and socialists were winning elections in Britain and other devastated parts of western Europe.

This threat affected American politics in conflicting ways. On the one hand, it led to a Red Scare and the persecution of Americans with left-wing views. The Taft-Hartley Act, for example, required union leaders to sign oaths stating they were not communists, and even liberal union leaders tried to root out radicals from their ranks. Eisenhower himself fed the Red Scare, refusing to denounce Senator Joseph McCarthy and selecting another fervent anticommunist, Richard Nixon, as vice president. On the other hand, the advance of communism and socialism in other countries made the New Deal model appear relatively attractive to many Republicans and business executives. They grew wary of scrapping a center-left economic model that seemed to be working at home. Sustaining that model was a way to show that capitalism could work and, by extension, to fight the Cold War. It was not a coincidence that Taft's wing of the Republican Party favored both isolationism and right-wing economic policies, while Eisenhower's wing favored international engagement and economic moderation.

Hoffman and the CED played a role in the new diplomacy of American capitalism. Before Eisenhower's presidency, Truman had created the Committee on Foreign Aid, to help Europe recover from the war, and five of the members came from the CED. The committee went on to design the details of the Marshall Plan, which sent billions of dollars overseas. For the first administrator of the Marshall Plan, Truman crossed party lines and chose a life-long Republican: Paul Hoffman. Rebuilding Europe, and persuading his fellow Americans to pay for it, became Hoffman's new sales pitch.

Once Eisenhower took office, he and the corporate executives who ran his administration validated the post-Depression changes to the domestic economy instead of reversing them. As *Time* magazine wrote in 1956, "By conserving and enlarging the social programs inherited from the New and Fair Deals, the Eisenhower Administration helped set a course for the new conservative." Eisenhower did move economic policy to the right, cutting federal spending and reducing some taxes, and he offered rhetorical paeans to small government and free enterprise. But the actual shift was modest. The top marginal tax rate was 92 percent in 1952, which meant that individuals kept only eight cents of each dollar of taxable income beyond $200,000. Under Eisenhower, the rate fell by a single percentage point, to 91 percent. Labor unions grew at roughly the same pace as the workforce did. Eisenhower's main labor policy consisted of lobbying behind the scenes to persuade businesses and workers to compromise with each other and sign contracts without costly strikes. His strategy largely worked. Wages continued to rise, and strikes happened less frequently than during the Truman administration.

The more conservative elements of Eisenhower's coalition were bitterly disappointed. "We cannot see what purpose was served by Republicans fighting the New Deal for 20 years if they were going to wind up by embracing the New Deal," the editorial board of the *Chicago Tribune* wrote. The John Birch Society, a far-right group, spread the lie that Eisenhower was a secret communist. Eisenhower's most conservative brother, Edgar, told him that his administration was validating unconstitutional expansions of government and that Edgar's friends wondered whether the president was even a Republican. Dwight Eisenhower had some fun in the letter he wrote Edgar in response, pointing out that he was the president and, as such, defined what it meant to be a Republican. It meant accepting the cultural shift among corporate executives and in the American economy.

· · ·

THE PUREST SIGN of the shift could be seen in the compensation that top business executives received.

The market for executive salaries has long been a clubby one. Officially, a board of directors, with a fiduciary duty to represent the interests of a company's shareholders, determines how much money a chief executive receives. In practice, a CEO helps choose the members of the board, some of whom are friends or former colleagues. Many board members are themselves executives at other companies and so are willing to err on the side of overpaying a peer. CEO pay, as a result, tends to be influenced as much by the culture of corporate America at any given time as by market forces.

One executive who rose through corporate America during its post-Depression period of moderation was George Romney. An extrovert who had honed his confidence during his time as a young Mormon missionary in London, Romney moved to Washington in the late 1920s and became a lobbyist for the aluminum industry. The leaders of the auto industry, including Hoffman, noticed Romney and hired him to lobby for them. He spent World War II helping the industry work with the federal government to manufacture military equipment. In 1948, the chairman of one of the carmakers Romney represented, the Nash-Kelvinator Corporation, recruited him to become a top executive at the company.

Romney was soon a star. He pioneered a new kind of vehicle, the compact car. It was part of the burst of consumer goods introduced in the years after the war. Nash-Kelvinator marketed this car, the Rambler, as stylish and affordable, and many families were drawn to the idea of owning a smaller vehicle, especially as a second car. Romney enjoyed mocking Detroit's larger cars as dinosaurs, a reference to both their size and their supposed future extinction. Company advertisements asked, "Is your car a dinosaur to park?" Sales of the Rambler surged in the late 1950s, as did the company's profits and stock price. By this point, Romney was running the company.

As pleased as he was with its success, Romney also started to

Governor George Romney and his son Mitt look over the New York World's Fair grounds, including the Chrysler and Ford exhibits, 1964.

grow uncomfortable with all the money flowing into the company. He worried that executives might become distracted by what he called "the temptations of success" rather than focusing on the business's long-term health. To avoid that problem, he went to the board of directors with a suggestion: The company should establish an annual cap on pay of $225,000 for any executive. That seemed like plenty of money. It was roughly forty times as much as a typical American household was earning at the time. The board—which included Romney's close friend J. Willard Marriott, a restaurant entrepreneur who had recently opened his first hotel—agreed to the cap.

But the board soon found itself with a dilemma. Romney's original contract called for him to receive a $100,000 bonus if the company reached certain financial benchmarks, and, because of how well the Rambler was selling, the company had done so. The bonus would have put Romney over the cap. To him, the solution was obvious: He forfeited the bonus. As the company continued to thrive in the early 1960s, new bonuses kicked in, and Romney asked the board to cancel them as well. Over a five-year period, he refused $268,000 in pay.

He was not the only executive to turn down higher pay during these years. John Ekblom, who ran the Hupp Corporation, an appliance manufacturer, turned down a $110,000 bonus in 1959. The sum, he said, "far exceeds my needs and appetite." Ekblom explained that he was refusing the money partly to call attention to low-level corporate managers who had been crucial to the economy's success yet did not earn enough money to save for retirement. The decisions by Romney and Ekblom were sufficiently unusual to receive press coverage at the time, but they were also consistent with a larger trend: Many executives did not try to grab every last possible dollar during the postwar decades.

The pay of the typical CEO of a large company rose only modestly from the 1940s through the 1970s, according to corporate records later analyzed by the economists Carola Frydman and Raven Molloy. CEO pay rose faster than inflation, meaning that the executives were receiving real raises, but these raises tended to be modest. Stock prices, the gross domestic product, and the median family income all rose more quickly. As a result, the gap between CEO pay and everybody else's pay shrank during these years. Executives accepted this situation without much complaint. They also accepted a top marginal tax rate that was above 90 percent in the 1950s. They did not start think tanks or advocacy groups whose mission was to argue that increasing the incentives for standout corporate performance would benefit the entire American economy.

Why not? The answer cannot have involved only pure economics. No doubt Romney, Ekblom, and their fellow CEOs could have found enjoyable ways to spend more money. They could have set aside great sums for their heirs or given a sizable donation to their alma mater, perhaps getting their name on a building. To anybody who believes that human beings naturally maximize their own income and living standards, these titans of capitalism were acting irrationally. Yet it did not seem irrational to them. They were acting in accordance with the culture, rejecting the ostentation that could have caused their fellow executives and citizens to lose respect for them. As Adam Smith argued, respect and pride are powerful drivers of human behavior.

Executives like Romney viewed themselves as a benevolent elite who rejected the Darwinian business conservatism of the early twentieth century for a more paternalistic and patriotic capitalism. They were part of a shared project to overcome existential threats to the United States—first the Great Depression, then World War II, and finally the Cold War. To do so, the executives moderated their self-interest. They still often fought with labor unions and government bureaucrats, but the different sides came to see their opponents as loyal opposition, ultimately interested in the same goal of creating a prosperous America to lead the world.

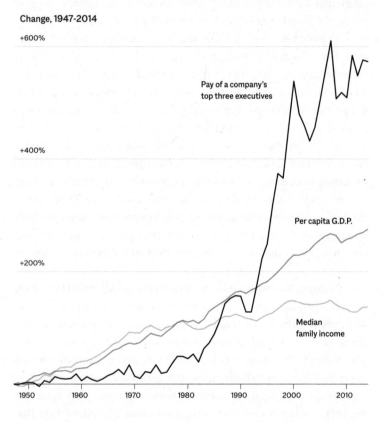

Change, 1947-2014

In hindsight, it can be seductive to treat these midcentury leaders as more virtuous than their successors. It would also be a mistake. The CEOs of the postwar decades were deeply flawed. They presided over an economy that excluded the great majority of the population—women, people of color, Jews, and openly gay

Americans—from many positions of authority. Few corporate leaders used their own influence to fight injustices like the Red Scare and racial segregation. What the executives did do was help to create an economy that reduced inequality and lifted living standards for virtually every group of Americans. That was no small thing. It reflected not the individual virtues of the executives but the prevailing culture of their era.

The Romney family underscores this point. George's youngest child was named Willard, after George's close friend J. Willard Marriott. The boy, born in 1947, went by his middle name, Mitt. He would grow up to be remarkably similar to his father. Each became a leader in the Mormon Church. Each first had a successful business career and then entered Republican politics, serving as a governor (George in Michigan, Mitt in Massachusetts) and running unsuccessfully for president. Each displayed an unusual willingness to buck his own political party, George by overseeing a redistricting process in Michigan that reduced the advantages for rural areas and Mitt by being the only Republican to vote to convict Donald Trump in both of his impeachment trials. Each Romney showed more interest in alleviating poverty than most Republican politicians, with George helping to open childcare centers in Detroit and Mitt pioneering an expansion of health insurance in Massachusetts. Both Romneys displayed a mix of conservatism, heterodoxy, and principle.

Yet there was also a glaring difference between their business careers. The elder Romney capped his annual salary at $225,000 in the early 1960s—the equivalent of about $2 million in today's terms. The younger Romney earned many multiples of that in the 1980s and 1990s as an executive at Bain & Company, a consulting firm where he helped start a spin-off private equity firm. The firm had a habit of buying a company, laying off some workers, reducing the pensions of other workers, and then selling the company at a profit. After decades at Bain, Mitt Romney's net worth approached $250 million. Unlike his father, he showed little concern about being corrupted by the "temptations of success." It would have been unusual if he had. By the time he was running Bain, the culture of corporate America had shifted again. Other

CEOs and private equity investors were making similarly huge sums.

Alan Greenspan, the longtime chairman of the Federal Reserve, later explained the shift by saying that human beings had not become any greedier than in generations past. Instead, Greenspan said, "the avenues to express greed have grown enormously." It was true of the Romneys. Mitt was not inherently more selfish than George. They were both products of their times.

CULTURE CAN BE difficult to think about because it is so amorphous. No single event shifted the culture of American business in the middle of the twentieth century (and no single event shifted it again decades later). There was no start date to the new era. The transformation was enormously consequential and a bit murky.

For anybody wondering whether the United States might someday experience another shift like the one in the 1940s—toward a more inclusive economy, with more patriotic and less self-interested corporate executives—two underlying ideas are important. The first stems from Ann Swidler's insight about settled and unsettled periods. During a settled period, major culture changes are unlikely. In the late twentieth and early twenty-first centuries, individual corporate executives occasionally initiated campaigns to persuade their peers to reduce their own compensation, increase the pay of their workers, keep jobs in the United States, and take other actions in society's interest. Typically, these efforts had little impact. The culture was too settled.

It is true that the past few decades have included traumatic events, such as the September 11 attacks, the financial crisis that began in 2007, and the Covid pandemic. But none challenged people's economic assumptions as much as the combination of the Great Depression, World War II, and the Cold War. Most corporate executives continue to believe in the current model of rough-and-tumble capitalism and oppose a return to democratic capitalism. Some of their rationale is legitimate: The industrialization of lower-wage countries and the rise of global trade in recent decades mean that American manufacturers need to be more competitive than they were in the 1950s. They cannot necessarily be as accommodating toward unions as they were then. On the other hand, much of today's aggressive approach by corporations does not stem from competitive necessity. It instead reflects a self-seeking culture that accepts enormous CEO salaries and high inequality at the expense of workers. The unsettling of that culture will apparently require a larger disruption—or at least a more effective political response—than anything from the past few decades.

The second idea involves the interaction between culture and political power. The executives who ran American business in the middle of the twentieth century did not switch to a more inclusive economy completely voluntarily. Even after the Depression gripped the country, many executives fought desperately against labor unions and New Deal regulations. Hoffman, as you will recall, initially described Roosevelt's recovery act as "a thoroughly vicious experiment in the fascist control of business." But as unions grew and Roosevelt kept winning elections, many of the leaders of corporate America accommodated themselves to the changes. They accepted defeat, or at least partial defeat. They came to see that a high-wage economy had advantages. Slowly, some executives began to change their own behavior, and more followed suit over time.

The Committee for Economic Development embodied this shift. It started as a weaker alternative to hard-line business groups like the Chamber of Commerce, yet it grew to shape postwar economic policy and help staff both the Truman and Eisenhower administrations. Liberal critics claimed that the overlapping membership between the CED and the Chamber proved that there was no difference between the two. In truth, the overlap showed how American business evolved during these years. Over time, the changes gathered momentum, and the CED outlook became the dominant one. But the critics were right about something vital: Corporate executives were not changing their worldviews out of pure altruism. They were responding to a shift in political and economic realities.

In the decades after World War II, power and culture in the

American economy were distinct forces that nonetheless fed off each other. They transformed the country's low-wage, high-inequality model of the 1920s into the high-wage, low-inequality model of later decades.

As grand an accomplishment as that was, it was not the only way in which the dual forces changed the economy. In addition to changing how the economic pie was divided, they also helped expand its size. They contributed to a more optimistic vision for the economy, one in which the country was willing to set aside substantial resources for creating a better future. Those investments would create modern America.

CHAPTER 3

Sacrifice for the Long Term

THE TWENTY-EIGHT-YEAR-OLD LIEUTENANT COLONEL WOKE up on July 7, 1919, at Fort Meade in Maryland, excited about the adventure he was about to undertake. He needed the distraction. He missed his wife, Mary, and their baby son, who were living back in Denver with her family. And he was in an emotional funk about never having made it to Europe to fight in the recently concluded Great War.

The army had instead assigned him to oversee various troop preparations in the United States. Many of his peers in the West Point class of 1915 had achieved battlefield glory, and he assumed that his military career would never recover from having missed the action. He imagined a future in which he would put on weight "in a meaningless chair-bound assignment, shuffling papers and filling out forms," as he wrote. "If not depressed, I was mad, disappointed, and resented the fact that the war had passed me by." When word began to spread in the summer of 1919 that the army was organizing a caravan to drive across the country—trucks, cars, and motorcycles, traveling from Washington to San Francisco—he volunteered. It sounded much more exciting than what the lieutenant colonel had been doing: sitting around Fort Meade and playing bridge with other officers while the army demobilized.

The caravan was called the Trans-Continental Truck Train, and it was both a promotional campaign and a tactical drill. Motorized vehicles had helped the United States and its allies win the war, and military leaders wanted the public to understand their importance. The leaders hoped to increase public support for the construction of new roads, which could strengthen the domestic

Scenes from the Trans-Continental Truck Train, 1919.

economy and the country's internal defenses. As a bonus, the caravan would serve as a training exercise. It would teach soldiers how to operate vehicles over long distances and would allow the army to test how quickly it could move troops west in case of a foreign invasion from the Pacific Ocean.

The answer, it soon became clear, was not quickly.

Motorized vehicles were so new in 1919 that many soldiers did not know how to drive them. This inexperience, the lieutenant colonel complained at the end of the trip in a seven-page memo to his supervisors, "resulted in excessive speeding of trucks" as well as "unauthorized halts" and "unseemly conduct." The condition of the roads and bridges was also a problem. Once the caravan crossed into Illinois, dirt roads became the norm. "Practically no more pavement was encountered until reaching California," the lieutenant colonel wrote. During the journey, eighty-eight bridges collapsed, and the troops had to rebuild them before continuing. Nine of the convoy's vehicles were destroyed. Many more had to be pulled out of the mud after rainstorms made dirt roads impassable. The Truck Train averaged six miles an hour while it was moving, covering only fifty-eight miles a day. At the end of each day, soldiers set up camp, often on fairgrounds, and rarely slept well.

For all this unpleasantness, the trip was a triumph. Dozens of towns staged celebrations to welcome the caravan, and the army estimated that 3.2 million Americans saw it firsthand. Millions more read about it in glowing newspaper stories. A paper in Iowa called it "the longest trip of the kind ever undertaken in the history of the world." In Pittsburgh, city leaders declared a half-day holiday. Salt Lake City asked local factories to blow their horns for four minutes, echoing the celebration of war victory in 1918. In Fort Steele, Wyoming, the town's only four families strung welcome banners across the highway and made enough coffee and doughnuts to serve all three hundred travelers. Other towns staged barbecues or banquets, with speeches by local politicians. On some nights, the soldiers would entertain people by lighting up the sky with the searchlights they had used during the war to track German planes.

Throughout, the officers leading the caravan promoted their political cause: the Good Roads movement, as it had come to be known. The army did not pretend to be above politics on the subject of roads because it considered their construction vital to the national interest. Military leaders wanted the United States to embark on its next great investment project, in the tradition of the canals, railroads, and telegraph lines of the nineteenth century. The national network of roads they envisioned would include five east-west highways and ten north-south highways, together costing about $1 billion. Many existing roads, the lieutenant colonel told his superiors, also needed improvements.

At the end of his memo, the lieutenant colonel included a summary of the trip. There had certainly been problems, he wrote. Still, the caravan had accomplished its mission: "The truck train was well received at all points along the route. It seemed that there was a great deal of sentiment for the improving of highways, and, from the standpoint of promoting this sentiment, the trip was an undoubted success."

Underneath this summary, the young officer typed his name: *D. D. Eisenhower.*

THE NEXT TWO decades of Dwight David Eisenhower's military career went better than he had feared. After the Trans-Continental Truck Train, he became an aide to a series of more senior officers. He was known for his intelligence and his ability to make superiors feel comfortable. After Japan attacked Pearl Harbor, the army chief of staff, General George Marshall, began looking for talented staff members to bring to Washington and help him plan the war. Eisenhower, then fifty-one years old and working at Fort Sam Houston in Texas, was among them. At one of their first meetings, he impressed Marshall with his directness and willingness to make decisions. Marshall put him in charge of planning the defense of the Philippines and gradually gave him other responsibilities.

Even so, few people saw Eisenhower as a future battle commander. He was an adviser rather than a leader. Eisenhower had been correct that his lack of battlefield experience during World War I had set him back. But then a series of remarkable circumstances catapulted him over dozens of other officers in the span of a few months.

Marshall was the obvious candidate to oversee the final assault on Nazi Germany, and he sent his trusted aide Eisenhower to oversee American operations in London until he could arrive. Instead, Eisenhower proved so adept at the role that he never had to give it up. He got along better with Winston Churchill than Marshall did, and President Roosevelt liked having Marshall by his side in Washington. When the time came for the Allies to begin planning their invasion of Europe, Roosevelt chose Eisenhower over Marshall as the commander. The selection was so surprising that the army dispatched George Patton—a more likely commander, in the Nazis' view—to the British region of East Anglia as a decoy. Patton's presence there seemed to suggest that the D-Day assault would take place farther east than was the case. In reality, Eisenhower had become Patton's superior by that point.

As a tactician, Eisenhower made significant mistakes. He had two great advantages, however. He was an effective leader of people. And he could summon the unmatched productive might of the American economy. The United States manufactured 44 percent of all bullets made during World War II. By the war's end, American factories were able to build a warship in less than three weeks, down from eight months at the war's start. Lucius Clay, an American general close to Eisenhower, said, "We were never able to build a tank as good as the German tank. But we made so many of them that it didn't really matter." The Nazi general Erwin Rommel lamented, "The battle is fought and decided by the quartermaster before the shooting begins." (The quartermaster is the military officer responsible for providing equipment.)

Twenty-five years earlier, on his cross-country road trip, Eisenhower had spent a summer enduring the consequences of the country's failure to invest in itself. He bumped along dirt roads, watched vehicles fall into rivers, and spent hours waiting for bridges to be repaired. In World War II, he helped that same country defeat fascism on two continents, thanks to an investment program like no other. The federal government had poured tremendous resources into wartime mobilization. It had helped channel the creativity of private companies into accomplishing a larger goal than those companies could have accomplished on their own. The central lesson of Eisenhower's military career was the awesome power of American investment.

INVESTMENT, IN THE simplest terms, involves using some of today's resources to make life better tomorrow. It is a form of short-term sacrifice, an optimistic bet on what the future can bring.

For a family, investment can involve skipping a vacation or cutting back on restaurant meals to save up for a home purchase or a child's college education. For a society, it can mean raising taxes to build roads that will take years to complete. In World War II, it meant shutting down the production of many consumer goods—and telling Americans to scrimp—so factories could retool and manufacture military equipment instead. The war also brought a sharp increase in federal debt, to be repaid by the taxpayers of the future.

Investments are not guaranteed to pay off. Families sometimes buy houses that decline in value, and college students sometimes fail to graduate, ending up with debt but no degree. Governments sometimes waste taxpayer dollars on programs that accomplish little. Still, successful people and societies have always understood that these risks are unavoidable. Failing to invest enough resources in the future tends to be the bigger mistake. Historically, the most successful economic growth strategy has revolved around investment.

Rome built its empire partly by investing in roads, bridges, aqueducts, and weapons. Renaissance societies invested in the development of the printing press and weapons. The Industrial Revolution brought the steam engine, the cotton gin, and the factory. Each of these examples depended on sacrifice—on devoting resources to the uncertain prospect of long-term gain when those same resources could have been used for immediate gratification.

The private sector often plays a crucial role in making these investments. Companies see an opportunity for eventual profit and make the necessary investments: in a medical laboratory to develop a new drug, in a factory to build a better vehicle, in an oil rig or wind turbine to produce new energy. But if the first historical lesson about investment is its crucial contribution to prosperity, the second lesson is that the private sector tends to do less of it than a healthy economy needs.

Why? Because investments are expensive and only a fraction of the returns typically flows to the original investors and inventors. Despite patents, other people find ways to copy or mimic the invention. Sometimes, these imitators build on the original in ways that are perfectly legal but would not have been possible without the initial breakthrough. Johannes Gutenberg did not get rich from inventing the printing press, nor did Nicolas-Joseph Cugnot from designing the first automobile in eighteenth-century France. More recently, Tim Berners-Lee did not become wealthy after creating the World Wide Web in 1989.

The earliest stages of scientific research are particularly problematic for the private sector. In these early stages, the commercial possibilities are unclear. An automobile company cannot justify spending money on basic engineering research that may end up being useful only to an aerospace company. A technology company cannot justify research that may make obsolete its own products. Yet such basic scientific research can bring enormous benefits for a society. It can allow people to live longer, healthier, richer lives and can lay the groundwork for unforeseen commercial applications that are indeed profitable. A well-functioning capitalist economy depends on large investments in research that the free market, on its own, usually will not make.

The government can make these investments because it can take the long view. It can spend money on research that may not turn a short-term profit but does have the potential to yield a big return for society. A government can also ensure that researchers collaborate and share their findings, rather than keeping them secret for commercial advantage.

During the laissez-faire years leading up to the Great Depression, the United States invested relatively little money in scientific research, and the country fell behind. Europe dominated the Nobel Prizes during this period, and European countries, including Nazi Germany, began World War II with a technological advantage over the United States. In the North Atlantic Ocean, German U-boats were able to move without detection, threatening American efforts to supply Britain. Once the United States entered the war, U-boats sank more than two hundred ships in the Atlantic and killed five thousand Americans, in attacks that sometimes occurred within sight of land on the East Coast.

Recognizing the threat from this technological gap, a small group of scientists and government officials began pushing for a major investment program even before the United States entered the war. The most prominent was Vannevar Bush, an engineer and entrepreneur who had recently left the Massachusetts Institute of

Technology to run the Carnegie Institution in Washington. Bush's campaign to change the country's approach to science had some similarities to Hoffman's campaign to change corporate America's approach to the economy. Like Hoffman, Bush considered himself conservative and hated much of the New Deal. But he was committed to the principles of empirical inquiry. He understood that only the government could devote the resources necessary for a major investment in science. "What was needed was not incremental improvement or marginal adjustments; it was fundamental breakthroughs and at great speed," Jonathan Gruber and Simon Johnson, two MIT economists and the authors of a history of American investment, have written. The private sector would never devote the resources required for these breakthroughs.

The resulting government effort, called the National Defense Research Committee, grew to be vast. It funded research into radar, planes, ships, vehicles, guns, and protective gear. It included a furious race to develop an atomic bomb before the Nazis did. It also included an effort to develop a machine that could perform mathematic equations more quickly than human beings.

Math was central to much of the wartime scientific research conducted by the government. At first, the military assigned human beings to solve the thousands of equations, and these mathematicians tended to be educated young women, ineligible to serve in combat roles because of their sex. The military referred to them, intuitively enough, as computers. For centuries, however, scientists had dreamed of building a mechanical counting machine, akin to an automated abacus, that could perform calculations more quickly than the human brain. In the 1600s, the French mathematician Blaise Pascal had designed a crude machine along these lines with a system of wheels. By the 1900s, automated counting machines were becoming more sophisticated, and they took on the same name as the human beings that they were meant to replace: computers. As part of its wartime mobilization, the United States government hoped to rapidly accelerate the development of these counting machines.

. . .

GRACE HOPPER WAS clearly lost. It was a summer day in 1944, and she had spent more than two hours crisscrossing the Harvard University campus. Wearing her navy uniform as she walked around Harvard's brick buildings, Hopper was looking for something called the Computation Lab.

At the time, Hopper was a thirty-seven-year-old mathematics professor at Vassar College who had recently joined the navy to help with the war effort. She had grown up in a comfortable family in New York City, one of three children of parents who believed in educating both boys and girls. She wanted to become an engineer and loved solving practical problems, like taking apart the family's clocks and reassembling them. (Her mother told her to limit her projects to one clock at a time.) But women in the 1920s were largely barred from engineering, so Hopper chose math. She majored in it at Vassar, was the first woman to receive a doctorate in math from Yale, and then became a professor at Vassar.

Hopper was intensely curious. As a Vassar professor, she audited classes in physics, chemistry, economics, architecture, philosophy, and other subjects. She then infused her math classes with practical problems from these other fields, sometimes upsetting her colleagues in the math department. "They disapproved of practically everything I did," she said. "I was going off into things which were not mathematics." After the attack on Pearl Harbor, Hopper saw an opportunity to help the country solve the problems of war, and she tried to enlist in the navy. It was her family's branch of the military: She grew up hearing stories about her great-grandfather, an admiral in the Union navy during the Civil War.

Getting into the navy was not easy for her. At first, Vassar administrators would not grant her leave. Her job as a wartime professor, teaching young women who could help the military solve math problems, was more important, the administrators told her. Eventually, Hopper threatened to quit and join the navy anyway. Her marriage, to a literature professor, was breaking down, and she was ready for a fresh start. Vassar finally yielded and approved her leave in 1943. She then had to wait several months for the navy to grant her a waiver to its usual age maximum and weight minimum: She was thirty-seven years old and only slightly more than one hundred pounds. In the training course for new officers that she attended in western Massachusetts, Hopper received the best grades among the roughly eight hundred attendees, and she was named battalion commander, the highest rank among trainees. When the training ended, she headed east, to Cambridge, to join the Computation Lab at Harvard.

When she finally found the right building, she walked into the lab and was greeted by Howard Aiken, a business executive turned navy commander, who was almost a foot taller than Hopper. "Where in the Hell have you been?" he asked.

She began to explain, but he cut her off. "I mean for the last two months?"

Aiken knew the answer. When he had first heard about Hopper—a math professor enrolled in a nearby training course for new officers—he asked the navy to release her early so she could join his team immediately. The navy rejected his request. Aiken's gruff question was his way of welcoming Hopper and underscoring the urgency of her new work.

Inside the Computation Lab, Aiken was overseeing the development of one of the world's first computers, the Automatic Sequence Controlled Calculator, nicknamed the Mark. Aiken had designed it himself while working at IBM, before he joined the Harvard faculty, effectively as an adjunct professor. Kept in the basement of a science building and protected by navy guards at all hours, the machine was fifty feet long and eight feet tall. It weighed five tons and had 750,000 parts, including visible gears, chains, and an electric motor.

The Mark was less sophisticated than some other early computers, because it was mechanical, rather than using the emerging technology of vacuum tubes. But the Mark's relative simplicity made it more efficient. And during the war, short-term performance mattered more than technical elegance or long-term potential. *The New York Times* described the Mark as the "Algebra Machine," and a Boston newspaper called it the "Robot Brain." Aiken referred to it as "a lazy man's dream" and a "land-based ship." The military came to rely on it so heavily that the lab operated twenty-four hours a day. The lab had a red phone connected to the Bureau of Ordnance in Washington so the military could demand the immediate solution of the most pressing problems.

"We used to shake every time that darn thing rang," Hopper recalled. The person on the other end would ask, "When are you going to have the numbers ready?" As Hopper said, "The pressure was terrific." Some nights, Hopper slept at her desk.

The intensity of the work and the high stakes fostered a quirky esprit de corps in the lab. The people who had found their way there were attracted to the unorthodox. They were part of something new—the beginning of the computer age. Aiken, for all his haughtiness, was an outsider himself, having spent thirteen years working in the electric utility business before going back to graduate school to study physics, hardly a typical background for an Ivy League faculty member. Other Harvard professors viewed him as a fledging inventor with an unproven project, not an intellectual worthy of a full-time position.

Nobody in the lab was more of an outsider than Hopper, the only woman on the staff. To get there, she had relied on the sort of rebelliousness that is common among trailblazers. She understood when to defy her superiors just enough to get something done without going so far as to lose their support. Early on, she had realized that the lab could save time by programming the Mark to add page numbers to its long printouts of equations. It would prevent confusion when the staff was looking through them. But Aiken refused to devote programming time to something as mundane as teaching the computer to number its pages. One day, Hopper waited until he had left for his daily hot lunch—complete with two cold martinis, served by his mother, at the Cambridge home they shared—and she taught the Mark to number its pages. When Aiken saw how little time it had taken, he conceded that Hopper had been correct. In later years, she would call him the best boss she ever had, somebody who cared above all about results and who let his subordinates make any mistake once without penalty.

Hopper also became the lab's leading comedian. She decorated her desk with drawings of gremlins and other beasts that she joked were sneaking into the computer and causing it to malfunction. (Later, some accounts would credit Hopper with coining the term "computer bug," but that story appears to be apocryphal.) When the Mark broke down, she loaned colleagues her vanity mirror—an accessory that none of the men owned—so they could reach into the computer and look for the problem. It was one of her many "dirty methods," as another programmer called them, for getting results any way possible.

Grace Hopper and three other programmers gather around the operator's console of a Univac computer, 1957.

All the good feelings inside the lab depended on the sense that it was succeeding. Hopper and her colleagues were helping the United States reverse the scientific gap that had existed in 1940 and win the war. Shortly after Hopper's arrival, the Hungarian mathematician John von Neumann, who had fled Europe for the United States during Hitler's rise, arrived at the lab bearing a long set of complex problems. He did not say why he needed them solved, and the lab's officers were used to such secrecy. Together, Hopper and von Neumann pored over long printouts full of partial differential equations. Eventually, he left, with the answers he needed and returned to his own lab in New Mexico, where he was working on the atomic bomb.

By the end of 1944, the United States and its allies seemed on the verge of victory in Europe. Hopper, meanwhile, had transformed herself in less than a year from an unhappy college professor into a navy officer working on a crucial part of the war effort in an exciting new scientific field. Among other accomplishments, she had helped devise a shortcut that allowed the lab's staff members to avoid reprogramming the Mark from scratch each time they started work on a new problem. Because many problems used the same series of formulas, she and a colleague began writing down what they called "subroutines" in notebooks. When one of them needed a subroutine to solve a problem, they could retrieve it from their own notebook or call out to the other and ask something like, "Can I have your cosine routine?" Hopper, who had played basketball in college, compared it to passing the ball to a teammate.

It was one of the first instances of computer programming. Hopper's preferred term, which would become popular again decades later, was "coding."

For Christmas 1944, she took a twenty-four-hour leave and returned home to see her parents in New York. When she described the Mark to her father, an insurance executive, he mentioned an idea that had not occurred to Hopper—or to very many other people. He said that he thought the machine she was working on could have major implications for business after the war. In the insurance industry, it could revolutionize how firms calculated risk and ran their operations. "That was the first mention that I ever heard of using the computer in industry," Hopper later said. With their ability to perform high-volume calculations rapidly, computers might also be able to transform banking, transportation, construction, and medical care.

Yet corporate America seemed strangely uninterested in the potential. Even leading technology companies were wary of computers. IBM's executives were focused instead on the mundane punch-card system that made up a large portion of company sales.

The executives had been so skeptical of the newfangled computers that they had allowed Aiken—one of their own employees—to leave the company and take his new machine to a Harvard laboratory. The attitude was not merely a reflection of wartime myopia, either. Into the 1950s, executives at IBM and other major companies remained wary of investing in the development of a large new computer. "It didn't move me at all," Thomas Watson, Jr., IBM's chairman, said. "I couldn't see this gigantic, costly, unreliable device as a piece of business equipment."

HOW COULD WATSON and other executives have been so mistaken? They were not ignorant or uncreative. They were among the most successful businesspeople in the country. Their failure was structural, stemming from the resources at their disposal and the financial incentives that constrained them.

Developing a new technology required large amounts of money, sometimes more than any individual company could muster. And the returns for such an effort were highly uncertain. The research might fail, or it might succeed in scientific terms but not lead to a marketable product. In the case of IBM, the computer also risked undermining its lucrative sales of punch-card machines, which helped other companies keep track of their operations. It was a classic case of an entrenched leader in an industry being unable to see a coming revolution.

Only one organization had enough money and a sufficient long-term horizon to bankroll the creation of the computer industry: the federal government.

It could afford the inevitable failures and setbacks that basic research involved. The federal government could insist that researchers build on one another's ideas, rather than working secretly in separate laboratories, unaware of related breakthroughs. The government could dictate collaboration when collaboration made sense. It could patiently finance research that was making progress but was not yet ready for commercial applications. As soon as an invention was shown to be useful to the largest organization in the country—the military—the federal government could guarantee huge amounts of revenue through military contracts. As Gruber and Johnson have written, "The military had to lead where the private sector was unwilling to tread." Given the enormous resources of the United States government, a few big investment successes could cover the costs for dozens of failures.

For all these reasons, the computer industry owed its creation to the government, particularly the military. After the war, the navy signed a new contract with Aiken, paying his Harvard lab to build more advanced versions of the Mark. The military also supported research at MIT, Penn, Princeton, the University of California, and other universities. As late as 1959, federal agencies financed about 85 percent of the country's electronics research, including at private companies like Bell Telephone. The military also made possible IBM's belated entrance into computing: After its top executives realized their company would otherwise wither, they made it their top priority to win a bidding competition to create the computers needed for a network of radar stations across Alaska and Canada that would watch for a Soviet attack. Thomas Watson, Jr., would later say that the contract saved the company. IBM hired more than eight thousand engineers for the project, and the company soon came to be known as Big Blue, a reference to its logo color.

Government investment does bring one major downside. A government is by nature a monopoly, prone to groupthink and bureaucracy. It is not an open system, like a market economy, in which an iconoclastic idea can prevail over safer ideas. A government needs to find ways to create a merit-based process in which the best ideas can triumph over the ideas being promoted by the scientists with the best political connections.

Hopper was well suited to address this problem. She advocated a democratic, interdisciplinary approach that encouraged ideas from almost anywhere. From the start of her career, she had enjoyed making connections across academic fields. That is why she had audited classes in other Vassar departments and brought their insights into her math classroom. "People sort of stayed in separate boxes, but if you combined the boxes, you had the answer," she said. As part of this philosophy, she had tried to make computers accessible to outsiders. "I always wanted to let people use computers," she explained. She believed that opening the field to a larger pool of users would lead to discoveries that nobody had yet imagined. As another early computer programmer said, Hopper "saw the need for bringing this thing out of the vast wilderness and back into where it became a tool and didn't require a 20-year apprenticeship."

In Hopper's biggest battle, she spent years fighting for the creation of a programming language that relied on English words rather than symbols and technical jargon. Symbols and jargon alienated people who might have something to contribute to the discussion, she believed. She wrote parts of the new language herself, and she made the case for it at industry conferences. On the other side of the debate were programmers who wanted to tailor computer language to themselves, an elite community of scientists. For them, jargon truly was more efficient. In the end, the military sided with Hopper—and it had the ability to make her preferred approach the standard one because it was funding so much of the country's postwar computer work. The conversational language, known as COBOL, would become the world's most widely used programming language. By the end of the twentieth century, more than 80 percent of businesses around the world used it. It was more successful than its own designers fathomed: They created only a two-digit system for denoting years—62 for 1962, as an example—never imagining that COBOL would still be in use in the next century. This system led to the Y2K problem of 1999, when computer systems needed to be reprogrammed to avoid being confused by the year 2000.

In another attempt to democratize computing, Hopper published a mischievous article in the magazine *Popular Electronics* that took advantage of sexist stereotypes to encourage computer use. For the article, she conducted an experiment in which she gave a nineteen-year-old Philadelphia woman, Marilyn Mealy, a computer to use. Hopper described Mealy as "a trim, attractive blonde" who was "prettier than average" and liked to go dancing and window-shopping. Nevertheless, Mealy proved herself capable of using the computer, which, Hopper explained, would open new job opportunities for her. The article offered an unstated challenge to the overwhelmingly male audience of *Popular Electronics:* If a young woman can learn to use a computer, surely you can too.

Because Hopper was a woman, Harvard did not offer her a faculty position after the war, but she had plenty of alternatives in the private sector. She chose the Eckert-Mauchly Computer Corporation in Philadelphia, a start-up that relied largely on federal funding. The company, with Hopper's help, used the money to develop a giant new computer that would become known as a mainframe and that government agencies and companies could use to solve problems, much as the navy had used the Mark during the war. The computer was called the Univac (for Universal Automatic Computer), and the Census Bureau ordered the first one to analyze results from its 1950 survey of the population.

The Univac became the first working computer that many Americans saw for themselves. In the run-up to election night in 1952, the executives at Eckert-Mauchly offered to let CBS News use a Univac on air to calculate election results. The executives wanted to demonstrate that a computer was not a magical device but rather a tool for solving everyday problems, as Hopper had long believed. They wanted to expand their market beyond the government to private companies. The goal was to "bring computers down to earth," one executive argued in a memo. CBS had its own reasons for wanting the election broadcast to be special. That night, the network was debuting a new anchor for its coverage, Walter Cronkite. Together, a new anchor and a powerful computer might give CBS an advantage over NBC, which dominated television news at the time. In the weeks before the election, CBS bragged that the computer's fifty-five hundred electronic tubes had the combined mental capacity of four hundred trained clerks. "A robot computer will give CBS the fastest reporting in history," one network affiliate announced.

Eckert-Mauchly and CBS devised a specific mission for the Univac. Instead of reporting the raw vote totals, as was standard, the computer would adjust them based on geography. These adjustments could offer insight into the election's likely outcome more quickly than raw vote totals alone. If the Democratic candidate won 60 percent of the vote in a precinct that normally voted

70 percent Democratic, for example, the other networks would report the Democrat as leading. The Univac, in contrast, would know that this result was in fact good for the Republican candidate. Any Republican keeping the race close in a heavily Democratic area would probably win. The Univac could quickly process vote counts from hundreds of precincts and allow CBS to offer a more accurate snapshot than the other networks.

The main significance of election night in 1952, of course, was not its effect on the public's understanding of computers. It was the presidential campaign decided that night. The Democratic candidate was Adlai Stevenson, the governor of Illinois, who was trying to win the party's sixth straight term in the White House, dating back to the Depression. The Republican candidate was the young lieutenant colonel from the Trans-Continental Truck Train who had risen to become a World War II hero, Dwight Eisenhower.

As the early returns came in, the Univac offered an emphatic prediction. Eisenhower was beating expectations almost everywhere. In traditionally Democratic areas, like Cleveland, Baltimore, and western Tennessee, he was trailing by only narrow margins. In Republican areas, he was winning easily. Shortly after nine o'clock that night, with about 5 percent of nationwide votes counted, the Univac reported that Eisenhower's chance of winning was roughly 99 percent. The most likely result was a landslide, 438 electoral votes to 93, the computer said.

The numbers were so different from the pre-election polls, which had pointed to a close race, that CBS refused to air them for hours. The delay became one more example of large companies' discomfort with a breakthrough technology. But Hopper and the other programmers knew what they were doing: When all the votes were counted, Eisenhower had won a landslide nearly identical to the Univac's early forecast, 442 electoral votes to Stevenson's 89.

The Democratic Party's twenty-year rule in Washington was over. The Republicans would now be in charge. The party that had long been skeptical of government interference in the economy would have an opportunity to implement its vision.

.   .   .

EISENHOWER, AS YOU already know, did not dismantle the New Deal. He tinkered with parts of the federal safety net and left most of it in place. He was the Republican president who solidified the country's new approach to economic policy. He also left his own mark on that policy. There was one way in which Eisenhower made the government even more activist than it had been under Truman and Roosevelt: investment in the future.

Although Eisenhower's instinct was to keep government involvement to the minimum necessary, he understood that some involvement was indeed necessary. He had come to believe that government had a vital role in ensuring that American society took the long view. "The principal contradiction in the whole system comes about because of the inability of men to forego immediate gain for a longtime good," he once said. "We do not yet have a sufficient number of people who are ready to make the immediate sacrifice in favor of a long-term investment."

Eisenhower's career had been one long lesson in the power of investment. It began with the cross-country trip after World War I, when he saw firsthand the costs of not investing in the future. During World War II, the industrial capacity of the United States, made possible by a crash program of spending, innovation, and mobilization, allowed him to lead the Allies to victory in Europe. The lesson continued after the war, as he toured defeated Germany and marveled at its highways, which were far more advanced than America's; the United States had still not engaged in the highway construction that the army had hoped to inspire with its 1919 caravan. When Eisenhower came home from World War II, he lobbied for the biggest infrastructure project under discussion at the time, the St. Lawrence Seaway. Once built, it allowed ships to travel from the Atlantic Ocean to the Great Lakes. His only significant job in the private sector had been the presidency of Columbia University, starting in the late 1940s, and his legacy there also involved a long-term investment. He was the president who finally persuaded New York City to close 116th Street, which ran through the campus. The quiet, green oasis that replaced the street transformed Columbia.

When Eisenhower spoke of these investments, he did so with

words like "cooperation," "sacrifice," "common purpose," and "collective good." The historian Robert Griffith coined a phrase to describe Eisenhower's worldview: the corporate commonwealth. "Although he typically expressed these ideas in platitudes," Griffith wrote, "he did create, beyond the banality of his language, a fairly coherent vision of how society ought to operate." Large corporations were at the center of this society, providing jobs that in turn allowed Americans to enjoy rising living standards, and Eisenhower's administration was often deferential to corporations. But the government had a central role. It had to prevent both business leaders and workers from behaving too selfishly, descending into conflict, and being overly focused on the short term. Government, Eisenhower believed, had to step in to accomplish things that the private sector could or would not.

The result was one of the great ironies of the twentieth-century American economy. The man who ran for president promising to unwind the excesses of Democratic government energetically expanded that government's investment in the future. While Eisenhower was making modest cuts to other parts of the budget, he sharply increased spending on research and development. As a share of the country's total economic output, federal spending on R&D more than doubled. It continued to rise for a few years after Eisenhower left office in 1961, under John F. Kennedy and Lyndon Johnson, before beginning a gradual six-decade decline.

The Eisenhower investment boom has no peer in U.S. history, at least not outside of wartime. He called for a forty-thousand-mile highway network that he said would accelerate economic growth, make the country more secure, and reduce traffic deaths. Congress initially said no but, after a few years of back-and-forth, passed a bill in 1956 to build the system. The annual budget for the National Institutes of Health increased almost tenfold under Eisenhower. The National Science Foundation budget rose even more sharply. Sometimes, Congress passed bills with more spending than the Eisenhower administration had originally requested. Other times, the administration had to push Congress. Either way, investment, in both physical infrastructure and knowledge, surged.

Federal spending on research and development

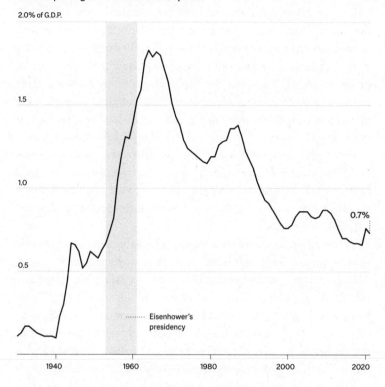

2.0% of G.D.P.

1.5

1.0

0.7%

0.5

Eisenhower's
presidency

1940   1960   1980   2000   2020

The Cold War created an important rationale for this investment boom. The United States felt threatened by the Soviet Union
and needed to keep pace, economically and technologically. Early
in Eisenhower's second term, a stunning Soviet accomplishment
created further pressure to increase investment. On the evening of
October 4, 1957, from a mountain range in Kazakhstan, the Soviet military launched the first satellite into space. It was called
Sputnik, and it created what Eisenhower called a "wave of near-
hysteria" in the United States. Two months later, the United States
launched its own satellite. It exploded almost immediately and became known as "Kaputnik."

Many Americans feared, reasonably, that they had fallen behind the Soviets in the technology race. The panic had echoes of
1940, when a foreign adversary seemed to be making more prog-

ress in developing weapons that could dominate the world. "We have been complacent and we have been smug," Vannevar Bush, the scientist who had helped inspire the World War II investments in research, said after Sputnik. Once again, Washington responded with a campaign to catch up. Eisenhower quickly appointed the president of MIT to be the first White House science adviser. Over the next two years, the administration and Congress allocated new money for education, especially in science. A school construction bill that had failed in 1957 passed in 1958. The military created a research group, the Advanced Research Projects Agency, known as ARPA. (It would later add "Defense" to its name and be called DARPA.) On October 1, almost exactly one year after the Sputnik launch, a new agency, the National Aeronautics and Space Administration, opened.

These programs were surprisingly affordable relative to the rest of government. Although basic research is too expensive for many individual companies to perform, it is far less expensive than many other federal programs, like the military or Social Security. When Eisenhower left office, R&D spending represented less than 1.7 percent of the federal budget. While he was increasing spending on research, he nonetheless managed to run a budget surplus during some years of his presidency. He did so by squeezing spending in other parts of the government and, above all, by winding down the Korean War and cutting military expenditures. He was able to be both a fiscal conservative and the president who more than doubled R&D spending.

Eisenhower has been a vexing president for historians to assess. He was immensely popular with voters during his two terms, only to drift toward irrelevance after he left office. He was the square old man of an earlier era who stood in contrast to Kennedy's glamour. Eisenhower also made profound errors as president. He supported anti-democratic coups in Iran and Guatemala that had long and damaging legacies. At home, his deference to corporate leaders allowed them to choose many of the routes of the new highway system, and these routes destroyed thriving neighborhoods, which were disproportionately Black. His administration missed the opportunity to make some investments that would have brought big returns, like better public transportation and universal basic healthcare. Yet even with these substantial mistakes, Eisenhower had a successful presidency, especially on economics. After Franklin Roosevelt, Eisenhower had arguably the second-best economic record of any twentieth-century president. He presided over good times during his own tenure. The broad-based prosperity continued for years after he left office. And the legislation he signed as president helped make that prosperity possible. None of his successors—including Kennedy, Johnson, Reagan, and Clinton—could make all those claims.

IT IS WORTH pausing to reflect on how many global industries were dominated by American companies by the late twentieth century. It happened not only in the computer business, with IBM, Microsoft, Apple, Amazon, and Google, but also in pharmaceuticals (Pfizer, Johnson & Johnson, Eli Lilly, and Merck), aviation (Boeing, American, United, and Delta), automobiles (General Motors, Ford, and, later, Tesla), energy (Exxon and Chevron), telecommunications (AT&T and Verizon), and more. The United States came to dominate higher education, with American universities occupying more than half of the top spots in various rankings of the world's best research institutions. American citizens dominated the Nobel Prizes, too.

None of this was inevitable. While there are multiple causes—including the country's large consumer market and a vibrant private sector shaped by a national ethos that celebrates risk-taking—the postwar investment boom was vital. That boom fit the historical pattern of successful government investments. First, the government paid for basic scientific research that the private sector was not conducting. Then the government helped create an early market for new products by buying them. Think of the Census Bureau's purchase of the first Univac or the military's role in the early computer market. Finally, the government's role receded over time. Once the market for a new product was established, the sprawling private sector—with its reliance on market feedback and the wisdom of crowds—often did a better job allocating resources than any government agency could. When a company made a better version of a product, it gained market share. The incentives for selling goods that improved people's lives were enormous. Free-market capitalism may not have done an adequate job of subsidizing basic scientific research, but it was very efficient at spreading the eventual fruits of that research.

The computer industry followed this path well beyond World War II and its immediate aftermath. Federal funding was crucial to most major advances. It helped the pioneer of the semiconductor industry, Fairchild Semiconductor, get its start in the late 1950s, when Fairchild won a contract to supply IBM with transistors for a new air force bomber. Fairchild, based in Northern California, then helped spawn Silicon Valley. Later, NASA's spending led to the creation of computer networks, in which individual machines became connected to one another. Eventually, DARPA created a physically remote network of computers: the original internet. Nearly every aspect of modern computing stems from federal research funding.

But the government did not continue to operate most of these networks and products. Private companies did. They helped bring down the costs of production and allowed many more people to afford their innovations. Companies found creative new uses for these scientific innovations.

There are similar stories in many other industries. Government-funded research led to the development of penicillin, cortisone, chemotherapy, vaccines, and cardiac treatments, which the private sector then produced and distributed. In transportation, the government built the air traffic and interstate highway systems, which private companies used. Government funding helped develop the satellite, the jet engine, the snowmobile, and the microwave oven.

These products fostered remarkable improvements in living standards. New medical treatments cured diseases. The daily drudgery of housework was substantially lessened by postwar appliances. Travel was transformed, with airline flights and the highway system reducing travel times, shipment costs, and traffic deaths. The postwar investment that boosted many of the other investments was education. High schools for the masses were already common in the early twentieth century, and they became universal after World War II. Thanks partly to the GI Bill, college also expanded well beyond its elite roots. The United States had the world's most educated population during these decades, and the country's educated workforce became the fuel for the rapidly growing, innovative economy. Relative to its economic rivals, the country could call on more college graduates to fill its professional ranks and more high school graduates to fill its blue-collar ranks. These educated workers made their companies more productive and received higher wages as a result.

By the end of the 1960s, the United States had become the most broadly prosperous country the world had known. Its success was a reflection of both the size of the economic pie and the way it was being divided. The economy had become less unequal than it had been at the start of the twentieth century as a result of the acquisition of political power by workers and the changed culture of corporate America. And economic growth had surged, with help from an investment program that began during World War II and continued for almost two more decades. Americans had faith that the future could be better than the past, and they then forged that future.

CHAPTER 4

Enforcing Racial Democracy

WHEN THE STEEL MILL IN FONTANA, CALIFORNIA, FIRED ITS first blast furnace at an opening celebration in the final days of 1942, it embodied the new era of American capitalism. Its owner was Henry Kaiser, a construction magnate who had once been a bare-knuckle capitalist opposed to labor unions and willing to impose harsh working conditions on his employees.

Over time, Kaiser realized that he would need to change if he wanted to continue winning federal contracts from the Roosevelt administration. Kaiser was also coming to see the ways in which a more humane approach to business could increase efficiency. After his company, Kaiser Steel, hired doctors to provide low-cost medical care for workers, absenteeism fell while productivity rose. Soon the term "Kaiserism" would come to describe a vision for business that was similar to the one that Paul Hoffman was spreading: a high-wage economy, in which workers shared in the growth and contributed to that growth as consumers.

The steel plant in Fontana, about fifty miles east of Los Angeles, was part of that vision. The federal government had helped select its location: The plant needed to be close enough to the West Coast to supply the war factories in major coastal cities but still far enough inland that Japanese ships could not launch missiles at it. To attract workers, the company placed advertisements in newspapers asking for "surveyors, designers, draftsmen, quantity engineers, inspectors, blueprint men." The pay was high enough to lure workers from elsewhere.

One of the people drawn to Fontana was a welder named O'Day Short, who had been living in Los Angeles. He and his wife, Helen, were originally part of the Great Migration of Black Americans from the South; she was from Georgia, he from Mississippi. By 1945, they had two children, nine-year-old Barry and seven-year-old Carol Ann. The family made a $1,000 down payment on a plot of land near the center of Fontana and built a house. They moved into their new home late that year, in time to celebrate Christmas.

The war was over, and millions of American workers were enjoying rising living standards. In Fontana, the Shorts saw an opportunity to become part of the boom and build a middle-class life for their family.

A few days after they moved in, it was clear that there was a problem. A deputy sheriff came to the house to tell the Shorts that they needed to move. The property they had bought was south of Base Line Road, which ran for miles at the base of the foothills of the San Gabriel Mountains. The road acted as a dividing line between developed areas in town, with streetlights and sewers, and rural areas in the foothills. The Shorts' property was in a developed area. Only White people were supposed to live there, explained the deputy sheriff, Cornelius "Tex" Carlson. If the Shorts refused to leave, Carlson said, there could be "disagreeableness."

Not long after Carlson's visit, a real estate agent came by to reinforce the message. The agent said he had attended a meeting the previous night with a rough bunch of men who would attack O'Day Short if he did not leave. A representative of the Fontana Chamber of Commerce followed up and told the Shorts that it would buy back the land for the price they had bought it for.

But the Shorts would not be intimidated. O'Day contacted a lawyer about the threats, and the lawyer urged him to tell the FBI, which he did. He also drove to Los Angeles and met with journalists at three Black newspapers to tell them what was happening. The newspapers had been reporting on, and encouraging, a nascent civil rights movement in Southern California. Many Black Californians had worked in wartime defense factories or served overseas and were increasingly unwilling to accept second-class citizenship.

"They're just trying to bluff me out," Short told the *Los Angeles Sentinel*. "I recognize the old Texas technique when I see it." It was not an accident that he mentioned Texas. Some of Fontana's White residents had recently moved from the South, looking for better-paying work, just as Short had.

On Sunday, December 16, 1945, two weeks after the Shorts had moved in, the family spent the day back in Los Angeles. Helen's father and sisters lived there, and the family's Catholic church was in Los Angeles too. Fontana's church was not an option for them because it was all-White. The Shorts arrived home in Fontana around five-thirty, just after sunset. As O'Day entered the dark house, he picked up a kerosene lamp in the living room and struck a match to light it. At virtually the same moment, a massive explosion rocked the house. Three-quarters of a mile away, a driver saw the sky light up.

The details of the fire were sickening. The explosion blew O'Day from the living room into the yard and lit his clothes on fire. He stood up and charged into the house to find his family. Together, they escaped into the yard, where Helen—her hair burned off and her face bleeding—summoned the strength to extinguish the fire on her children's clothes while they screamed in pain.

"That family is burning, run down there quickly," one neighbor told her husband. "Everything was on fire," another recalled. Neighbors drove the Shorts to the local Kaiser Permanente hospital, with the children screaming. By the next morning, Helen, Barry, and Carol Ann had all died. O'Day was in critical condition.

The police never conducted a serious investigation. They called the fire an accident, caused by the kerosene lamp that O'Day had lit when he entered his house, and the case received little attention in local White newspapers. Black newspapers and civil rights groups would not allow the case to disappear quietly, though. The National Association for the Advancement of Colored People hired a retired fire department investigator, who found evidence of foul play. The Shorts' house and yard had been soaked with gas, and O'Day, from his hospital bed, told a family member that he had smelled something unusual when he arrived home. The investigator also discovered that the kerosene lamp was intact, indicating it had not caused the explosion. The most likely explanation was either that O'Day's lighting of the lamp had ignited the gas doused inside the house or that the lamp was an unrelated coincidence and the attackers had started the fire after the Shorts entered the home.

The Fontana police and the district attorney ignored the investigator's findings. They ignored the pleas from O'Day, and from Helen's sisters and their husbands, to investigate. The sheriff assigned his deputy—Carlson, the same man who had threatened the Shorts—to conduct the inquiry, and Fontana officials quickly closed it, classifying the explosion as an accident. On the night of January 21, after five weeks in the hospital, O'Day Short died. The attackers had murdered an entire family and gotten away with it.

In the years to come, the Kaiser plant became the largest steel mill in the West, employing thousands of people. The pay of the plant's workers kept rising, thanks both to the company's success at finding innovative ways to produce steel and to the labor union's success at negotiating contracts. Japanese steel executives visited Fontana to learn from Kaiser's production methods. The Kennedy administration recommended that companies in other industries study the profit-sharing plan in Fontana. The mill was a beacon of prosperity, just as Helen and O'Day Short had foreseen.

But Black workers never got much of a chance to be a part of it. After the Shorts, no Black family moved to central Fontana for another twenty years.

AS THE UNITED STATES built the great middle class of the postwar years, the country went to extraordinary lengths to exclude Black citizens. The effort included both legal and illegal methods, violent and nonviolent ones. Lawmakers in Congress and state legislatures, as well as police officers, school administrators, business executives, and citizen vigilantes around the country all played a part. Trying to prevent Black Americans from joining the middle class was government policy, sometimes written into law and other times, as in Fontana, informally enforced by government officials.

In Washington, the central players were southern Democrats

who supported redistributive economic programs so long as those programs maintained a racial caste system. These southerners were not completely fake populists. They supported many laws and programs that narrowed the gap between rich and poor, including Social Security, minimum wages, union protections, antitrust regulations, and education and housing programs. The southerners even employed pugnacious class-based rhetoric. Theodore Bilbo, campaigning for a Mississippi Senate seat in 1934, promised to "raise the same kind of hell as President Roosevelt" and make "noise for the common people." But the southerners' progressive economic vision was exclusionary. The historian C. Vann Woodward described their views as a "paradoxical combination of white supremacy and progressivism." Crucially, these southerners held an effective veto over Roosevelt's agenda because of their numbers and their congressional seniority.

They used their power to build a new middle class that would be as White as possible. The constitutional amendments ratified after the Civil War prevented this effort from being explicit, but the goal was nonetheless obvious. The minimum wages established by the National Industrial Recovery Act during the Depression did not cover farmworkers or domestic workers, two categories that together accounted for roughly two-thirds of Black southern workers. Social Security also excluded them.

Many other federal programs gave local officials latitude to decide who received benefits, and those officials—not just in the South—often excluded Americans who were not White. (At the time, more than 99 percent of the population was either White or Black.) Local officials frequently rejected Black applicants for unemployment benefits, sometimes with a manufactured reason and sometimes with no reason at all. The result, as the NAACP put it when opposing an unemployment insurance bill in Congress, was "a sieve with holes just big enough for the majority of Negroes to fall through." The Civilian Conservation Corps, another New Deal program, promised not to create programs for young Black Americans in towns that did not want them; the governor of New Jersey did not allow any CCC work sites for Black corps members in the entire state. Once World War II began, the military told

Black troops that it could not train them for specialists' jobs because it did not have barracks where they could sleep. The navy was particularly hostile, usually assigning Black sailors to be stewards. The GI Bill did help Black veterans in much of the country attend college after the war, but local officials in the South were able to restrict the program's benefits largely to Whites.

The housing market was the premier example of government-enforced racism. Residential segregation in the United States can sometimes appear to stem from a mix of economic factors and personal choice: Many Black Americans lack the money to move into predominantly White neighborhoods, and many people, of all races, prefer to live among those who are similar to them. In reality, though, residential segregation has been much more top-down and deliberate.

Across the country, federal and local governments built all-White public housing that was far superior to the housing available to Black families. Outside St. Louis, a relatively progressive developer tried to build two different communities for working-class families, one Black and one White; the Federal Housing Administration would fund only the White one. Near the East River in Manhattan, the city government cleared eighteen square blocks for a moderate-income development called Stuyvesant Town and bestowed twenty-five years of tax breaks on it. The development rented only to White families. After years of legal fighting, Stuyvesant Town finally said it would allow a Black family. By then, the apartments, with their below-market rents, were filled, and many White families remained in the apartments for decades. Among the residents of Stuyvesant Town who went on to national prominence were the authors Mary Higgins Clark and Frank McCourt, the political guru David Axelrod, and the actor Paul Reiser. Stuyvesant Town was an American success story, but not everyone was allowed in.

The segregationist policies extended to the private mortgage market. Before the New Deal, most Americans did not own their home. The required down payment was too large, often 50 percent of the purchase price, and home loans had to be repaid over only a few years, making monthly payments onerous. The New

Deal, along with the GI Bill and other programs, changed this, creating the modern system of modest down payments and thirty-year mortgages. The federal government decided that it had an interest in encouraging home ownership, and it used government funds—that is, tax dollars—to both subsidize and guarantee mortgages. This, in turn, made banks willing to lend to middle-class families. The postwar housing boom was in many respects a government program. When William Levitt, the creator of Levittown, the iconic community on Long Island, appeared before Congress in 1957, he acknowledged as much. "We are 100 percent dependent on government," Levitt told his benefactors. Without government-backed mortgages, Levittown and other communities could not have existed. And Levittown was segregated, at the insistence of its founder. The contracts to buy or rent a home stated that residents could be only "members of the Caucasian race."

Even in communities without explicit Whites-only policies, homebuyers who hoped to receive a government-subsidized mortgage first needed a seal of approval indicating that they represented a good credit risk. Government agencies, working with local real estate agencies, awarded the seals of approval, and they automatically designated Black neighborhoods as poor risks. They also judged integration of a White neighborhood to be a threat to property values and, by extension, a repayment risk. The government produced color-coded maps, using green to denote acceptable neighborhoods and red to denote unacceptably risky ones. Black neighborhoods, by definition, were red. Those maps are the origin of the term "redlining."

The combination of redlining and segregated public housing was not sufficient to prevent all residential integration. Some Black families managed to amass enough savings to buy homes in booming, largely White neighborhoods. When they did, there was one final way in which the government enforced segregation: Law enforcement allowed or participated in efforts to force out Black families.

In 1951, a war veteran and Chicago bus driver named Harvey Clark rented a home in the suburb of Cicero for his family. The Cicero police tried to prevent the Clarks from moving in, and after local White residents rioted, a grand jury indicted Clark and his real estate agent, rather than any of the rioters. In Berkeley, California, the Federal Housing Administration informed a White teacher who had rented an apartment to a Black colleague that he would never again qualify for a subsidized mortgage. In Bucks County, Pennsylvania, a White mail carrier organized neighborhood opposition to a Black family's presence; demonstrators threw rocks at the family's house, burned a cross on the lawn, flew a Confederate flag, painted a Ku Klux Klan sign on a wall, and blared loud music at night. When a sergeant tried to interfere with the harassment campaign, the police department demoted him.

In the Los Angeles area, the killing of the Shorts was one episode in a yearslong campaign of terrorism intended to keep neighborhoods segregated. Among the dozens of incidents was the predawn bombing of two homes in the West Adams neighborhood. Identifying suspects did not seem especially difficult, given that pro-segregation picketers had surrounded the home days before the bombings. But the police never made any arrests, which was the norm in such cases. The Los Angeles police chief during this period was William Parker, known for making racist remarks about Black and Mexican American residents. Under Parker's leadership, the police department sanctioned vigilante violence, so long as it was done in the name of racism.

The combined economic impact of these policies was enormous and long-lasting. The federal government helped White families build up housing wealth that passed down from one generation to the next. The government trained White military troops for skilled positions that allowed them to get high-paying jobs after their service. It gave financial aid to White teenagers attending largely segregated colleges. It created a federal retirement program mostly for White workers. The entire time, Black Americans were paying taxes, serving in the military, and helping build a world-leading economy with their labor and ingenuity, while being denied the return on their loyalty and investment. If you are a White American today, you have almost certainly benefited from the racially exclusionary efforts to build the middle class; if you are a Black American, you have almost certainly been harmed by them.

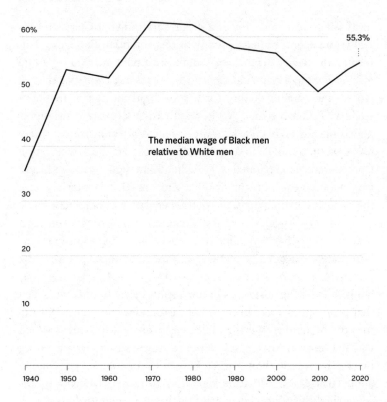

The median wage of Black men
relative to White men

55.3%

But there is also one surprising—and inspiring—caveat to the story of midcentury racial exclusion in the United States. Despite the government's efforts, Black Americans managed to climb the economic ladder between the 1940s and 1970s. They participated in the long boom, as incomplete and unfair as that participation was. Black workers received larger raises on average than White workers, and this shrinking of the pay gap began well before the passage of 1960s civil rights laws. Most surprisingly, the pay gap shrank more in the decades before the passage of those laws than it has since the 1970s. The gap in life expectancy between Black and White Americans also declined in the postwar decades. Even as racism remained a dominant feature of everyday life and the government enacted policies meant to exacerbate racial inequity, that inequity instead narrowed.

The period since 1980 has looked very different: Racial gaps have largely stopped narrowing, with only brief exceptions (including the past several years, because of a tight labor market and minimum-wage increases, among other factors). Nonetheless, the White-Black wage gap was larger in 2020 than in the final decades of the twentieth century and almost as large as it was in 1950.

This chapter—the final chapter tracing the rise of the American dream—is devoted to solving the mystery of Black progress during the postwar decades. The narrowing of racial gaps is perhaps the best testament to the potency of the long postwar boom and the forces that created it. Those forces were strong enough to make progress possible despite the racism that was America's original and enduring sin.

ONE OF THE largest private employers of Black Americans in the early twentieth century was the Pullman Company. It made and operated sleeping cars during the heyday of railroad travel, and it employed Black men to work as porters and Black women to work as maids on the cars.

The company had gotten its big break in 1865, when government officials were looking for an opulent railroad car to transport Abraham Lincoln's body to Illinois for burial. The officials discovered the Pullman car—with red carpeting, silver-trimmed lamps, and exquisite woodwork—in a Chicago rail yard, and they selected it. The resulting fanfare lifted the company's business. In the following years, Pullman continued to link itself with Lincoln and Black emancipation, hiring Lincoln's son Robert as its top executive and employing formerly enslaved people as porters and maids.

A job as a Pullman porter was among the highest-status work available to Black Americans in the early twentieth century. They traveled the country and met celebrities. They would bring back newspapers from faraway cities for their relatives and neighbors to read, and their friends treated them as experts on national affairs. "Everybody listened," E. D. Nixon, a porter, told the writer Studs Terkel. "We were able to let people know what was happening."

Pullman work was so important that a leading Black newspaper, *The New York Age,* ran a regular column called "Things Seen, Heard and Done Among Pullman Employees." A porter's job also paid relatively well, albeit mostly in tips, which allowed some Black families to buy a home or send a child to college.

But if the work seemed elite, it was only in comparison to most opportunities for Black families. Porters worked grueling hours and were not paid for the time they spent arranging a Pullman car before it left the station. Porters also had to pay for their own uniforms and equipment, including shoe polish for the passengers. "The work was hard, the hours long, and the pay poor," one porter said. To receive good tips, porters often had to play into the stereotype of a servant cheerfully accepting humiliating treatment from his master. Many travelers referred to every porter as "George," after the company's founder, George Pullman. It was shorthand for "George Pullman's boys" and an echo of slave culture, in which people were stripped of individual identity. The practice was so well known that a group of prominent White men named George formed the Society for the Prevention of Calling Sleeping Car Porters George. Its members included the kings of both England and Greece, George Herman Ruth (better known as Babe), and several entertainers. The society's members seemed more concerned with the potential damage to the prestige of their own name than with the porters' working conditions.

In the 1920s, some porters in New York decided to take action to improve those conditions. Influenced by the intellectual energy of the Harlem Renaissance, they talked about forming a labor union. One of the budding activists had an idea of somebody who might be able to help: a man named Asa Philip Randolph, who had developed a reputation as one of Harlem's finest soapbox orators—amateur speakers who held forth about pressing matters of the day on local street corners, especially Lenox Avenue and 135th Street.

People sometimes described Randolph as the most graceful man they had ever met. He was slender and stood erect, making him seem even taller than he was. He spoke in a rich baritone, enunciating each syllable in an accent that sounded almost British.

He eschewed money but dressed well on a tight budget. "His only vanity," a newspaper columnist would write, "is his manners."

He inherited those manners from his parents. Randolph had grown up in Jacksonville, Florida, where his father, James, was a preacher in the African Methodist Episcopal Church and his mother, Elizabeth, ran a small sewing and clothes-dyeing business out of their home. The couple had only a modest amount of formal education but a deep intellectual curiosity. They insisted that their two children—Asa and his older brother, James—read every day, not just the Bible but also Austen, Dickens, Keats, Shakespeare, and Darwin, as well as African and American history. The boys would often do so on the front porch of their rented two-story house. Elizabeth Randolph said that she always felt more comfortable when the boys were reading on the porch rather than playing ball in the street, where a passing car might hit them.

Her husband's lack of college training meant that he could not rise through the hierarchy of the AME Church. His parish consisted mostly of servants and laborers, and he also ministered to rural parishes outside Jacksonville. He traveled there on riverboats with segregated seating, often bringing along his sons. Even overseeing multiple churches, James did not make enough money to pay the family's bills, and Elizabeth's clothing business was their main source of income. They also maintained a fruit and vegetable garden in their backyard and kept a few chickens and hogs to help feed the family. Each Christmas, the Randolphs bought a straw carpet to decorate their living room and threw it out a couple of months later, once it had frayed.

Years later, it became clear how well Asa's childhood had prepared him for political leadership. He grew up experiencing both the everyday struggles of working-class Americans and the particular humiliations of racism. He also grew up with parents who were leaders in their community and who had even bigger ambitions for their children. Asa and his brother attended the Cookman Institute, one of the first private high schools for Black children. At home, Asa heard that many of the world's great leaders were Black and that he should follow their path. Don't merely try to make a dollar, his father would say; dedicate your life to lifting up Black America. Speak clearly and stand tall—shoulders back—as you go about your work.

After Asa read W. E. B. Du Bois's *The Souls of Black Folk,* he became impatient with the lack of options in Jacksonville, and he moved to New York in 1911, when he was twenty-two years old. He worked a series of menial jobs—like scrubbing floors and operating the switchboard in an apartment building—and did some acting with local theater troupes. Increasingly, he found himself drawn to politics. He and his friends would stay up late into the night in their apartments arguing over current affairs, and sometimes they would participate in formal public debates. He enrolled in night classes at City College of New York, which were free, and became attracted to the radical ideas that were popular on campus.

From those City College classes and from the European history books he read during visits to the New York Public Library, Randolph decided that the problems of Black Americans were similar to the problems of many other workers around the world. The only solution, he concluded, was political power. Black Americans would never achieve decent pay and working conditions merely by asking for them. They had to organize themselves into a sufficiently powerful force to demand them. "There is no hope for any group of workers without some power, and history has shown that the labor movement is the source of power for workers," Randolph said. He was intrigued by the situation in Europe, where unions were helping form new political parties, like Britain's Labour Party and Sweden's Social Democrats.

Randolph thought that few existing organizations in the United States were viable options. He admired his parents' religious devotion and saw how faith could move people emotionally. But he did not believe religion was the mechanism for political change. He also had no interest in Marcus Garvey's Black separatist movement, which was narrower in its appeal—focused on only one race—than successful workers' movements around the world. The Democratic Party, for its part, was dominated by southern racists, including the president at the time, Woodrow Wilson, who segregated federal agencies and demoted Black workers. The Republican Party had a better historical record on civil rights, but it was the party of big business, with an agenda dedicated to keeping wages low. "The Republicans knew they had the Negroes in their pockets, and the Democrats looked down on them," Randolph said. "Neither had a program for the Negro."

Before the porters approached him, Randolph's success as a soapbox orator had helped him and a friend get jobs editing a magazine for hotel waiters, the *Hotel Messenger*. They broadened its subject matter and renamed it *The Messenger*. The cover announced that it was "a journal of scientific socialism." Randolph stopped calling himself Asa and began using the writerly byline A. Philip Randolph. His wife, Lucille, who ran a successful hair salon, subsidized the magazine and introduced him to leading figures in Harlem. *The Messenger* published work by Langston Hughes and other Harlem Renaissance writers. The Justice Department, as part of its surveillance of political radicals, described *The Messenger* as "by long odds the most able and the most dangerous of all the Negro publications." That combination explained why the Pullman porters thought that Randolph might be able to help them.

The porters asked him to lead their campaign to form a union, and Randolph said yes. Several weeks later, he presided over a meeting at an Elks lodge in Harlem to announce the formation of the Brotherhood of Sleeping Car Porters.

IT WAS THE underdog labor union of all underdog labor unions. Pullman was a corporate colossus, with a board that at one point included J. P. Morgan, Alfred Sloan, and members of the Mellon, Vanderbilt, and Whitney families. The Brotherhood of Sleeping Car Porters hoped to become the country's first meaningful union for Black workers.

"The history of all groups in America and everywhere else who are at the bottom of the economic ladder," Randolph said at the Brotherhood's first meeting in 1925, was that they "raise themselves up and are able to provide for themselves a viable life only through organization." He explained that while the Black church was a great institution—Randolph's own father was a preacher, he mentioned—it was not enough. Religion would not fix their earthly lives. The porters needed something else, he told them. They needed a union. On their behalf, the Brotherhood would demand a 40 percent reduction in hours, as well as a wage increase and an end to the insecurity that came from depending on tips. The Brotherhood would give them power, Randolph said. His case proved persuasive. By 1928, the union had signed up almost seven thousand members.

But in the 1920s, union-organizing drives were usually doomed. Companies could simply ignore a union or take steps to eliminate it, and Pullman followed this strategy. It sent spies to organizing meetings and threatened or fired union members. The company labeled Randolph "a Bolshevik hustler" and his allies "wormy Pullman fruit." Executives lobbied Black ministers and newspaper editors, reminding them that a porter who lost his job faced bleak employment alternatives. "Any Sunday you went to church, the preachers touched on the Brotherhood," one porter said. "Their slogan was 'Don't rock the boat, don't bite the hand that feeds you.' They said Randolph was just a glib orator, whereas the Pullman Company was a million-dollar outfit." Once the Depression hit, these tactics succeeded, and the Brotherhood's membership shrank by almost 90 percent. Lucille Randolph's hair salon collapsed during this time, leaving her and Phil (as he was known) without their main source of income. Porters noticed that Randolph's normally impeccable clothes began to look tattered. In Harlem, the Brotherhood could no longer pay the rent on its headquarters, and the landlord evicted it, leaving the furniture on the street.

Then came the New Deal revolution in labor policy. After the passage of Section 7(a) and the Wagner Act, Pullman porters streamed back into the union. The company resorted to new stall tactics, making meaningless contract offers to the Brotherhood while hoping that the Supreme Court would undermine the union's ability to organize. For several years, the delays succeeded, and nothing changed for the porters. But as part of the Supreme Court's new moderation on economic issues after Roosevelt's landslide reelection and his searing criticism of the court, the justices issued a decision in 1937 supporting organized labor in the railroad industry. Only three days after that decision, Pullman made its first substantive offer to the Brotherhood. Several months later—on a summer day that happened to be the twelfth anniversary of Randolph's kickoff meeting at the Elks lodge in Harlem—the company and union signed a contract. It included a 40 percent reduction in hours for both maids and porters, a 30 percent wage increase for maids, a 15 percent wage increase for porters, and time-and-a-half pay for overtime. Once again, grass-roots organizers, with the ultimate backing of government officials, had succeeded in reshaping the economy.

"No labor leadership in America has faced greater odds," the civil rights activist Elmer Anderson Carter wrote about the Brotherhood. "None has won any greater victory."

THE PORTERS' VICTORY was a turning point for the unionization of Black America. In the 1920s and early 1930s, when unions had been shrinking, Black workers were even less likely to belong to one than White workers. Only about 1 percent of Black workers were unionized in 1930, compared with almost 10 percent of White workers. Collective bargaining was yet another political right denied to Black Americans, and both business executives and union leaders were responsible. Executives wanted to maintain a pool of very low-wage workers to do menial work, while many labor leaders favored segregated unions. Some unions were explicitly White-only; others simply refused to admit Black members. Samuel Gompers had initially called for the unionization of Black workers when he founded the AFL in the late 1800s, but he did little to make that happen. He instead supported the right of individual unions to exclude Black workers and then blamed those workers for having low unionization rates. With Black workers shut out of unions, companies could use them to break strikes. If unions remained segregated, employers could always call on a reserve army of replacement workers who had no reason to support the union.

Over the course of the 1930s and 1940s, however, a growing number of union leaders saw integration as a moral imperative or at least a matter of self-interest. The CIO, with its strategy of industrial unionism that tried to recruit all types of workers, led the way. At an early CIO convention in the 1930s, it adopted a resolution called "Unity of Negro and White Workers" that promised "uncompromising opposition to any form of discrimination." At labor conventions, John L. Lewis, the mineworkers' leader and CIO founder, sometimes sat with Randolph and other Brotherhood officials as a show of support while racist union leaders taunted them. The United Auto Workers, led by Walter Reuther, also pushed for integration, with White and Black organizers working together to overcome Ford's longtime hostility to unions. The historian Ira Katznelson has described the relatively progressive unions of the CIO as "the most racially integrated institutions in American life." The openness to integration even spread to parts of the more conservative AFL. Its president amended the organization's charter so that Randolph's Brotherhood, rather than an all-White union, had jurisdiction to organize the porters.

Virulent racism remained common in many unions during the postwar years, but the changes were nonetheless significant. After the Wagner Act established the right to collective bargaining and wartime mobilization accelerated unionization, Black workers began rushing into unions. Many had been part of the migration from the South and found industrial work in the cities of the North and West. A few unions even managed to integrate southern workplaces, as *Fortune* magazine reported in 1946. Throughout the South, Blacks and Whites "live in different sections, go to different schools, worship in different churches, read different newspapers, shop in different stores, seek different places of amusement, live separate lives, and are buried in separate cemeteries," *Fortune* wrote. "The only local institution that southern whites and Negroes have in common today is the labor union." In the late 1940s, W. E. B. Du Bois was able to proclaim, "Probably the greatest and most effective effort toward interracial understanding among the working masses has come about through the trade unions."

By the 1960s, the racial gap in unionization had reversed: About 33 percent of workers of color were in unions, compared with about 28 percent of White workers, later research would show. (The research did not distinguish among Black, Latino, and Asian workers, but Americans of color were still overwhelmingly Black in the 1960s.) Frequently, Black workers received an even larger financial benefit from membership than White workers did. White workers still made significantly more on average, but unionization tended to shrink the difference. A unionized Black worker often made at least 20 percent more than a nonunionized Black worker doing similar work.

That pattern makes sense if you recall the idea that wages exist in a "range of indeterminacy," influenced by factors other than pure economics, including psychology and political power. In nonunionized workplaces, racism, whether explicit or subconscious, can keep the wages of Black workers in a lower part of the range than those of White workers. A union contract, by contrast, both lifts workers' wages and standardizes them. A union contract makes it less likely that employees from a disadvantaged group will receive lower pay than their colleagues.

Combined, the surge of Black unionization and the large financial benefits of unionization are the first part of the solution to this chapter's mystery. The United States remained a deeply racist society during World War II and the decades immediately after it. Across the South, Black citizens lacked the most basic democratic right of all—the right to vote—and were consigned to inferior, segregated schools, hospitals, transportation, and more. Many workplaces and universities outside the South were segregated. Anti-Black violence was common, often ignored by police officers and sometimes committed by them. The federal government enacted a sprawling set of economic policies that simultaneously tried to create a new middle class and exclude Black Americans from joining it. And yet, amid all this oppression, racial inequality declined during these same decades.

How could that possibly have been the case? Because the American economy of the postwar decades benefited lower-income families more than it benefited the affluent, and Black Americans were much more likely to have low incomes. Even as many other forms of American racism remained intact, the decline in overall economic inequality helped shrink the racial wage gap.

RANDOLPH'S AMBITIONS HAD always been larger than building a union. He had joined the porters' cause because he saw it as a way to improve life for Black Americans, but he knew that labor organizing alone could not dismantle the country's racism. That task would also require sweeping changes to government policy. Randolph knew something else, as well: In the Brotherhood of Sleeping Car Porters, he had helped create the potential foundation of a national political movement.

The union's triumph had turned Randolph into "the most popular black political figure in America," as the journalist Jervis Anderson wrote. The porters, meanwhile, were an unusual group of workers. A porter spent his life traveling around the country, making connections with other people. "His home is everywhere," as

Protesting against military segregation, A. Philip Randolph leads the picket line outside of the Democratic Convention in Philadelphia, 1948.

Randolph said. Porters could build a movement by spreading the gospel of civil rights and economic justice.

The movement's first target, Randolph decided, would be the huge jobs program that World War II mobilization seemed destined to bring. As the world descended into war in the late 1930s, Black leaders understood that America's wartime factories were likely to be segregated, as so many New Deal programs had been. The magazine of the NAACP printed an illustration on its July 1940 cover showing an aircraft factory, with captions reading "For whites only" and "Negro Americans may not build them, repair them, or fly them." Randolph, no longer needing to focus all his efforts on a Pullman contract, lobbied the Roosevelt administration to integrate both military units and wartime factories. The administration signaled that it was open to making changes, and Eleanor Roosevelt became Randolph's main point of contact. But the encouraging words never led to action. After President Roosevelt handily won a third term in 1940, he stepped up the preparations for war and showed no sign of integrating the country's armed forces or its wartime production.

Several weeks after the election, Randolph and Milton Webster, a hulking, cigar-smoking Chicago porter who served as the union's second-ranking official, were on a train trip through the South to visit Brotherhood locals when Randolph raised an idea. "I think we ought to get 10,000 Negroes to march on Washington in protest, march down Pennsylvania Avenue," Randolph said. "What do you think of that?"

"Where are you going to get 10,000 Negroes?" Webster asked.

"I think we can get them," Randolph said.

Soon they settled on a name for their protest: the March on Washington. And they settled on a theme: racial justice in the name of patriotism. "We loyal Negro American citizens demand the right to work and fight for our country," Randolph wrote in a statement to the press. In the early months of 1941, Brotherhood officials visited restaurants, bars, barbershops, beauty salons, and other gathering places to promote the march. Black newspapers wrote about it. The NAACP and the National Urban League signed on, despite their traditional wariness of confrontational protests. The response was so positive that Randolph stopped talking about 10,000 marchers and began using the number 100,000.

It was a spectacularly audacious plan. Randolph was asking Black Americans to march on the nation's capital, a city that was located below the Mason-Dixon line, where many local businesses still included "Dixie" in their name. "It scared everybody to death," Webster said. When he and Randolph described the idea for the march during public appearances on their southern tour of Brotherhood locals—in Savannah, Jacksonville, Tampa, and Miami—they noticed that a few members of the audience would sometimes stand up and leave. They did not want to be seen at a meeting where speakers were discussing a Black march on Washington.

Randolph believed the protest was worth the risks because the war had presented Black Americans with a rare political opportunity. The United States and Britain were portraying themselves as defenders of democracy and freedom. The image was crucial to maintaining morale in Britain, which was fighting the European war virtually alone by late 1940, and to building popular support in the United States. The treatment of Black Americans undermined this image. If thousands of people marched on Washington demanding freedom within their own country, it would be a public relations windfall for Japan, Germany, and the Soviet Union, which was allied with Germany until 1941. "We cannot inscribe on our banners: 'For Democracy and a caste system,'" *The Nation* magazine later wrote. "We cannot liberate oppressed peoples while maintaining the right to oppress our own minorities."

One Washington columnist wrote that the prospect of Randolph's demonstration had caused a panic inside the White House. Roosevelt had to choose between angering the pro-segregation forces in his party on the one hand and damaging his war preparations on the other. Randolph confronted the president with a dilemma that lacked an easy solution.

The White House tried to avoid the problem by persuading Randolph to cancel the march. Eleanor Roosevelt told Randolph that it was "a very grave mistake" that could set back civil rights—

a cause she believed in—by heightening opposition to integration. She asked Randolph where all the marchers would sleep and reminded him of the Washington police force's brutal treatment of Black people. The administration also tried to mollify Randolph by sending letters to military contractors encouraging them to hire Black workers and by suggesting that Congress form a committee to investigate discrimination in the defense industry. Randolph responded by making one major concession, dropping his demand that the military integrate its units, but otherwise held firm. Unless the president ordered the integration of wartime factories, the march would proceed.

Less than two weeks before the march's planned date of July 1, 1941, Roosevelt finally invited Randolph and Walter White, the head of the NAACP, to the White House for a meeting. Three military leaders attended, as did New York mayor Fiorello La Guardia, who was close to Randolph.

When Randolph entered the Oval Office, Roosevelt began the meeting with one of his attempts at bonhomie. "Hello, Phil," he said. "Which class were you in at Harvard?" Roosevelt had been in the Harvard class of 1904, and he was not the first person to confuse Randolph's florid speaking style with an Ivy League education. In truth, Randolph had no college degree, only some night classes at City College of New York and years of self-education.

"I never went to Harvard, Mr. President," Randolph replied.

"I was sure you did," Roosevelt said. "Anyway, you and I share a kinship in our great interest in human and social justice."

"That's right, Mr. President," Randolph said.

At that point, knowing that a meeting with a president could end at any moment, Randolph made his case: Black workers wanted to work in defense industries. They deserved the right to do so. Only an executive order by Roosevelt could make it happen.

Roosevelt responded with the same arguments that Randolph and White had already heard. The president told them that he would personally ask contractors to hire Black workers. He also warned of the chaos that the march could cause. "You can't bring 100,000 Negroes to Washington," he said. "Somebody might get killed."

Randolph parried that violence was unlikely if Roosevelt spoke at the march, as they had invited him to do. Roosevelt replied brusquely: "Call it off, and we'll talk again."

The pressure on Randolph in this moment was immense. The president of the United States was giving him an order in the Oval Office. Some of Randolph's allies had advised him to call off the march or risk violence against the people he was leading. And he was a Black man at a time when Black people were not supposed to defy White people, let alone Franklin Delano Roosevelt. But Randolph did not yield. "Gentlemen," La Guardia said to the room, "it is clear that Mr. Randolph is not going to call off the march, and I suggest we all begin to seek a formula."

Over the next six days, Roosevelt's aides negotiated a solution with Randolph. It required Roosevelt to surrender without acknowledging that he was doing so. His aides began drafting an executive order to integrate factories and telephoned Randolph in New York to read him initial versions. Randolph rejected them as lacking teeth. "Who the hell is this guy Randolph?" Joseph Rauh, a member of Roosevelt's staff, said to his colleagues during the process. "What the hell has he got over the President of the United States?"

The answer was one that Roosevelt understood well: political power.

Randolph referred to it as "mass power." He had assembled a movement strong enough to change national policy. He had made sure that the political cost of continued segregation of the defense industry would be greater than the cost of integration. On June 25, Roosevelt issued Executive Order 8802, and it was less than two typed pages, double spaced. "The democratic way of life within the Nation can be defended successfully only with the help and support of all groups within its borders," it read. All workers, "without discrimination because of race, creed, color, or national origin," could participate equally in defense industries. (Roosevelt himself had suggested the addition of "national origin" to prevent discrimination against ethnic groups, especially Poles.) Du Bois, Randolph's hero, called the order "most astonishing."

As soon as Roosevelt issued it, Randolph canceled the march, saying it had achieved its objective. Some other civil rights activists criticized him for doing so, arguing that Black Americans still had many reasons to march. Randolph replied that he had made a deal with the president of the United States and would stick to it. To do otherwise, he said, would be "a lamentable specie of infantile left-ism." Instead, Randolph announced that the march's organizers would form a permanent group, called the March on Washington Committee, to advance civil rights.

One of its first projects would be to make sure that the Roosevelt administration enforced the executive order. That was important because nobody knew how effective it would be. Segregated workplaces were an ingrained part of American life, and many people did not expect the executive order to be a turning point. *The New York Times* covered it with a short story—"President Orders an Even Break for Minorities in Defense Jobs"—on page 12, next to stories about a planned fire drill in Queens and a decline in venereal diseases among military men. Other newspapers ran one-paragraph items from wire services. Black newspapers did give the order extensive coverage, but their tone was circumspect. "There is manifest confusion," Emmett J. Scott of *The New York Age* wrote. Some employers were following the order, while the others were defying it.

These acts of segregationist defiance would continue for years, from both companies and all-White labor unions. Some workers staged so-called hate strikes in 1941, walking off the job in protest of integration. Some companies retained an overwhelmingly White workforce for years. Elsewhere, residential segregation, often enforced violently, prevented many workers from moving close enough to a job to take it. By any definition, Executive Order 8802 failed to fulfill its promise to provide for the full and equitable participation of all workers in the American economy.

But the order still made a major difference Many companies voluntarily followed it. Wartime labor shortages soon meant that some had to choose between integrating their workforces and failing to meet their production goals. In other cases, the Committee

on Fair Employment Practice, a five-member presidentially appointed board created by the executive order, investigated companies for discrimination and ordered them to stop.

Together, Executive Order 8802, World War II, and the changes
inside labor unions began to integrate America's industrial economy. Along with Randolph's Brotherhood, the CIO played a central role. It emerged as "the leading edge of New Deal liberalism,"
as the political scientist Eric Schickler has written, pushing the
Democratic Party to endorse both economic progressivism and
civil rights, and the party increasingly did so. In response, Black
voters—almost 40 percent of whom supported Republicans into
the 1940s—shifted decisively toward the Democrats. This dynamic
was the same self-reinforcing one that had occurred with White
workers in the 1930s. The Democratic Party's policies had lifted
their living standards and won their political loyalty. That loyalty
made the party more responsive to the workers' interests. The
Great Migration deepened the connection because many of the
states to which Black voters were moving, including New York,
Pennsylvania, Illinois, and California, were swing states during the
mid-twentieth century. The Democratic Party, outside of the South
at least, needed Black voters.

Around the country, a Black middle class began to grow—in
Harlem and South Philadelphia, along the U Street corridor in
Washington, on the South Side of Chicago, in Detroit suburbs like
Inkster, in the West Adams neighborhood of Los Angeles, and elsewhere. The early civil rights movement, allied with labor unions
and with Randolph at the forefront, had cracked open the door of
the country's industrial sector to Black Americans just as that sector was lifting living standards for the masses.

IT CAN BE difficult to make sense of the dueling realities of the postwar decades—both the rapid progress of Black Americans and the
era's huge and enduring injustices. They seem like a contradiction,
and historians have sometimes struggled to keep both realities in
mind. There is a long-running academic debate, for example,
about whether labor unions were agents for racial equality or ex-

clusion. Some scholars have emphasized the integration of unions and their role in the civil rights movement, while others have countered by noting the bigotry and exclusion that remained inside so many unions. Similarly, some scholars have focused on the Democratic Party's lingering discomfort with civil rights into the 1960s, while others have stressed the party's growing support for civil rights starting in the 1940s. These debates persist because each side has a legitimate point. The subject is not either-or. Both parts of the apparent contradiction are true.

Two economists—Patrick Bayer of Duke University and Kerwin Kofi Charles, the dean of Yale University's management school—have developed an idea that makes sense of the contradiction. Bayer and Charles argue that there are two different sets of forces that can narrow the racial gap. They describe one category as "positional." It describes changes in the relative position of Blacks and Whites. If there is a pay gap between a Black worker and a White worker who are similarly experienced and productive, that gap is positional. Any shrinking of that gap is a positional change. Positional differences often reflect outright discrimination.

The second category of forces is "distributional," and it is a little less intuitive. It measures whether economy-wide changes disproportionately affect workers from different racial groups. An increase in the minimum wage may seem like a racially neutral policy, but it can still shrink the wage gap by affecting a greater share of workers from one race than another. Rising unionization among low-wage workers, and the pay increases that come with it, is another such policy. As a hypothetical example, imagine that the federal government were to send a $5,000 check to every American family. That would narrow the racial wealth gap because it would represent a larger percentage increase in net worth for Black families than White families—even though it would seem like a racially neutral policy and would do nothing to reduce discrimination. Bayer and Charles would describe $5,000 checks as an example of distributional convergence rather than positional convergence.

The narrowing of the wage gap in the three decades following the Depression was due almost entirely to distributional factors. Positional convergence was close to zero on net: The wage gap between otherwise similar Black and White workers—that is, those in the same region, in the same industry, and with the same experience—held fairly steady. So did gaps in educational attainment and home ownership.

The idea takes a minute to grasp but explains a lot. In some ways, racial discrimination increased during the postwar decades. Just think of the housing subsidies and other segregationist government programs that lasted for decades. In other ways, racial discrimination receded, through the early victories of the civil rights movement in the 1940s and 1950s, such as the integration of wartime factories and the Supreme Court's 1954 *Brown v. Board of Education* ruling on schools. These various forces—the positional forces—roughly canceled one another out in economic terms. On net, the economic effects of racial discrimination did not change much during the 1940s and 1950s.

Yet the distributional forces were so strong that they substantially shrank racial inequality. Unions expanded and integrated. The culture of corporate America shifted in ways that caused workers' wages to rise more quickly than CEO pay. The federal government invested billions of dollars in roads, schools, and other programs that lifted incomes. As a result, the narrowing of racial gaps in income and life expectancy during these years reflected class-based changes more than explicitly race-based changes.

The story changed again in the early 1960s. The civil rights movement achieved larger victories, including federal laws banning discrimination and a new commitment by Washington to enforce those laws in the South. Black children attended better schools in many communities, and Black workers got jobs long denied to them. For a decade starting in roughly 1964—the year that Lyndon Johnson signed the Civil Rights Act—positional gaps between Black and White workers narrowed, modestly in most of the country and substantially in the South. To be sure, distributional factors continued to play a role during this decade. A single law was especially important, as research by the economists Ellora Derenoncourt and Claire Montialoux has found. In 1966, Congress both increased the federal minimum wage and expanded it to cover farming, restaurants, schools, hospitals, and other service industries that together employed roughly one-third of Black workers. The law said nothing about race, but it nonetheless decreased racial inequities.

All the while, racism continued to oppress Black Americans. The wage gap never disappeared, or even came close, nor did the gap in life expectancy. Progress can be real and still outrageously insufficient.

When Americans think about racial justice, they sometimes overlook the distributional factors—the ways in which declining economic inequality can reduce racial inequality. These factors are not the whole picture, obviously: A society can never become equal if it does not also achieve positional convergence. But economics plays a crucial role in the struggle for racial equality.

The leaders of the civil rights movement understood the connection. "Negroes are almost entirely a working people," Martin Luther King, Jr., said in 1961. "Our needs are identical with labor's needs: decent wages, fair working conditions, livable housing, old-age security, health and welfare measures, conditions in which families can grow, have education for their children and respect in the community." Randolph, likewise, became one of the most successful civil rights activists by understanding this relationship. "The great movements that achieve justice and also make the world a better place to live in are movements that are based upon economic facts and economic problems and economic conditions," he said. He built an economic movement—the Brotherhood of Sleeping Car Porters—and used it to launch a movement for racial equality.

After World War II ended, the union remained a political force. Randolph first turned his attention back to the desegregation of military units, the issue he had temporarily abandoned when he pushed Roosevelt to integrate wartime factories. Randolph believed that ending military segregation would be politically easier to accomplish in peacetime, when critics could not argue that any resulting turmoil would distract the war effort. In 1948, he testified before Congress that he would rather face a charge of treason than serve in a "Jim Crow army." He and other Black leaders picketed the Democratic National Convention in Philadelphia that nominated Harry Truman, with Randolph carrying a sign that read: "Prison is better than Army Jim Crow service." Truman, needing to win Black votes to help his underdog campaign, issued Executive Order 9981, integrating the military, less than two weeks later. That order delivered victory on the second goal of the original 1941 March on Washington movement.

As the civil rights movement made progress in the 1950s and 1960s, the Brotherhood played a central role. The local Brotherhood leader in Montgomery, Alabama, was E. D. Nixon, who knew virtually every political leader in the city. (Nixon was quoted earlier in this chapter, explaining that porters were respected in their community because they had traveled the country.) In 1955, when Black residents of Montgomery got fed up with surrendering their bus seats to White riders, Nixon saw that the issue might offer a way to challenge segregation in the courts. He began looking for the ideal case on which to fight. He soon became aware of two arrests of riders who had refused to give up their seats, but he believed both of their personal backgrounds were too complicated for them to become sympathetic public figures. Nixon helped them quietly resolve their cases instead. The third person to be arrested, however, seemed perfect. She was an unflappable forty-two-year-old seamstress whom Nixon had recruited to join the local NAACP chapter years earlier. Her name was Rosa Parks.

Only after Parks said that she was willing to fight did Nixon try to start a movement. Early on the morning after her arrest, he telephoned King, then a twenty-six-year-old reverend who had recently arrived in Montgomery, and asked him to endorse a boycott of the city buses. King said he would mull it over. After their conversation, Nixon reported for duty at the train station in Montgomery and boarded a Pullman car for a round trip to New York. In the midst of planning one of the great campaigns of civil disobedience in modern history, Nixon was still working as a porter. Soon, King agreed to support the boycott, and it launched him to national prominence.

Eight years later, King and Randolph worked together to make the March on Washington finally happen, more than two decades after Randolph had come up with the idea and name for it and threatened Roosevelt with it. King was the face of the civil rights movement by this point, and Randolph was a senior statesman. Once again, a president—Kennedy, this time—told Randolph during a White House meeting that a march would hurt the cause of civil rights, but in 1963, Randolph thought the time had arrived. Executive orders were no longer enough. Congress needed to pass civil rights laws to establish voting access and bar workplace discrimination. A march would increase the pressure as nothing else could.

Leaders of the March on Washington, including A. Philip Randolph, center, and John Lewis, second from right, 1963.

When the marchers reached the National Mall on August 28, the first speaker from the steps of the Lincoln Memorial was Randolph. He organized his speech around the two ideas that had guided his adult life. First, neither racial justice nor economic justice could exist without the other. Second, only a mass political movement could deliver progress. "Those who deplore our militants, who exhort patience in the name of a false peace, are in fact supporting segregation and exploitation," Randolph said, in his stentorian voice. "They would have social peace at the expense of social and racial justice. They are more concerned with easing racial tension than enforcing racial democracy."

When the event ended—after a parade of other speakers, culminating in Randolph's introduction of King as "the moral leader of our nation"and King's soaring "I Have a Dream" speech—Randolph stood by himself on one end of the speakers' platform and watched the marchers leave the Mall, many of them singing as they dispersed. He was seventy-four years old at the time. Another organizer, Bayard Rustin, seeing Randolph standing alone, walked over to put his arm around his mentor and saw that tears were streaming down his face. It was the only time Rustin had ever seen Randolph unable to contain his emotions.

The day was a glorious one. It would help lead to the Civil Rights Act of 1964, whose language—outlawing discrimination based on race, color, and national origin—echoed Roosevelt's executive order on wartime factories. In 1965, Congress passed the Voting Rights Act. Congress would also pass a series of laws in the mid-1960s to reduce economic inequality. One created Medicare and Medicaid. Another increased federal aid to schools. A third was the increase of the minimum wage and its expansion to new sectors. Randolph had mentioned each of those economic issues in his speech from the Lincoln Memorial.

The March on Washington and the legislation that followed were an affirmation of Randolph's vision. Working people had come together to form a powerful democratic movement. They had demanded change, endured setbacks, and ultimately accomplished more than almost anybody expected. It was a version of the same story that had transformed so many parts of the American economy in the 1930s and 1940s.

But if the March on Washington marked the apex for this movement, the march also happened as the coalition was starting to show signs of strain. It would not survive the 1960s. By the end of the decade, the alliance between political progressives and working-class Americans would split apart. Labor unions grew self-satisfied and self-interested. The political left focused increasingly on the preferences of college graduates and professionals. The civil rights movement became more insular. With memories of the Depression fading, business executives and conservative politicians began to embrace a rough-and-tumble version of capitalism that harked back to the 1920s.

When the nation endured a deep recession in the 1970s, many Americans believed that this laissez-faire approach offered a solution. Political power shifted back to the wealthy. The culture of corporate America grew more self-interested and less patriotic. The country's investments in its future declined. The result would be the America we know today, with high economic inequality, large racial gaps, slow-growing living standards, and widespread frustration.

The victories won by A. Philip Randolph, Grace Hopper, Paul Hoffman, Floyd Olson, Frances Perkins, and their many allies were formidable. They transformed the United States and created an American dream more real than any before it. Yet this reality would not last.

PART TWO

The Fall

CHAPTER 5

The Young Intelligentsia

SINCE HE WAS A BOY IN TEXAS IN THE 1920S, C. WRIGHT MILLS had felt like an outsider.

Mills was a rebellious budding intellectual growing up in a conservative place during a conformist time. His friends and neighbors were outwardly religious. While he was still in high school, Mills wrote a letter to the *Dallas Morning News* criticizing a local fundamentalist for rejecting science. As a freshman at Texas A&M, he refused to stand up when upperclassmen walked past him, as was the campus custom. During World War II, he was a rare pacifist, repulsed by the country's militarism. He did not enlist, and his high blood pressure kept him from being drafted. Summarizing his attitude toward the world, Mills wrote in his journal at one point: "There are so many people left that I've got to tell to go to hell."

He finally found his niche at the University of Texas, where he transferred for his second year of college. On his new campus, he discovered that the academic field of sociology offered an outlet for his skepticism of mainstream America. He eventually earned a doctorate in it at the University of Wisconsin and was hired by Columbia University in 1945. Along with many other young people on the political left, Mills became fascinated by the labor movement. It was a new force in American life. To better understand it, he conducted a survey of 410 union leaders and spent many hours interviewing them.

In the book that resulted from that research, *The New Men of Power*, Mills argued that the country's labor leaders "lead the only organizations capable of stopping the main drift towards war and

slump." He feared both that the country was headed toward another military conflict, this time with the Soviet Union, and that
the postwar boom was unsustainable. To create a healthier peacetime economy, he urged labor leaders to demand seats on corporate boards from which they could shape company strategies (as
would happen later in Europe). But Mills was not optimistic that
labor leaders would take his advice. He ended the book by criticizing them for being unlikely to adopt the combative stance that he
considered necessary. In the years ahead, his view hardened, and
he came to see union leaders as guardians of the status quo and
junior partners to corporate executives.

C. Wright Mills at Columbia University, 1950s.

This pessimism made Mills an outlier among liberal intellectuals at the time, most of whom celebrated the cooperation and limited conflict among labor, business, and government. The economist
John Kenneth Galbraith coined the term "countervailing power"
to describe this dynamic. The three groups kept one another in
check while promoting the national interest. The Eisenhower years
represented the apex of Galbraith's vision: The countervailing
powers were running a healthy economy, investing in the country's
future, and helping contain the Soviet Union.

Mills viewed this attitude, scornfully, as "the great American celebration," and he reveled in his disagreements with other intellectuals. He was not a typical Ivy League professor, anyway. He was a hulking Texan who rode a motorcycle from his home in the Hudson River Valley to Columbia's Manhattan campus. He had built much of the home with his own hands. He described himself as the opposite of a bureaucrat and his attitude toward life as "Take it big, boy!" He liked to cook and to drink bourbon. He traveled around Cuba with Fidel Castro. He was the father to three children with three different wives, one of whom he remarried after their divorce. In his writings, Mills engaged in vicious arguments with other academics about postwar American life.

He believed that the United States was not truly a democracy because a small group of elites ran each of the countervailing powers. Together, the government and large companies were stifling individuality and creativity. The elites who ran these organizations became the subject of Mills's best-known book, *The Power Elite,* published in 1956. In his view, labor union leaders were part of the elite, pushing the country toward more war and suffering. He rejected the idea, long popular on the political left, that the working class was the mechanism by which progressive change necessarily happened. Mills dismissed it as "the labor metaphysic."

During a yearlong sabbatical in Copenhagen in the 1950s, Mills developed an alternative. Students, he decided, could play the galvanizing political role that workers once had. In Europe, they were already doing so. Organized labor was in crisis there, sparked by the leaking of a secret speech that Nikita Khrushchev, the Soviet premier, had given to other Soviet leaders, condemning Josef Stalin's rule by terror. The speech humiliated many socialists, including those connected to labor unions, who had long made excuses for Stalin. Looking around the world, Mills noticed that the energy on the left seemed to be with young intellectuals, not the old guard of trade union officials. In parts of the Soviet bloc, like Hungary, students defied Moscow. In Britain, young socialists led an anti-nuclear movement. In Japan, students protested American military bases.

After Mills returned home, he noticed a similar energy in the United States. On February 1, 1960, four students at the Agricultural and Technical College of North Carolina, a Black college in Greensboro, staged a sit-in at a segregated Woolworth's lunch counter. The four—Ezell Blair, Jr., Franklin McCain, Joseph McNeil, and David Richmond—had acted on their own, without having told civil rights leaders about their plans. Something about their bravery, combined with the political atmosphere, sparked a reaction unlike that which had followed 1950s civil rights protests. Within days, sit-ins spread to other North Carolina cities and beyond. Those protests led to the creation of the Student Nonviolent Coordinating Committee, which began a campaign to topple Jim Crow.

To Mills, the lesson was clear: Young intellectuals, in the West and the Soviet bloc, were the new agents of political change. In the summer of 1960, he published an essay in a British journal, *New Left Review,* that synthesized these events into a theory of political change. The essay was titled "Letter to the New Left." In it, he criticized radicals who "cling so mightily to 'the working class' of the advanced capitalist societies as *the* historic agency, or even as the most important agency, in the face of the really impressive historical evidence that now stands against this expectation." He continued: "Who is it that is thinking and acting in radical ways? All over the world—in the bloc, outside the bloc and in between—the answer's the same: it is the young intelligentsia."

Mills's agenda was somewhat vague. He criticized the banality and apathy of modern society and praised radical utopianism. His essay alluded to civil rights protests only briefly and did not mention women's rights, environmentalism, or other causes that would become central to the 1960s. Nonetheless, his essay electrified young progressives on university campuses and in major cities across both Europe and the United States. Finally, they thought, somebody had captured their frustration with the conservative 1950s and the old liberals who helped maintain its stultified order.

Mills encouraged them to be hopeful. "The Age of Complacency is ending," his essay concluded. "We are beginning to move again."

. . .

A PROGRESSIVE AGENDA, from the political left, is not the only plausible way to lift the living standards of most members of a society. One alternative is the one preferred by libertarians and other conservative advocates for a laissez-faire economy, in which market forces, rather than government intervention, supposedly bring broad-based prosperity. Another alternative is a heterodox approach that might be called populist nationalism, mixing social conservatism with economic progressivism.

Populist nationalism has a long history. It was part of the appeal of William Jennings Bryan, the three-time Democratic nominee for president. On economic policy, he moved the party well to the left and earned the nickname the Great Commoner. But he was also deeply religious and, later in his career, became an advocate for Prohibition and the most prominent opponent of the theory of evolution. After Bryan's death in 1925, southern Democrats picked up this approach. Huey Long, the Louisiana governor and senator, took one of Bryan's lines—"Every man a king, but no one wears a crown"—and made it his motto. Long favored a steep wealth tax, inveighed against gambling and prostitution, and opposed American involvement in Europe's troubles during the 1930s. Even as his critics called him a right-wing demagogue, he helped inspire the creation of Social Security. He was a populist nationalist.

Similar ideologies have attracted support in other countries. The details differ substantially by country, but there is a common theme: Social and cultural conservativism can be paired with government intervention in the economy to lift mass living standards. The best modern examples are in Asia. In the late twentieth century, the governments of Singapore, South Korea, and Taiwan were not politically progressive by most definitions of the term. At times, they used authoritarian methods to impose conservative social mores. Yet they also built capitalist economies in which the government intervened to deliver rising living standards for most citizens. Since the 1980s, China has become another example. While calling itself communist, it has practiced interventionist capitalism and rejected Western liberal ideals.

In the United States, this combination of economic populism and social conservatism has rarely achieved national power. Neither Bryan nor any of the southern populists who followed him won the presidency. Instead, Democratic presidents have been more broadly progressive, while Republican leaders have been more consistently right wing. Republicans have combined conservative social policies and a hawkish foreign policy with a more laissez-faire economic agenda that defers to big business. The modern Republican Party has shown more hostility to economic intervention than many other right-leaning parties around the world. Republicans often claim that such policies create prosperity in ways that government never could. But the record suggests otherwise: Living standards rose much less during the Gilded Age and Roaring Twenties than after World War II.

All of which means that the political left has played a crucial role in creating broad-based economic progress for Americans. When the Democratic Party and progressive groups have focused on improving working people's living standards, they have often succeeded. When that focus has drifted to other matters—say, to fighting a war, as was the case with Woodrow Wilson, or to opposing war, as was the case with Mills—lower- and middle-income Americans have lost their best economic champions.

This chapter and the next tell the story of how the American left splintered—into an insular, blue-collar old left dominated by union leaders and an idealistic, privileged New Left molded by intellectuals like Mills. That splintering helped the Republican Party capture the allegiance of a growing number of workers and eventually allowed Republicans to reorient the economy in ways that ended up hurting many of the same workers who voted for the party. In the 1930s and 1940s, American workers gained political power and used it to improve their living standards. In the 1960s, they began to lose that power—partly because they surrendered it, partly because it was taken from them—and the ideals of the American dream suffered as a result.

The New Left and the old labor left deserve plenty of criticism, and I will not shy from it. Still, I have tried to tell the story of each with empathy. The New Left recognized deep problems in American society and helped create a better, fairer society in numerous ways. The old left tried to prioritize the interests of its own union members at a time when rising global competition made that task very difficult. In any circumstance, the political coalition that came together in the 1930s and survived into the 1960s, a coalition that spanned workers and professionals, the North and the South, urban and rural, and White and Black, could not have lasted forever. My argument is that many of the political leaders who emerged in the 1960s hastened its decline rather than trying to forge a new majority coalition that could have continued to protect the economic interests of most Americans.

THE UNIVERSITY OF Michigan was one of the country's largest schools in the late 1950s, and life there typified the postwar rigidity that Mills's essay had highlighted. The nightly curfew for students was eleven, and the cafeteria food resembled military rations. Freshmen lived in cramped doubles, with two beds and two desks, on long dormitory hallways. "Making us feel like dots on a grid, the dorms, called quadrangles, were divided into floors, corridors, and numbered cell-like rooms just large enough for two persons," wrote Tom Hayden, a middle-class teenager from Detroit who arrived at the University of Michigan in September 1957. Hayden described the campus as having a "barracks culture, with its twin lacks of privacy and community."

Compared with what their parents and grandparents had endured, the college students of this period were obviously fortunate. Many had no memories of the Great Depression or World War II. To them, American power and prosperity were the norm, and the Eisenhower-era government investments were pouring resources into university campuses and enabling many more students to attend college. But human beings do not usually evaluate their day-to-day experiences by considering how much worse life might have been. They live in the moment. When the college students of this period looked around, they saw problems.

Postwar life felt "boring and prearranged," as Hayden put it. Some of the early signs of rebelliousness and individuality were evident in popular culture, through the movies of James Dean, the books of Jack Kerouac and the Beat generation, and the music of Chuck Berry and Elvis Presley. John Kennedy's 1960 presidential campaign tapped into the desire for change. He was unlike any president before—Catholic, glamorous, only forty-two years old when he announced his campaign. He promised to "get the nation moving again." The slogan was almost identical to the final line of Mills's essay.

The students' two biggest political concerns involved nuclear war and civil rights. "We thought that, like the fictional citizens in Camus's *The Plague,* Americans were going about business as usual while denying the existence of pervasive and threatening evils," Hayden wrote. The nuclear arms race, with its satellites hurtling above the earth, had made human extinction seem possible. College students of this generation had grown up crawling under school desks during bomb drills. They had also grown up in a society in which more than half of Americans—women, people of color, gay and lesbian people and members of some religions—endured oppressive bigotry. The Greensboro sit-in excited many students because it showed that they did not need to meekly accept the status quo. They could fight back. "Here were four students from Greensboro who were suddenly all over *Life* magazine," Rennie Davis, a student at Oberlin College, said. "There was a feeling that they were us and we were them, and a recognition that they were expressing something we were feeling as well." Within a few months of that first Monday afternoon sit-in at Woolworth's, civil rights groups had sprung up on more than a hundred campuses.

One of the most active groups outside the South was in Ann Arbor. It was connected to a nationwide left-wing group called the Student League for Industrial Democracy, whose roots dated to 1905 and which had the unfortunate acronym of SLID. By the late 1950s, its leaders wanted a better name, and they rechristened the group Students for a Democratic Society. The new name, without the word "industrial," seemed fresher and broader, less grounded in their parents' New Deal era. At the time, almost nobody outside the group took notice of the change. SDS had only three active chapters, at Michigan, Columbia, and Yale, and many of its members had already graduated from college.

The group scheduled a conference in Ann Arbor for May 1960, and Hayden, by then a junior and the editor in chief of the campus newspaper, *The Michigan Daily,* attended. He had come to Michigan on a tennis scholarship before gravitating toward journalism and politics. He had an unusual charisma. He managed to be simultaneously circumspect, curious, and polite, and despite his athletic background, he often stood with slumped shoulders. He was also an uncommonly elegant writer, able to give voice to the frustration and idealism of his generation.

He soon moved to Atlanta as the national field secretary for SDS and wrote dispatches that were mailed to students around the country. In McComb, a small city in Mississippi where civil rights activists were trying to register voters, a White supremacist pulled Hayden out of a car when it stopped at a traffic light and beat him. A newspaper photographer captured the moment when a fist landed on Hayden's ear. Weeks later, police in Albany, Georgia, arrested him, and while he was sitting in a jail cell that reeked of urine, he wrote a letter to other SDS leaders. He told them that he did not want to remain a lone correspondent in the South, enduring attacks and imprisonment mostly so that the members of a national mailing list could remain informed about the civil rights movement. It was time for SDS to become more ambitious. It should use the tactics of the civil rights movement to confront a broader set of social problems, Hayden believed.

His timing was excellent. There was a self-conscious generation of young Americans ready to be stirred, and their numbers were about to explode. Like Hayden, the baby boomers on the cusp of going to college had grown up in a postwar prosperity that allowed their parents to focus on the future—and on their children—in ways that previous generations could not. This focus gave the children more educational opportunities and imbued them with greater confidence and righteousness. Corporate America, in marketing goods to these families, described their children as a distinct generation, helping to give baby boomers a shared identity.

When Hayden returned to Ann Arbor, he and other SDS leaders decided that they needed to draft a manifesto that would spell out an agenda for their generation. Their aim was to finish the work of the Roosevelt era while also moving beyond it, creating an economy and society that were more equal, just, and decent. Hayden started writing the manifesto, and Mills's work was its central inspiration. "He seemed to be speaking to us directly," Hayden said. While Hayden was working on the SDS manifesto, Mills died of a heart attack at age forty-five, becoming even more of a hero to young activists.

The sixty or so SDS members who gathered at a lakeside retreat in Port Huron, Michigan, in June 1962 to edit and approve Hayden's draft had a more expansive vision of the New Left than Mills. They were open to working with labor unions; the Port Huron retreat was owned by the United Auto Workers, a union whose leaders shared some of the students' critique of the national labor movement. The SDS manifesto also put racial equality at the center of progressivism, a change from the 1950s, when many leftists, including Mills, had minimized race. And the SDS leaders bravely rejected McCarthyism. They made clear that they were not Marxists but welcomed people who were or had been. But while the students' vision was more inclusive, it shared Mills's core belief that the young intelligentsia would define and lead the political left. That belief would shape the new movement and ultimately limit its effectiveness.

The final version of the manifesto, known as the Port Huron Statement, was a sixty-six-page, single-spaced pamphlet that both described an emerging movement—the New Left—and sought to shape it. The document was up-front about its origins. The opening sentence read: "We are people of this generation, bred in at least modest comfort, housed now in universities, looking uncomfortably to the world we inherit." The tone of the document was almost spiritual. It celebrated human independence and authenticity, arguing that reason, freedom, and love could overcome loneliness, estrangement, and isolation. As Kirkpatrick Sale wrote in a sympathetic history of SDS, the statement "was unabashedly middle class, concerned with poverty of vision rather than poverty of life."

The progressive movement of the 1930s and 1940s was organized around material concerns: available jobs, rising wages, decent retirement, and an end to the powerlessness and unpredictability that many people felt in their workplaces. The New Left was at least as focused on the psychic concerns of people fortunate enough to take material comfort for granted. It rebelled against the conformity of the mid-twentieth century by calling for a new individualism without acknowledging that individualism was often a better deal for privileged members of a society than for everybody else.

The New Left did not ignore economic class. Many of its members spoke about the exploitation of the oppressed. Hayden, reflecting his thoughtful idealism, moved to Newark for three years in the mid-1960s to be a community organizer, while a Marxist offshoot of SDS founded a "worker-student alliance" based on the notion that students were the less important of the two groups. But these efforts tended to speak *to* workers rather than with them. Few American workers were attracted to the New Age spirituality of the Port Huron Statement or to Marxist theory. They were more likely to be traditionally religious and patriotic.

In a sign of the disconnect, the New Left included an anti-American strain that set it apart from some other twentieth-century progressive movements. The labor unions that rose out of the Depression and the civil rights movement that followed both consciously connected themselves to American ideals. They flew large flags at their rallies and argued that their goals were fundamentally American: democracy, opportunity, liberty. The New Left was more agnostic about the virtues of the United States. Mills rejected the notion that the country was a pluralistic democracy and took more inspiration from Castro's Cuba. The Port Huron Statement described "the hypocrisy of American ideals" as the source of its authors' disillusionment.

The New Left believed that much of American life, including some of the institutions that had made up the old left, was too compromised to be saved.

. . .

LIKE MILLS, BETTY GOLDSTEIN had tried to enter progressive politics through labor unions. She had grown up in Peoria, Illinois, in a prosperous family that owned a local diamond store but that also frequently experienced antisemitism. Eager to get away from Peoria, Goldstein attended Smith College in Massachusetts and was one of the top students in her class. Afterward, she moved to New York City as an idealistic young leftist. There, she began dating a theater director named Carl Friedman, who had decided that he wanted a more distinct last name and dropped the letter *m* from his. When the couple got married in 1947, Betty began using the new name, too. Her byline became Betty Friedan.

In New York, Friedan was hired by a news agency that produced stories for publications friendly to labor unions. As in Peoria, she was treated like an outsider. The editors excluded her from meetings, saying they were for men only, and later fired her for becoming pregnant. When she turned for help to the head of the local chapter of her own union, the Newspaper Guild, he told her that it was her fault for getting pregnant twice in a short period of time. She was understandably disillusioned. "I no longer bought the Marxist illusion that the working class 'were the only ones capable of revolution,'" she wrote.

Friedan spent the 1950s writing freelance articles for women's magazines and raising her and Carl's young children, with help from a maid who watched them three days a week at the family's Victorian house overlooking the Hudson River north of New York. The articles followed a formula, with saccharine lessons and upbeat endings. When Friedan tried to introduce more substance into the articles and grapple with the difficulties facing women, the editors cut that material to keep the articles cheery. The experience contributed to Friedan's sense that she was not doing meaningful work and not living up to the expectations that people had of her when she had been a student leader at Smith. She described the feeling as "an existential guilt." In search of something more substantive, she agreed to take the lead role writing a survey of her

Smith class, the class of 1942, as it prepared for its fifteenth reunion.

She filled the survey with blunter questions than the recipients were accustomed to hearing: Is your marriage truly satisfying? Do you talk to your husband about your deepest feelings? Do you have fun with your children? Do you feel you are a good mother? Do you feel almost over and done with sexuality, or are you just beginning the satisfaction of being a woman? Are you a good cook? Did you have career ambitions? Are your politics the same as your husband's? Do you believe in a personal God? How much time do you spend alone? Have you had psychotherapy? How many books have you read in the last year? What are the chief satisfactions in your life today?

The responses helped Friedan make sense of her own complicated attitude toward her adult life. Much like Friedan, many classmates felt at least partly satisfied with their lives, juggling motherhood, community involvement, and an intellectual life. They also lamented that their choices were so restricted. Friedan came to describe it as "the problem that has no name." After presenting the survey results to her classmates, she chose to do more research and write an article about her findings for a women's magazine. When none would publish it, she managed to get a modest book contract and spent the next five years writing *The Feminine Mystique.*

By the time it appeared in February 1963—less than a year after the Port Huron Statement—the cultural unrest of the decade had begun, and many more people were receptive to her message than when she had started the project. Two of the women's magazines that had turned down Friedan's original article on the same subject now published excerpts of the book. The following year, it was the country's top-selling paperback. Two years later, Friedan helped found the National Organization for Women and became its first president.

Friedan had given millions of women, and men, a language to understand the sexism that the country had unthinkingly accepted. She had exposed a dark underside of the postwar prosperity. "The problem that has no name," she wrote, "is simply the fact that American women are kept from growing to their full human capacities." Women were confined to a narrow group of job opportunities. When they had young children, they were expected to care for them full-time even if they would prefer to hold a job. When women did enter the workforce, they held jobs that were usually subservient to men—secretaries assisting executives, nurses taking orders from doctors, stewardesses supporting pilots. Sexual harassment was a daily reality.

By forcing the country to confront these injustices, *The Feminine Mystique* became one of the most influential American books of the twentieth century. It launched a movement, often described as second-wave feminism to distinguish it from the push for voting rights that culminated with the Nineteenth Amendment in 1920. Friedan's work helped open opportunities in education, business, government, sports, and almost every other realm of society. It began to overturn repressive attitudes toward gender and sexuality. It is one of the great reform movements in American history, and it affected daily life in a way that few others have. It moved the country closer to its ideals of offering opportunity for all by demanding equality for women.

Betty Friedan, right, at an early conference for the National Organization for Women, 1967.

From the beginning, however, feminism's second wave had a particular class dynamic. Like the Port Huron Statement and SDS, this new feminism had sprung from an affluent slice of America and reflected its concerns. The first paragraph of *The Feminine Mystique* described its subject as the "suburban wife." No wonder: The book had grown out of a fifteenth-reunion survey for Smith College, whose alumnae roster included Anne Morrow Lindbergh, Julia Child, Margaret Mitchell, Sylvia Plath, Nancy Reagan, and Barbara Bush (even if not all of those names were famous by 1963). At the time, only 7 percent of American women and 11 percent of men had a bachelor's degree. "I was, admittedly, investigating a middle-class phenomenon," Friedan would later say. That phenomenon overlapped with the sexism experienced by working-class and poor women; both suffered diminished opportunities, casual bigotry, harassment, and worse. But there were major differences between Friedan's experiences and those of most American women.

Friedan often viewed the world in individualistic terms. Her book emphasized empowerment and achievement. Describing a typical young girl, Friedan wrote, "She must learn to compete then, not as a woman, but as a human being." Friedan encouraged women to summon the confidence, discipline, and effort to commit themselves to a profession. She was critical of many women's approach to parenting, and her language could be harsh. She blamed omnipresent, watchful mother love for producing infantile, neurotic, immature, and unproductive children, as well as an increase in "overt manifestations" of homosexuality. In a passage about which she later expressed regret, she compared the homes of suburban housewives to a "comfortable concentration camp" where trapped women had become "dependent, passive, child-like."

Many working-class women recoiled from this message. For one thing, Friedan was not describing their reality. She was urging women to get jobs outside the home, even though many working-class women already had jobs. They did not have much choice since they were unmarried or their husbands did not make enough money for the family to live on. In 1960, slightly more than half of

Black women were in the labor force. So were about 40 percent of White women. Most could not afford to hire a maid to watch their children while they worked. They often relied on extended family or informal neighborhood daycare. Their main challenges were material, not attitudinal.

Friedan's criticism of mothers also proved to be quite unpopular. *McCall's,* one of the magazines that published an excerpt of *The Feminine Mystique,* received hundreds of letters in response, and 87 percent were negative, according to an analysis by the historian Jessica Weiss. Some of the letter writers were angry. Others felt demoralized.

Almost immediately, critics of *The Feminine Mystique,* some friendly and some less so, pointed out its bourgeois assumptions. Gerda Lerner, a historian, wrote privately to Friedan both to call the book "splendid" and to urge her not to ignore working-class women and Black women. Excluding them, Lerner said, "is something we simply cannot afford to do." Later, the feminist bell hooks (who did not capitalize her name) would write of Friedan, "She did not discuss who would be called in to take care of the children and maintain the home if more women like herself were freed from their house labor and given equal access with white men to the professions."

Over time, Friedan and her allies did pay more attention to issues that were important to working-class women. In the founding manifesto for NOW in 1966, Friedan—the group's first president—called for a national network for childcare centers and retraining programs for mothers returning to the workforce. But, as with SDS and other parts of the New Left, second-wave feminism never tried very hard to recruit working-class women or join forces with groups that represented them. NOW tried to speak for less advantaged women rather than speaking with them. And less privileged feminist groups did exist. The welfare-rights movement came together in the mid-1960s and was led mostly by Black women like Johnnie Tillmon. It called for a guaranteed income so that children would not grow up in poverty and so that welfare recipients would not have to endure humiliating questions—about whether they had a boyfriend, for example—to qualify for assistance. "For a lot of middle-class women in this country, Women's Liberation is a matter of concern," Tillmon wrote in *Ms.* magazine. "For women on welfare, it's a matter of survival." To lower-income women, collective solutions, like access to decent-paying blue-collar work, were more important than individual notions of empowerment.

Abortion was another hot-button issue because many less affluent women favored abortion restrictions, often on religious grounds. A few NOW activists, including some who opposed restrictions, encouraged the group not to emphasize the subject in its early years because of its potential to divide women. A larger feminist movement would require compromises, but it could ultimately accomplish more, these activists argued. They wanted NOW to become a mass organization focused on the needs and views of women across classes. The founders of NOW disagreed. They consciously chose to create a group of professional women. It would not make tradeoffs to find common ground with less elite women. It would try to remold the country by working inside the corridors of power.

The privileged cast of the second wave of feminism extended into popular culture. A 1983 movie, *Silkwood,* told the story of Karen Silkwood, a worker at a plutonium plant operated by the Kerr-McGee company in the early 1970s, who tried to strengthen the labor union there and call attention to the unsafe working conditions. She died under mysterious circumstances during the effort. The movie told much of the story truthfully, but it also turned Silkwood into a New Left–style figure focused on stopping the spread of nuclear weapons. As another labor organizer said, "She has been portrayed as an anti-nuclear activist. She wasn't. She was involved in one simple activity; it was to save a local union at Kerr-McGee where the company was hell bent on destroying it." But Hollywood, an increasingly influential part of the American left, told the story it wanted to tell. The popular image of A. Philip Randolph—as well as that of Cesar Chavez, the farm labor pioneer—would also be subtly altered. In their own minds, they had been both union organizers and civil rights leaders, with the second role flowing from the first. Their modern admirers often overlooked their union roots. For the new American liberalism, labor activism was not enough to be heroic.

Friedan's own path offered a similar lesson. In the two decades since she had graduated from Smith, she had traveled a political journey that reflected the larger changes in liberalism. As a young woman in the 1940s, she had devoted herself to making the United States a fairer society. To do so, she spent her early years as a writer covering union-organizing drives, McCarthyist attacks on union leaders, and more. But like Mills and his SDS protégés, she soured on the idea that working-class organizations were the agents of political progress. In her experience, they were often the opposite. They were insular and sexist. Organized labor had shown little interest in women, and Friedan's new movement would show little interest in organized labor.

The old working-class left felt so stale that Friedan did not acknowledge her ties to it in *The Feminine Mystique*. The book never mentioned her years working for labor publications. She instead described spending her twenties in "the usual kinds of boring jobs that lead nowhere." She embraced her suburban image and tried to leave behind her labor ties. She had become an avatar of the upscaling of the American left.

ONE SIGN OF the larger shift was the central role of written argument in shaping the New Left. Grassroots organizing, mostly by political parties and labor unions, created the old left. Essays, pamphlets, and books went a long way toward creating the movements of the 1960s.

Mills's essay influenced the Port Huron Statement, which in turn influenced many young activists. *The Feminine Mystique* led to NOW. *Silent Spring,* a 1962 book by the conservationist Rachel Carson, helped launch the environmental movement. And *Unsafe at Any Speed,* Ralph Nader's 1965 exposé of the automobile industry, spurred a sprawling new effort called the consumer movement.

The son of Lebanese immigrants who owned a restaurant in Connecticut, Nader was a student at Harvard Law School in the late 1950s when he became interested in the dangers of automobiles. The auto safety campaign of the 1930s, run by Paul Hoffman, had sharply reduced the death rate, but Americans were driving so much more in the 1950s that crashes remained a leading cause of death. Nader went to work as a consultant to Daniel Patrick Moynihan, then a Labor Department official who viewed crashes as a workplace hazard. That stint led Nader to write *Unsafe at Any Speed*. At first, the book received only modest attention. But it spooked General Motors executives, and they hired a private detective who harassed Nader with threatening telephone calls and attempts at sexual entrapment. After the detective's hiring became public, GM's president apologized, and Nader's book became a bestseller. He formed a nonprofit organization devoted to consumer safety, on the roads and elsewhere.

From the beginning, Nader's consumer movement reflected the worldview that Mills had described in his letter to the New Left. Nader identified his enemy as big institutions of all kinds, including big business, big government, and big labor. He, too, rejected Galbraith's model of countervailing power, in which workers and corporate executives would balance each other out. Nader's vision deemphasized economic class. He idealized an economy in which small businesses competed in open markets and an active citizenry guarded the public interest. It was similar to Thomas Jefferson's vision of the ideal economy.

To create this society, Nader formed advocacy groups like Public Citizen. They relied on volunteers in their early years, and they soon attracted dozens of idealistic graduates of selective colleges, the same demographic that had built SDS into a national movement. One year, roughly a third of all Harvard Law School students applied for a summer internship with Nader. A young Naderite said that his colleagues resembled the elites who would have traveled in a Pullman railroad car in an earlier era. Two of the employees included William Howard Taft IV, who would go on to a long career in Republican politics, and Edward Cox, a blue-blooded Long Island native who would become Richard Nixon's son-in-law.

Nader's organizations were not politically conservative, but they were elite. They trusted well-credentialed experts over members of Congress and career government officials. The Naderites focused on the problems of consumers, a group that included the well off, instead of emphasizing less privileged workers. Nader vilified "big government" in ways that influenced Democratic politicians, including Jimmy Carter, who was elected president in 1976 and moved the party away from Franklin Roosevelt's class-based approach toward a more technocratic one.

These criticisms of government would play into the arguments of the rising conservative movement later led by Ronald Reagan. When Nader and his acolytes decided that a Democrat was insufficiently committed to their consumer protection cause, they criticized him or her, as happened with Edmund Muskie, a Maine senator with a long list of environmental accomplishments who nonetheless became a Nader target. During the 1980 presidential campaign, when the television host Phil Donahue asked Nader whether he preferred Carter's energy policies or Reagan's, Nader declined to distinguish between them and instead praised the nominee of the obscure Citizens Party. That nominee received 0.3 percent of the vote on Election Day.

In much of his work, Nader identified genuine problems in American society. The automobile industry built unsafe vehicles. Coal mines were outrageously dangerous for their workers. The nation's water and air were polluted. The political establishment, including Democrats and labor unions, had overlooked these problems for decades, and Nader's passionate young followers refused to accept the apathy any longer. Their advocacy helped lead to new laws in Congress and victories in court. Similar idealism animated other parts of the New Left and was also influential. Friedan called out the economy's pervasive sexism. Hayden and his fellow SDS organizers demanded an end to the doomed Vietnam War. Each of these new movements offered accurate critiques of society, and their work led to changes that made life in America better and more just.

What the New Left failed to do was to create an enduring mass political coalition. It did not really even try. It claimed to speak for workers without doing much to recruit them or reflect their views. Nader's strategy was typical. As the historian Paul Sabin has written, "Few Black activists found Nader's approach appealing, or were actively recruited by him." During these same years, the civil rights movement also became more insular. In 1966, the Student Nonviolent Coordinating Committee dumped John Lewis as its leader and expelled all its White members. In doing so, the movement moved toward a version of Marcus Garvey's Black nationalist approach that A. Philip Randolph had rejected decades earlier because he believed that it was too narrow to achieve political change. SNCC's new leaders had a different outlook. Like the more elite parts of the political left, they focused more on purity than persuasion. American progressivism had atomized.

In the decades to come, the New Left would emphasize winning cases in court, where judges—who frequently had elite backgrounds themselves—made the decisions, rather than building coalitions that could win elections and pass legislation. This disdain for institutional politics, with all the accompanying compromises, helps explain why the Democratic Party and progressive groups put so little emphasis on state and local politics in the decades after the 1960s. The political right, especially the religious right, stepped into the void and gradually won grassroots victories.

The right was able to do so partly because of the New Left's arithmetic problem. The Port Huron Statement declared, "We believe that the universities are an overlooked seat of influence." The authors believed that if college students and professors led the way, the rest of the country would follow. But less than 10 percent of Americans held a bachelor's degree in the mid-1960s (and even today the share is less than 40 percent). College graduates were not the makings of a new majority unless they won over many more people. And the New Left's vision was not especially attractive to most Americans. It was too liberal and secular. It was uncomfortable with patriotism. It sometimes preferred the apparent neatness of expert opinion to the messiness of democratic negotiation. The New Left represented an early stage of today's Brahmin left. Despite Mills's criticism of elites, he and his disciples created an elite movement.

Since the 1960s, college graduates have continued to move to the left, and working-class voters have moved right. The left flank of the Democratic Party has become especially Brahmin. The Pew Research Center, which conducts national polls, categorizes Americans as belonging to one of nine ideological groups based on their views on major issues. The most liberal group is called the Progressive Left, and Pew points out that it is by far the most heavily White and highly educated of the left-leaning groups. The pattern holds for both specific policy questions and general beliefs about society. Highly educated liberals are more likely than most Americans to say that the United States is not the best country in the world and that success in life is beyond any individual's control. This phenomenon helps explain why a broad cross section of working-class voters, including Asian, Black, and Latino Americans, have drifted away from the liberal wing of the Democratic Party.

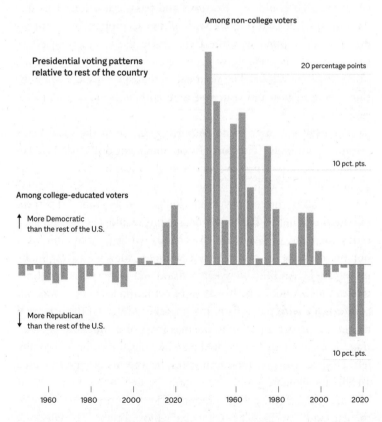

Among non-college voters

Presidential voting patterns
relative to rest of the country

20 percentage points

10 pct. pts.

Among college-educated voters

↑ More Democratic
than the rest of the U.S.

↓ More Republican
than the rest of the U.S.

10 pct. pts.

1960   1980   2000   2020   1960   1980   2000   2020

The split has been evident in several recent elections. During the 2021 mayoral race in New York City, Eric Adams, a moderate Democrat focused on reducing crime, won four of the city's five boroughs. The only one he lost, to a more liberal candidate, was Manhattan, the city's most affluent borough. Similarly, in the 2020 presidential primaries, more affluent and educated Democrats initially showed little interest in Joe Biden. His campaign was saved by South Carolina's predominantly Black, working-class voters. Biden himself was first elected to the Senate in 1972, a year when the Democratic presidential nominee, George McGovern, who was influenced by the New Left, lost forty-nine states to Richard Nixon. Reminiscing about that election recently, Biden said that his party had made the mistake of listening too closely to "limousine liberals" and not enough to voters from more modest backgrounds. "We didn't pay nearly as much attention to working-class folks as we used to," he said. "And the same thing is happening today."

Sabin, the historian, has compared the old version of liberalism, before the rise of the New Left, to a bicycle. It was a bicycle badly in need of repair, and the reformers of the 1960s accurately diagnosed many of its problems. But after taking it apart, they could never figure out how to reassemble it and get it moving again.

THE NEW LEFT may have been focused on a relatively narrow slice of the population, but the movement was at least dynamic. It offered fresh ideas that changed the public debate on big issues and inspired young people who had not previously considered themselves political. The old left, dominated by the labor unions that had grown so much during the 1930s and 1940s, offered little such energy. It emphasized the protection of its existing members instead of expansion to new groups of workers. It tried to protect the status quo rather than change with the times.

There was an irony to this position. In the 1930s, the two dominant organizations in American labor, the AFL and the CIO, had been divided over the question of whether to focus on existing members or to expand. The AFL had taken the narrower view. It was based on craft unionism, in which specific groups of skilled workers came together to bargain for higher pay. These guilds were exclusionary by definition. They restricted membership to keep wages high. They believed that economic output was constrained and workers had to battle not only employers (over the balance between profits and wages) but also other workers (over a fixed number of jobs).

The CIO, by contrast, believed in industrial unionism, in which workers with different jobs would belong to the same union. They would bargain for higher pay and, crucially, serve as a force for larger political change that would benefit their members. The workers would make up the backbone of a growing high-wage economy. They would not have to fight with other workers over a fixed piece of the pie because the pie would grow. When Minneapolis's truck drivers chose to include other workers around the city in their 1934 unionization drive, they were practicing industrial unionism. The industrial approach largely won the debate during the New Deal, making possible the surge in unionism during the 1930s and 1940s, including among many lower-skilled workers. But the original AFL outlook never disappeared, and it reasserted itself during later decades.

William George Meany was born into the AFL tradition, in New York City in 1894, and he was born into a particularly conservative strain of it: New York's building trades. Meany's grandparents had escaped the Irish potato famine of the mid-nineteenth century and immigrated to the city. His parents raised him in the relative comfort of a working-class Bronx neighborhood called Port Morris, where residents lived in single-family homes rather than tenements. During the early 1900s, Meany's father, Michael, was president of Local 2 of the plumbers' union. It practiced a version of what today would be called legacy admissions, admitting mostly the sons and other relatives of existing members. Local 2 also tried to keep other plumbers off its jobs rather than recruit them into the union. "They could drop dead," Michael's son, who went by George, would later say. George started working as a plumber at age sixteen, when he was also a semipro baseball catcher, and left plumbing to become a full-time union official at twenty-eight.

George Meany was a hulking man, at least 220 pounds, with "an immense neck and huge, square-fingered hands," as one newspaper wrote. He spoke in the "dems and dose" patois of the Bronx and rose through the ranks of the AFL in his thirties, thanks to a superior understanding of what motivated people. He put a high priority on clear, direct communication and inspired loyalty in those around him. At one point, Meany took nighttime Spanish classes so that he could talk with labor leaders from Latin America. He summed up his leadership philosophy as "Never beg, never threaten, never think you're right all the time." By the 1940s, he had moved to Washington as a senior AFL official and helped shape the wartime cooperation between management and labor. By the 1950s, he was running the AFL, and in 1955, he negotiated a merger between the AFL and CIO. Because the AFL was larger, Meany got the top job in the combined organization.

His basic vision remained the same as it had been in the plumbers' union in New York: Unions were guilds that fought fiercely for their members. As a national union leader, he helped to raise the pay and benefits and improve the working conditions of millions of workers. He could also be principled, as when he ejected the Teamsters from the AFL-CIO for corruption in the 1960s. Nonetheless, Meany had something in common with the New Left student activists he despised as effete hippies: He too was much more interested in building a narrow movement than an expansive one. He did not think that labor's primary mission was to put together a national coalition that could create a more prosperous working class and a more equal economy.

"Ideology is baloney," Meany said. He bragged that he had never walked a picket line. He did not devote much AFL-CIO money to recruitment efforts. He considered protest marches to be mere showmanship. He was largely uninterested in recruiting women, and although he supported the civil rights legislative agenda of the 1960s, he sent mixed signals about efforts to expand unions among Black and Latino workers. During one large union conference, he publicly insulted Randolph by asking, "Who the hell appointed you spokesman for the whole Negro race?" Race and gender would play major roles in the marginalization of the labor movement. White men, who made up almost two-thirds of the labor force in the 1950s, were on their way to becoming a minority. But many union leaders were unwilling to recruit workers from the growing parts of the workforce.

Even as Meany publicly dismissed the importance of the ideology, he embraced it in another respect. He built a public image as a committed Cold Warrior and a foe of communism. It was politically useful to the labor movement during the McCarthyism of the 1950s, and Meany genuinely abhorred communism. He aligned the AFL-CIO with right-wing unions in Latin America that cooperated with the CIA, including during the 1954 coup in Guatemala, and he strongly supported the Vietnam War.

He was also unapologetic about living the good life. He wore European suits and appeared on magazine covers with a cigar in his mouth. He lived in Bethesda, Maryland, near Burning Tree Country Club, an all-male golf club where presidents played. After a lunch together in Paris, a *New York Times* columnist wrote in his diary: "I must say that although Mr. and Mrs. Meany still talk like a plumber and his wife, they look and dress more like big business. She was wearing a mink cape." Each year, Meany turned the AFL-CIO convention into an extended retreat in Miami Beach, sometimes lasting more than a week. To opponents of organized labor, the event became an easy way to portray union members as being part of a privileged blue-collar aristocracy. In many ways, that was Meany's vision too. The AFL's narrower focus ultimately triumphed over the CIO philosophy, which viewed organized labor as a tool for building a broad workers' movement. Labor would instead look out for its own.

Throughout, Meany remained effective at implementing his vision. He built relationships with other union leaders, and they kept him atop the AFL-CIO for twenty-four years. He also became close to Washington politicians. Lyndon Johnson liked Meany so much that he sometimes sent a car to fetch Meany from his home for nighttime chats at the White House. After the Democratic landslide of 1964 gave the party its largest congressional majorities since Franklin Roosevelt's second term, Johnson began to push for the most ambitious package of legislation since Roosevelt's presidency. Known as the Great Society, it included Medicare, Medicaid, and major bills on voting rights, education, transportation, immigration, consumer protection, and the arts. Initially, it also included a bill intended to expand union membership by repealing the part of the Taft-Hartley Act of 1947 that allowed so-called open shops. Its repeal would have helped unions organize workers in the South.

Officially, the bill became the AFL-CIO's top priority. Meany and other labor leaders visited the White House shortly after the election to remind Johnson of its importance and of labor's support for him during the campaign. Johnson then publicly reiterated his support for repeal of the provision. The House passed a bill doing so in 1965, and the bill moved to the Senate, where business lobbyists hoped to kill it. But it had enough support among the newly liberal Senate that Capitol Hill observers were unsure what would happen. They believed that a push by Meany, Johnson, and Democratic leaders in Congress would give it a good chance of finding enough votes to pass.

The push never materialized. Meany did not tell Johnson that the bill's failure might jeopardize their relationship and labor's support for other parts of Johnson's agenda, like the Vietnam War. Johnson did little to lobby his old colleagues in the Senate. Senate Democrats never held an all-night session that might have overcome a filibuster. "Somebody might drop over and we'd never quit apologizing to ourselves," a top Senate Democrat explained. Filibusters to block the bill succeeded twice, and the bill died. The bill's failure was the only major legislative defeat of Johnson's Great Society program.

A few years later, as Meany neared the end of his tenure, he sat down for an interview in the conference room of *U.S. News &*

World Report's Washington headquarters and explained his philosophy. At the time, the share of workers in labor unions had fallen to 25 percent, from 33 percent when Meany took over the AFL. When a journalist asked Meany why the decline was happening, he replied, "I don't know, I don't care." Meany added that he did not necessarily want the share to be higher. "With all of our complaints, we have the highest standard of living in the world. Why should we worry about organizing groups of people who do not appear to want to be organized? If they prefer to have others speak for them and make the decisions which affect their lives, without effective participation on their part, that is their right," he continued. "Frankly, I used to worry about the size of the membership. But quite a few years ago I just stopped worrying about it, because to me it doesn't make any difference."

It was a spectacular miscalculation. Meany had created a labor movement that represented workers in a shrinking share of the economy. "In my opinion, the labor movement with which I have had such close and warm ties all my working life is cutting its own throat," said Joseph Rauh, a former Roosevelt administration official who became a civil rights and labor activist. As labor's share of the workforce declined, its political influence did as well, and it was less effective at fighting policies that hurt all workers, including union members. It was also less effective at fighting policies that further shrank unions. One economist described the situation as "the Cheshire Cat phenomenon," a reference to the Lewis Carroll character that slowly disappears, leaving only its smile. The workers whom unions failed to recruit were the cat's body. The shrinking share of workers still earning union wages were the smile.

The New Deal had included a two-pronged approach to lifting living standards. The first involved direct government efforts to do so. It spanned benefits like Social Security and regulations like the minimum wage, all of which increased take-home pay. The second prong focused on the longer term through policies to help workers build political and economic power, like the Wagner Act. By strengthening organized labor, the New Deal both allowed workers to negotiate with their employers for higher wages and gave them a stronger political voice. Crucially, the second prong helped protect the first: Large labor unions could help elect presidents and members of Congress, ensuring that programs like Social Security thrived while creating new programs in the future.

Johnson's Great Society included only the first of these two prongs. It expanded health insurance and created a raft of anti-poverty programs, but it did little to expand the political power of ordinary Americans. In the decades to come, this one-pronged approach became the norm for Democrats. When Carter had to choose between prioritizing the passage of a bill to strengthen unions and a treaty to hand over control of the Panama Canal to Panama, he chose the treaty, and the labor bill died. Bill Clinton and Barack Obama appointed regulators and signed executive orders to protect collective bargaining, but they too failed to pass legislation empowering unions. Biden, who vowed to be "the most pro-union president you've ever seen," followed the same pattern in the first years of his presidency. In many of these cases, congressional Democrats were at least as responsible as the presidents were. The Senate filibuster also helped block pro-union bills. In 2021 and 2022, when Democrats narrowly controlled Congress, they passed major bills on Covid, climate change, healthcare, infrastructure, China policy, and gun control—but not labor policy.

Of course, corporate America and its allies in government played a crucial role in the shrinking of unions. The Taft-Hartley Act had made it hard for them to expand into the South and parts of the West, and corporate lobbyists fought every effort to repeal the law, with help from the filibuster. Federal judges continued to side with employers more often than workers. In the latter parts of the twentieth century, companies became increasingly aggressive about trying to shrink or eliminate unions. Even if Meany and the Democratic Party had been more focused on expanding the labor movement, they would not have had an easy time doing so. The strangest part of the story, however, is that they never joined the battle. They instead contributed to a vicious cycle in which the declining membership of labor unions reduced their political power and contributed to future declines.

Dolores Huerta, 1965.

AN INTRIGUING ALTERNATIVE to Meany's vision emerged from the farms of central California. In 1960, Edward R. Murrow of CBS News made many Americans aware of the plight of the workers there with his prime-time television documentary *Harvest of Shame*. It was filled with scenes of families living in run-down shacks, and Murrow described the workers as underfed, under-clothed, and forgotten. He went so far as to compare them to slaves. In the show's opening minutes, Murrow interviewed Eisenhower's secretary of labor, who called the workers "the excluded Americans." CBS aired the program the night after Thanksgiving to contrast the nation's bounty with the workers' poverty.

Agriculture remained an industry largely untouched by the country's widening prosperity. Many labor laws, like minimum wage requirements, did not apply to the farm sector, partly at the insistence of southerners in Congress who did not want New Deal reforms to cover Black workers. This exclusion meant that a diverse mix of workers around the country—Black, Latino, Asian, Native, and White—were left out of the postwar boom. In the service sector, many workers, including maids, janitors, waiters, store clerks, and hospital aides, also made low wages. These workers were rarely unionized, which both helped explain their situation and presented an opportunity for labor unions to expand in rapidly growing parts of the economy.

In Delano, a small California city near the farms of the San Joaquin Valley, a group of community activists began trying to organize the agricultural workforce in the early 1960s. Their leaders included Cesar Chavez, who had grown up in a family of itinerant farmers, and Dolores Huerta, whose parents had been involved with labor unions. They started not by trying to sell workers on grand visions of political change, or even on union membership, but by focusing on everyday problems. In exchange for monthly dues of $3.50 (about $35 in today's terms), members received a form of life insurance modeled after the informal policies that community groups in Mexico offered. The organization also created a credit union, giving families access to loans previously unavailable to them, as well as a literacy program and a program to distribute contraceptives to women. The activists helped people respond to traffic tickets and file complaints about police brutality. A minister who worked with the group bought a large fuel tank and formed a cooperative that sold gas cheaply, reducing one of the biggest costs for migrant workers.

Eventually, the organization—which went by the aspirational name of the National Farm Workers Association—organized a rent strike to protest the condition of the cabins where workers lived. Each cabin had only one electrical outlet, forcing families to alternate using lamps and kitchen appliances. At one point, ninety people living in a labor camp had to share two working toilets. The rent strike was a galvanizing event, attracting dozens of families to the NFWA. "They began seeing us defending the small victims," Chavez said, "and each member in a way became an organizer." The residents staged a march, with one woman holding a sign that read "The rich get richer and the poor get the rent raise." An organizer gave speeches around the area comparing the strike to the Boston Tea Party and saying that the shacks were in such disrepair that most farmers would not house their pigs there. In response, the local housing authority reduced the rent increase but did not eliminate it, and the residents took their case to court.

To achieve lasting improvements in their lives, Chavez knew that the workers would need to form a labor union, but he was wary of demanding union recognition only to have the growers fire their members. The group needed to be larger and stronger before it acted, Chavez believed. Yet events forced his hand. In a nearby farming community, another labor organizer announced that a group of Filipino workers were going on strike. Once they did, Chavez decided that the NFWA had to support them. Within weeks, a few thousand workers across the San Joaquin Valley had walked out.

The strike grew to include a rare alliance between organized labor and the New Left. The strikers received help from SDS, civil rights groups, and progressive Catholic priests. These outside allies helped bring attention to the union's call for a consumer boycott of grapes—the farms' main product and an optional purchase for many families, easily replaced by other fruit. Established labor unions helped too, with the Teamsters refusing to unload grapes when they arrived at stores and warehouses. The boycott spread, and grape sales declined. Chavez's campaign had the feel of a grassroots campaign with the potential for national impact, like the strikes of 1934 and Randolph's organization of the Pullman porters.

At the center of the alliance supporting the farmworkers was Walter Reuther, the head of the United Auto Workers, the same union that had allowed SDS to use its Port Huron retreat a few years earlier. Reuther was frustrated that George Meany was not doing more to support the farmworkers, and the Auto Workers helped pay for Chavez's organizing campaign. Reuther also visited the town of Delano early in the strike and persuaded Robert Kennedy, then a New York senator, to visit too. To Reuther, California's grape fields offered a model for how American workers could expand their political power in a new era, and he publicly compared them to the autoworkers who had broken Detroit's opposition to collective bargaining. "You are leading history," Reuther told a rally in Delano. The effort involved a multiracial, cross-class coalition that placed a priority on both meeting working people's needs and winning over public opinion. It focused on immigrant groups, Hispanic and Asian, who would make up a growing share of the population in coming decades. The farmworkers' campaign drew on the best part of the Roosevelt era while also addressing that era's injustices.

But the early progress did not last, mostly because of the short-sightedness of other leaders within organized labor, specifically in the Teamsters. During the strike's initial weeks, support from the Teamsters had been crucial. Its members had joined picket lines outside grocery stores and disrupted the distribution network for grapes. These moves seemed consistent with the Teamsters' history. After its seminal victory in Minneapolis, the union had grown to include almost two million members, which meant that one out of every forty American workers was a Teamster. The Teamsters' leaders won large pay increases, transforming truck driving from a job that paid poverty wages to one that allowed a middle-class life. It was a common story for union members in the 1960s.

Along with this prosperity, however, came a new kind of self-interest among union leaders. Some used the growing pool of members' dues to finance lavish lifestyles and build ties with organized crime. One Teamsters president diverted union funds to buy silk shirts, golf equipment, football tickets, a heated pool for his Seattle home, and a house next door to it for his son. As the farmworkers' strike seemed to be succeeding, the leaders of the Teamsters saw an opportunity to push Chavez's group aside and expand their own ranks. The Teamsters had already organized the drivers who transported the farms' crops. If fruit pickers and other field workers were going to be organized, the Teamsters wanted to organize them and receive their dues. Even as some members continued to support the grape boycott, Teamsters officials began a campaign to undermine Chavez.

"I don't think he has the strength to win," said Jimmy Hoffa, the Teamsters president, who was out of jail while appealing a fraud conviction. "I'm sure he can't do it."

Above all, the Teamsters tried to persuade farmworkers that the NFWA was more of a left-wing interest group than a labor union focused on their well-being. Teamsters officials pointed to the priests, student volunteers, and civil rights leaders who had joined their cause. Bill Grami, a top Teamsters official, told reporters that while NFWA organizers might pretend to be downtrodden farmworkers, they were really "highly sophisticated people from the New Left with a liberal sprinkling of kooks." The Teamsters also spread rumors that Chavez's union was a front for a "Mexican Power Movement" that would "get California back and give it to the Mexicans." The *San Francisco Examiner,* a newspaper owned by the Hearst family that had long been sympathetic to California's farm owners, trumpeted the Teamsters' false accusations. In one article, the *Examiner* printed the conspiracy theory about a Mexican power grab and then added this less-than-helpful rebuttal: "An N.F.W.A. organizer denied the existence of any plan to create a massive Mexican-American revolutionary pressure group."

At one point, Grami made a remark that encapsulated the fundamental change in the American labor movement since its New Deal growth. He criticized the NFWA for trying "to build a power base for political action." This was true, of course. It was exactly how labor unions had been so successful over the previous three decades. They had built a power base larger than any one workplace, job category, or industry. They had supplied the political support for an overhaul of the American economy so that it would provide rising incomes and living standards for most of the population.

The Teamsters had once played a central role in building that power base for political action, but the union was no longer interested in doing so. The union began to see itself not as part of an interconnected working class but as an independent organization focused on itself, even at the expense of farmworkers. This outlook led it to commit the ultimate union betrayal: The Teamsters formed an alliance with a major fruit company. The company did its part by encouraging workers to choose the Teamsters over the NFWA. When workers were voting on which union to join, the company distributed a leaflet calling the Teamsters a tough, fair organization that fought hard for its members. The leaflet failed to mention that the Teamsters were willing to accept lower wages than the NFWA.

The Teamsters spent much of the next decade battling for control of the California grape fields, using every possible tool, including politics, public relations, intimidation, and violence. One Teamster beat an NFWA member with brass knuckles, leaving a permanent dent in her face. Another person with ties to the Teamsters shot and killed a worker walking a picket line. The NFWA won some victories during these years, but it never lived up to its early potential. It faced not only the usual obstacles to organizing— companies with extensive resources; police departments and newspapers hostile to unions; workers fearful for their livelihoods—but also one of the country's largest unions. The Teamsters cared more about the Teamsters by this point than the larger labor movement.

THE FARMWORKERS' UNION demonstrated what an alternative path for the old left might have looked like. It would have involved an expansive vision of organized labor that changed along with the American economy.

The places where unions were already strong—factories in the Northeast, Midwest, and a few places on the West Coast—made up a declining share of the American economy. By this point, western Europe and Japan had rebuilt their industrial bases and were starting to challenge the manufacturing dominance of the United States. Imports made up a growing share of the American economy starting in the mid-1960s. In later decades, some Americans would nostalgically wish that manufacturing could have remained as large a part of the economy as it had been in the immediate postwar years, but that was almost certainly impossible. The rest of the world was going to recover at some point, and its factories would become more competitive. Inside the United States, economic growth would need to shift toward the service sector and the Sun Belt. If unions did not expand, they would become less relevant and less able to influence government policy and the economy. The hard-won gains of previous decades would be at risk.

It is impossible to know whether this approach would have

succeeded had it been tried. It surely would have faced obstacles, including a growing ability of companies to shift labor to low-wage countries as the rest of the world developed in the second half of the twentieth century. But the advocates of this alternate approach were certainly prophetic about the weaknesses of the path that the old left had chosen. American labor was confining itself to a shrinking portion of the workforce and dooming itself to diminished political power.

Nobody recognized the problem as clearly as Walter Reuther. The red-haired son of socialist German immigrants, he was born in West Virginia and moved as a teenager in the 1920s to a booming Detroit, where he found a job as a mechanic. The family's leftist roots led him and his brother Victor to organize protests against racial discrimination at Detroit City College and the Whites-only policy of local pools. Walter soon became a union activist and devoted his life to expanding organized labor. He helped lead the 1937 sit-down strike at General Motors, the one that Michigan's governor resolved in favor of the workers by refusing to use the National Guard against them. That same year, Reuther was beaten by company-hired hooligans outside Ford's River Rouge plant. Eleven years later, he survived an assassination attempt inside his home, in which he was hit by five shotgun blasts that permanently damaged his arm. The police never arrested anybody for the crime. By that point, Reuther had risen to become the president of the United Auto Workers, and he later ran the national umbrella group of which it was a part, the CIO.

A gifted public speaker, Reuther traveled the world, arguing that the United States—with its high-wage, unionized economy, where workers' spending fueled growth—could be a model to countries trying to recover from World War II or from colonialism. His vision resembled the one that Paul Hoffman and George Kaiser were selling to their fellow business executives. Reuther soon became the country's best-known labor leader. George Romney, during his time as an auto executive, called Reuther "the most dangerous man in Detroit because no one is more skillful in bringing about the revolution without seeming to disturb the existing forms of society."

George Meany, left, and Walter Reuther discuss a merger of
the AFL and CIO, 1953.

When Reuther and Meany negotiated the merger of the AFL
and CIO, combining the two biggest parts of organized labor,
Reuther saw it as a huge opportunity. A united labor movement
could leave behind internecine battles and devote itself to growth.
He called for a nationwide doubling of union membership. He
pushed for more spending on organizing drives and a crackdown
on the kind of raiding that the Teamsters had done to the NFWA.
But Meany was always the senior partner in the relationship, because of the AFL's larger size, and he never bought Reuther's ex-
pansionist visions.

At the conference to celebrate the merger, the philosophical differences between the two were already apparent. In Reuther's
speech, he proclaimed, "This is an unparalleled opportunity to
begin to lay the basis for moving forward, for organizing the millions of unorganized workers who are still denied the protection
and the benefits that only trade union membership can give them."
Meany, speaking from the same stage, said, "Let all of our actions
be keyed into that simple, plain principle that a trade union has no
other reason for existence than the job of carrying out and carrying forward and advancing the interests and welfare of its members."

As the two worked together, they clashed both philosophically and stylistically. Reuther avoided displays of ostentation that conflicted with the lifestyle of an ordinary American worker. He would fly coach to meetings and refuse to stay in rooms as nice as the other leaders did. "We don't have a labor movement," he complained. "We have a club. It's a very exclusive club: stays in the best hotels, in the finest resorts in the Western Hemisphere. But it isn't doing the job." One year, Reuther managed to persuade Meany to move the annual AFL-CIO conference out of its lush Miami Beach setting. But instead of going with Reuther's suggestion of Washington, Meany chose Puerto Rico. During the conference, Reuther joined a picket line of striking workers at a local lighting fixtures plant, while Meany appeared in a *Life* magazine photograph sunbathing shirtless. Still, Reuther ended up being the one who was embarrassed. After he publicly suggested during the conference that unemployed workers plan a march in Washington to protest the looming expiration of jobless benefits, Eisenhower, who was in Washington, tartly noted that the call came from the "sunny beaches" of Puerto Rico. Reuther seethed.

The other prominent labor leader arguing for growth during these years was Jerry Wurf, a Jewish native of Brooklyn who had survived polio as a child. While confined to a wheelchair, he immersed himself in books, many about the Depression and its causes. He learned to walk with a limp, although he was frequently in pain. Wurf wore thick glasses and had a full head of tousled hair. He was, as one journalist wrote, ebullient and volatile, and he turned himself into a soapbox orator in Greenwich Village, as A. Philip Randolph had done in Harlem. After getting a job in a cafeteria, Wurf set about organizing his co-workers, many of whom were immigrants from Eastern Europe, Ireland, Italy, and Mexico. "You are *men*," he declared, urging them to fight for decent wages and working conditions.

Wurf eventually took over a union of government workers—the American Federation of State, County and Municipal Employees, known as AFSCME (pronounced "AFF-skmee")—and he believed it had potential for rapid growth. Traditional unions had long ignored janitors, nurses, teachers, garbage collectors, and other government workers, partly because of laws barring them from joining unions. As a result, many of these workers lived in poverty or on the edge of it. But in 1958, Wurf helped persuade the mayor of New York to issue an executive order giving government workers limited rights to join a union. President John Kennedy signed a similar federal order in 1962.

Both Wurf and Reuther made civil rights central to their push for expansion. They recognized that the initial progress that unions had made toward racial integration was not enough. To remain strong, unions needed to recruit more workers of color and many more women. Reuther used United Auto Workers funds to pay for the sound system at the March on Washington and was the only White speaker on the Mall that day. During the California grape strike, he marched alongside Chavez with a sign bearing the word "Huelga," Spanish for "strike."

Wurf, in a decision that would alter American history, tried to organize Black sanitation workers in Memphis in 1968. A local sanitation worker had started the effort, and Wurf brought national attention to it and helped finance it, with some of the money coming from Reuther's United Auto Workers. At the time, Memphis's sanitation workers had no paid holidays, no health insurance, and no formal way to request changes to their routine. They had to go to city hall during their off-hours, in soiled work clothes, and wait in line to ask for an appointment with the mayor. Once they went on strike, the workers carried signs that echoed Wurf's old exhortations to cafeteria workers in New York: "I Am a Man."

A turning point came when Wurf and AFSCME formed an alliance with local ministers, whose support helped persuade the Reverend Martin Luther King, Jr., to travel to Memphis three times during the spring to support the strike. During his first visit, he spoke to thousands of people at a Masonic temple. During his second visit, he marched with workers. During King's third visit, while he stood on the balcony of the Lorraine Motel, a White supremacist shot and killed him. Less than two weeks later, while much of the country mourned, Memphis's mayor reversed his prior opposition to the union and agreed to raise the workers' wages. At the ceremony to sign the contract, Wurf told the crowd never to forget that King's mission to Memphis and his martyrdom had made the victory possible.

The sanitation strike raised AFSCME's profile and helped turn it into a national force. A few months later, *Fortune* magazine profiled the union and described the "exuberant atmosphere in its Washington headquarters reminiscent of the CIO organizing drives of the Thirties." It continued: "There is an élan to the organization, an air of bustle and excitement, a sense of great plans underfoot, and an evangelical zeal that one rarely encounters these days in the stately mansions of Big Labor."

Wurf and Reuther understood that an expansion of labor unions during these years would not be easy. But they also knew that such an expansion was never easy. Similar efforts had failed in the nineteenth and early twentieth centuries. The successes of the 1930s and 1940s had required years of grassroots organizing and had included many setbacks. A campaign to expand unions in the 1960s would be more difficult in some ways because there was no depression or world war to unify workers. And factories could more easily move to low-wage countries or to the largely non-unionized South, which was more developed by the 1960s. But the latter-day organizers also had some advantages that their predecessors lacked. The legal right to collective bargaining was enshrined, thanks to the Wagner Act. The economy was shifting toward the service sector, and its main employers, like restaurants, retailers, and hospitals, could not relocate the way factories could. As important, many workers, especially low-wage service workers, including many women, were eager to join unions, if only unions would welcome them. Wurf called the recruiting ground "fertile beyond belief," and Reuther said, "There is nothing wrong with the American labor movement excepting that we haven't mobilized it."

WHY, THEN, DID the attempts to modernize the old left fail?
The personal weaknesses of its reformers played a role. All were better at analyzing problems and developing visions than

managing large organizations. Wurf had a notorious temper. He raged frequently, which some people believed was related to the physical pain with which he lived. Even an admirer described him as "petty, mean-spirited and extremely jealous" and said that his personality drove away would-be allies. Chavez, after becoming an icon, turned into an autocratic leader who created a cult of personality. He insisted that his staff participate in group therapy exercises, and he made a friendly visit to Ferdinand Marcos, the Filipino dictator. Reuther was the most effective manager of the three, but he was still flawed. He preferred traveling the world to spending time at the AFL-CIO's Washington headquarters. He made frequent threats about confronting Meany without following through, and Meany came to ignore them. Both inside and outside the union, some people lamented that Reuther tended to give speeches even in one-on-one conversations. President Kennedy was one of the lamenters. While he admired Reuther and would rather spend time talking to him than Meany, Kennedy also found Reuther condescending.

Meany, despite his crassness, was extremely skilled at reading people around him. Reuther, who was thirteen years younger, assumed he would ultimately succeed Meany atop the organization. "What Reuther wants of me is to die," Meany said, "and I mean die." Instead, Meany stayed on the job into his eighties, in control of the union votes he needed. After a frustrated Reuther finally pulled the Auto Workers out of the AFL-CIO, Wurf remained on the executive committee. Sometimes, as *Time* magazine reported, the committee would vote in favor of a Meany-backed policy 25 to 1; other times, the vote would be 34 to 1. The margin depended on how many committee members were attending the meeting. Regardless, Wurf was a minority of one.

As much of an obstacle as Meany was, the structural impediments to the reinvention of American labor were even larger. By the 1960s, the United States was enjoying what the historian Arthur Schlesinger, Jr., called "an economy of abundance." The desperation of the Depression and the fear that it would return after World War II had long since passed. Americans were enjoying the comforts of modern life, and those comforts were improving every year. For much of the 1960s, the economy grew faster than 5 percent a year, a boom with little precedent. Many workers, along with the unions that represented them, were satisfied with the status quo. They did not recognize that the economy was irrevocably changing and that the labor movement needed to expand into the service sector. They did not see the need to devote themselves to overhauling a political movement that had been so good to them.

They did not understand what Chavez, Reuther, and Wurf did: The status quo was not an option. The choice was between growing and withering.

THE NEW LEFT had its own Cassandras. Much like Reuther and his labor allies, these internal critics recognized the dangers of focusing on purity rather than coalition building. They understood the inherent weakness of a movement that revolved around intellectuals to the exclusion of the majority of the population.

The feminists who urged Friedan to adopt a more inclusive approach were among these critics, as was John Lewis, the deposed leader of SNCC, who believed that the civil rights movement should continue trying to recruit outside allies. A few of the earliest members of SDS also foresaw the inherent weakness of the New Left, including Michael Vester. He was a German student activist who had come to the United States to study sociology at Bowdoin College in Maine during the 1961–62 school year. Like Hayden, Vester would eventually write an academic thesis on Mills. Vester attended the Port Huron conference and wrote much of the manifesto's section on the Cold War. Before the conference, Hayden had sent Vester an early draft of the document, asking for feedback. Vester immediately recognized its central political weakness. In a letter, he told Hayden, "The intellectuals by themselves can be a motor of social change, but *not the agency,* the moving power itself." The moving power still had to be the labor movement, because of its size.

Western Europe had its own New Left at the time; the phrase had come from Europe, partly because of Mills. The European New Left, however, made a bigger effort to appeal to workers than the American movement. In Germany, student leaders like Vester—whose group was also known as SDS, a German acronym for socialist students' league—worked with union officials whose job it was to communicate with workers about politics. "For us, the role of critical intellectuals in the media and in politics was not to *replace* the working classes but to help them to understand that their private grievances had political causes," Vester later wrote. "The left could only leave its complacent ghetto when it tried to mobilize people by raising issues germane to their everyday experiences and grievances."

This approach helped build an agenda that resonated with German workers. In 1969, as Richard Nixon settled into the White House, Germany's Social Democratic Party won an election and implemented many progressive policies, including expanded education, healthcare, pensions, housing, and transportation. The broadly prosperous German economy of the late twentieth century grew out of those policies, which in turn had grown out of the alliance between West German intellectuals and workers. Similar coalitions existed in other European countries. In Scandinavia, the Social Democrats moderated their once radical agenda calling for revolution, as the historian Tony Judt notes. They understood that radicalism doomed them to minority-party status. To win elections, they had to appeal to farmers, loggers, fishermen, and other rural voters who were often poor and culturally conservative. The Social Democrats did so by forming "red-green coalitions," with "red" referring to economic leftism and "green" to agricultural interests. These coalitions dominated politics in Denmark, Norway, and Sweden for decades after World War II and built the world's most renowned social safety nets.

The political dynamics obviously varied between those countries and the United States, and the European New Left had some advantages that its American counterpart did not. Most importantly, labor unions were historically larger in western Europe, creating a stronger political base. But building coalitions between workers and intellectuals was not easy in Europe. As in the United States, student activists and labor leaders often came from different class backgrounds and were skeptical of one another. The Europeans also had to overcome the traumas of World War II. Many of the rural voters who made up the center-left's postwar majorities had been part of the fascists' political base in the 1930s and 1940s. The European New Left, scarred by the horrors of genocide and war, responded with a pragmatic approach, understanding that the path to power did not run through university campuses and affluent suburbs. It ran through the places where most citizens lived.

The leaders of the American New Left were more prone to seeing the world that they wanted to see. They had not suffered the horrors of war on their own soil. They had watched history mostly move their way since the Depression. They did not distinguish between the parts of the old Roosevelt coalition that would eventually need to be jettisoned, like hardcore Dixiecrat segregationists, and the parts that could be won over even if they were less socially liberal than well-to-do college students. The European left made such distinctions and was rewarded with the votes of many workers and farmers. In the United States, many progressives did not see the need to do the hard work of coalition building because they had never experienced long-lasting political defeat.

But a few members of the American left were beginning to contemplate the prospect of it. David Riesman was a Harvard sociologist with stellar left-wing credentials. He had been a law clerk to Supreme Court Justice Louis Brandeis and the lead author of *The Lonely Crowd,* a 1950 book that was among the first bestsellers to criticize the conformity of postwar life. It was enough of a cultural sensation that *Time* magazine put Riesman on its cover and Bob Dylan mentioned "this lonely crowd" in his 1967 song "I Shall Be Released." In the 1960s, Riesman founded *The Correspondent,* an anti-nuclear journal that helped push the issue to the core of progressive politics. The journal also criticized the Vietnam War. But while Riesman shared many of the New Left's goals, he was worried about its strategy.

In essays, media interviews, and public talks, Riesman argued that the New Left was too insular. It viewed mainstream politics as so broken that it rejected the idea of working within the existing system, he argued. "Among members of the Students for a Democratic Society and other groups on the student left, hostility to the concept of 'power politics' reflects a general hostility toward 'politics,' 'bureaucracy,' 'organization'—all of these symbols being seen as aspects of the corruption of our society," he wrote. He urged his fellow activists to overhaul the country's political institutions, as Randolph, Perkins, and earlier progressives had done, rather than reject those institutions as hopelessly corrupt, as Mills and Nader often suggested.

Riesman was particularly worried that the New Left was alienating Americans who could be its allies. "I have always felt it important to look for allies in places which might seem unlikely to the purist," he wrote. At one point, he and Hayden wrote essays debating this issue in the pages of *The Correspondent*. Riesman believed that the rejection of traditional politics, as well as the confrontational tactics of student protesters, could cause parts of the Roosevelt coalition to defect to the Republican Party.

To get people's attention, Riesman raised an alarming scenario. He described the actions of protesters at the University of California, Berkeley, as "uncivil disobedience" and said they had played into the hands of Ronald Reagan, California's new governor, whose views had once been considered too right-wing for him to be electable. But in his first political campaign, in 1966, Reagan had proven the doubters wrong and beaten the incumbent Democratic governor by 15 percentage points. He had done so partly by turning the Berkeley protesters into the bogeymen of his campaign message and promising to restore order.

Riesman predicted that if his friends on the political left kept alienating people, they might cause a political reaction that once would have seemed outlandish. They might help elect Reagan as the president of the United States.

BY THE LATE 1960S, millions of American workers had no political home.

The labor movement, the heart of the old left, was not much of a movement anymore. Its leaders did not view themselves as the political representatives of the American masses, nor did they consider it their mission to serve as a bulwark against a return to a highly unequal, 1920s-style economy. The New Left was more energetic, but its energy was not focused on building political power for economic purposes. It was mostly a movement of and for college students, intellectuals, and professionals. That was evident in the causes it picked and did not pick and in its emphasis on individual fulfillment and rights over group action and coalition building.

One legacy of the New Left, perversely, was its affirmation of the effectiveness of political organizing in a democracy. The movement motivated thousands of Americans to become politically active. These new activists tried to shift public opinion and pressure Congress to pass new laws—and they often succeeded. Their success has had triumphant legacies, protecting consumers from harm, reducing pollution, and winning new rights for women and people of color. What the New Left tried to do, it often succeeded at doing. Yet the movement never made much of an attempt to improve the pay, benefits, and job conditions of working-class Americans, including many of the same women and people of color whom the New Left claimed to be representing. And it is very difficult for a movement to succeed at something that it does not attempt to do.

The combination of the old left's torpor during the 1960s and the New Left's narrow focus meant that the country no longer had a mass movement centered on lifting most Americans' living standards. It had split into two movements: a progressive, elite movement and a group of largely self-interested labor unions. The sum of the parts did not come close to equaling the whole. Many workers, not surprisingly, were starting to wonder where their political loyalties should lie.

CHAPTER 6

The Problem of Crime

T HE CRIME WAS SO AUDACIOUS THAT IT ALMOST IMMEDI-
ately acquired a name: the Great Plymouth Mail Robbery.
On a Tuesday night in August 1962, a group of armed robbers
executed the perfect heist.

One of them, posing as a police officer, closed off an entrance
to a divided highway south of Boston, to keep a stretch of the road
in Plymouth, Massachusetts, nearly empty. Another, also posing as
a police officer, pretended to help travelers who were supposedly
having car trouble on that same stretch of the highway. When a
Postal Service truck approached the fabricated scene of car trouble, the second man dressed as a police officer waved at the truck
to stop. He and the travelers then took out machine guns and surrounded the truck. "Open the door, or I'll blow your head off," the
phony police officer said. The truck was carrying $1,551,277
(more than $15 million today) in cash, collected from Cape Cod
businesses after a busy summer weekend. By the next day, newspapers across the United States and Canada had put the crime on
their front pages and said it might have been the largest heist in
American history.

From start to finish, the robbery made government officials and
bank executives look incompetent. To save money, the Cape Cod
banks were using a Postal Service truck to transport the cash,
rather than an armored truck. The Postal Service had allowed
word of the new route to leak. After the robbery, the FBI and Boston police conducted a chaotic investigation, changing their minds
about who the suspects were, and did not bring charges until almost five years after the crime. The prosecutors' case had so many
holes that the jury needed only an hour of deliberations before

acquitting the defendants, and the judge announced that he agreed with the verdict. To this date, the closest thing to an authoritative account of the crime is a novel written by a former *New York Times* editor who had previously written the screenplays for the movies *Shaft* and *The French Connection*. Based on his reporting, the author believed that one of the trial defendants was indeed the mastermind and lead robber.

It was not clear at the time, but the Great Plymouth Mail Robbery happened at almost exactly the moment that American crime had reached a turning point. After years of having been low, crime was beginning to surge. By the early 1960s, the numbers of robberies, burglaries, and murders were all rising, and spectacular crimes like the mail robbery became common events.

On May 22, 1962, a Continental Airlines flight exploded over Iowa, killing all forty-five people on board, the result of a suicide bomb carried by a man who was about to be tried for armed robbery. On the night of June 11, three Alcatraz prisoners staged a daring escape. Three days later, a twenty-three-year-old man in Boston found his mother murdered in her apartment, the first of at least eleven women whom the Boston Strangler would kill over the next year and a half. In Chicago, an alderman who had just been reelected in a landslide was found handcuffed and shot execution-style in his office. In New Jersey, three jewel thieves beat to death the wife of Chile's consul general. In Queens, New York, a twenty-eight-year-old woman named Kitty Genovese was stabbed to death while walking home from work, and the police claimed (wrongly, it eventually became clear) that neighbors who heard the crime failed to come to her rescue. The most notorious crime of the period occurred on November 22, 1963, when John F. Kennedy was killed in Dallas. Two days later, Kennedy's assassin was himself shot to death inside the Dallas police headquarters, another sign of law enforcement's fecklessness. "Crime," Orlando Wilson, the superintendent of the Chicago Police Department, said that year, "is overwhelming our society."

The national crime rate continued to rise for most of the next three decades. By 1976, crime had increased so much in Detroit that Jimmy Carter, the Democratic nominee for president, abandoned decades of tradition and did not hold a rally on Labor Day weekend in that city's Cadillac Square. The potential for trouble that might sully Carter's speech seemed too large, his aides believed. The decision was doubly symbolic, given that the event had long demonstrated the Democratic Party's closeness to organized labor. Nationally, the murder rate more than doubled between 1962 and 1980, while the assault rate more than tripled and the robbery rate nearly quadrupled. All remained high into the 1990s. Crime also rose in many other countries during this period, but not by nearly as much.

U.S. homicides per 100,000

The increase in violence was both shocking and confusing. People often assume that poverty drives crime, but poverty could not explain the trend. The trend had made more sense during the previous three decades, when the country was becoming more prosperous and crime was falling. By the 1960s, the boom was still going strong, and measures like employment and GDP growth reached new heights. Yet crime was rising. "Here was an explosion in crime that seemed to be occurring at a time when many economic variables looked favorable," Gary LaFree, a sociologist, wrote. James Q. Wilson, a prominent social scientist, described it as a paradox of "crime amidst plenty."

In this chapter, I hope to explain that paradox because it is part of a much larger story. The crime increases reflected a rising sense of disorder in American society—and, in turn, contributed to that sense of disorder. Things seemed to be falling apart in the 1960s. Leading political figures were assassinated. The country was losing a war. Major cities were engulfed in flames. Younger and older Americans felt an intense generational divide.

This period is critical to the history of the American economy because it is when large parts of the working class changed their political allegiance. They turned against the party that had delivered rapidly rising living standards—the Democrats—and embraced Republicans. Much of the shift has endured. Just as the 1930s started a new political era, so did the 1960s. It was the decade when the coalition that had built democratic capitalism and allowed millions of families to achieve the American dream unraveled.

In the standard progressive telling, the explanation for this political shift is race. By abandoning their segregationist past and pushing through civil rights legislation, Democrats took a heroic stand that cost the party the support of millions of White Americans. And that version of the story has a great deal of truth to it. You will be reading more about it in this chapter—about George Wallace, Spiro Agnew, and the southern strategy of Richard Nixon. Democrats could never have avoided paying a political price for their push for racial equality. A significant number of White voters would have abandoned Democrats no matter what else was happening.

But the rightward shift of the working class is not only about race, and Democrats do a disservice both to themselves and to many Americans by claiming otherwise. For one thing, telling voters that they are irredeemably bigoted is not an effective way to win their support. For another, the focus on race to the exclusion of other explanations has sometimes led progressives to misread the electorate. Because of that misreading, the Democratic Party has ignored political strategies that could have allowed it to win back some working-class voters without softening its support for civil rights.

One other figure highlighted in this chapter is Robert Kennedy. In death, he became a liberal icon. In life, he was something more complex. He was a passionate advocate for civil rights who also avoided misreading public opinion in ways that other liberals often did in the 1960s—and still do today. More than any other politician, Kennedy tried to bring together the blue-collar old left and the idealistic New Left. To do so, he combined a commitment to civil rights, a populist economic agenda, and a surprisingly conservative stance on some other issues. He did so because he recognized that many Americans were focused on one issue above all others in the late 1960s: the country's growing disorder.

THE CRIME WAVE that began in the 1960s became the subject of intense academic study in the following years. Eventually, scholars discovered a pattern that existed across multiple societies and eras: Crime waves tended to coincide with periods of social discord. When political consensus came apart—when people questioned whether their society was fair and whether they could trust their fellow citizens—more began to break the law. Most of the crime was without any political motive. But societal instability nonetheless seemed to change people's behavior. They became more likely to lash out and ignore established rules.

Ted Robert Gurr, a political scientist and a member of a 1968 federal commission on rising crime, noticed the pattern dating back to the early nineteenth century. When Gurr studied records from cities like London, Calcutta, and Stockholm, he saw that political turmoil and crime tended to move in tandem. Another scholar found that when Ireland became less politically stable in the 1910s, crime there rose. The same held true in Belgium, France, and Italy before World War II.

It also had been true in early periods of American history. In the tumultuous periods leading up to both the Revolutionary War and the Civil War, crime rose. It climbed the most in places where the political disagreements were most intense, like the contested frontiers in the 1700s. "People responded violently not only to threats to their property or person but also to disrespect," Randolph Roth, a historian at Ohio State University, has written. "They killed over a word, a gesture, a glance." The opposite seemed to be true as well. During periods of cohesion and patriotism, when people viewed the social hierarchy as legitimate, crime often fell.

Roth developed an innovative way of documenting the relationship. He compared crime rates with the trends in the naming of American counties back to the 1600s. In some periods, he noticed, many counties were named for national heroes, and these periods coincided with events that fostered national cohesion. During the surge of patriotism that followed the War of 1812, for example, officials named counties for Washington, Monroe, and other founders. During periods of political friction, such as the years before the Revolutionary War and before the Civil War, officials were less likely to choose national symbols. They instead named counties after local heroes or geographic features. Officials in New Jersey created Ocean County in 1850, and Georgia officials established Gordon County, named for the first resident of the state, the same year. The most surprising finding from Roth's research was that the share of counties named for national heroes tended to move in the opposite direction as crime. When people were feeling less national unity, they also committed more crimes. Both variables, Roth argued, were reflections of social cohesion.

This argument had historical antecedents. In the nineteenth century, the French sociologist Émile Durkheim popularized the term "anomie" to describe a breakdown in cohesion that can occur during periods of rapid social and political change. In the 1930s, the American sociologist Robert Merton applied the idea specifically to crime, arguing that rising anomie could lead to rising crime. In stable periods, people reflexively accept society's code of conduct, enforced by government agencies, employers, schools, neighborhoods, social networks, and families. People fear the shame and consequences of violating these rules and encourage their fellow citizens to abide by them as well. But when cohesion frays and anomie rises, the dynamic can flip. Once citizens question the justness of a system, many of its rules can come to seem illegitimate, as the sociologist Elijah Anderson explained. Social trust, or what philosophers call "fellow feeling," is like the air that citizens breathe. It can affect how angrily somebody responds to a disagreement with a neighbor, how willing somebody is to steal, and much more.

Crime is a complex subject, and rising anomie is far from the only reason that crime rose in the early 1960s. Another factor, researchers agree, is demographics. Male teenagers and young adults commit an outsize amount of crime, and the number of American teens rose in the late 1950s because of the baby boom. But demographics could not be the entire explanation because the age structure of the population changes by just a small amount each year. Crime, by contrast, held fairly steady until the early 1960s and then spiked. The timing of the demographic changes and the crime trends do not quite match.

A third factor appears to have been an increase in what sociologists call concentrated poverty. In the 1950s, middle-class White residents began to leave cities like Detroit and Philadelphia partly because they had access to government-subsidized mortgages that allowed them to buy suburban homes. Factories moved out of central cities during these same years, as did some middle-class Black families. And government planners, like Robert Moses in New York, built highways through long-established city neighborhoods, destroying some of them. This combination created clusters of urban poverty even as the national economy was thriving and likely contributed to the crime increase. But the concentration theory also seems to be only a partial explanation. It does not explain why crime also surged in suburbs, rural areas, and heavily White neighborhoods in the early 1960s. As with demographic changes, the trends in concentrated poverty appear to have played a meaningful role but not a dominant one.

The explanation that lines up most consistently with historical events is anomie. The 1960s were a period when many Americans were questioning long-held beliefs, including the legitimacy of the government and the social order. College students rebelled against conformity. One student activist famously urged young people not to trust anybody over the age of thirty. Republicans left behind the moderate Eisenhower era and turned toward the conservative Barry Goldwater. Civil rights organizers highlighted the hypocrisy and injustice of racism and themselves split into dueling factions. Liberal authors helped to found new movements that questioned society's approach to gender roles, the environment, consumer safety, and sexual activity. Music listeners and moviegoers embraced rebellious new stars.

It is important to emphasize that rising anomie can be a rational reaction to serious problems. After decades of accepting injustices, including racism, sexism, religious bigotry, and intolerant conformism, Americans began to challenge them in the early 1960s. You can think of those injustices as a harmful disease afflicting society and anomie as a medical treatment to combat the disease. Treatments, however, often have side effects. Consider this jarring sentence from Roth's work: "Nothing increases homicide rates more surely, at least in the short term, than an effort by a dedicated minority to create a more just society, as happened during the Revolution and in the struggle against slavery in the mid-nineteenth century."

The early 1960s saw a confluence of movements challenging the status quo, from the political left and right and especially from younger Americans. That crime rose on a nearly identical timetable may have seemed mysterious in the moment. Even today, the connection between the two trends can feel fuzzy. But it was consistent with a strong historical pattern.

In response to the crime wave, conservatives and liberals tended to make two different mistakes. Many conservatives claimed that the only problem was the social turmoil of the time and dismissed the underlying problems causing that turmoil. As crime rose, conservatives like Goldwater, J. Edgar Hoover, and southern Democrats were quick to denounce it. They blamed student radicals and civil rights demonstrators for fomenting a culture of lawlessness and argued for a return to what they considered the good old days. A longer historical lens exposes the weakness of this position. It was akin to arguing that the colonists of the 1770s should not have rebelled against British tyranny, or that the abolitionists of the 1850s should have not fought slavery, because challenging the status quo caused social turmoil that in turn led to increases in crime. The conservatives were correct that turmoil fed crime, but they ignored the injustices of the status quo.

Liberals made a different error. Many denied that crime was in fact increasing and tried to dismiss the trend as an invention of the political right. *The Nation* used quotation marks to signal its skepticism, writing about "the school 'crime wave'" and "the problem of 'crime.'" The magazine suggested that the media was creating a false narrative by sensationalizing individual crimes. One *Nation* writer disingenuously pointed out that crime was lower in 1964 than it had been in 1930. That was true but beside the point: The increases had only recently begun in 1964, while crime was on the cusp of declining in 1930. *The New Republic* also tortured statistics, emphasizing that violent crime was not rising as rapidly as property crime, as if that were reassuring. President Johnson was among those who did not seem to take the problem seriously. When he talked about crime, he tended to portray it as an extension of poverty and another argument in favor of his War on Poverty. He ignored the fact that crime was rising while poverty was falling.

These dismissals ran counter to what Americans experienced. "A steep, decade-long rise in violent crime has begun to alter patterns of life," a national magazine reported in 1970. By that point, many Americans knew somebody who had been a victim of street crime. People made decisions about where to live, walk, and shop based on fear of crime. When they turned on their television or picked up their morning newspaper, they saw further reason to believe that the country was descending into a violent new era.

Violence was not the only way that disorder seemed to dominate American life, either. As the country left behind the conformism of the 1940s and 1950s, Americans argued over the Vietnam War, race, marijuana, pornography, and sex education. Divorce became more common. The share of Americans who said that they trusted the federal government to do the right thing most of the time declined from its lofty postwar levels. "In the public perception, all these things merged," James Sundquist, a political scientist and former aide to President Harry Truman, wrote. "Ghetto riots, campus riots, street crime, anti-Vietnam marches, poor people's marches, drugs, pornography, welfarism, rising taxes, all had a common thread: the breakdown of family and social discipline, of order, of concepts of duty, of respect for law, of public and private morality." In early 1968, James Reston, a *New York Times* columnist, wrote, "The main crisis is not Vietnam itself, or in the cities, but in the feeling that the political system for dealing with these things has broken down." The experts at Gallup reported that during the firm's 32 years of existence, the American public had never before been so disillusioned and cynical as it was in 1968.

This rising anomie upended presidential politics. Less than four years after Johnson had won a landslide, he decided that he was too unpopular to win again. On the night of March 31, 1968, in a televised address from the Oval Office that surprised even senior members of his administration, he withdrew from the campaign. Johnson had served as president less than five years at the time. Other sitting presidents had entered campaigns in weak positions— including Truman in 1948, Hoover in 1932, and Taft in 1912— but few had thought that they were too unpopular to attempt a comeback.

All the while, the economy continued to boom. When Johnson made his announcement, the unemployment rate was below 4 percent, and the country had not experienced a recession for more than seven years. Nonetheless, he seemed to understand that the country was more dissatisfied than it had been in a long time. That dissatisfaction inspired some of the leading names in American politics—including Richard Nixon, George Wallace, Robert Kennedy, Ronald Reagan, Hubert Humphrey, Nelson Rockefeller, and George Romney—to run for president. The 1968 campaign, in turn, would reshape the country's political landscape for decades.

FOUR DAYS AFTER Johnson quit the campaign, Martin Luther King was assassinated. Within hours of his death, infuriated residents of Washington, New York, and several other major cities rioted, and the riots continued, on and off, for days. In Baltimore, the Republican governor of Maryland, Spiro Agnew, responded by calling a meeting with about a hundred local Black leaders, many of whom had been his allies. Once he began speaking, they realized that the event was a political ambush.

With the leaders still mourning King, Agnew had invited them to a state office building in Baltimore to lambaste them. He told them that they had not done enough to prevent the riots. "You know who lit the fires," Agnew said. "They were not lit in honor of your great fallen leader. Nor were they lit from an overwhelming sense of frustration and despair." Instead, he argued, they were a response to calls for violence from radical activists like Stokely Carmichael, and Agnew told the leaders they had not spoken out against those calls (even though some had). Most of the leaders walked out of the room in anger.

The speech was a piece of opportunism, intended to raise Agnew's national profile. Until then, he had been known as a moderate Republican. In his race for governor, less than two years earlier, he won partly by criticizing his Democratic opponent for being too close to the Ku Klux Klan. In office, he supported several civil rights measures, including the first fair housing law in a state south of the Mason-Dixon line. By 1968, however, Agnew had come to believe that support for civil rights was not the path to national prominence in the Republican Party. His humiliation of local civil rights leaders was his attempt to get noticed.

It worked. Four months later, Nixon chose Agnew as his vice-presidential nominee. Nixon's aides portrayed the choice as part of their candidate's outreach to conservative southerners who had long voted Democratic. It was consistent with a strategy that Nixon had developed during the primaries in large part to prevent

Reagan, a conservative darling then in his first term as California's governor, from winning the nomination by sweeping southern delegates. Nixon's team referred to the plan as the southern strategy. Central to it was the wooing of Strom Thurmond, the segregationist senator from South Carolina who four years earlier had switched his affiliation from Democrat to Republican. At a meeting in Atlanta during the 1968 primaries, Nixon told Thurmond and other southern leaders that he opposed busing to desegregate schools and that they would have a say in his vice-presidential selection. They later used that say to block northern moderates like George Romney and Nelson Rockefeller and to boost Agnew instead.

The southern strategy showed how important race—and racism—had become to the Republican Party's campaign plan. Republicans recognized that Johnson's signing of civil rights legislation had given them an opening to win over working-class White voters. Many of these voters were in the South, but others were not. Some were unhappy with school busing plans, particularly because those plans tended to avoid affluent suburban areas and desegregate only lower-income White and Black urban schools. Other voters were turned off by the spate of riots that had begun in the Watts neighborhood of Los Angeles in 1965 and surged again after King's murder. Often, as had been the case in Watts, the disturbances were sparked by police brutality, which had afflicted Black neighborhoods for decades.

The conservative politicians who sought to capitalize on these issues did not usually grapple with the nuances. They instead tried to capitalize on White fears. They linked crime, riots, busing, and more, using code words to suggest that Black Americans presented a threat.

The master of White fright politics was George Wallace, the forty-eight-year-old former governor of Alabama who had announced an independent 1968 presidential campaign even before Johnson withdrew from the race. Wallace had grown up during the Depression as the son of a "dirt farmer," as he put it, and he escaped his background through a combination of schoolwork, high school debate, boxing, and World War II service. As a young

Alabama politician, he was a southern populist like the members of Congress who had made possible the New Deal, both insisting on segregation and supporting redistributionist economic policies to help White families. He pushed for the building of modern trade schools and hospitals, larger pensions for the elderly, and free textbooks for students. As governor, he became the embodiment of the White South's opposition to racial integration and equality. In his 1963 inaugural address, he thundered, "Segregation now, segregation tomorrow, and segregation forever," and later that year he stood in a doorway at his alma mater, the University of Alabama, in a failed attempt to block Black students from registering.

In 1964, Wallace entered a few Democratic presidential primaries, traveling to campaign stops in a plane with a Confederate flag painted on it to protest Johnson's civil rights push. He lost by wide margins all three primaries he entered, in Indiana, Maryland, and Wisconsin, but fared better than many experts had expected. Wallace had demonstrated that the Deep South was not the only part of the country where racism could win votes. Four years later, in 1968, Wallace ran as an independent, believing that the Democratic Party was no longer a congenial home for a segregationist.

This history explains the widespread perception on the political left that the working class's rightward shift since the 1960s is almost entirely about race: Some White voters are unwilling to vote for a party that advocates for racial equality and drawn to one that plays to racial animosities. When the Democratic Party switched from the latter category to the former, it damaged its electability for the sake of higher principles. Under almost any conceivable scenario, large parts of the American South would have switched to the Republican Party once Democrats embraced civil rights.

But it is a mistake to imagine racism is binary—that people are either racist or not and that this characteristic determines their vote. The distinction I am making here is subtle and can feel awkward, given the moral opprobrium that racists like Wallace deserve. Racism is a stark American injustice that has shaped so much of the country's history. Yet to say that racism has been a central force is not the same as saying it is the dominant cause of every political trend. Race can sometimes obscure other forces affecting politics.

The 1968 presidential race was an example. Wallace and Nixon both used race, obviously. Yet their campaigns devoted less attention to it than is sometimes assumed. If anything, Nixon, Wallace, and their advisers believed that subjects besides race offered more promising ways to win votes during the general election campaign that year.

Wallace made a conscious effort to run a different campaign than he had four years earlier, one aimed at a broader section of the electorate. In 1964, he told voters that he was a segregationist but not a racist. In 1968, he said, "I'm not running on segregation." Wallace instead emphasized his opposition to the New Left: "bearded professors, liberal judges, beatniks, incompetents—even in the pulpit—and editorial writers on the newspapers." He told Californians that too many of their tax dollars were going to pay UCLA professors, and he described intellectuals who supported the Vietcong as traitors. "You young people seem to know a lot of four-letter words," he said during one speech. "But I have two four-letter words you don't know: S-O-A-P and W-O-R-K." He told crowds that student protests, riots, and rising crime were all part of the same story and that Americans were right to be sick of it. He mocked liberals for blaming crime on poverty, saying he had grown up poor without becoming a criminal.

In part, he was playing into voters' preferred self-image. Wallace recognized that many racists did not like to think of themselves as such and was giving them another rationale to support him. But he was also filling a void in American politics. The leaders of the Democratic and Republican parties had not been speaking to the frustrations of many voters. The Republicans often seemed like the party of the country club, while the Democrats were the ones governing a nation that seemed to be breaking down. Wallace promised to stand up to the elites who had allowed disorder to spread. He promised to speak for "the glassworker, the steelworker, the autoworker, and the textile worker, the farmer, the policeman, the beautician and the barber, and the little businessman."

Wallace's approach to the 1968 campaign altered his image. During his 1964 campaign, local organizations that typically hosted candidates' speeches refused to do so for Wallace. By late 1967, the situation had changed. Rotary clubs and other groups were sending him invitations. "This new-found respectability among the luncheon set may be the most significant development yet in his unannounced third-party bid for the Presidency," wrote Gene Roberts, a *New York Times* correspondent who had made his name covering the civil rights movement. "Civic club members who would not have been caught in the same room with him four years ago, now find him interestingly provocative, even when they do not agree with him." Wallace did not expect to win many votes at these lunches, but they made him look like a more legitimate candidate to the beauticians and steelworkers he was courting.

In the national polls, Wallace peaked during the summer of 1968 around 20 percent, an unusually strong showing for an independent. The number of voters drawn to parts of his message was much larger. One poll found that roughly half of American adults appreciated Wallace "for saying it the way it really is." More than half agreed that "liberals, intellectuals, and longhairs have run the country for too long."

Nixon's campaign also emphasized these issues instead of race. The southern strategy was a larger part of his primary campaign, when he needed to box out Reagan, than his general election campaign. Nixon told his aides that he did not want to compete with Wallace to win the Deep South. "Forget the Goldwater South," he said, referring to the five states in the Deep South that Goldwater had won in 1964. "You can't just echo Wallace." Sure enough, Wallace won four of the five states in November.

Nixon's speeches and advertisements were also light on racist dog whistles. The villains of the Nixon campaign were anti-war radicals, not civil rights protesters. In a minute-long television ad, set to nerve-jangling music, his campaign showed scenes of war and violent protest while Nixon, the off-camera narrator, proclaimed, "It is time for an honest look at the problem of order in the United States." Nearly every one of the dozens of faces shown at chaotic rallies was White. At the Republican National Convention, his speech added "organized crime" and "loan sharks" to the list of villains.

Nixon's 1968 presidential campaign echoed the themes that had dominated his life: exclusion, resentment, and envy, usually connected to social class. After he was admitted to Harvard and Yale as a high school senior in Southern California and offered partial scholarships, his family decided that it nonetheless did not have enough money to send him east. He instead attended nearby Whittier College, where the entering class had about a hundred students. During college, he would sometimes rise at three-thirty in the morning and drive to Los Angeles to buy goods for his parents to sell at their general store. Unable to gain admission to Whittier's most desirable fraternity, Nixon helped found a rival group, the Orthogonians, whose motto was "Beans, Brains, Brawn and Bowels." As John A. Farrell, a Nixon biographer, wrote: "The lives of American presidents are often cast as Horatio Alger tales, and the stories of their rise barnacled with myths. Yet few came so far, so fast, so alone, as Nixon."

Once he entered politics, populism became his trademark. He first won election to the House of Representatives running on the slogan "Richard Nixon is one of us." He defeated an incumbent Democrat who was a Yale graduate and the son of a wealthy automobile executive. To win a Senate seat, Nixon defeated a Hollywood actress who had a privileged background and was a favorite of liberal activists. In both campaigns, Nixon truthfully portrayed his opponents as elites and falsely suggested that they were communist sympathizers. "Every campaign had taught Nixon the same lesson: mobilize resentment against those in power," Garry Wills, a writer who spent time with Nixon, explained.

Once Eisenhower chose Nixon as the vice-presidential nominee in 1952, his anti-elitism helped save his career. Newspaper stories accused Nixon of improperly using campaign donations to underwrite personal expenses, and Eisenhower was leaning toward pushing him off the ticket. (The accusations were largely unfair; Nixon used his expense account less aggressively than Eisenhower or Adlai Stevenson, the Democratic nominee.) To defend himself, Nixon bought a half hour of television time on NBC and delivered a speech that became known for his mention of Checkers, the family dog. "It's essential in this country of ours that a man of modest means can also run for President, because, you know, remember Abraham Lincoln, you remember what he said: 'God must have loved the common people—he made so many of them,'" Nixon told viewers. Many media commentators found the speech to be cringeworthy: the columnist Walter Lippmann, watching with a foreign guest, apologized on behalf of the United States. But most Americans loved it. They flooded the Eisenhower campaign with supportive telegrams and phone calls, and Eisenhower had no choice but to keep Nixon on the ticket.

Robert Ruark, a syndicated columnist from North Carolina with a homey style, offered an insightful analysis. Yes, Nixon's performance was like a soap opera, Ruark wrote in a column shortly after the speech, but life for many Americans also resembled a soap opera. They had debts and had to cope with unexpected crises. "The sophisticates, the dwellers in big cities who live off expense accounts and accrued wealth before present taxes, would be inclined to sneer at Nixon's frank abasement over the huge seeing eye of television," Ruark wrote. Still, Nixon's speech "came closer to humanizing the Republican party than anything that has happened in my memory." Democratic politicians often presented themselves as ordinary Joes, Ruark explained, while Republicans cultivated the aura of supermen. Nixon flipped the script.

The Checkers Speech foreshadowed a reordering of American politics. Democrats had long defined America's class divide in economic terms. Farmers and laborers were on one side, while business executives and financiers were on the other, as one Nixon speechwriter explained. The Checkers speech offered a dichotomy based not so much on economics as on lifestyle and mindset. It pitted "the highbrow and the heretical" against "God-fearing, none-of-your-highfalutin-nonsense, all-American common sense," as a historian wrote. This contrast was vaguer and less connected to government policy, but it resonated with many people, especially in the prosperous years when economic desperation had waned but class envy remained.

Nixon largely abandoned populism while serving as Eisenhower's vice president, but he returned to it in 1968. He closed his acceptance speech at the Republican convention by recounting his humble origins and his setbacks. "You can see why I believe so deeply in the American Dream," he said. "For most of us the American Revolution has been won; the American Dream has come true. And what I ask you to do tonight is to help me make that dream come true for millions to whom it's an impossible dream today."

It is difficult to know the precise mix of reasons that so many voters were drawn to Nixon and Wallace in 1968. For some, racial animosity was no doubt the main reason. In the case of Wallace, his voters at least had to be comfortable with his long history of White supremacy. But when Democrats dismissed Nixon's appeal as based on nothing other than racism dressed up as anti-elitism, they missed a crucial part of the story. They misread the national mood and did Nixon a favor. The clearest proof came from another 1968 candidate, one who wanted to take the country in a very different direction than Nixon did.

ROBERT KENNEDY WAS not an outspoken champion of civil rights early in his political career, but he had become one by 1968. As attorney general earlier in the decade, he increasingly sided with the movement as it gained momentum after the 1960 Greensboro sit-in. It was one of Robert Kennedy's Justice Department deputies who confronted Wallace in the doorway at the University of Alabama. As a New York senator, Kennedy toured rural Mississippi to call attention to poverty there, and he traveled to South Africa to denounce apartheid. After he spoke, a multiracial group of seventeen thousand students responded with a five-minute ovation.

By the eve of the 1968 presidential campaign, Kennedy was the most popular White politician in Black America. In a national poll that asked Black voters to choose among twelve potential candidates, Kennedy finished first and Wallace last. Behind the scenes, King encouraged Kennedy to enter the presidential campaign. The head of the National Welfare Rights Organization—the group that advocated for low-income women and that more affluent feminists had largely ignored—signaled its support in a letter to Kennedy's wife, Ethel. When Kennedy traveled to Black neighborhoods, residents sometimes held signs reading, "Kennedy White But Alright."

King's assassination deepened Kennedy's connection with civil rights. Hearing the news of King's death shortly before he was to give a talk in a Black neighborhood in Indianapolis, Kennedy understood that he would be informing the audience of a hero's murder. He delivered an impromptu speech in which he connected his own rage over his brother's death five years earlier to the rage that so many people felt about King's death. He then asked his listeners to overcome their understandable hatred and dedicate themselves to working toward a more compassionate country. John Lewis, the civil rights activist who was then a Kennedy supporter and had organized the Indianapolis visit, later said, "He had the capacity, perhaps more than any other White politician in America, to sort of vent the feelings and . . . the hopes and the dreams and aspirations of African-Americans." Coincidentally or not, there were no riots in Indianapolis on the night of King's murder. At King's funeral in Atlanta, Kennedy was the only White politician the crowd greeted with cheers when he entered the church.

Kennedy was in Indiana on the night of the assassination because he had decided that the state's upcoming primary would be his first major stand in the campaign. He had entered the race late, at first unwilling to challenge Johnson. By the time of Indiana's primary, the Democratic field seemed to have narrowed to three candidates: Kennedy; Eugene McCarthy, an anti-war senator from Minnesota; and Vice President Hubert Humphrey, who became the closest thing to an incumbent in Johnson's absence. (Humphrey did not formally enter the Indiana primary, but the state's governor, Roger Branigin, did, and voters understood that he was a stand-in who would later transfer his delegates to Humphrey. It was a common practice at the time.)

In this field, Kennedy faced a strategic decision: What kind of coalition should he try to build? He knew he could count on strong support from Black Democrats, but they alone could not carry him to the nomination. Only 9 percent of Indiana's residents were

Black. And it was unclear which White Democrats he should target. One possibility was to pursue the vision that Tom Hayden and the other authors of the Port Huron Statement had described, with a coalition that linked working-class Black voters and young, college-educated progressives. By 1968, campuses were filled with political energy against the Vietnam War, and thousands of students were ready to devote themselves to organizing. These were the bearded protesters Wallace liked to mock, and they were eager to join the fight.

Kennedy decided against this approach. For one thing, he had missed his chance to win over most young activists when he declined to challenge Johnson earlier in the campaign, believing that no challenger could deny the nomination to the incumbent. Many activists understandably thought that Kennedy had prioritized political calculation over principle and viewed him as cowardly. They supported McCarthy, who had entered the race earlier, when Johnson was still running. At Kennedy rallies, pro-McCarthy protesters held up signs reading "Sell out." McCarthy had become the candidate of the New Left, and hundreds of student organizers went to Indiana to campaign for him. Liberal celebrities also supported McCarthy. The singers Peter, Paul, and Mary performed at a rally in Indiana, as did Simon and Garfunkel, who had just released a new album with the hit song "Mrs. Robinson."

Even if Kennedy had been able to win over these educated voters, he understood the arithmetical weakness of the Port Huron vision. He had run a winning national campaign for his brother in 1960, and he was known for his unemotional approach to political analysis. An adjective that many people associated with Robert Kennedy was "ruthless." He knew that college graduates represented a small minority of the population. There were many more votes to be won among the working class. At a meeting with aides at Kennedy's home in northern Virginia shortly after he entered the race, they agreed to pursue a modern version of Franklin Roosevelt's coalition, including farmers, economic progressives, White and Black industrial workers, and immigrants and their descendants. "I think there has to be a new kind of coalition to keep the

Democratic party going, and to keep the country together," Kennedy told an interviewer.

This approach had its own challenges. Blue-collar White voters remained largely supportive of the Vietnam War, making them likely to back Humphrey. Many were moderate or conservative on social issues. Many also viewed the civil rights movement skeptically if not hostilely. In Indiana, Kennedy would be running directly into these challenges. It was one of the states where Wallace had competed in 1964, and he had won roughly a third of Democratic votes in the primary, a surprisingly good showing. Branigin, the governor, had warned Senator Edward Kennedy, Robert's younger brother and a top campaign strategist, that anti-Catholic prejudice remained common in Indiana. In the 1920s, the Ku Klux Klan had signed up more members there than in any other state. In the 1960s, Indiana lagged other Northern states in enacting anti-discrimination laws.

Despite all this, Kennedy—Black America's favorite White politician—had chosen Indiana as the place to prove himself.

THE STANDARD DEMOCRATIC approach to winning over working-class voters was the same in 1968 as it would be in later decades. It involved focusing on economic issues and trying to avoid the social issues on which these voters often held conservative views. McCarthy avoided saying the phrase "law and order," which many liberals considered to be racist code words.

Kennedy thought this approach was madness. He agreed that Wallace and some other politicians were stoking racial animosity, but Kennedy believed that the demagogues would be more likely to succeed if liberals ignored rising crime. It was a real problem, and not only for White Americans. Crime disproportionately beset Black neighborhoods. Democrats needed to speak to people's legitimate fears and concerns, he believed, rather than pretending that they could change the subject and remain credible.

He decided to embrace the idea of law and order, turning it into a central theme of his campaign and developing a message that was progressive without being soft. He described violence as a sickness of the national soul that undermined Americans' shared humanity. He expanded the definition of the problem—and tried to link the fears of White and Black Americans—by talking about the "violence of institutions." It was an acknowledgment of the suffering that many poor Americans, particularly Black Americans, endured at the hands of the police and other parts of the government. Kennedy was also careful to talk about both his belief in law and order and his support for civil rights in every speech he gave. The latter position did not always receive applause from White residents of Indiana, but Kennedy kept repeating it. "We can't tolerate the lawlessness and violence of the riots that take place in our cities," he said during a question-and-answer session with voters, which his campaign turned into a thirty-minute television ad. "I also know in the United States that there's no role and no place for injustice." One of Kennedy's few aides who was from Indiana summarized the combination as "favor civil rights but oppose disorder."

After making clear that he understood the problem of disorder, Kennedy hoped to persuade voters that he was tough enough to solve it. He made self-deprecating allusions to his reputation for ruthlessness and described himself as having served as "the chief law-enforcement officer of the United States," a reference to his time as attorney general. "I promise if elected, I will do all in my power to bring an end to this violence," he told voters. To emphasize his commitment, he said that he cared more about Americans being able to walk their streets safely at night than about any Americans walking on the moon; his brother had started the moon program as president, and it was on the verge of triumph in 1968. In newspapers across Indiana, Kennedy's campaign bought full-page ads containing an open letter from a group of former prosecutors and a former New York City police commissioner. They called Kennedy "the only man seeking the presidency who has the experience, the ability and the compassion to understand and deal effectively not only with the problems of law enforcement, but with the causes of crime." A Kennedy aide joked that he sometimes seemed to be running for sheriff of Indiana.

In later decades, Kennedy would be remembered as more liberal than Democrats who followed him, because of his focus on poverty, economic opportunity, and civil rights. But during his presidential campaign, he upset many liberals. His message sounded strange to them. It sounded tough. Liberal commentators compared it to Barry Goldwater's message from four years earlier. Mary McGrory, a syndicated columnist, called Kennedy "a good Republican." *The New Republic* accused him of using "the euphemisms of the backlash." *The Village Voice* said he offered merely "the illusion of change." A *New York Times* headline read, "Kennedy: Meet the Conservative."

A few of his young, liberal campaign aides brought these criticisms to Kennedy and urged him to stop talking about crime, violence, law, and order. Kennedy overruled them. "We're going to talk about what people will listen to," he said. "You have to get them listening by talking about what they're interested in, before you can start trying to persuade them about other matters." Theodore White, a journalist who was close to the Kennedys, later wrote, "Law-and-order? That was what the *people* wanted him to talk about. Everyone—even the labor unions. The labor people were telling him that their unions were more worried about riots and crime than they were about wages and hours."

The focus on law and order was the core of Kennedy's larger strategy to signal to working-class voters that he stood apart from the New Left. Yes, he thought the Vietnam War was a disaster, but he was no pacificist. He wanted the United States to train the South Vietnamese military and help negotiate a truce. During a speech at Notre Dame in South Bend, Indiana, he called for the end of student draft deferments, which allowed well-off young men to avoid the war while less affluent men were dying. He also tried stylistic appeals to Indiana's voters. Kennedy had his hair cut shorter and made fun of himself for having done so. He stopped wearing his usual tailored suits from a Washington, D.C., haberdasher and instead campaigned in slightly baggy suits that seemed to come off a department store rack. He boasted about how much he and Ethel were doing to support farmers because they had ten children. Kennedy was a millionaire, but he tried to signal to his audiences that he shared their values.

To all these political messages, Kennedy added a similarly populist economic policy. It included several nods to the political center, a recognition that many Americans were wary of government. Kennedy praised "private enterprise" and pointed out that, as a senator, he had pushed for anti-poverty programs that involved private employers. He said that local control of government spending was usually better than centralized control in Washington and that paying jobs were preferable to "welfare handouts." He also criticized some labor leaders as selfish, a stance that was consistent with his history as a Senate staff member in the 1950s who had investigated corruption in the Teamsters.

Overall, though, Kennedy's agenda was strikingly progressive. He left no doubt that he was on the side of people who had less, and he did not mind annoying people who had more. He began his Indiana campaign with a speech focused on hunger, and he frequently reminded his audiences about (as he put it) poor Whites in Appalachia, struggling Indians on reservations, and jobless Negroes in cities. When private companies were not providing enough jobs, he said that government should step in. He asked how the country could own seventy million television sets while children went hungry—"*American* children, starving in *America*." When he campaigned at Indiana University and a medical student asked where the money for Kennedy's proposed expansion of healthcare would come from, he replied, "From you." He added, "You are the privileged ones."

Kennedy called for a minimum tax on the affluent to prevent them from using loopholes to avoid taxes. Referring to tax avoidance by the wealthy, he said, "It's unjust and unreasonable." In one of his campaign brochures, the entire section on tax policy read, "We must reform the flagrant tax loopholes which enable too many Americans to escape their fair share of the cost of shaping our nation's destiny."

Liberal editorialists may have criticized the Kennedy campaign as right wing, but conservatives and business executives understood his economic agenda was more progressive than that of his rivals. The largest newspapers in Indiana—on the orders of their conservative publisher, Eugene Pulliam (the grandfather of an Indiana college student at the time named Dan Quayle, who two decades later became vice president of the United States)—tried to undermine Kennedy's campaign by paying little attention to him in their news coverage and denigrating him in their opinion pages. A cartoon depicted Kennedy as a lecher, and an editorial accused him of being a racist, implying that he was anti-White because of his emphasis on civil rights. Pulliam's newspapers published more favorable coverage of McCarthy, the New Left's preferred candidate. Outside of Indiana, many corporate executives also saw Kennedy as a threat. *Fortune* magazine published a survey of executives showing that Kennedy was the least popular presidential candidate among that group since Franklin Roosevelt.

Kennedy was trying to put together a "have-not coalition," as one reporter covering the campaign wrote. Another writer referred to the approach as "inclusive populism." Unlike many other attempts to build a working-class coalition across racial lines, Kennedy's did not focus only on economic issues and ignore the cultural issues on which so many workers held less liberal views. He embraced those views. He venerated hard work and poked fun at intellectual philosophizing. He considered American power to be a force for good in the world. "He believed in sacrifice, family, community, and love of country," one journalist wrote. As Robert Coles, the child psychiatrist, who worked on Kennedy's campaign, said, "The very qualities that the upper-middle class liberal intelligentsia did not like about him are what working-class White people liked."

Those qualities helped Kennedy win the Indiana primary with 42 percent of the vote, electrifying his campaign. The state's governor, Branigin, the stand-in for Vice President Humphrey, finished second, with 31 percent. McCarthy was third, with 27 percent. Political analysts, historians, and Kennedy's own campaign aides have long debated how successful his working-class appeals were, and there is no question that he failed to win over many of Indiana's White voters. For some, his commitment to civil rights was a dealbreaker, regardless of his other positions. Their refusal to vote for Kennedy was a reminder that the Democratic Party's support for racial equality brought some unavoidable electoral costs. But the magnitude of those costs was not predetermined. The results in Indiana demonstrated that a progressive version of populism could attract a significant share of blue-collar and rural voters who might otherwise be attracted to a candidate like Wallace or Goldwater. And Kennedy did not need to hold on to every part of the New Deal coalition to vindicate his strategy. He needed to hold on to enough to win the primary—and offer an updated model for his party to win general elections.

He succeeded in doing that.

He finished first among Indiana's industrial workers, well ahead of Branigin and McCarthy, according to a survey conducted by Louis Harris, a leading pollster at the time, and Kennedy won Black voters by even more. Among white-collar professionals and highly educated voters, Kennedy finished last and McCarthy first. Not only that, but Harris's polls showed that Kennedy had lost ground among more affluent voters over the course of the Indiana campaign. His message had alienated the well off and appealed to the working class, which is almost always a worthwhile electoral tradeoff given the relative sizes of the two groups. "In a painful era of racial polarization in the U.S.," *Newsweek* magazine wrote days after the Indiana primary, "he managed to bridge the chasm separating the gut elements of the traditional Democratic coalition." Paul Cowan, a progressive writer who had initially supported McCarthy, described Kennedy as "the last liberal politician who could communicate with white working class America."

He had even won most of the counties where Wallace had posted his best showings in Indiana's Democratic primary four years earlier. Kennedy prevailed in Lake County, which included the city of Gary and was the only large Indiana county Wallace had won, as well as in the counties that were home to smaller cities like Anderson and Terre Haute. In the southern part of the state, which bordered Kentucky, Kennedy won seventeen of the twenty-five counties.

Kennedy had recognized a distinction that other Democrats, then and since, missed. Wallace himself may have been irredeemably vile, but many of his supporters were not. They were open to voting for a racist candidate, and they were open to voting for an anti-racist candidate. Their vote depended on more than race. Still other voters who refused to consider Wallace nonetheless believed that disorder was a dire problem. These voters' decisions, in turn, depended on more than pocketbook issues. Democrats could win these voters, but doing so required effort and respect. Ignoring their moderate views on many issues and talking only about economic policy did not qualify.

On the same night Kennedy won Indiana, he won the primary in Washington, D.C., where the electorate was largely Black. In the following weeks, he won Nebraska before losing Oregon to McCarthy and then heading to California for its primary. There, he joined forces with Cesar Chavez and Dolores Huerta, the leaders of another attempt to build a working-class coalition in the 1960s, and together they implemented a West Coast version of the Indiana strategy. Chavez and Huerta formed the "Viva Kennedy" group and went so far as to pause a grape strike so that workers could focus on the campaign. "The poor people are very excited about Senator Kennedy," Chavez said. When student hecklers taunted Kennedy during a rally by asking where he had been when the 1968 presidential campaign began and Johnson was still running, Chavez replied, "He was walking with me in

Cesar Chavez, right, with Senator Robert Kennedy as Chavez ends his hunger strike in support of the United Farm Workers, 1968.

Delano." The line was somewhat beside the point: Kennedy could have entered the presidential race while also supporting California's striking grape pickers, but Chavez did not mean the retort literally. He just wanted to remind people of Kennedy's longtime support for workers.

Kennedy's relationship with labor unions was a microcosm of the schism within organized labor: Established union leaders did not like him. George Meany referred to him as "that jitterbug" (a word associated at the time with immature teenagers), and the AFL-CIO geared up to prevent him from winning the nomination. But many labor reformers who wanted to expand unions to new parts of the workforce supported Kennedy. Chavez and Huerta made their support public, while Walter Reuther worked behind the scenes to help the campaign. Kennedy also received the backing of March Fong Eu, a leader of the Chinese American community and a member of the California State Assembly. Unlike much of the country in 1968, California was home to substantial numbers of Latino and Asian American voters, and they were central to Kennedy's attempt to overcome McCarthy's popularity in the state's suburbs. As in Indiana, the strategy carried Kennedy to a narrow victory.

Kennedy and his aides celebrated the win in a suite at the Ambassador Hotel in Los Angeles on the night of June 4, 1968. When it was time to go down to the ballroom to deliver his victory speech, Kennedy turned to Huerta and asked if she would escort him to the stage. He delivered his celebratory remarks with Huerta and Ethel Kennedy standing next to him. In the speech, Kennedy pointed out that he had won not only heavily urban California that night but also heavily rural South Dakota. "What I think is quite clear," he said, "is that we can work together in the last analysis, and that what has been going on within the United States over the period of the last three years—the division, the violence, the disenchantment with our society; the divisions, whether it's between Blacks and Whites, between the poor and the more affluent, or between age groups or over the war in Vietnam—is that we can start to work together. We are a great country, an unselfish country, and a compassionate country." It was time, he told the crowd, to take their campaign to Illinois, the site of the year's final primary.

He never made it. As he walked through the hotel's kitchen after the speech, Sirhan Sirhan, a Palestinian citizen of Jordan who was angry about Kennedy's support for Israel, shot him three times. It was shortly past midnight in Los Angeles, which made it the first anniversary of the start of the Six-Day War between Israel and Arab countries. Kennedy died in a Los Angeles hospital the next day.

Nobody can know what would have happened in the 1968 election had he lived. Despite his victories, Kennedy was not assured of the Democratic nomination. Humphrey had substantial support among the party's delegates, including those close to Meany and the AFL-CIO leadership. After Kennedy's death, Humphrey won the nomination easily. Kennedy also might have become the Democratic nominee but lost the general election. Voters were frustrated, and he would have been trying to win a third consecutive term for the Democrats. Nixon and Wallace could have used Black voters' enthusiasm for Kennedy to imply that White voters should be wary of him.

Yet it is also reasonable to think that Kennedy might have won the presidency. The general election ended up being close, and Kennedy would have had an easier time distancing himself from Johnson than Humphrey. Kennedy was also more dynamic and more appealing to many swing voters. Tellingly, in the weeks after Kennedy's assassination, Wallace rose in the national polls, suggesting that Kennedy appealed to some voters who did not support most other Democrats at the time.

More than anybody else, Kennedy had tried to forge an alliance across the country's racial divide and between the old left and the New Left. He did so aggressively and joyfully, without apology. He offered a message that mixed toughness and compassion and that tried to redefine American progressivism with both soaring idealism and shrewd pragmatism. He reflected many of the actual views of the working class, and he vowed to make the country's economy more inclusive. When Kennedy died, that effort died with him.

. . .

NIXON, OF COURSE, went on to become the most disgraced American politician of the twentieth century. In retrospect, it can be difficult to remember him in any other way. But for the purposes of understanding American politics—and how politics reshaped the economy—the pre-Watergate version of Nixon is a vital figure. He is the bookend to Franklin Roosevelt. While Robert Kennedy attempted to reshape the Democratic Party's message to protect and update Roosevelt's vision of mass prosperity, Nixon set out to dismantle Roosevelt's majority and construct a different one. Nixon succeeded, too. In many ways, the United States is still living in the Nixon era.

As part of Nixon's 1968 campaign, he set up a small brain trust of political strategists in a Midtown Manhattan building separate from the campaign's main operations. These strategists were supposed to remain focused on the big picture. Among them was Kevin Phillips, a twenty-seven-year-old who had grown up in New York City politics and who believed that Nixon had a historic opportunity.

The Roosevelt coalition—a coalition that helped the Democrats dominate American politics since the 1930s—had grown rickety, Phillips knew. Americans were anxious about the country's condition, and the Democratic Party seemed unable to respond. Johnson had no evident solutions to crime, war, and disorder, much as Herbert Hoover had lacked answers to the Depression decades earlier. The Democrats of the 1960s were also burdened by the New Left's alienation of many voters. Phillips and other Nixon aides were fascinated by a referendum that Madison, Wisconsin, had held early in 1968 about whether the United States should withdraw from Vietnam. Even though Madison was a liberal college town that had been home to anti-war protests, its residents voted against withdrawal. Americans may have been sick of the war, but most did not want outright defeat, either. Nixon began speaking of a "silent center" (which would later become the "silent majority") exhausted by turmoil.

"Who needs Manhattan?" Phillips told an interviewer while

sitting in his Manhattan campaign office. "We don't need the big cities. We don't even want them." Referring to Humphrey, who was Nixon's opponent, and an avenue on Manhattan's Upper West Side, Phillips said, "Sure, Hubert will carry Riverside Drive in November. La-de-dah. What will he do in Oklahoma?" In Phillips's mind, 1968 resembled five previous elections when enduring coalitions had formed: 1800, 1828, 1860, 1896, and 1932. The Nixon campaign had an opportunity to add a sixth election to that list.

Phillips also believed that liberals were naïve about the role of ethnicity in American politics. It was almost as if they wanted to imagine a world in which different cultural groups did not have distinct political opinions and interests. In truth, he thought, race and religion were inescapable parts of democratic politics and always had been. He referred to the subject as "the secret." Phillips's experience in New York politics had taught him that any candidate who set out to win Catholic voters usually hurt himself among Jewish voters. The same was true with Protestants and Catholics. People tended to vote for a candidate they thought was on their side, and cultural identity played an important role in that calculation. By embracing civil rights, Democrats were winning the loyalty of Black voters. That embrace also caused others—like the Irish, Italian, and eastern European voters who had been part of the New Deal coalition—to wonder if Democrats still cared about them.

Phillips recognized that his boss was not a charismatic politician. Yet he thought that Nixon's ordinariness might be an advantage, much as it had been during the Checkers speech and his early campaigns. "In his gut he understood the middle class and the working middle class," another Nixon aide said. "He understood when they felt they were being put upon." Richard Goodwin, an adviser to Democrats who competed against Nixon, said, "He could reach, with uncanny intuition, the buried doubts, the secret dreads, the nightmare panic of the threatened soul." Nixon had figured out how to speak to large sections of the American working class in ways that no other Republican had and in ways that Democrats increasingly struggled to do.

. . .

IN 1968, IT was just enough to win. Nixon won the popular vote by less than 1 percentage point, after Humphrey had made a late surge, aided by his belated efforts to distance himself from Johnson's Vietnam policy. The AFL-CIO also helped Humphrey by running an outreach campaign that criticized both Nixon and Wallace as anti-worker. Still, the race was not as close in the Electoral College. One problem was that Humphrey failed to excite many voters of color, and their turnout declined in much of the country.

Phillips believed that the closeness of the popular vote obscured the true picture. Together, Nixon and Wallace won almost 57 percent of the vote. Shortly after the election, Phillips published a book, *The Emerging Republican Majority,* which proved prescient. The opening sentence declared "the end of the New Deal Democratic hegemony and the beginning of a new era in American politics." Phillips predicted that the New Left forces within the Democratic Party would take it over during Nixon's first term and that Wallace's voters would not return to the Democrats. Inside the White House, Nixon encouraged his aides to read another book with a similar message: *The Real Majority,* by Richard Scammon and Ben Wattenberg, two political analysts. It argued that Democrats had long won the votes of "plain people" through economic appeals but that these appeals were less effective in an affluent society. The battleground had shifted to cultural issues, like patriotism and crime, and Democrats did not speak the cultural language of the mainstream. Democrats mistakenly imagined that the typical voter was a twenty-four-year-old political science instructor at Yale University, Scammon and Wattenberg wrote; in reality, it was a forty-seven-year-old woman married to a machinist in Dayton, Ohio.

As if to follow Phillips's script, the Democratic nominee in 1972 was George McGovern, who ran a New Left–style campaign despite his own humble background and record as a World War II hero. Hollywood celebrities like Warren Beatty, Barbra Streisand, and Peter, Paul, and Mary campaigned for McGovern, and his aides described them as the "Mighty McGovern Art Players." Nixon's campaign caricatured McGovern as the candidate of "the three A's"—acid, abortion, and amnesty (the last being a reference to draft dodgers). McGovern also called for a guaranteed income for all Americans, and the idea was so unpopular that he distanced himself from it before the campaign was over. The plan allowed the Nixon campaign to run a television ad explaining that McGovern would make almost half of all Americans eligible for welfare. With the tagline "Democrats for Nixon," the ad centered on a construction worker in a hard hat eating his lunch, meant to symbolize the workers whose taxes would allow other people not to work. The issue played into an argument that had gained credence during Johnson's War on Poverty—namely, that the Democratic Party had become focused on the poor at the expense of the working class and middle class.

Despite McGovern's stellar record on labor issues, Meany despised him as a figure of the New Left, and the AFL-CIO stayed neutral in the election. It was the first time that the country's largest labor organization had failed to endorse a Democratic presidential nominee since the 1920s. On Election Day, McGovern fared better in affluent neighborhoods like the Upper East Side of Manhattan than working-class neighborhoods like those in Queens, and Nixon won the largest landslide since Franklin Roosevelt's first reelection, in 1936.

Within two years of his 1972 victory, Nixon was gone from Washington, having resigned in disgrace to avoid impeachment and conviction. Yet he had remade American politics. Nixon persuaded millions of working-class Americans to believe that the Republican Party was the "one of us" party. Starting in 1968, Republicans would win five of the next six presidential elections, losing only during the post-Watergate backlash of 1976, and barely losing that year. Nixon wrote the playbook that other Republicans used to dominate this period. With their power, they refashioned the American economy.

CHAPTER 7

A New Way of Looking at
the World

N OT LONG AFTER THE FOUNDING OF A NEW MAGAZINE
called *New York* in 1968, its editors published an essay by
a young writer who was emerging as a signature voice of that city.
His name was Pete Hamill, and he was thirty-three years old.
Hamill's parents had immigrated from Belfast to Brooklyn because, as he wrote, "they believed America was a place where a
human being would be judged on his merits, not his religion." The
oldest of his parents' seven children, Hamill dropped out of high
school to work as a sheet metal apprentice but eventually wrote so
many letters to the editor that the *New York Post,* then a liberal
newspaper, hired him. Hamill's article in *New York* was called
"The Revolt of the White Lower Middle Class," and while he did
not like the term, it was what sociologists had begun using to describe a group that had previously been known as the White working class. These were Hamill's people, residents of the northern tip
of Manhattan and the city's outer boroughs, he explained. He also
informed the magazine's upscale readers that they did not understand quite how unhappy Hamill's compatriots had become.

They felt trapped, Hamill wrote. They were not poor enough
to qualify for welfare, but they made much less money than professionals did. Politicians seemed to care more about those other
groups. Working-class neighborhoods had grown dirty and dangerous, "a dumping ground for abandoned automobiles, which
rust and rot for as long as six weeks before someone from the city
finally takes them away." The air in these neighborhoods was polluted. The White lower middle class had for years sent its sons to
fight in wars and proudly flown American flags in its neighborhoods, but now patriotism was out of fashion because of the Viet-

nam War. Popular culture tended to ignore these "ethnics" and "blue-collar types," Hamill added, except when it mocked them.

The article did not glorify the residents of these neighborhoods. It unstintingly described the racism present in many of them, and Hamill pointed out that the Black working class had it even worse than the White working class. In truth, he wrote, Black and White workers had much in common. His central message was that the fury that had led to riots in Black neighborhoods during the 1960s could soon spread to White neighborhoods. "A large reason for the growing alienation of the white working class is their belief that they are not respected," Hamill wrote. "For now, they see a terrible unfairness in their lives, and an increasing lack of personal control over what happens to them. And the result is growing talk of revolt."

Hamill's article, published in the spring of 1969, quickly made its way to the White House, where Nixon was in his first few months in office. As Nixon had been as a younger man—nicknamed "Iron Butt" by his Duke Law School classmates for his study habits—he remained a dedicated reader as president, and he found Hamill's article compelling. It offered the same diagnosis that Nixon's 1968 campaign strategists had. Nixon directed his aides to circulate the magazine article among the White House staff. Now that he was the president, rather than just a candidate, he would have to decide what to do about this working-class frustration.

This chapter will tell the story of how Nixon ultimately followed an approach similar to that of Dwight Eisenhower, the only previous Republican president since World War II. Both endorsed a version of democratic capitalism in which the government played a central role in trying to raise living standards. In doing so, Nixon reflected the prevailing culture among business executives and Republican politicians, the same culture that Paul Hoffman, George Romney, and Eisenhower had shaped. This was the culture that accepted relatively high taxes rates for the wealthy, a strong safety net, substantial government regulation of business, and limited confrontations with labor unions. It treated the American economy as fundamentally sound, and it emphasized moderation in the name of the national interest.

President Richard Nixon greets workers at the National Steel and Shipbuilding Company, 1972.

Within just a few years, however, this culture would change. With it, the Republican Party's economic agenda would change, and so would the nation's economy. The country abandoned the long post–New Deal consensus and replaced democratic capitalism with rough-and-tumble capitalism. The transformation came to be known as the Reagan revolution, and it happened quickly.

Moderation dominated the Republican Party's approach to economics through the Nixon and Gerald Ford presidencies. As late as 1976, when Ronald Reagan failed to wrest the nomination from Ford, the old consensus reigned. By 1980, moderation was passé. The revolution that occurred during those four years has shaped the American economy ever since.

AFTER NIXON READ Hamill's article, the job of responding to working-class alienation fell to the secretary of labor, George Shultz, an economist by training. Shultz, in turn, asked Jerome Rosow, an assistant labor secretary, to study the problem. Rosow was a classic figure of the postwar corporate world. He had served in the army and then held a series of civilian jobs at the Pentagon before joining Standard Oil of New Jersey (which later changed its name to Exxon). He had worked his way up to a middle-management post in London in 1969 when Shultz, who had met him while doing economic consulting work for Standard Oil, asked him to come to Washington. At first, Rosow demurred. "I was a registered Democrat and I didn't believe that the Nixon Administration would be too happy with me as an assistant secretary," he said. But Shultz wanted him and asked Nixon to approve the appointment. Nixon did, urging Shultz to hire the best people regardless of political affiliation. One of Rosow's first assignments was to write a report that offered a rigorous analysis of the problems that Hamill had described as well as potential solutions. The result, known as the Rosow Report, was a clairvoyant analysis of the country's emerging class divide.

Unlike many other analysts of working-class anger at the time, Rosow paid significant attention to both women and Black workers. His first paragraph argued that the non-White working class "shares the same concern as white workers for law and order and other middle-class values." Both White and Black workers, Rosow wrote, were struggling with state and local taxes that were higher on them than on the rich. Inflation was also a problem, having risen to 5 percent in 1969. Families often found their expenses rising as their children reached teenage years, which tended to be the same time that their incomes were leveling off because the creeping effects of middle age made blue-collar work more difficult. Working-class women, for their part, had a hard time contributing to family income because of sex discrimination and high childcare costs. The problems seemed likely to persist in future generations because relatively few children in these families were among the growing number of college graduates.

Adding to their anxiety, working-class Americans were hearing the message that they were part of a fading culture. "To a considerable extent, they feel like 'forgotten people'—those for whom the government and the society have limited, if any, direct concern and little visible action," Rosow wrote. He elaborated:

The American working man has lost relative class status with the growth of higher education. Changes in the nature of the labor force have dramatized the professional and technical experts to the relative detriment of the skilled worker. Skilled workers also have hostility toward those below them at semi-skilled and un-skilled levels and the feeling is mutual. But all blue-collar work-ers, skilled or not, have been denigrated so badly—so harshly—that their jobs have become a last resort, instead of decent, respected careers. Manual and skilled occupations have become almost in-visible in terms of the propaganda of today. Fathers hesitate—and even apologize—for their occupations instead of holding it up as an aspiration for their sons.

To address the problem, Rosow called for a range of policies, including expansions of community colleges, mass transit, afford-able housing, and disability insurance. He also pointed out that some of Nixon's existing domestic proposals would help: The ad-ministration's tax plan would cut taxes for middle-earning fami-lies, and an initiative called the Family Assistance Plan would expand childcare for mothers on welfare. Both programs, Rosow argued, could be broadened to benefit more people.

The report was intended to be internal, but it soon leaked to the media. Once that happened, it sparked an intense debate inside the Nixon administration over what the federal government should do about blue-collar anomie. On one side were most of Nixon's advisers, including Rosow and Shultz. On the other was a gregari-ous Texan named Charls E. Walker.

THE POLITICAL CULTURE of American business has never been uni-form. Since the early industrial days of the nineteenth century, there have always been executives who favored a freewheeling ver-sion of capitalism and a more confrontational approach to work-ers and government regulators. They have argued that American power and prosperity depend on free-market dynamism; to do anything else is to imitate European-style socialism. Until the 1920s, this philosophy dominated American business (with excep-tions for the support of tariffs that protected companies from for-eign competition). During World War II, corporate moderates began to win more battles. But the rough-and-tumble approach never went away. Its adherents, like the du Pont family of Delaware, financed sympathetic advocacy groups, radio shows, and magazines during the 1940s and 1950s. And this faction won some victories, like the Taft-Hartley Act of 1947, which made it difficult for labor unions to expand into the South. Still, the rough-and-tumble advocates lost more battles than they won during these years. When Eisenhower's conservative critics, including his brother Edgar, complained that he was following in Roosevelt's footsteps, they expressed the frustration that stemmed from defeat.

Charls Walker was not a laissez-faire true believer, but he was sympathetic to parts of the argument. He was born in 1923 in Graham, Texas, about 120 miles west of Dallas, and his mother left the letter *e* out of his first name in the hope that it would lead people to call him Charls, which seemed more distinguished than Charlie. Walker's grandfather had been a successful oil prospector, and Walker grew up in Texas's business culture, where unions were weak and executives tended to be conservative. Although his family struggled financially after his father died young, his mother still owned enough oil-producing land to send Walker to the University of Texas, where he studied economics as an undergraduate and then a graduate student.

More social than many academics, he found himself drawn to a job at the Federal Reserve Bank of Dallas after graduate school, rather than a faculty position. At the Fed, he traveled the region working with bankers to keep credit markets functioning smoothly. "A tall, lean and balding Texan," as a newspaper profile described him, "with oversized L.B.J. ears and a Bob Hope ski nose," Walker soon became a prominent figure in banking circles. He enjoyed talking with business associates over bourbon-and-water cocktails, and he was a licensed pilot who visited his Texas vacation home by landing an amphibious plane on Possum Kingdom Lake.

From the Fed, Walker moved to Eisenhower's Treasury Department and later to a job as the top lobbyist for the American Bankers Association. Those two jobs introduced him to the political and corporate elite. He belonged to Burning Tree Country Club in Maryland, the club where Eisenhower, George Meany, and other Washington grandees played golf. Soon, Walker was on a first-name basis with powerful members of Congress and younger officials on the rise like George H. W. Bush and Paul Volcker. One rising politician, Lyndon Johnson, described Walker as an "S.O.B. with elbows." Walker reveled in the description. "Where I come from, that's a term of endearment," he said. Despite his mother's wishes, his friends and business associates called him Charlie.

On the political spectrum, Walker was on the conservative side of mainstream corporate America. He spoke frequently about the importance of economic stability and sometimes favored tax increases to hold down the deficit, much as Eisenhower did. But Walker also believed that companies should fight for their interests. He worried that the economy was becoming unbalanced during the 1950s and 1960s, with big companies too weak and labor unions and government agencies too strong. In speeches representing the banking industry, he warned of the country's "awesome" tax burden and "seemingly inexorable rise" in federal spending. At times, Walker did battle with Wright Patman, a populist member of Congress from Texas who was Washington's most aggressive advocate for antitrust enforcement. Walker, by contrast, thought that big companies were not powerful enough.

In 1969, after Nixon's election, Walker left his job as a lobbyist to return to the Treasury Department, this time as undersecretary, one of the department's top jobs. From that perch, Walker became the leader of a group of officials within the Nixon administration who argued for a more aggressive approach to economic policy. After the Rosow Report circulated, these officials set out to undermine it. Tom Charles Huston, a young conservative activist who had joined Nixon's White House as a speechwriter, described the report as a blueprint for a bigger welfare state, which he did not mean as a compliment. Trying to bolster the conservatives, *The Wall Street Journal* editorial board, long an advocate of rough-and-tumble capitalism, devoted an editorial to criticizing the Rosow Report as wrongheaded and depressing.

Walker channeled ideas like these into a counterproposal that he sent to Nixon in a five-page memo in November 1970. He urged the president to take a more confrontational approach toward organized labor and help elect business-oriented candidates to Congress. Cracking down on unions had both economic and political benefits, Walker told the president. New laws and regulations that reduced unions' bargaining power could spark a virtuous cycle. Smaller wage increases could allow business to slow price increases. With inflation falling, the Fed could stop raising interest rates, and unemployment, which was starting to rise, might fall. Just as important—especially to Nixon, who enjoyed political maneuvering more than economic policymaking—unions were one of the main forces that seemed likely to be working against Nixon's 1972 reelection. If Nixon pursued anti-union policies, he could weaken one of his biggest political enemies.

"The legitimate question is whether or not this Administration should 'take off the gloves,' and enter open battle," Walker wrote. His memo made his answer clear. "There is therefore little to lose—and perhaps much to gain—by getting 'tougher.'"

Nixon scrawled "I agree" on some of Walker's individual points, adding a caveat: "But with us on National Defense." Union leaders, and Meany in particular, continued to support the Vietnam War, which meant a great deal to Nixon. The most telling reaction from the president appeared on the memo's cover sheet. He listed three of his top economic advisers—Shultz, James Hodgson, and Charles Colson—and wrote next to their names, "What are your views on this?"

All were on the other side of this debate from Walker. Schultz, before joining the government, had developed a reputation as one of the country's best mediators between labor and management. Inside the Nixon administration, he was known as a member of the more liberal faction. Hodgson, the new labor secretary, held similarly moderate views. And Colson was a White House aide whom Nixon had assigned to cultivate labor leaders, in the hope of splitting off some of them from supporting Democrats in 1972 and ensuring Nixon's reelection. Earlier in 1970, Colson had worked behind the scenes to encourage the so-called Hard Hat Riot, a pro–Vietnam War rally by construction workers in New

228   The Fall

York. (Colson's affinity for the dark side of politics later led him to hire E. Howard Hunt, a former CIA agent, to spy on Nixon's political opponents. As part of that assignment, Hunt led a June 1972 break-in of the Democratic National Committee headquarters in the Watergate building.) Nixon loved the construction workers' demonstration and hosted its organizers in the Oval Office, where they presented him with a hard hat.

In Colson's response to the Walker memo, he explained why a "take the gloves off" strategy would be a mistake. "I agree with what George Shultz recommended some weeks ago," Colson wrote, "an 'even-handed approach' by this Administration to labor and business." Many union leaders and members were more politically moderate than the Democratic Party, and the administration could work with them, Colson argued. Union members were not the extreme figures of the past, trying to restructure American society. "They want to protect the system in which they have now acquired a vital stake," he wrote. "Labor is today middle America. It is no longer resentful over what it has not; it is concerned with protecting what it has." If anything, Colson concluded, blue-collar union members offered Nixon his best opportunity for expanding his support beyond the 43 percent of Americans who had voted for him in 1968.

Nixon never explicitly resolved this debate. He did not publicly endorse the Rosow Report. Most of its specific proposals did not become law, and Nixon had an up-and-down relationship with labor unions during his presidency. Still, Nixon's record left no doubt about the outcome of the struggle for control of economic policy inside his administration. Rosow's side won, and Walker's side lost.

Nixon governed as an economic moderate. When members of Congress began working on progressive legislation, Nixon often looked for ways to moderate their proposals instead of blocking them—and then take credit for them. He raised the capital gains tax (the main tax on stock holdings) and created the alternative minimum tax, which limited the number of deductions that the affluent could use. That tax was a gentler version of the one on which Robert Kennedy had campaigned. Nixon increased Social

Security benefits and food stamps, as well as federal funding for education, medical research, and the arts. He oversaw the creation of the Environmental Protection Agency and the Occupational Safety and Health Administration. He tried, but failed, to pass both a large expansion of health insurance and the Family Assistance Plan mentioned in the Rosow Report, which would have increased anti-poverty funding. The tax credits in the Family Assistance Plan later became the model for the earned income tax credit, which has since become a major way the federal government redistributes income.

Despite his selection of Agnew as vice president and Nixon's own use of slurs in private, he even governed as a moderate on several issues related to racial and gender inequality. He made clear to his southern supporters that he would enforce the law on school desegregation, against their wishes; Tom Wicker, a Nixon biographer and longtime liberal columnist at *The New York Times*, concluded that more southern desegregation occurred under Nixon than under Eisenhower, Kennedy, and Johnson combined. Nixon endorsed "self-determination" for Native Americans, reversing long-standing federal policy that gave tribes more control over their affairs. He signed Title IX, barring sex-based discrimination in schools, which changed the lives of millions of American girls. As Herbert Stein, one of Nixon's economic advisers, said, "Probably more new regulation was imposed on the economy during the Nixon administration than in any other presidency since the New Deal."

Nixon also continued to court labor unions. On May 4, 1972, a handful of union leaders came to see him and Colson in the Oval Office, and Nixon opened the meeting by lavishly thanking them for their stance on foreign policy. "I just want to say while you're here in a bunch that I'm very grateful above all for the support," Nixon told them. "The most important thing is we need people, at a time when there are so many softies in this country, who have a bigger dedication to the principles of—well, just basic character that we need. And your fellows, whatever issue has come up in terms of a strong or a weak America, an America that is going to surrender, an America that is going to see something through, you've always come on the right side, and I appreciate it." He added that the support would run both ways. "We don't want the impression that this administration is pro-big business and anti-labor," Nixon told his guests. "The only way we can do it frankly is to have a good relationship."

Walker had asked Nixon to take the gloves off with organized labor, but Nixon instead extended his hand in friendship. The long era of economic moderation continued. The culture had not yet shifted.

YET THERE WAS a rising intellectual movement trying to shift it.

The center of this movement was at the University of Chicago. During the 1930s and 1940s, the university had begun to attract a growing number of young economists who considered themselves classical liberals, in the European meaning of the term. They were skeptical of government, and they valorized the efficiency of the free market. They drew inspiration from the eighteenth-century writings of Adam Smith and David Ricardo and the nineteenth-century emergence of the Austrian school of economics. Among the researchers who arrived at Chicago in the 1930s were a brother and sister named Aaron and Rose Director, Jewish immigrants from present-day Ukraine, who had grown up in Portland, Oregon. The Directors became two of the most influential figures in classical liberalism even though neither published much academic work under their own name.

Having studied in London with Friedrich Hayek, a leader of the Austrian school, Aaron convinced the University of Chicago Press to publish Hayek's recent book, *The Road to Serfdom*, in the United States in 1944. It was a jeremiad warning that Britain's use of government planning to run the economy was leading the country toward totalitarian control. Despite being published by an academic press, the book attracted a wide audience, thanks partly to excerpts published by *Reader's Digest*. After Aaron persuaded Rose to join him at Chicago, she met and married another student there, Milton Friedman. Rose recognized the importance of spreading their ideas beyond the academy, and she pushed Friedman to do so. In later decades, she edited and rewrote his work—initially under only his name, later under both of their names—into books intended for a general audience. They sold millions of copies.

The central idea of classical liberalism, which came from Adam Smith, revolved around voluntary exchange. "If an exchange between two parties is voluntary," Milton and Rose Friedman wrote, summarizing Smith, "it will not take place unless both believe they will benefit from it." If one person hires another, it is because both think they gain from working together. One will receive productive work, the other income and experience. The same logic applies to a consumer buying an item from a shopkeeper. One will gain a valuable item, the other money. Multiply these voluntary exchanges—which make up the market economy—and human well-being increases.

Crucial to this system is the language that people use to communicate in a market economy: the language of prices. A price signals how much one person values an item and allows other people to decide if they want to engage in a voluntary exchange. Over time, prices change, enabling a society to produce more of what people want. If a baby boom causes a run on pencils used by schoolchildren, as the Friedmans explained in one of their favorite examples, pencil prices will rise, and companies will start to make more pencils. If the existing pencil companies cannot keep up with demand, an entrepreneur can start a new company, providing jobs for workers and pencils for children. If that company finds a more efficient way to make pencils, it can cut prices and gain market share, allowing families to spend less of their money on pencils and more on other items, raising their standard of living. Prices, by incorporating a vast array of information across the market's voluntary exchanges, allow people to make rational decisions. Prices make possible the magic of Smith's invisible hand.

The biggest problem in modern economies, the Chicago economists argued, was that outside forces too often interfered with the price system. "Anything that prevents prices from expressing freely the conditions of demand or supply interferes with the transmission of accurate information," the Friedmans wrote. The most common source of this interference was the government. Government imposed rules on business, artificially raising the price of desired goods and thereby reducing their production. Government protected labor unions to the detriment of workers not in a union. Government prevented human beings from immigrating from the country where they were born to the country of their choice, further limiting voluntary exchange. Government taxed successful people to redistribute income and create welfare benefits, and incomes were just another form of prices. Without high tax rates, the hypothetical pencil entrepreneur might work harder, manufacture more pencils, and discover new innovations.

Classical liberals did not believe in eliminating all government interference, but they thought that such meddling should be kept to a minimum. In postwar America, the amount of interference was clearly much more extensive. Chicago's economists devoted their careers to arguing that the government bureaucrats who imagined that they could outwit the genius of the price system were wrong. Throughout the 1950s and 1960s, this argument failed to win over many converts. The economy was thriving. Americans saw no reason to abandon the policies that had helped create the prosperity. But the Chicago economists believed that this prosperity could not last. And whenever the next economic crisis occurred, they would be ready to make their case.

AS WORLD WAR II was winding down, Elizabeth Bork was becoming concerned about her only child. He seemed to be drifting toward far-left politics. Elizabeth, a schoolteacher in Pittsburgh, and her husband, Harry, a purchasing agent for a steel company, were New Deal Democrats. Their son, Robert Heron Bork, known as Bob, was attracted to something more radical. He identified as a socialist and once brought a high school friend to a local meeting of the Communist Party.

Throughout Bob's childhood, Elizabeth had been his intellectual mentor, encouraging him to read highbrow magazines like the *Saturday Review* and debate books with her. "My mother and I used to argue far into the night about all kinds of things," Bob Bork said later. "My father would yell down at us from the bed-

Robert Bork (second from left) with Edward Levi (seated, left) and Aaron
Director (seated, right) at a law and economics conference at the University of
Chicago, 1953.

room: 'This is not a debating society. Go to sleep!' " As Bob's flirtation with socialism continued, Elizabeth asked one of his teachers how she could ensure that he would wrestle with a range of ideas when he went to college. The teacher suggested that the Borks look at the University of Chicago, where its dynamic president, Robert Hutchins, had created an exciting intellectual environment. Hutchins encouraged students to read great works of literature, history, and philosophy and to debate them vigorously. Hutchins also encouraged students to engage with the world and made sure the university that he ran did so as well. He helped launch the Committee for Economic Development with Paul Hoffman during World War II and contributed to the development of the atomic bomb.

The young Bork enrolled at Chicago, first as an undergraduate in the late 1940s and then, after serving in the marines, as a law student. In college, he again began to consider himself a liberal Democrat and admired Adlai Stevenson, Illinois's governor. In law school, however, Bork started to work with a new mentor, Aaron Director, one of the first economists to join the law school faculty.

Director was brilliant and spirited. He asked students to challenge accepted wisdom. He had a grand theory of how the world should work: with as little government involvement in the economy as possible. Over tea, beers, and meals with his students, he pointed out logical flaws in the arguments made by the advocates of regulation and taxation. Bork soon found Director's unified theory appealing, much as he had once found socialism appealing. "It was a new way of looking at the world, and an enormously rigorous and logical way," Bork said, "a method that seemed to promise further explanations of things if one pursued it." Working with Director, Bork added, was "a little bit like a conversion experience."

Director and his fellow classical liberals seemed to have fun with their ideas. They were not boring academics. At one point, after Milton Friedman traveled to the Soviet Union and sent home a postcard with Karl Marx on the front, Director and George Stigler, another Chicago economist, wondered why there were no postcards in the United States with the heroes of capitalism. They decided to have an Adam Smith postcard made. But the press they found insisted on printing a minimum of five different postcards and charged them only modestly more to buy hundreds of these postcards than to buy a few. Responding rationally to these incentives, Director and Stigler ordered two thousand sets of five postcards, depicting Smith, Ricardo, John Stuart Mill, Alfred Marshall, and Henry Simons. In subsequent years, Director would often send Bork short notes on one of the postcards.

Director brimmed with ideas for research papers but rarely wrote any himself. He preferred suggesting topics to students and then overseeing their work. One of his biggest ideas involved antitrust laws: He believed that they were counterproductive. Big companies, like Rockefeller's Standard Oil, which the government had broken up, were often more efficient than small companies. This efficiency allowed them to sell their goods at lower prices. Antitrust regulators worried that a large company could use its market power to raise prices after having driven out the competition, but Director believed this worry was overblown. If a company raised prices artificially, a competitor could enter the market and win over customers with lower prices. Director encouraged Bork to dig into the subject, and Bork stayed at the University of Chicago for a year after law school to work on a law review article about antitrust.

While doing so, he benefited from the school's tough-love approach to big ideas and political engagement. He received help from both Director and Edward Levi, the law school's dean (and a future attorney general), who told Bork that he needed to write more clearly. "I cannot believe that you cannot polish this paper," Levi wrote to Bork about an early draft. "It is preposterous that this is not better written." Levi added: "If necessary, you ought to take two hours on every paragraph and perhaps a day or so on some of them. I feel most strongly about this."

Antitrust came to dominate the early stages of Bork's legal career, and his writings ultimately overturned the consensus on the subject in both academia and government. The paper that Levi and Director had helped him write, published in *The University of Chicago Law Review,* attracted attention from established scholars around the country. In it, Bork argued that regulators were usually wrong to worry about "vertical integration"—a term that described the merger between two companies operating in different parts of an industry, such as a manufacturer and a distributor. These mergers did not create antitrust problems, he wrote. Both parts of the business would still face the rigors of market competition.

Soon after the paper's 1954 publication, Bork took a job at Kirkland & Ellis, a Chicago law firm, where he defended companies in antitrust cases. After becoming a partner there, he decided that he missed academic life—"the leisure of the theory class," as he joked—and began looking for a job as a law professor. Levi wrote letters to his faculty contacts around the country, urging them to hire Bork, and Yale Law School soon offered Bork a position. He eagerly accepted, even though it cut his income by about two-thirds. At Yale, Bork published more papers and, eventually, a book on antitrust, *The Antitrust Paradox: A Policy at War with Itself.*

All the while, Director remained a mentor. He sent letters and postcards, complimenting Bork's work, suggesting new ideas, mocking their intellectual opponents, and simply checking in. After Bork joined the Yale faculty, Director sent Bork a note teasing him for still addressing his elder as "Professor Director." Subsequently, Bork began to use "Aaron."

Like his mentor, Bork reveled in the world of ideas. He could be a generous mentor himself, going out of his way to help younger colleagues. Six feet tall, with curly red hair and, later, a beard, he smoked heavily and drank martinis. He liked debating people with whom he disagreed and co-taught a seminar at Yale Law School that revolved around him and another professor disagreeing in front of students. Years later, *The Washington Post* would describe Bork as having "uncommon charm, intellect, introspection and emotion."

Bork's views were not uniformly conservative. As a young lawyer at Kirkland & Ellis, he had risked his career to confront the partners about their refusal to promote a Jewish associate. The partners yielded, and the man eventually rose to become the firm's managing partner. Bork also broke publicly with other conservatives when he thought their arguments were legally weak. Although he also worried about government spending, he opposed a constitutional amendment that would have required a balanced budget, a favorite conservative idea in the 1970s. (During a war or recession, a balanced budget can be ruinous, preventing a government from taking immediate action to solve an emergency.) Bork also opposed a bill that would have classified a fetus as a person, despite his belief that *Roe v. Wade* represented a major overreach by the Supreme Court. "The deformation of the Constitution is not properly cured by further deformation," Bork explained.

But while Bork had many admirers, he also had detractors. Famously disorganized, he struggled to keep up with the paperwork of his various jobs and frequently had to apologize to colleagues for being so late to respond to questions. His intellectual confidence could lapse into arrogance. Once, at the end of an interview, Steve Lohr, a *New York Times* reporter, asked Bork, "Would it be accurate to describe you as a leading antitrust expert?"

"Yes," Bork replied, "but I would change the *a* to *the*."

Despite his occasional political unorthodoxy, Bork considered himself part of a movement. He was a member of the Chicago School, and he and his fellow laissez-faire believers wanted to persuade the country that the old left-wing status quo embraced by government officials, union leaders, intellectuals, and college students was wrong. After giving a graduation speech in the 1970s at Carleton College in Minnesota, he sent a transcript to the conservative columnist George Will and added a note: "The president tells me it stirred up the animals." Bork recognized that he was engaged in a political struggle. He intended to win it.

TO BORK AND the Chicago School, antitrust law had become the primary way in which the government distorted the price system.

Antitrust had its roots in America's historical skepticism of large institutions, a tradition that included Thomas Jefferson, Andrew Jackson, and Theodore Roosevelt. Many Americans had long worried about private enterprises becoming so large that they would inhibit freedom. "The avenues to wealth and preferment are continually blocked by the greed of combinations of men and by monopolists, and individual effort and initiative are thus discouraged," one of the founders of the American Economic Association, which would become the field's premier professional group, wrote in 1886. The government, he argued, needed to take actions "to keep the avenues open for those who would gain a livelihood by their own exertions." The same idea guided political leaders during the Progressive Era and led to the passage of the Sherman and Clayton antitrust acts. After World War II, skepticism of corporate concentration guided the reconstruction of Europe's economy, as Eisenhower and Truman ordered the breakup of German conglomerates like IG Farben, out of a belief that their power had contributed to the rise of fascism. In the United States, the Supreme Court under Chief Justice Earl Warren expanded the reach of antitrust regulators during the 1950s and 1960s. With their new authority, the regulators restrained American capitalism.

One example was a government order requiring AT&T to

share its transistor technology with rivals to prevent the company from dominating the nascent electronics industry, as the author Binyamin Appelbaum has noted. In response to pressure from regulators, AT&T brought engineers from smaller companies to its New Jersey headquarters in 1952 to demonstrate the technology. In the years that followed, the companies given access to that technology helped create Silicon Valley. A similar federal mandate required IBM to invite other companies to write software for IBM computers. As a result, Paul Allen and Bill Gates, two childhood friends from Seattle, were able to start a new software company in 1975, then called Micro-Soft. For decades, antitrust enforcement has been associated with both freedom and prosperity.

Bork took a darker view of antitrust regulation. He agreed that it was sometimes vital: Rivals should not be allowed to conspire to set prices, and a company could theoretically become so big as to be economically dangerous. But he believed that actual monopolies were rare. Bork pointed out that the Supreme Court's antitrust standards were nebulous, lacking a clear definition of excessive market power. In one decision, the court had prevented a merger between two shoe companies out of concern that they would have an unfair advantage if they combined. Bork considered that notion ludicrous, given that one had a market share of 4 percent and the other of 1 percent.

Bork thought that the only rigorous way to conduct antitrust policy was to base it on the language of capitalism: the price system. If a merger could be proved to lead to higher prices, it was harmful. But few mergers truly led to higher prices, he argued. Most mergers were beneficial, in Bork's view. They created economies of scale, which allowed companies to cut the cost of manufacturing, distribution, and marketing. With their costs reduced, the companies could sell their goods for less. If a large company did try to charge artificially high prices, the market would solve the problem, Bork believed. Had the two shoe companies been allowed to merge and tried to exploit consumers, they would have failed, he argued. A competitor could have charged lower prices, stolen market share, and still made a profit. Otherwise, the American economy would have been dominated by the same companies for many generations. It wasn't. Old behemoths faded, and new ones emerged.

As a lawyer at Kirkland & Ellis, Bork had seen how much time and effort his corporate clients devoted to adhering to antitrust policy. As a law professor, he continued to advise companies on the side. He came to believe that antitrust was part of a larger problem. Government regulation of business had mushroomed in the postwar decades. Ralph Nader's consumer movement had been particularly influential, successfully pushing for laws protecting personal safety, the environment, and more. Director, Bork, and the Chicago School believed that much of this legislation was needlessly paternalistic and that consumers usually understood their interests better than bureaucrats. "A free economy, within obvious limits, produces greater wealth for people in general than a planned economy does," Bork said. If a product was unsafe, people would not buy it.

The new regulations lowered living standards by needlessly raising the cost of many items, according to the Chicago School. In one of Director's handwritten letters to Bork, he encouraged his former student to consider writing an article about the problems that would flow from a new consumer law that Congress was considering in the 1960s. "The title," Director wrote, "should be the consumer law is socialism."

Parts of Bork's argument were reasonable. Antitrust policy in the postwar decades could be arbitrary. The merger of two modest-sized shoe companies was surely less threatening than the Supreme Court feared. But Bork's philosophy had its own blind spots. It was based on the notion that the real world operated much as the elegant theories of academic economists imagined. If a company tried to take advantage of its customers by charging an artificially high price or selling an unsafe product, Bork claimed that market competition would quickly solve the problem: A new company would enter the market and customers would flock to it. In truth, the world often did not work this way. Consumers did not always have enough information to act in their own best interests. And big business could sometimes amass enough political and economic power to prevent new rivals from entering the market.

For decades, advocates of a forceful antitrust policy had viewed it as a way to constrain the power of large corporations. Bork dismissed this concern. For one academic paper, he studied the legislative history of the Sherman Act of 1890 and argued that even its authors had not been worried about corporate bigness for its own sake. They were focused on economic efficiency and what Bork called "consumer welfare" rather than corporate power, Bork wrote. Other historians soon debunked this argument and documented that the Sherman Act was indeed an attempt to limit the size of companies, but Bork continued to make his case. Corporations were much less powerful than their critics thought, he claimed. If anything, they were too weak, and government had grown too strong.

OTHER CONSERVATIVES SHARED this view in the 1970s. They were alarmed by the growth of regulation and called for more aggressive efforts to reverse it. Their alarm often focused on Nader, whose advocacy had made possible much of the regulation that Nixon had signed. "Perhaps the single most effective antagonist of American business is Ralph Nader, who—thanks largely to the media—has become a legend in his own time and an idol of millions of Americans," Lewis Powell, a corporate lawyer in Richmond, Virginia, and a member of Philip Morris's board of directors, wrote in a 1971 memo. Powell had become worried about corporate America's political weakness and frequently complained to his neighbor, who happened to be a top official at the U.S. Chamber of Commerce, about it. The neighbor told Powell to put his thoughts in writing.

The result was a thirty-four-page manifesto, meant to persuade the Chamber to take action. "The American economic system is under broad attack," Powell wrote. "We are not dealing with episodic or isolated attacks from a relatively few extremists or even from the minority socialist cadre. Rather, the assault on the enterprise system is broadly based and consistently pursued. It is gaining momentum and converts." In the face of this assault, most executives had responded with apathy, Powell continued. They went on the defensive rather than confronting their opponents.

Powell's memo laid out a strategy for fighting back. The Chamber could insist that colleges devote equal time to explaining the benefits of the free-enterprise system. It could establish a speakers' bureau to send pro-business lecturers to campuses and could monitor television, newspapers, and scholarly journals for anti-business bias. Individual companies could devote a portion of their advertising budgets to defending capitalism rather than pitching specific products. Most important, corporate America should try to shape government policy. "Business must learn the lesson, long ago learned by Labor and other self-interest groups," he wrote. "This is the lesson that political power is necessary; that such power must be assiduously cultivated; and that when necessary, it must be used aggressively and with determination—without embarrassment and without the reluctance which has been so characteristic of American business." This effort to build political power would cost money, he acknowledged, but it could save businesses much more.

The memo echoed the arguments that Walker had made privately to Nixon the previous year: Business should take off the gloves. Government and labor were becoming too powerful. Europe and Japan were becoming more competitive. "Business leaders like Paul Hoffman," the journalist John Judis has written, "attempted to be above both party and class." That approach had worked in previous decades. Powell and Walker believed that it no longer did. In the face of increasing government regulation and growing global competition, American business needed to fight harder to protect its interests.

Powell's memo had an immediate impact, but only on a small number of executives and lobbyists. It helped persuade several right-wing business owners who had inherited companies from their families, including Joseph Coors and the Koch brothers, to donate money for think tanks that would promulgate their views. Both the Cato Institute and the Heritage Foundation were established with help from these donations. Executives at larger companies, meanwhile, began taking gradual steps to become more involved in politics. The National Association of Manufacturers soon moved its headquarters from New York to Washington. The chairmen of General Electric and Alcoa traveled to Washington to meet with Walker and several other top Nixon administration officials about corporate America's political problems. Walker and his colleagues told the executives that they should start a new organization composed of major chief executives who were willing to take the time to personally lobby Congress, the White House, and cabinet departments. The executives agreed to do so, and the result was the Business Roundtable, which became one of corporate America's most effective interest groups.

Powell himself also decided to become more political. In 1969, two years before writing his manifesto, he had turned down Nixon's offer of a Supreme Court nomination. The seat instead went to Harry Blackmun, who became one of a handful of Republican-appointed justices during the second half of the twentieth century to vote on the liberal side of many cases. Powell had said no in 1969 because he enjoyed his private practice in Virginia, and it paid much more than a seat on the court. But he was torn. The month after he sent the memo, two more court vacancies opened up, and this time Powell accepted Nixon's nomination. He decided it was his duty to the country.

Just as notable as what changed after Powell's memo, however, was what did not.

Most chief executives continued to remain distant from politics. Into the mid-1970s, only six hundred registered lobbyists worked in Washington. Today, more than twelve thousand do. Corporate executives also remained skeptical of the rising conservative movement that included the Chicago School economists, William F. Buckley's *National Review,* and think tanks like Cato and Heritage. "What we did was way too controversial for corporations," one think tank executive said. The support for this newly energized wing of conservativism instead came largely from executives and entrepreneurs in the West and South, not the established companies of the Northeast and Midwest. It was no accident that Coors ran a Colorado brewery and the Kochs owned an oil company based in Kansas—or that the movement's star politician, Reagan, was the governor of California at the time. The establishment still preferred politicians who embraced a moderate approach, as both Nixon and Ford did. The American public seemed similarly comfortable with the status quo. Many of the new consumer laws seemed to be making life better. Deaths from vehicle crashes fell after Nader's safety movement took off, and the new environmental laws reduced pollution. The economy continued to grow.

Chicago's classical liberals understood that they were not winning the argument. In 1962, Rose Friedman turned a series of Milton's speeches into a book called *Capitalism and Freedom*, published by the University of Chicago Press. It appeared around the same time as the books that shaped the New Left—books by Nader, Betty Friedan, Rachel Carson, and others. Yet while those books appeared on bestseller lists, won prizes, and changed policies, the Friedman book received little attention. Milton, frustrated by the lack of attention, kept a list of publications that did not even review *Capitalism and Freedom*. The list included *The New York Times*, the *Chicago Tribune, Time,* and *Newsweek*.

Even so, Friedman believed that he was playing a long game. Bork did as well. The two of them shared a specific view about how to win that game. To change the American economy, they first had to change the intellectual climate.

IN HIS STUDY of regulation, Bork had noticed something important. The laws that Congress passed were often vague about the extent to which the government could or should interfere with business. As a result, courts played a dominant role in shaping the law. Antitrust law, like much of regulatory law, was "primarily judge-made," Bork wrote. This was an exciting realization because it meant that he and his allies did not need to persuade Congress to spend months holding hearings and debating new laws to reduce the regulation of American business. The Chicago School intellectuals needed to do something less daunting: persuade judges, especially the nine who sat on the Supreme Court.

During the early 1900s, the Supreme Court had often prevented the government from regulating business. The court had blocked laws on child labor, minimum wages, and the pricing of goods. In later years, Bork lamented, it "gave way under intellectual and political assault." But this history also suggested that an assault from the opposite direction could succeed. A new movement could reverse the court's positions.

To accomplish the goal, Bork decided that he had to reach audiences larger than those reading academic journals. He adopted as a personal motto a line that he had heard from an academic mentor who had originally heard it from Justice Felix Frankfurter: "Wreak yourself upon the world." With that in mind, Bork wrote newspaper op-eds and developed relationships with conservative journalists like George Will and William Safire. One of Bork's friends from the marines was a writer at *Sports Illustrated,* and the friend encouraged the managing editor of *Fortune,* a sister publication, to commission an essay from Bork on antitrust in the 1960s. At the time, *Fortune* was not only a bible of corporate America but also a forum for long articles making provocative arguments, and Bork ended up writing several over the years. After one ran, Chief Justice Warren Burger sent Bork a note to say he enjoyed it and hoped it would reach the academic community. Later, Bork became friendly with another Supreme Court justice, William Rehnquist, and the two spent time together with their wives at Rehnquist's Vermont vacation home. In his thank-you note for the visit, Bork included three of his recent articles for Rehnquist to read.

Bork settled on a word—"culture"—to describe what he was trying to change. "Capitalism is the name not merely of an economic system but of a complex of institutions and attitudes, a culture," he wrote in the first sentence of one of his articles aimed at a general audience. "Perhaps it is best to think of capitalism as a matter of degree, located on a segment of the spectrum from laissez-faire to what one supposes the economic organization of Cambodia to be. The question for us is not a choice between either of those extremes, but whether we are and wish to remain in the range where capitalism and its institutions are healthy and vigorous."

Friedman took a similar view of the importance of changing the culture, using phrases like "climate of opinion" to describe the underlying mechanism for changing policy. To do so, the classical liberals gathered at conferences and published articles in mainstream publications. They launched publications of their own, like *Regulation,* a magazine published by the Cato Institute, with an inaugural board of editors that included Bork and his friend Antonin Scalia, a law professor at the University of Chicago.

These legal theorists and social scientists made up one part of a two-pronged movement. They were making an intellectual argument in favor of a market-based economy with less government regulation and lower taxes. At the same time, political operatives like Powell and Walker were trying to persuade business executives to abandon their postwar accommodation and to become bolder about fighting for their own interests. Karl Marx might have said that Powell and Walker were urging executives to develop a stronger class consciousness. If they did not, they would continue to lose political battles with workers and government bureaucrats. These new corporate activists and the Chicago School professors were natural allies. Corporate groups helped finance academic research and its dissemination, while the intellectuals provided a moral justification for executives who were willing to get more involved in politics.

Surely, an element of self-interest drove this new movement. The executives were lobbying for policies that would increase their companies' profits and their own compensation, while the economists acquired benefactors to finance their conferences and hire them as consultants. But most political movements involve a mix of self-interest and ideology. The rising group of classical liberals was no different. What was good for them, they believed, was good for America.

By the early 1970s, the movement had not yet succeeded. But it had sharpened its worldview and was slowly attracting converts. The goal, as Friedman put it, was to allow the United States to keep its options open. He and his allies were helping to develop an alternative set of policies that would be ready for Washington to implement when circumstances changed. "There is enormous inertia—a tyranny of the status quo—in private and especially governmental arrangements," Friedman wrote. "Only a crisis—actual or perceived—produces real change. When that crisis occurs, the actions that are taken depend on the ideas that are lying around. That, I believe, is our basic function: to develop alternatives to existing policies, to keep them alive and available until the politically impossible becomes politically inevitable."

Walker may have lost the struggle over economic policy within the Nixon administration, and Bork may still have been a lonely voice calling for a new legal approach. But a crisis was about to occur.

CHAPTER 8

Clear the Track for Business

THE CRISIS BEGAN ON THURSDAY, OCTOBER 18, 1973, WHEN A spokesman for King Faisal of Saudi Arabia came on the radio in Riyadh to read a statement from the palace. The Saudi government would be cutting its oil production by 10 percent immediately and would soon halt all oil shipments to the United States unless Washington stopped sending military equipment to Israel. In hindsight, it was the day that a new economic era began.

Almost two weeks earlier, an Arab coalition led by Egypt and Syria had invaded Israel to reclaim territory lost in the Six-Day War of 1967. The Soviet Union quickly sent military equipment to two of its allies, Egypt and Syria. The United States responded with an airlift of equipment for one of its allies, Israel. The American airlift was supposed to be a secret so all countries could pretend that Washington was not choosing sides between Israel and the United States's own Arab allies, like Saudi Arabia. But changes in the weather forced the planes to land in Israel during the day rather than at night, and any hope of plausible deniability was lost as huge American aircraft began descending from the sky toward Tel Aviv. The United States was publicly aligning itself with Israel, and the Saudis decided to fight back. To pressure the Nixon administration into taking a more neutral position, King Faisal and his aides turned to a new weapon. They called it the oil weapon.

The economic trends of the previous few years had made oil-producing countries like Saudi Arabia realize that they had global leverage. The world economy grew rapidly in the 1960s and early 1970s, creating enormous demand for oil, and oil production struggled to keep pace. Prices had begun to increase sharply in the summer of 1973, before the war. When the fighting began, the

Saudis recognized that they could cause global prices to rise further by reducing their shipments. The price increases would be particularly large in any countries on which the Saudis imposed an oil boycott. "His majesty's government is making efforts so the government of the United States of America will modify its current positions toward the Arab-Israeli war," the king's spokesman announced over the radio on October 18. "If these efforts do not quickly bring about tangible results, the Saudi Arabian kingdom will stop the flow of oil to America." Other Arab countries quickly announced their own cutbacks. Two days later, with Washington continuing to stand by Israel, the Saudis made good on their threat and halted oil shipments to the United States.

Oil prices soared, more than doubling within a few months. The spike caused overall inflation, which had been a gradually building problem in the United States, to become a crisis. Annual inflation had been below 2 percent when the 1960s began. It reached 5 percent in 1969, almost 9 percent by the end of 1973 and 12 percent by late 1974. Even though the Arab-Israeli war ended after just a few weeks and the oil embargo ended several months later, oil-producing countries had learned how much power they had. By restraining production, they could keep prices high enough to enrich their countries. In the following years, they did so, and prices remained near embargo levels. After Iran's 1979 revolution disrupted its production, prices rose higher still.

For American families, the result was a stagnation in purchasing power. Median family income in 1979 was lower than it had been when the 1973 embargo began. There had not been such a protracted economic slump since the Great Depression.

This stagnation would eventually change how Americans thought about the economy. Dissatisfaction had already been building during the 1960s, focused on crime, the Vietnam War, and disorder. Later, the Watergate scandal and mistrust of government joined the list. But this unhappiness had generally not extended to the economy. Even with inflation rising during the 1960s, most Americans felt good about the economy.

One way to understand the relative lack of economic anger before the embargo is to look at the conservative movement. Its attempts to win over Americans to a vision of a low-tax, laissez-faire policy continued to fail well into the 1970s. The Republican Party's internal polls showed that many Americans believed that both taxes and benefits should remain roughly at present levels. When Ronald Reagan challenged Ford, the sitting president, for the Republican nomination in 1976, Reagan cast himself as the conservative to Ford's moderate. Even so, Reagan spent little time talking about a tax cut because he and his aides did not believe the issue would resonate. He did call for cuts to government spending—and lost the nomination. That same year, anti-tax ballot initiatives failed in several states. In Michigan, voters resoundingly rejected a referendum to limit taxes, 57 percent to 43 percent. Milton Friedman had campaigned for it, to no avail.

The more successful issues for the conservative movement tended to be social rather than economic. Reagan won the California governorship in 1966 partly by campaigning against student protesters at Berkeley who had been demonstrating about the Vietnam War, civil rights, and a university policy banning speakers from a street corner popular with student activists. Reagan began to emphasize the mayhem of the protests, he said, after hearing repeated complaints from voters in his one-on-one conversations with them. In the 1968 presidential campaign, Nixon adopted a version of this strategy by calling for law and order. In the early 1970s, conservatives expanded the theme by focusing on the spread of pornography, and school busing. Two Supreme Court decisions contributed to the conservative focus on social issues, one invalidating all existing death sentences and the other establishing a constitutional right to abortion. Economic policy, if anything, was a weak spot for the conservative movement.

Then the oil embargo happened. A recession began within weeks and continued for sixteen months. Consumer confidence—a term pollsters use to describe Americans' attitudes about the economy—plunged, falling well below any level during the brief recessions that occurred in the 1950s and 1960s. The recessions of 1973 and 1974 did not immediately change the political landscape: Some of the conservative movement's struggles on economic policy, like the Michigan tax referendum, occurred later. But political attitudes rarely shift quickly. They tend to do so gradually, as voters question long-held beliefs. As the economic troubles of the 1970s lingered, these doubts started to spread.

Oil was the lifeblood of the economy, and the price increases made seemingly everything more expensive. A typical new car had cost about $3,500 in 1973; it cost almost $7,000 in 1980. The price of groceries and clothing rose more than 50 percent over the same period. Many Americans felt as if they were watching their living standards deteriorate. The decade's two oil crises, first after the Saudi embargo and then after the Iranian revolution, also caused frustrations that were not financial. Because of the oil shortages, people had to organize their weekly rhythms around buying gas and often had to wait in long lines at gas stations. The experience made people angry and anxious. "The notion that Americans were going to run out of gas was both new and completely terrifying," the historian Meg Jacobs said. "If Vietnam and Watergate taught Americans to mistrust their leaders, the energy crisis taught them that government didn't work."

Historically, experts had believed that an economy could be either too strong or too weak. When it was too weak, people hoarded their money, leading businesses to cut back on production and employment and causing the country to lapse into recession and stagnation. When the economy was too strong, people spent so much money on goods and services that business could increase their prices, leading to spiraling inflation. The 1970s somehow combined stagnation and inflation, and the resulting misery came to be known as stagflation.

As these conditions persisted, more Americans became open to the idea that the country should try a different approach to running the economy. This was the moment for which Friedman and the Chicago School had been waiting. The Great Depression had created an opening for Roosevelt's overhaul of the economy. Now a new crisis raised the possibility that the country would finally move on from the long New Deal era. The politically impossible was no longer so.

. . .

THE ANTI-TAX MOVEMENT enjoyed the starkest turnaround. In 1978, only two years after its defeat in Michigan and its near irrelevance to Reagan's losing presidential campaign, the movement transformed into a political leviathan.

In California, a businessman named Howard Jarvis organized a petition campaign to place a referendum on the ballot that would sharply cut property taxes and limit future increases. It was called Proposition 13. When the campaign began, Jarvis looked like a one-man symbol of conservatism's postwar failures. He had been a press officer for Hoover's 1932 presidential campaign and supported Goldwater in 1964. Jarvis himself ran unsuccessfully for various political offices in California, including in a Senate primary bid that he lost to a more moderate Republican. He had repeatedly advocated for lower taxes to little effect. But 1978 turned out to be different. The economy had been struggling for five years by this point. Consumer prices had risen sharply, and a tax cut was one way the government could help people pay their bills. Jarvis's anti-tax campaign adopted as its slogan a newscaster's rant from the popular movie *Network:* "I'm as mad as hell and I'm not going to take this anymore." As in Michigan two years earlier, Friedman campaigned for the referendum. This time, the measure passed, 65 percent to 35 percent, and Jarvis became a national celebrity.

Anti-tax sentiment also rose in Washington, and Charls Walker helped foment it. By this point, Walker was Washington's top Republican lobbyist. In the Nixon administration, he had risen to deputy secretary of the Treasury and left when it became clear that he would not get the department's top job. He wanted to focus on making money or, as he put it, "refurbishing my estate." He set up a lobbying shop, Walker & Associates, on Pennsylvania Avenue, a block from the White House. From his thickly carpeted office, with photographs of Eisenhower, Johnson, and Ford (but not the disgraced Nixon) on the walls, he entertained clients with stories and cigars from his humidor. Walker commuted in a stretch sedan, a burgundy Buick Electra, driven by a chauffeur. The car had a telephone in the back seat at a time when car phones were rare enough to merit mention in magazine profiles. He used the phone to make calls on behalf of the most impressive client list in Washington, including U.S. Steel, General Electric, Ford, Procter & Gamble, and DuPont.

Walker was an effective lobbyist partly because he made a point of building relationships with both Republicans and Democrats on Capitol Hill, as well as with journalists with whom he would swap information. He helped start a series of dinners, which he called salons, where his clients could genially explain their views to policy makers and journalists. It was lobbying disguised as socializing. Otherwise, Walker tended to skip Washington's nighttime social scene. At the end of the day, his chauffeur would drive him home while he made a few more phone calls, and he and his wife, Harmolyn, would eat dinner together in their suburban Maryland home.

At the encouragement of one of his clients—the chief executive of Weyerhaeuser, a family-run timber company—Walker formed a new advocacy group to argue for lower taxes on businesses and stock holdings. If taxes were reduced, Walker argued, the cost of building a new factory and investing in new equipment would fall, and investments that were unprofitable at the existing tax rates would become profitable. The resulting surge in corporate investment would lift economic growth and create jobs, he predicted. Walker named his new group the American Council for Capital Formation. One of its employees happened to be a former aide to William Steiger, a moderate Republican congressman from Wisconsin. Steiger did not look like a typical crusader for lower taxes; he had sponsored the 1970 bill that created the Occupational Safety and Health Administration. But Steiger's former aide convinced him that reducing the capital gains tax could jump-start the economy, and Steiger soon offered a bill. It passed with bipartisan support in 1978, another sign that the anti-tax movement was on the march.

Momentum to cut income taxes grew, too. A key advocate was Jack Kemp, a Republican congressman from an economically struggling district around Buffalo, New York, who was less than a decade removed from his pro football career. Kemp had long been a conservative. He grew up in a Los Angeles family that owned a small trucking company, and he spent one football off-season as a celebrity intern to Reagan, then California's governor. While in Congress during the mid-1970s, Kemp was intrigued by a series of editorials in *The Wall Street Journal* calling for a large tax cut. He had already been thinking about such a policy, and he proposed a bill in 1977 to reduce income tax rates by 30 percent across the board. At first, the bill seemed like the sort of fringe conservative policy that even most Republicans rejected. The bill received little support from corporate groups like the Business Roundtable and the National Association of Manufacturers. Business executives favored a balanced budget, and Kemp's bill would have added to the deficit.

Yet Kemp was savvy enough about the country's economic dissatisfaction to turn the opposition to his bill into an advantage. He accused the lobbying groups of supporting a "zero-sum society," invoking the title of a recent book by a left-leaning economist at the Massachusetts Institute of Technology. Kemp said that Jimmy Carter believed in those same zero-sum ideas, which held that one person could benefit economically only if another person suffered. Kemp dismissed that philosophy as uptight and outdated. He called it green-eyeshade austerity, suggesting it was appropriate for fusty old accountants, who were known for wearing green visors above their eyes, rather than for bold political leaders. He pointed out that Hoover, the president who ushered in the Depression, had also favored a balanced budget. Kemp instead offered optimism in the form of a tax cut that would benefit everybody.

With tax rates reduced, people would have an incentive to work harder and start new businesses, Kemp said. The resulting activity would expand the size of the economy, creating more dollars for the government to tax and preventing the deficit from soaring. Each dollar would be taxed less, but there would be more dollars to tax. It was the same argument that Walker was making about corporate taxes and the core idea behind the policy that became known as supply-side economics. Some conservatives, notably Arthur Laffer, a University of Chicago economist, went so far as to argue that a tax cut would lead to so much new activity that the deficit would decline. If that were true, Kemp's bill would be akin to a free lunch. Most experts found this idea ludicrous, and Kemp himself was careful to avoid getting bogged down in technical details, but he was happy to reap the political advantages of Laffer's claims. Advocates of tax cuts no longer felt the need to pair them with proposed spending cuts, as Eisenhower and generations of fiscal conservatives had. The supply-side economists could retain the politically appealing part of the policy—the tax cut—and still claim to be fiscal conservatives. Kemp sold his idea as a hopeful antidote to the frustrations of the 1970s. He wanted to let Americans keep more of their money. He was putting his faith in them.

"I really think the social fabric of the nation is based upon good will and when the pie is shrinking, when you perceive that your gain must come at my expense or that my gain is coming at your expense, then this whole special interest environment builds up," he said. "I'm convinced that the needs of all of the American people, if not the needs of the rest of the world, are inextricably linked to economic opportunity and social mobility and what we used to call the American Dream." Kemp emphasized that he was responding to a new economic problem—stagflation—with a new solution. Liberals, by contrast, just seemed confused. "Liberalism has not come up with any new ideas to resolve the dilemma of stagflation," he said.

Kemp's enthusiasm was infectious. He offered an economic theory that sounded plausible to many Americans. It did not hurt that he proposed a windfall for taxpayers, especially for the wealthy, who tended to have political connections in Washington. Each time his tax cut came up for a vote in the 1970s, Congress rejected it, but the bill usually attracted more supporters than it had in the previous vote. By 1978, the chairman of the Republican Party had come to see the political potential of a tax cut and adopted Kemp's plan as official party policy. The chairman explained that Kemp had finally allowed the Republicans to embrace a positive vision rather than being the party of negativity, or, as he put it, the "anti-women, anti-minority, anti-union, anti-poor" party. A big tax cut would allow Republicans to move beyond the traumas of the 1960s and 1970s.

.   .   .

THE ANTI-TAX MOVEMENT signaled a shift among the advocates for a return to rough-and-tumble capitalism. Until the late 1970s, many of the Republican politicians and corporate executives calling for less regulation and lower taxes favored only modest changes. They tried to keep organized labor from expanding. They sought to moderate the most aggressive efforts of the Naderite consumer safety movement. They hoped to tweak the tax code. They favored gradual change, and they prioritized stability. But as the economy continued to flail in the 1970s, these same constituencies became open to sweeping changes. Not only were conservatives winning more debates over economic policy, but they were also becoming much more ambitious in their goals.

In 1978, Robert Bork published a pamphlet called *The Danger of Great Nations,* which summarized the case for major changes. It was the text of a speech he had given at a conference held by General Motors. "If the Dow Jones had merely kept pace with inflation since 1965, it would now be approaching 3,000 instead of hovering around 800," he wrote. The main reason for the slump, he argued, was an explosion of laws and regulations pushed by an intellectual class of academics, journalists, government officials, and even corporate managers who were more liberal than the country. Many of their goals were admirable, rooted in egalitarianism, meant "to require business to serve a wide variety of social ends—environmentalism, consumerism, racial equality, safety and health, investor protection, small business protection, and so on," Bork explained. Yet these egalitarian goals were destroying American capitalism.

A pessimist, Bork wrote, might conclude that Washington's many regulatory agencies presented a greater threat to American interests than anything the Soviet Union was doing. But Bork was not a pessimist. "Trends do not always run forever in one direction and there are hopeful signs that the ones I have been describing will not," he wrote. Three of the four most widely syndicated newspaper columns in the country were written by conservatives, Bork noted. The Chicago School of economics had also ceased to be what he called "a despised curiosity." The Supreme Court had begun to restrict the authority of antitrust regulators. In one ruling, Chief Justice Burger cited Bork's writing. Perhaps most important, Bork concluded, "businessmen are beginning to realize that their future—the future of the American corporate system—depends upon the intellectual and political atmosphere of the country, and some of them are beginning to speak out. That more of them do so is indispensable."

Bork could sense it: The culture was changing. Nixon had shown the party of business and markets how to win power in the late twentieth century, but he had governed as another government-friendly moderate. Carter, who was president when Bork published his pamphlet, was not going to implement the agenda of the new conservative movement. Carter was a Democrat. But the changes in the political culture meant that conservatives could imagine a future in which a Republican president would abandon the approach of Eisenhower, Nixon, and Ford.

By the end of the 1970s, the identity of that potential president was becoming clearer. It was Reagan. He had been the great hope of conservatives for more than a decade but had never been able to win over enough mainstream Republicans to secure the presidential nomination. Nixon, the establishment candidate, had won the nomination in 1968, and Ford had similarly triumphed in 1976. In 1980, however, the party's voters decided that they were ready for something different.

IN LATER YEARS, Reagan's critics cast him as a simpleton actor merely playing a part, while some of his admirers claimed he was a secret genius with a masterful grasp of policy. Neither caricature was accurate, but both were based on real traits. Reagan was more detached from policy specifics than many politicians. His own aides found him shockingly unconcerned with details. He frequently deferred to them, and he was willing to invent anecdotes and statistics to persuade audiences of his arguments. Still, he had abiding principles that had guided him for decades. He pursued them even when other Republicans dismissed them as unrealistic or wrong, and he could be very tough when he ran into obstacles. As Martin Anderson, one of his top economic aides on the 1980 campaign, put it, Reagan had "a calculating, imaginative mind governed by a steely will." Anderson called Reagan "a warmly ruthless man." After years of failing to persuade their own party of their views, many other politicians might have altered those views. Reagan did not. He stuck to his principles.

Just as important, he was a talented performer, well cast for the role of politician. He was handsome enough to have been a Hollywood actor but ordinary enough never to have become a major movie star. In the final days of the 1980 campaign, when a reporter asked Reagan what voters saw in him, he replied, "Would you laugh if I told you that I think, maybe, they see themselves and that I'm one of them?" He could tap into Nixon's "one of us" approach, yet he was more appealing than Nixon.

Reagan also embodied the twin forces that came together to create a policy revolution—the ideas-based movement of the Chicago School and the increasingly assertive self-interest of corporate lobbyists. First, Reagan genuinely believed in the ideas of Friedman, Hayek, and others who argued for individual freedom over government collectivism. Reagan enjoyed reading conservative publications like *Human Events* and *Reader's Digest* and using anecdotes from them (albeit in embellished form at times). True, he had been a Democrat and Roosevelt supporter as a young man. But his supposed political transformation is sometimes exaggerated, as Lou Cannon, Reagan's biographer, has noted. The strains of conservatism had always been lurking. Reagan had grown up in a conservative religious community in small-town Illinois, with a devout mother and an alcoholic father. His favorite novel as a child was *That Printer of Udell's,* an ode to Christian virtue, hard work, and Horatio Alger–style upward mobility. As a young actor, he had been repulsed by the leftists around Hollywood's unions, and he later ran the Screen Actors Guild as an anti-communist. His political philosophy remained strikingly consistent from the late 1950s onward.

The second part of Reagan's background was important too: He was a member of America's postwar nouveau riche. His Hollywood success brought him and his wife Nancy into contact with a rising generation of corporate executives in California. Some became close friends and eventually political supporters. They were his peers, and he came to see the world as they did, unhappy with regulations that constrained their companies and taxes that reduced their profits and compensation. Like his affluent friends, Reagan chafed at the 90 percent marginal tax rate on top incomes.

The business relationship that most influenced Reagan was with General Electric, for which he became a spokesman in 1954. When he arrived, the company was already a stronghold of conservative thought. GE coined the term "business climate" to describe a community's wage levels and union presence, and its head of labor relations, Lemuel Ricketts Boulware, argued for a confrontational approach to labor, including moving factories to the largely non-unionized South. Boulware saw the issue in ideological terms. He believed in free-market capitalism without interference from union and government bureaucrats, and he circulated conservative articles about economics to other company executives. As part of Reagan's GE role, he traveled the country talking with employees, and he absorbed the worldview of Boulware and his internal allies. Reagan too came to believe that the company should fight back against the growing power of unions and government agencies. Over his years working for GE, the stump speech that he gave at its factories and offices became more political, so much so that GE's top executives—Boulware's and Reagan's bosses—became uncomfortable with it. Most of them still accepted large parts of the mainstream economic consensus. "Reagan's appeal is not to the Fortune 500," Kemp would say later. "It never was." The tensions between Reagan and GE contributed to his departure in 1962.

Two years later, Reagan used his GE talk as the basis for a televised speech on behalf of Goldwater's presidential campaign, and the speech launched Reagan's political career. "Well," Reagan said, using one of his favorite words of emphasis, "I think it's time we ask ourselves if we still know the freedoms that were intended for us by the Founding Fathers." Taxes were too high, and thousands of regulations were throttling ingenuity, he said.

Watching him, many conservatives began thinking that they had nominated the wrong conservative for president. After Goldwater lost, California Republican leaders, including Reagan's friends in business, began urging him to run for governor, and he won the 1966 election easily. The economy's continuing prosperity and the country's basic satisfaction meant that Reagan was unable to implement many of his preferred economic ideas as governor. But as he and his advisers planned his 1980 presidential campaign, they knew that the country's mood had darkened, and they set out to create a platform that reflected his beliefs.

IN THE SUMMER of 1979, Reagan's campaign aides produced Policy Memorandum No. 1, describing the economic agenda of a would-be Reagan administration. The memo's number signified the new primacy of economic policy.

The memo used a sleight of hand that was common to the conservative movement during this time: It downplayed the role of oil prices in causing high inflation and instead blamed the federal government, arguing that excess spending had sparked inflation. The claim was not entirely wrong. High levels of government spending, without the taxes to pay for it, and loose monetary policy during the Johnson and Nixon administrations had begun to increase inflation before oil prices surged. To keep pace with rising prices and avoid losing workers, many employers raised wages. This additional money became yet another source of inflation—a dynamic that economists refer to as the wage-price spiral. But Americans' purchasing power was barely rising because the price increases were erasing the pay increases.

Taxes were making matters worse. At the time, tax brackets were not adjusted for inflation. When inflation rose, it pushed families into higher tax brackets, treating them as if they had become richer when they had not. The phenomenon became known as "bracket creep." If anything, many families were losing ground, after taking into account inflation and taxes. As Alan Greenspan, another Reagan adviser, said at the time, inflation was making Americans more politically conservative by making tax cuts more appealing.

In response, Reagan called for a large tax cut—Kemp's tax

cut—even though many business executives and Republicans remained nervous about the plan. Cutting tax rates by 30 percent over three years without making accompanying spending cuts seemed as if it could cause the budget deficit to soar. Even Milton Friedman was wary. Yet Reagan believed in the plan and refused to make major changes. Instead, his campaign looked for ways to soothe doubters without altering the policy.

That job went to Walker. To the Reagan campaign, Walker offered the promise of establishment credibility. He had worked for both Eisenhower and Nixon and had close relationships on Capitol Hill and in corporate America. In the 1980 campaign, Walker had initially endorsed another candidate, John Connally, one of Nixon's Treasury secretaries. Had Walker been writing the campaign agenda, he would have come up with something more cautious than the tax cut that Reagan favored. But Walker was willing to change with the times and sell Reagan's vision.

Walker's new position was a microcosm of how much the Republican consensus had shifted. During the Nixon administration, Walker had been the conservative voice who lost a major policy debate to the political center. By 1980, the party had leapfrogged him to the right. Walker's job was to help other mainstream Republicans get comfortable with the shift. He joined the Reagan campaign as an adviser while continuing to run his lobbying firm, effectively becoming Reagan's ambassador to corporate America. "The Business Roundtable doesn't know Reagan, and they tend to identify him with right-wing positions and extremism," Walker told an interviewer. He explained to executives why they should feel comfortable with a Reagan presidency. As another tax cut advocate said about Walker, "He was able to take supply-side economics and decorate it with the veneer of establishment credibility."

On September 9, 1980, Reagan gave the centerpiece economic speech of his campaign at a Chicago business club. In it, he laid out his agenda and tried to reassure corporate America. "I know we can do these things, and I know we will," Reagan said. "But don't just take my word for it." Reagan explained that he had discussed his plan with "distinguished economists and businessmen," including Shultz, Greenspan, and Walker. Reagan was telling his audience that the Republican establishment had signed on to the revolution. Business executives gradually became more comfortable with Reagan's bolder approach and soon were full-throated supporters of it. "The events of the last few years have emboldened the corporate managers to be more conservative and socially conscious," Buckley, the editor of the *National Review,* said in the 1980s. To executives, being socially conscious now meant fighting for less regulation and lower taxes.

Charls Walker in his office near the White House, 1983.

During Reagan's 1980 campaign, Walker occupied a senior policy role, helping to design a package of additional business tax cuts to accompany Kemp's income tax cuts. After Reagan won the election, Congress passed both sets of cuts, and Walker's corporate clients received a windfall. When journalists asked him about the potential conflict, he denied any problem. Walker insisted he could distinguish between his clients' narrow concerns and the country's needs, and he believed the tax cuts would benefit the entire economy.

For decades after the Great Depression, the prevailing culture of corporate America called for restraining self-interest in the name of the national interest. That ethos explained why corporate executives helped build a high-wage economy and accepted high taxes on their incomes. They were willing to sacrifice their own short-term interests for what they considered to be larger causes, including political stability and American power.

By 1980, their outlook had changed. In the new culture, executives came to believe that there was no difference between their own personal interests and the national interest.

THE SECOND MAJOR plank of Reagan's economic agenda was deregulation of business. As with tax cuts, Reagan's team could point to recent events around the world to argue that the economy was overregulated.

Antitrust policy, as Bork noted, could be fuzzy, without clear standards to determine when a big company was too big. General Motors was an example that deregulation advocates liked to cite. Regulators had spent years debating whether the company was so powerful as to be a monopoly, yet by the 1970s GM was struggling to compete with Japanese rivals. "The whole time I was down in Washington, people there wanted to go after General Motors," said Nicholas Katzenbach, a senior Justice Department official under Kennedy and attorney general under Johnson. "Wouldn't that look ridiculous today?" GM seemed to be a case study of why antitrust enforcement was overrated: The free market would reward companies that provided products people wanted and punish those that did not. Size alone could not protect a company.

The burst of regulation inspired by Nader's consumer movement played a prominent role in the calls for deregulation. Several large new agencies like the EPA had sprung up shortly before the American economy entered its 1970s funk. The similar timing of the two developments was largely coincidence. High oil prices and low consumer confidence had much bigger effects on corporate profits than clean air rules. But the order of events nonetheless played into the arguments made by advocates for deregulation. The economic struggles of the 1970s had made many policy makers and voters eager to try new approaches.

Moreover, some recent examples of deregulation did seem to be working. In the United States, the Carter administration had deregulated the airlines, and prices fell, making airline travel accessible to more Americans. The full legacy of airline deregulation would be mixed, but the laissez-faire advocates were correct that the private sector was capable of choosing which airline routes to fly without government oversight. Free-market policies also seemed to be succeeding in other countries. West Germany's economic boom stemmed partly from loosening government rules, Reagan's economic advisers believed. Britain elected Margaret Thatcher, an acolyte of Chicago School economics, as its prime minister in 1979. Chile boomed after its dictator, Augusto Pinochet, took Friedman's economic advice and privatized state-owned enterprises. Even China's Communist Party loosened government control of the economy. Starting in 1978, under Deng Xiaoping, China pursued a policy of "reform and opening up," which included investment by foreign companies.

Once Reagan took office, his team set out to deregulate the American economy. They did so partly by pushing for bills in Congress, but their main attempts to reduce government intervention did not require new laws. Bork's writings during the 1970s had helped conservatives understand this reality. Reagan could take major steps to deregulate the economy by appointing the right people to both the executive and judicial branches. Regulations were broad enough that cabinet officials made many decisions about how to enforce antitrust policy, environmental rules, Wall Street regulations, and more. And the final say usually belonged to federal judges.

As simple as this approach may have sounded, Reagan's advisers knew that finding the right appointees would require work. The federal bureaucracy was filled with officials who were more sympathetic to regulation than Reagan was. So were the traditional places to recruit government appointees, such as state governments, think tanks, and universities. Reagan's advisers believed that Nixon had erred by not removing as many officials as he had the authority to and by appointing too many officials who believed in the postwar, pro-government economic consensus. To ensure

Reagan did not repeat that mistake, his campaign starting compiling lists of hundreds of potential appointees long before Election Day. Being a Republican was not enough. Top economic officials, as one aide said, needed "to agree completely with the main elements of the comprehensive economic policy he had set forth during the campaign." Given how recently Reagan's own party had favored a different policy, his administration would need to pass over many traditional Republican job seekers and identify those who were willing to come to Washington to change its culture.

COLORADO WAS ONE of the states where the conservative economic movement had made progress before Reagan's election. In 1976, Republicans gained control of both houses of the state legislature with much of the energy coming from a cadre of conservative candidates who campaigned on reducing property taxes that had been swollen by 1970s inflation. It was the same issue—bracket creep—that would fuel California's measure limiting property taxes, Proposition 13, as well as Kemp's call for an across-the-board federal tax cut.

Among the most dynamic new members of the Colorado legislature was a thirty-four-year-old lawyer named Anne McGill Gorsuch. She had grown up in a Catholic family in Denver, where her father was a prominent surgeon. A precocious student, she graduated from the University of Colorado at age nineteen, and from the university's law school at twenty-two, before winning a Fulbright scholarship to study in Jaipur, India. She married another Denver lawyer, David Gorsuch, and they began climbing Denver's legal ladder while raising their three children. Anne first worked as a prosecutor and then went into private practice as a lawyer for Mountain Bell, the regional phone company, where her specialties included antitrust and labor relations. She was smart, her colleagues noticed, and she was comfortable speaking in public.

In 1976, Gorsuch decided to challenge the Democratic incumbent who represented her Denver district in the state legislature. The district, home to many Jewish families, leaned to the left, and Gorsuch ran a less ideological campaign than some other Colorado Republicans that year. She knocked on hundreds of doors, sometimes bringing her children, Neil, J.J., and Stephanie, all under age ten. "Whether you contact my friends or my enemies, they'll tell you two things: I'm intelligent, and I'm capable of making hard decisions," Gorsuch said.

Despite her conservative politics, she won the endorsement of the Colorado Women's Political Caucus, to the frustration of Patricia Schroeder, then a Democratic congresswoman from Denver and one of the nation's most prominent female politicians. Schroeder argued that Gorsuch's opponent—David Gaon, the Democratic incumbent—had a strong record on women's issues and that the caucus should not endorse Gorsuch simply because she was a woman. The caucus did not listen. Gorsuch seemed like an exciting candidate, and she did not seem very ideological. She also benefited from Gaon's distraction. He was the Colorado Democrat in charge of trying to keep control of the legislature for the party and spent time strategizing about other races around the state. Once Gaon recognized that he was in danger, he tried to portray Gorsuch as a tool of big business by pointing out that she still worked for Mountain Bell and had refused to commit to recusing herself from legislation that would affect the company. But the charge did not stick, and Gorsuch won a close race.

In the legislature, she quickly showed herself to be more conservative than her campaign had suggested. She became the leading legal strategist for Colorado's new Republican majority. In response to the continuing crime wave, she helped draft a law to standardize criminal sentences. She and her colleagues ousted their party leader and replaced him with a more conservative member to serve as Speaker of the House. They also reduced the property tax, indexed the state income tax to inflation and eliminated the inheritance tax. "The government that governs least governs best," Gorsuch said. She also helped eliminate a state commission focused on closing gender gaps. "She did that almost single-handedly," another politician said. "She's very tough."

Some members of the local media began describing Gorsuch and the other newly elected conservatives as "the House crazies," and they proudly adopted the nickname. At the end of her first

legislative session, a Denver magazine named Gorsuch the out-
standing freshman of the year. She won reelection in 1978 but by
1980 was looking to do something else. She and her husband were
splitting up, and she said that she did not want to put her children
through a divorce and a campaign at the same time. Instead, she
began thinking about moving to Washington to work for a Reagan
administration if he won.

Gorsuch had just the credentials that Reagan's team wanted.
She was not just another Republican. She was a movement conservative who believed in shrinking government. She came recommended by Joseph Coors and James Watt, two conservative stars
from Colorado. Coors had used some of his fortune to found both
the Heritage Foundation in Washington and Mountain States
Legal Foundation in Colorado, which was trying to counteract
consumer and labor groups, much as the Powell memo had urged.
Watt, a conservative lawyer and Wyoming native who had worked
in the Nixon administration, ran the Mountain States Legal Foundation.

With these stellar endorsements, Gorsuch soon found herself
interviewing to become deputy administrator of the Environmental Protection Agency, a job that would allow her to restrain a
federal agency that she had battled in the Colorado legislature. But
a Reagan aide who interviewed Gorsuch for the job thought she
had set her sights too low. Impressed by her—and knowing that
the administration had a shortage of female job candidates—the
aide began encouraging other officials to name Gorsuch to the top
EPA job rather than as a deputy. Reagan signed off on the plan,
and Gorsuch became the administration's second-ranking woman,
after Jeane Kirkpatrick, the ambassador to the United Nations.
Once installed in her EPA office, with spectacular views of the Po-
tomac River, Gorsuch set about defanging the regulatory apparatus.

She ordered career EPA staff members, many of them Democrats, to stop making public speeches or talking to members of
Congress without her office's approval. She centralized decision-
making among a small number of top officials. After Reagan proposed cutting almost 25 percent of the agency's budget, she

suggested a cut of 40 percent. She reduced the number of investigations into pesticide and other pollutants. In the decade before Gorsuch arrived, the agency's first decade of existence, it referred an average of about two hundred cases a year to the Justice Department for further action; Gorsuch cut the annual pace to thirty.

Anne Gorsuch meets with President Ronald Reagan in the Oval Office, 1982.

Along the way, she attracted attention and made enemies. Some of it was sexism: In one Senate hearing, a Wisconsin Democrat compared her to Suzanne Pleshette, then a star of *The Bob Newhart Show,* and the senator described himself as "smitten." Some of the criticism stemmed from Gorsuch's ostentatious, confrontational style: She wore a mink coat and traveled around Washington in a gas-guzzling Oldsmobile. But much of the controversy surrounding Gorsuch was neither sexist nor stylistic. It was about the substantive stakes. The Reagan administration was overhauling the federal government's approach to regulation, with major consequences for the economy and society. Both the Reaganites and their opponents recognized as much.

The Interior Department, which Reagan had named Watt to run, pulled back in myriad ways. The Transportation Department conducted fewer investigations of automobile manufacturers. OSHA, the workplace safety agency, inspected fewer job sites. The Agriculture Department stopped rating meat-processing plants based on their compliance with federal rules. Financial regulators required fewer disclosures from banks about the loans they made. And just as the University of Chicago economists had urged, the administration implemented Bork's ideas about antitrust policy.

"Bigness in business does not necessarily mean badness," the attorney general, William French Smith, announced. His department ended the government's highest-profile antitrust case, which accused IBM of having grown too large, and issued new guidelines for when the government would try to stop a merger. Concerns that the combined company would be too large or powerful were not enough. Only when regulators could demonstrate that the company would raise prices for consumers would the government try to block the deal (and the Reagan administration did force the breakup of AT&T on these grounds).

The new policy was friendlier to business. But it was also less vague. The old standard depended on subjective judgments about what constituted too much market power. The new standard depended on the output of economic formulas. It was the approach that Bork had long recommended. One of the lawyers who ran the Justice Department's antitrust division under Reagan was Douglas Ginsburg, a former Harvard law professor and a deregulation advocate, and he knew who deserved credit for the theory shaping the country's new antitrust policy. The approach, Ginsburg said, "followed directly from the scholarly work of Judge Robert Bork."

With federal regulators stepping back, merger activity soared in the 1980s and 1990s. Texaco bought Getty Oil. General Electric bought RCA. Bristol-Myers bought Squibb. Warner Communications bought Time Inc. Dozens of local hospitals bought other hospitals. Kohlberg Kravis Roberts, part of the rising class of private equity firms, bought RJR Nabisco. Corporate raiders like T. Boone Pickens became famous. New investment firms started during these years, including Bain Capital, the Blackstone Group, and the Carlyle Group. Over the course of Reagan's presidency, the volume of merger activity in the United States increased thirteenfold.

It all stemmed from the idea that competitive market forces could discipline businesses better than government regulation. Bork, Director, the Friedmans, and other members of the Chicago School had changed the intellectual climate. Reagan and his appointees were taking the next step and changing reality. They were demonstrating why political culture and power play such important roles in shaping an economy.

REAGAN'S AIDES DID not want these changes to be temporary. They understood that the administration would not hold power forever. At some point, it would be replaced by a Democratic or a moderate Republican one, which would again regulate zealously. The best way to constrain future administrations, Reagan's team recognized, was to appoint federal judges with free-market views. Judges had lifetime tenure and broad leeway to interpret regulatory statutes. "Judges," as Bork had written, "make law to a far greater extent than laymen, or even many lawyers, realize."

For these reasons, the administration prioritized the appointment of like-minded judges. It held dozens of meetings at the White House and Justice Department to vet candidates. It looked for candidates with a solid record of free-market conservatism. "We must know what he thinks now, and he must have thought about issues enough that he will be unlikely to change his mind," one Justice Department official wrote in an internal memo. The administration focused on younger nominees, who would have longer careers on the bench. Among them were several professors at the University of Chicago, including thirty-six-year-old Frank Easterbrook, forty-two-year-old Richard Posner, and forty-six-year-old Antonin Scalia. Reagan also nominated Bork, who was fifty-four, to a seat on the federal appeals court in Washington, one level below the Supreme Court. In all, Reagan named eighty-three judges to appellate courts. No previous president had named even sixty appellate judges, and none of Reagan's successors has named more than sixty-six.

As influential as these appellate judges were, the nine justices of the Supreme Court mattered much more. They set the ground rules by which the rest of the legal system and the American economy had to play. Reagan's advisers believed that the Supreme Court was another area where recent Republican presidents had paid too little attention to ideology. The newest justice when Reagan took office, John Paul Stevens, was particularly galling to conservatives. Ford had chosen Stevens in 1975 over another finalist who already worked in the Ford administration: Bork. In the so-called Saturday Night Massacre during the Watergate investigation, Bork had been the Justice Department official who agreed to carry out Nixon's order to fire the special prosecutor, and two years later Ford did not want to refocus attention on the scandal by nominating Bork. Stevens, a moderate appellate judge, got the job instead and became one of the court's most liberal justices.

Reagan's aides did not want to name any justices like Stevens. When a court vacancy opened during Reagan's first year in office, he used it to fulfill a campaign promise to name the first female justice and chose Sandra Day O'Connor, an Arizona state judge whom prominent conservatives recommended. The second opening came in 1986, and the White House narrowed the choice to two leading figures from the judicial right, Bork and Scalia.

Bork had the better résumé. He remained the country's most influential conservative legal theorist. In addition to his work on antitrust, he had helped forge a new legal theory which argued that the Supreme Court should usually limit itself to narrow interpretations of the Constitution, consistent with the founders' original intent. This approach appealed to conservatives because it tended to curtail government authority; the federal government was small when the Constitution was written in the 1780s, almost entirely lacking the agencies that would later regulate capitalism and society. If the court hewed to the founders' intent, large parts of the modern liberal state might be in legal jeopardy. Reagan's longtime policy aide from California, Edwin Meese, adopted the idea after becoming attorney general in 1985 and called for "a jurisprudence of original intent." Later, the more popular term for this idea became "originalism," and it has guided Republican judicial philosophy for decades.

When Reagan's aides talked about Bork's legacy, they tended to be reverential. They believed that they had been able to implement deregulatory changes that would have been considered extreme only a decade earlier because of the intellectual movement that Bork led. The first sentence of an internal White House memo summarizing Bork's Supreme Court candidacy read: "Robert Bork has been the leading spokesman for an interpretavist theory of constitutional law and judicial restraint for over 20 years, spearheading the at-times lonely conservative reaction to the excesses of the Warren court." Another memo called him the godfather of Meese's originalism push.

Scalia had been much less influential. White House officials rarely mentioned originalism when talking about his candidacy because Scalia had not spent much time talking about the idea as a professor or appellate judge. Still, his credentials were dazzling, and he was almost a decade younger than Bork. Although Reagan's aides idolized Bork's contributions to their cause, they believed he had some weaknesses that complicated his Supreme Court candidacy. "He is 59 years old, smokes heavily, drinks somewhat and engages in little if any exercise," one memo reported. It added: "Conflicting views have been expressed on the warmth of his personality and the extent of his humility, but all agree on his eloquence and skills of advocacy."

Scalia had both a superb intellect and a warmer personality. He was better liked inside the federal courthouse in Washington where both he and Bork worked as appellate judges at the time. Scalia was a charming, courteous bon vivant. "He scares me," one liberal lawyer said, anonymously, in Scalia's entry in the *Almanac of the Federal Judiciary*. "Very smooth, bright and dead wrong on the big issues." Either way, White House aides believed that the Senate would confirm Reagan's choice, and they were probably correct. Republicans controlled the Senate in 1986, and several southern Democrats often voted with them. In the end, Reagan was attracted to Scalia's relative youth and the excitement that would accompany his status as the first Italian American justice. Bork, once again, was the runner-up.

Yet Reagan was sufficiently steeped in the conservative movement that he recognized Bork's significance. When a third Supreme Court seat opened in 1987—to replace Powell, author of the 1971 memo urging corporate America to fight back—Reagan made clear from the first White House meeting about the vacancy that he liked Bork for it. The nomination process that followed would become notorious. It would spawn a new word—"bork," a verb to describe a political campaign to defeat a judicial nominee on ideological grounds—and would overshadow every other part of Bork's career in the public memory.

In 1987, Democrats controlled the Senate for the first time during Reagan's presidency, and the chairman of the Senate Judiciary Committee, Joe Biden, had specifically warned Reagan about Bork during a meeting on the nomination. "If you nominate him," Biden said, "you'll have trouble on your hands." Bork's paper trail was so long and pugnaciously right-wing that Democrats thought they might be able to defeat him. Once Reagan submitted the nomination, liberal groups organized a grassroots campaign to defeat the nomination, and Biden took on the mission of persuading his colleagues that Bork was unfit for the job. Edward Kennedy played an important role, delivering a fiery speech on the Senate floor about "Robert Bork's America," which described back-alley abortions, segregated lunch counters, schools banned from teaching evolution, and rogue police officers breaking down doors during midnight raids. Harsh as they were, each of Kennedy's accusations was connected to one of Bork's writings, like his belief that *Roe v. Wade* should be overturned and his criticism of the 1964 Civil Rights Act (a position he later reversed) for forcing businesses to serve all customers. The Senate rejected the nomination, 58 to 42. He resigned from his appellate judgeship out of a mixture of bitterness and boredom.

Bork became a symbol of what Reagan failed to accomplish. So did Anne Gorsuch. Her EPA tenure was marred by mini-scandals, such as her refusal to give Congress records involving a toxic waste site, and Reagan's aides forced her out in 1983 to keep the controversies from damaging the president. She received the news from Coors, the beer executive, who summoned her to his Colorado home on a snowy night when she was in Denver to inform her that Reagan's advisers wanted her to resign.

One of the few people who counseled her to fight was her oldest child, Neil, then fifteen years old. "You didn't do anything wrong," he told her. "You only did what the president ordered. Why are you quitting? You raised me not to be a quitter. Why are you a quitter?"

THE DOWNFALL OF Gorsuch and Bork fit with a larger sense of disappointment that some conservatives felt about Reagan's presidency. He suffered failures and did not always govern as ambitiously as he spoke. In the 1960s, he had opposed Medicare as a form of socialism and had criticized Social Security. As president, he protected both programs from large cuts. He did not eliminate any cabinet departments. He signed a tax increase in 1982 that reversed a portion of his 1981 tax cut. His Supreme Court appointees, except for Scalia, were sometimes disappointing, too.

But these disappointments could obscure the big picture. The Reagan revolution was real.

Almost a half century earlier, Roosevelt and his allies in Congress had refashioned the American economy, raising taxes, regulating business, and strengthening labor unions in unprecedented ways. In the decades that followed, this basic structure remained intact. The scope of government fluctuated within a narrow range. Republican presidents accepted the consensus and sometimes expanded government's role. Eisenhower oversaw larger increases in government investments than any other modern president and appointed a liberal chief justice friendly to regulation. Nixon created more federal agencies than any president since Roosevelt.

Reagan ended that era. He ended it with help from intellectuals like Bork, power brokers like Walker, and government officials like Gorsuch. "Ronald Reagan changed the trajectory of America," Barack Obama said while running for president decades later. "He put us on a fundamentally different path." True, Reagan suffered setbacks, as all presidents do, and, true, Reagan was willing to compromise when he thought it benefited him and his cause. To refuse compromise, in his view, was naïve. "On nearly all issues, Reagan was simultaneously an ideologue and a pragmatist," Cannon, the biographer, wrote. Reagan occasionally complained to aides that some hardcore conservatives preferred to lose and remain pure than make progress. "I'd rather get 80 percent of what I want than go over the cliff with my flag flying," Reagan said. His 80 percent transformed the American economy.

The big exception was government spending. Reagan did not reduce spending on social programs as he had suggested he would. But his presidency was a turning point for tax policy and government regulation. The top marginal income tax rate was 70 percent when Reagan took office. It fell to 50 percent in 1982 and to 28 percent in 1989, when he left office. It has never again exceeded 39.6 percent. Tax rates on stock holdings, corporate profits, and inheritances also fell during his presidency. Together, these cuts produced a sharp decline in total tax payments by the wealthy. In 1980, rich American households paid almost half of their income in combined federal, state, and local taxes. Since Reagan, this combined rate has been closer to 35 percent.

Reagan also ushered in a new combativeness toward labor unions, starting with his firing the air traffic controllers in 1981. It helped him that they belonged to a distinctly unsympathetic union and typified labor's entitled attitude. After endorsing Reagan in the 1980 campaign, the controllers demanded a large raise, bigger pensions, a more generous disability policy, a thirty-two-hour workweek, and free airline trips. Reagan said he would fire and replace them if they went on strike. When they did, he did. The firing, along with Reagan's pro-management appointments to federal agencies and the judiciary, encouraged companies to take a harder line against unions. During the 1980s, union membership shrank more than twice as rapidly as it had in the late 1970s. When Reagan left office, less than 17 percent of American workers belonged to a union.

Beyond taxes and labor policy, Reagan deregulated the economy in the ways advocated by the Chicago School. Wall Street was a prime example. The Reagan administration gave banks greater flexibility to invest their holdings as they pleased. It also changed the rules on the taxation of stock options, making them a more attractive way for executives to be paid. These changes caused financial transactions to become a more important part of the economy and led to a Wall Street boom. The share of total compensation paid to the finance sector grew by roughly 50 percent between 1980 and 2000. Not even the financial crisis of the early twenty-first century reversed this increase. The deregulation of finance and the decline of income tax rates interacted in a crucial way: Bankers had more freedom to make large sums of money thanks to deregulation and more incentive to do so thanks to falling taxes on their income.

In a sign that Bork had been correct about the importance of changing the intellectual climate, many Democrats came to agree with at least some of Reagan's economic changes. They agreed that the New Deal consensus had put too much faith in government planning and not enough in the power of the market to allocate resources efficiently. The stagflation of the 1970s appeared to be the best evidence for this view. The new consensus became known as neoliberalism. In recent years, the term has turned into a catch-all epithet that progressives use to describe the views of moderate Democrats and conservatives. But the word is nonetheless meaningful.

It has its origins in Europe during the 1930s. Conservative intellectuals like Friedrich Hayek and Ludwig von Mises worried about the growing appeal of Marxism, but they also recognized that the laissez-faire approach of the early 1900s—called liberalism—had failed. It had helped lead to World War I and the Great Depression. These intellectuals sought to update the old version of economic liberalism, thus the use of "neo." They also wanted to differentiate themselves from Franklin Roosevelt and his fellow New Deal Democrats in the United States, who had begun describing themselves as liberals and were well to the left of classic European liberals. The prefix accomplished both distinctions.

Neoliberalism did not emerge as a fully formed worldview. Different neoliberals made competing arguments about its true meaning. Over time, though, the definition became clearer. Neoliberals believed that the government had a small number of crucial roles to play to ensure the smooth operation of a capitalist economy, such as the maintenance of a strong military to defend the country, a clear set of laws to protect property rights, and a powerful central bank to control the money supply. Otherwise, they believed the price mechanism of the market allocated goods more efficiently than government bureaucrats could.

Neoliberals also shared one of the New Left's main critiques about postwar life in the United States. It was too conformist, they said. Large corporations, labor unions, and government agencies stifled individuality and creativity. Although Ayn Rand was not exactly a neoliberal herself, her novels channeled and popularized this argument by describing the struggles of her talented heroes to overcome the "second-raters," who symbolized bureaucracy and conformism.

When Democratic intellectuals looked at the world in the 1970s and 1980s, they saw legitimate reasons to be skeptical of the old economic consensus that had been so comfortable with government intervention. The guns-and-butter policies of the 1960s—the Vietnam War plus the War on Poverty—had fed inflation. So had some labor unions' demands for large wage increases. Living standards were no longer rising rapidly for most families, and Japanese and German companies were outcompeting their American rivals in several industries. Neoliberalism seemed to offer a way forward. The Democratic Party rejected much of Reagan's agenda, but not all of it. Democrats also came to believe that less reliance on government and more on market forces could reinvigorate a turgid American economy.

Bill Clinton, an uncommonly talented politician, emerged as the champion of this view in the 1990s. Clinton's life in Arkansas, first as a child and then as the state's governor for more than a decade, had given him a visceral understanding that many Americans felt alienated from the modern Democratic Party. It was too liberal for them on social issues, and it no longer seemed capable of delivering the economic gains that it once had. He called himself a New Democrat, and he was careful to avoid coming off as another effete liberal. Clinton talked more about opportunity than fairness, more about helping the middle class than waging war on poverty. He could still sound like a populist because he knew that populism tended to be a more appealing message to most voters than pure neoliberalism. In his 1992 presidential campaign, he traveled to the Wharton School of the University of Pennsylvania, a top business school, and castigated it for prioritizing greed over Americans' well-being.

But Clinton was also a product of the elite networks that increasingly ran the Democratic Party. He had attended Georgetown and Yale and had been a Rhodes Scholar. He may have campaigned with populist poetry, but he governed with neoliberalist prose. He did for the Reagan revolution what Eisenhower had done for the New Deal: Clinton was the opposition-party president who endorsed much of the new approach rather than trying to reverse it. Reagan, upon taking office, had said, "Government is not the solution to our problem. Government is the problem." Clinton echoed him, telling Americans, "The era of big government is over."

Clinton did govern quite differently than Reagan had, much as Eisenhower had not simply mimicked Truman and Roosevelt. Clinton raised taxes on the wealthy and unsuccessfully attempted to expand health insurance. He reduced poverty by expanding the earned income tax credit—effectively a subsidy for low-wage workers—and creating a child tax credit. He also expressed frustration, at least briefly, about the overall direction of his agenda. "Where are all the Democrats?" he asked his aides at one point. "We're Eisenhower Republicans here, and we are fighting the Reagan Republicans. We stand for lower deficits and free trade and the bond market. Isn't that great?"

Nevertheless, much of Clinton's economic legacy was neoliberal. He continued to deregulate financial markets, repealing parts of the Glass-Steagall Act of 1933 and allowing mortgage-backed securities to grow unchecked. He signed a deregulatory telecommunications bill that largely absolved technology companies of responsibility for the material on their platforms. He continued the taming of antitrust enforcement. He did little to strengthen labor unions. He loosened trade rules with Canada, Mexico, and, most significantly, China. Doing so, he argued, would make America richer and other nations freer.

The first bill signed by Clinton embodied the new approach. It was the Family and Medical Leave Act, and it required large companies to give workers up to twelve weeks of unpaid leave. The bill was too liberal for Reagan Republicans but also far less ambitious than the programs that Democrats from earlier eras favored. The law did not provide paid family leave, as nearly every other country in the world does, which effectively would have given many workers a raise; it trusted market capitalism to pay people what they were worth.

Clinton was betting that his restrained version of neoliberalism could create the best of all worlds: rapid economic growth, widely shared prosperity, and expanded global influence for the United States.

SOME OF NEOLIBERALISM'S biggest triumphs occurred in the branch of the government on which Bork had urged his fellow free marketeers to focus: the courts. Bork's central idea—that consumer prices should become the yardstick of a policy's economic effects—went from fringe to dominant. Unless regulators could demonstrate that a merger would increase prices, judges became skeptical of antitrust actions to block it. The old system for evaluating mergers had been subjective and sometimes led to bizarre outcomes, like the Supreme Court's blocking of the merger between two modest-size shoe companies. Bork's method relied on the elegant formulas of academic economics. Most of the time, those formulas suggested that a merger would make a newly combined company more efficient and presumably reduce prices.

One example of the new consensus was the resolution of a 1986 lawsuit that accused the moving company Atlas Van Lines of abusing its market power in its treatment of truck drivers. Bork still served as an appellate judge in Washington at the time, and he was part of the three-judge panel that heard the case. He ruled in favor of Atlas and said that the market, not the legal system, could discipline a company that was abusing its power. Joining him in that decision was a judge whom Jimmy Carter had appointed: Ruth Bader Ginsburg. She, like Stephen Breyer, another Democratic judge who later joined the Supreme Court, had come to accept major parts of the Chicago School's arguments.

Even Bork's failed Supreme Court nomination ultimately underscored the success of the movement. After his defeat, Reagan nominated Douglas Ginsburg (no relation to Ruth Bader Ginsburg), the former head of the Justice Department's antitrust division. He was a Bork disciple on antitrust, and his selection underscored the issue's importance. When Ginsburg had to withdraw from consideration, after revelations that he had smoked marijuana with his law students, Reagan turned to Anthony Kennedy, a federal judge in California. In the White House memo summarizing Kennedy's candidacy, aides emphasized his pro-business record and his skepticism of antitrust rules. During the decades to come, Kennedy frequently disappointed conservatives with his Supreme Court decisions on social issues. But he was much more reliable on economic policy. He was skeptical of regulations and unions, and he often deferred to the wishes of corporate executives. Along with O'Connor, who also was more moderate on social issues than economic ones, Kennedy helped to undo the Supreme Court's pro-regulation legacy from the years when Earl Warren had been chief justice. On some issues, the Reagan revolution was indeed stymied. On economic policy, it succeeded.

Eventually, the conservative legal movement figured out how to avoid even partial disappointments on the Supreme Court. In 1982, in another attempt to change the intellectual climate, a group of conservative law students founded an organization, the Federalist Society. It would become a professional network for its members and provide a seal of approval that marked future judges as true conservative believers. At the society's inaugural conference in Connecticut, before almost anybody had heard of the group, two judges made the trip from Washington to speak: Bork and Scalia. "The court responds to the press and law-school faculties," Bork told the students. "The personnel of the media are heavily left liberal. Their values are quite egalitarian and permissive. Law school faculties tend to have the same politics and values." The speech was unusual, as media coverage noted, because sitting federal judges rarely criticized the Supreme Court. But Bork thought that conservatives needed to counteract the social pressure of the political left with their own approval and disapproval of federal judges.

This feedback became central to the Federalist Society's mission. Its members worked to reduce "the stigma associated with once-radical ideas," as the political scientist Amanda Hollis-Brusky wrote. The society would become one of the most influential groups in American politics. Like Bork, it set out to change the culture of American politics. By 2020, six of the Supreme Court's nine members had been part of the Federalist Society. The chief justice, John Roberts, was one of them, as were Samuel Alito, Amy Coney Barrett, Brett Kavanaugh, and Clarence Thomas. So was the justice who replaced Scalia: Neil Gorsuch, the oldest child of Anne Gorsuch. When the White House pressured her to resign in 1983, Neil was the teenager who urged his mother to stay and fight. She did not, but he would take up many of the same causes.

Neil Gorsuch excelled in college and law school and then became part of a conservative legal establishment that Bork and the Federalist Society had helped create. On the Supreme Court, he became part of an ambitious conservative majority, more willing than earlier justices to overturn court precedents on social issues, including *Roe v. Wade*. The new majority also continued to restrict the federal government's authority to regulate business, including the authority of the EPA, the agency Neil's mother had tried to tame in the 1980s.

As Roberts's influence over the court has waned because he is more cautious than the other five Republican appointees, legal observers have stopped referring to it as the Roberts court. They have had a hard time coming up with a new name. No one sitting justice has enough influence to seem worthy of the moniker. The five conservatives other than Roberts often vote as a bloc.

But there is a fitting name for this new court: the Bork court. Even though Bork himself never sat on the Supreme Court, his ideas have come to dominate its rulings. On issue after issue, a majority of justices vote as Bork would have.

THERE IS STILL one big question about the Reagan revolution—the biggest question, in fact: Did it create the economy it promised?

The revolution's advocates said that a shift toward a free-market economy would lead to a more prosperous country where living standards rose rapidly for most Americans. With bureaucrats marginalized and tax rates reduced, voluntary exchanges made possible by the price system would dominate economic life. The most innovative, efficient companies could grow, reducing the cost of goods, creating well-paying jobs for workers, and delivering strong returns for investors. The United States economy would outpace the collectivist economies of western Europe, Canada, and elsewhere.

In his first inaugural address, Reagan called the moment a new beginning. His administration, he said, hoped to build "a healthy, vigorous, growing economy that provides equal opportunities for all Americans." At his second inaugural, Reagan told the country that the renaissance had begun. "We are creating a nation once again vibrant, robust, and alive," he said. "Let history say of us: 'These were golden years—when the American Revolution was reborn, when freedom gained new life, when America reached for her best.'"

Any fair examination of Reagan's economic legacy should acknowledge his accomplishments and, by extension, the accomplishments of neoliberalism. The American economy could not have remained on its course from the 1950s and 1960s and continued to prosper. The global economy was becoming more competitive, and many American companies and unions had stultified. Parts of the regulatory apparatus of the postwar decades were inefficient and irrational. They created layers of regulatory review that could discourage the creation of new businesses and the construction of new projects. For these reasons, Jimmy Carter had deregulated some sectors before Reagan took office. The United States economy needed to become more flexible. It also needed to reduce the inflation of the 1970s.

Reagan's signature economic accomplishment was breaking the inflationary spiral, as had promised to do as a candidate. A calmer Middle East played a role, but the Federal Reserve, under Paul Volcker, deserved much of the credit. Volcker was a Carter appointee, reappointed by Reagan, who implemented a strategy that Chicago School economists had long favored. The Volcker Fed sharply raised interest rates, helping to cause the deep recession of the early 1980s. That recession reduced spending by enough that inflation finally began to decline and Americans stopped believing the problem was intractable. By 1982, inflation had fallen enough that Volcker could cut interest rates, sparking the boom that began in 1983. When Reagan ran for reelection the next year, he based his campaign on the economy's improvement. "It's morning again in America," a narrator pronounced in an iconic campaign commercial that showed people going to work, buying homes, and getting married.

Clinton's embrace of neoliberalism played a similar role in the 1990s boom. Instead of focusing his initial economic agenda only on federal spending, he reduced the federal budget deficit and calmed fears that the country might return to the inflation of the 1970s. The resulting rally in the financial markets fueled the formation of new businesses and the expansion of existing ones. Clinton's deregulation of the technology and finance sectors helped both grow. Given more freedom to behave as they wanted, American business executives created leading companies in many industries. Much as the Chicago School had insisted, the free market did a good job of directing resources toward profitable enterprises. The bleak situation for the stock market that Bork had described in the late 1970s, when prices did not even keep pace with inflation, came to an end. Stocks started soaring in 1982 and never returned to their previous levels. Reagan's defenders argued that he had started it all and deserved partial credit for the 1990s boom too. Anderson, one of his top aides, would describe the 1980s recovery as "the greatest economic expansion in history."

But that was not quite right.

A full accounting of Reagan's record finds two major weaknesses. First, the broadest measures of economic activity were solid on his watch but not spectacular. GDP per person—the combined value of the economy's output divided by the size of the population—grew more slowly under Reagan than during the combined Kennedy-Johnson administrations or Franklin Roosevelt's long presidency. Over the past century, in fact, economic growth has been somewhat faster under Democratic presidents than under Republican ones. Employment has also risen faster under Democrats. These simple comparisons should not be the final word on which party's economic policy is superior because a president has only limited control over the economy. At the very least, though, the macroeconomic statistics do not support the notion that laissez-faire policies produce better outcomes than progressive policies.

The second flaw in Reagan's record is larger yet. By many measures, his presidency was indeed a turning point for the American economy—in a negative way. Starting in the 1980s, an increasing share of the nation's economic bounty began flowing to a relatively small and affluent segment of the population. Incomes for everyone else grew quite slowly. To put it another way, Reagan helped end the weak overall growth of the 1970s, but he ushered in a new era of unbalanced growth. The combination meant that he failed to halt the slump in living standards that had begun in the 1970s. The increase in GDP growth could not overcome the sharp increase in inequality: The pie became somewhat larger, but a small share of wealthy families began to consume more and more of it, leaving less for most Americans. Reagan's presidency reinvigorated the stock market and the financial well-being of the wealthy. For most families, however, the Reagan revolution failed to deliver on its promise.

This can be seen in every widely used measure of income and wages, be it from the Census Bureau, the Bureau of Labor Statistics, the Internal Revenue Service, or academic researchers. Several years ago, I worked with Gabriel Zucman, an economist at the University of California, Berkeley, to compare the economy's performance before and after 1980, and the differences are stark. The analysis is based on a broad measure of income, subtracting taxes and adding government benefits like Social Security. For every part of the income distribution except the top 2 percent, the decades from World War II to 1980 produced faster income growth than the decades since. (A chart in the introduction, on page xxiii, shows this data.) Only for the affluent, and especially for the very affluent, has the post-Reagan economy created faster growth than the pre-Reagan economy.

The Clinton boom of the 1990s is also part of the disappointing modern era. For a few years during Clinton's presidency, incomes did rise at a healthy pace for the poor and middle class. But the trend did not last, and his record has not aged so well. Even while he was president, incomes for the rich were growing more quickly than for any other group, and some of the 1990s boom was the unsustainable product of a dot-com bubble that began deflating during Clinton's last year in office. Many of his promises—that his preferred mixture of free trade, deregulation, and tax credits would benefit ordinary workers—have gone unfulfilled.

Defenders of Reagan and neoliberalism respond to the statistics of recent decades in several ways. Some of the arguments are technical, claiming that the official numbers understate income growth for everybody because they exaggerate inflation. If the statistics accurately captured how low inflation has been, the past forty years look like a glorious economic era of rapidly rising living standards, according to this view. Most economists reject this argument and believe that the inflation data is not badly wrong. But the clearest refutation comes from noneconomic data, which paints as worrisome a picture of recent decades as the official economic statistics. Polls showing that Americans are unhappy with the economy's direction, for example, do not depend on highly technical inflation adjustments. Nor does data on health and lifespans. Starting around 1980, the United States became an outlier and today has the lowest life expectancy of any large high-income country. The slump in life expectancy among working-class Americans, even before Covid, is the main reason. The post-1980 period simply has not been a golden age for most Americans.

A more reasonable counterargument is that the past half century was destined to be a disappointing era for American economic performance because the postwar boom depended on the temporary struggles of the rest of the world. Once Japan and western Europe recovered from World War II and Asia developed, American growth was bound to slow. This argument has some legitimacy, but it still fails to qualify as a good defense of rough-and-tumble capitalism. For one thing, income growth since 1980 accelerated for the wealthy, which suggests the problem is not an inevitable slowdown in growth. Instead, the economy changed in ways that have benefited some Americans while harm-

U.S. life expectancy after age 25

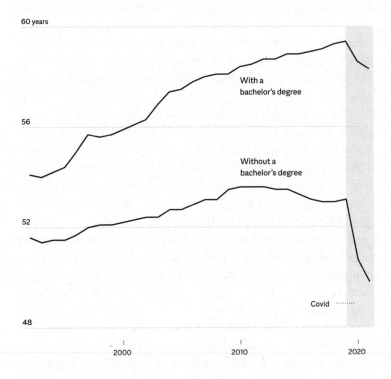

ing most. It is also notable that the United States moved closer to the neoliberal ideal than many other countries—and broad measures of national well-being, such as life expectancy, fared worse here than elsewhere.

As they were pitching their vision to the country, the members of the Chicago School made specific predictions. They claimed that an economy in which individuals could pursue voluntary exchange without much interference would produce the best results for the greatest number of people. It would do so because the free market was efficient and rational, allowing workers to enjoy the full fruits of their labor. In this vision, political power and cultural norms are relatively unimportant, and the real world resembles the market economy of economic theory. Companies pay workers what they are worth. Labor unions are pointless if not damaging.

Large companies cannot impose their will on consumers and workers. One of the ways Friedman made this point was to claim that
corporate profits made up too small a part of national income for
their fluctuations to matter much. Market forces, according to this
view, wring out excesses. Rough-and-tumble capitalism is supposed to produce faster growth and ensure almost everybody benefits.

That is not what happened. It did not happen partly because
power does matter in an economy. The decline of labor unions
pushed wages toward the low end of the range of indeterminacy.
The deregulation of many industries allowed companies to operate
with less government oversight. The soaring profits of the finance
sector, along with the financial crises of the early twenty-first century, were one legacy of that lack of oversight.

The economic importance of power also undermined many of
Bork's arguments about antitrust. He was correct that large companies could be so efficient that they reduced prices in the short
term. But with the market power that these companies acquired,
many could raise prices in the longer term. It happened in healthcare, with the merger of hospitals in many local markets leading to
higher prices. The merger of global pharmaceutical companies had
a similar effect. It also happened in the airline, cable television, and
mobile phone markets. Americans have fewer choices of phone
providers than many Europeans do and pay more for service. Rising corporate concentration helped employers hold down wages,
as well: A nurse in a region with only one hospital chain does not
have much bargaining power. And rising concentration gave companies more resources with which to influence government policy
by hiring lobbyists, making campaign donations, and subsidizing
advocacy groups. The elegant formulas evaluating a merger's effects, the ones that Bork believed should guide antitrust policy,
ignored many of these forces.

Global trade was another area in which neoliberalism offered
false promises to most Americans. Reagan, George H. W. Bush,
and Clinton all sold increased open trade as a win-win for the
country. American companies would gain access to new markets,
allowing them to hire more workers at good wages, while the

spread of market capitalism around the world would spread democracy. If some American workers suffered in the short term from the increased competition, Washington would come to their aid with retraining programs. These ideas led to the passage of the North American Free Trade Agreement with Canada and Mexico in the early 1990s and, more significantly, to the permanent lowering of tariffs on Chinese-made goods in 2001.

In hindsight, the China policy appears to have been one of the biggest failures of modern American economic policy. The shift of production to low-wage Chinese factories led to the loss of more than two million jobs in the early twenty-first century, according to an academic analysis. The professors who studied the problem referred to the phenomenon as "the China shock." The job losses were concentrated in the Midwest and Southeast and disproportionately harmed workers without a college degree. When researchers compared regions that had lost jobs to China to those that had not, they found that the places in the struggling category had become more politically polarized and more likely to support right-wing Republicans, including Trump.

As for China itself, the rapid expansion of factories in the 2000s had large economic benefits. Incomes rose, and poverty plummeted. But Chinese society did not change in the way that American presidents of both parties said that it would. Rather than becoming more democratic, China has become less so. Its new prosperity has enabled it to become the biggest global rival to the United States and one that favors authoritarianism at home and abroad. An irony is that China's rise has depended partly on trade protectionism, such as government subsidies for its companies and barriers to foreign entry. While the United States opened its economy to China, leaders in Beijing understood the value of a trade strategy that mixed market forces with government regulations.

Together, the neoliberal forces of recent decades—rising trade, increasing corporate concentration, declining unions, less regulation, and lower tax rates—have helped cause a decline in the share of American economic output going to workers' wages. Corporate profits, by contrast, have grown more rapidly than the economy.

By the early 2020s, profits accounted for more than 7 percent of national income, up from an average of 5.5 percent in the postwar decades. For a typical family, the increase translated to almost $3,000 every year that has flowed out of its own income and into corporate profits. That is a sizable amount of money, more than enough to undercut Friedman's claim that profits are too small a part of the economy to be significant.

Was there an alternate path that the American economy might have taken after 1980 with better results? There are reasons to believe so. After all, inequality has not risen as much in many countries as it has in the United States, and the American life expectancy trends have been uniquely bad for a high-income country. Better results certainly seem feasible. The neoliberal critique of the postwar American economy did contain important pieces of truth: The economy needed to become more dynamic. Government regulators and labor unions needed to recognize that rising global competition created challenges that had not existed in the 1950s and 1960s. Companies, unions, government agencies, and other organizations all stood to benefit by becoming more flexible. But instead of modifying the postwar economic model that had delivered such large increases in mass living standards, the country discarded it.

And who benefited?

In the 1940s, when the classical liberals at Chicago were still struggling to be noticed, the university's economics department included another faculty member who was less conservative and more prominent. His name was Paul Douglas. He had advised the Roosevelt administration during the New Deal and was later elected to the Senate, where he spent eighteen years. Long before Reagan implemented the Chicago School's ideas, Douglas offered a particular critique of those ideas: He said that the laissez-faire veneration of the market would benefit the wealthy and powerful at the expense of everybody else.

"The doctrine of non-interference with the market meant, in practice, clear the track for big business," Douglas wrote. American society would stop trying to prevent the excesses that resulted from inequalities in power, knowledge, and income. Government would return to a limited model out of the eighteenth century, which, Douglas argued, "had been insufficient even for that time and were certainly so for ours."

The most cynical view of the people on the other side of the argument—both free-market economists and their allies in business and politics—is that they promulgate their ideas out of raw self-interest. They want to make more money, and their intellectual justifications are fig leaves. That view strikes me as too cynical, at least in most cases. Robert Bork, Aaron Director, and the Friedmans seem to have believed that their ideas would create a better, stronger economy. So did Reagan, Anne Gorsuch, and Charls Walker.

But no matter how genuine their motives, they were wrong.

CHAPTER 9

This Little Village
Called America

ONE PART OF THE NEOLIBERAL REVOLUTION IN WASHINGTON long predated Ronald Reagan's arrival. It involved immigration policy.

In later years, many people did not associate a more welcoming immigration policy with neoliberalism. Political progressives came to celebrate the first and deride the second. Yet the two were indeed related. Neoliberalism calls for fewer laws restricting the behavior of businesses and citizens and greater deference to market forces. Freer movement of goods and capital, made possible by less regulation, is consistent with this vision. So is freer movement of people.

For much of the twentieth century, the United States tightly restricted who could enter the country. But when Senate hearings on the nation's immigration system opened on a winter morning in 1965, the identity of the senator in charge of the proceedings made clear that something had changed. It was Edward Kennedy, all of thirty-two years old, the youngest member of a political family that had become the country's most prominent advocate for overhauling the system.

Despite his role running the hearings, Kennedy did not chair the committee holding it. James Eastland, a Mississippi plantation owner and segregationist, did. For years, Eastland had helped block immigration reform as part of his belief that the United States should remain a White Anglo-Saxon nation. By the mid-1960s, however, Eastland recognized that he and the other opponents of reform were losing their ability to block bills. Rather than preside over the hearings likely to produce a bill he did not like, Eastland allowed Kennedy to do so. During Kennedy's short time in the Senate, he had gone out of his way to build good relationships with his colleagues, even those with whom he disagreed strongly, like Eastland. To reciprocate, Eastland let Kennedy become the face of the immigration bill in the Senate. The bill was the first that Kennedy tried to shepherd through the chamber.

The issue was a good fit for Kennedy, the Senate's youngest member. Other subjects, like healthcare and civil rights, were much more prominent in 1965 and took up the attention of more senior legislators. Immigration, by comparison, was "little noticed," as *The Wall Street Journal* reported. Yet immigration was a signature Kennedy issue. Teddy Kennedy, as he was known, was the descendant of Irish immigrants who had come to the United States in the mid-nineteenth century as part of a surge of people fleeing poverty and famine in Ireland. One of the children of those immigrants was John "Honey Fitz" Fitzgerald, Kennedy's maternal grandfather, who climbed Boston's political ranks and won a seat in Congress in the 1890s. Once there, he fought efforts to restrict the immigration that followed the Irish wave. "It is fashionable today to cry out against the immigration of the Hungarian, the Italian and the Jew," Fitzgerald argued on the House floor. "But I think that the man who comes to this country for the first time—to a strange land without friends and without employment—is born of the stuff that is bound to make good citizens."

Those on the other side of the debate—the immigration restrictionists—eventually triumphed over Fitzgerald's side and barred most immigration from eastern Europe and southern Europe, as well as Africa and Asia. They passed a bill in 1924 that set country-specific quotas for much of the world and sharply reduced overall immigration. The annual quota for Italy was only 3,845 immigrants. For Hungary, it was 473. For Greece, Turkey, Egypt, South Africa, and New Zealand, it was 100 each. The law virtually banned immigration from Asia, building off the Chinese Exclusion Act of 1882, the country's first major limit of immigration. The only region permitted to send large numbers of people to the United States was western Europe.

After the law's passage, one president after another viewed it as a blight on America's global image and tried to loosen the quotas, with support from a small band of Congress members with ties to immigrant communities, like Emanuel Celler of Brooklyn. The 1924 law, Celler said, was a piece of "gratuitous condescension" that claimed "one man is better than another." But Celler's efforts failed repeatedly. The restrictionist position remained so popular that after Truman vetoed a renewal and updating of the quotas in 1952, both the House and Senate overrode his veto. The quotas remained.

That same year, however, Massachusetts elected a senator who believed that the politics of immigration were changing: John F. Kennedy, one of Honey Fitz's grandchildren. Kennedy won his seat with votes from immigrant descendants, including the state's Greek and Italian communities. Many of them understandably objected to a law that treated them as inferior and that prevented their friends and extended family from joining them in the United States. As Kennedy searched for issues that could raise his national profile—especially among liberals, who often played a decisive role in choosing a Democratic presidential nominee and who distrusted the Kennedy family, given the conservatism and wealth of John's father—he saw promise in immigration.

Kennedy's advocacy of an overhaul of the law caught the attention of the Anti-Defamation League, a Jewish civil rights group, and it invited him to write a pro-immigration book that it would publish. Kennedy, happily accepting the offer, assigned one of his aides, a first-generation Ukrainian American, to write a draft. The book was called *A Nation of Immigrants* and appeared under Kennedy's name in 1958. It was a paean to American immigration, citing the work of Oscar Handlin, a Harvard historian who had been making the then novel argument that the United States should view itself as a nation of immigrants. Before Handlin, many scholars, and much of the American public, had thought of immigration as a footnote to the country's Anglo-Saxon legacy. The new school of history instead portrayed the British colonists as an initial wave of immigrants, not so different from those who followed. Along with the early British settlers came enslaved Africans. Then came Germans, Scandinavians, and Irish, followed by Chinese, Italians, Greeks, Poles, and Russians, until Congress first restricted Chinese immigration in 1882 and then shut the gates on most nationalities in 1924.

The resulting system, Kennedy explained, was grossly unfair. Two-thirds of all immigration slots were given to only three countries—Britain, Germany, and Ireland—and these slots often went unclaimed because relatively few western Europeans wanted to leave home in the 1960s. After winning the presidency, Kennedy assigned his brother Robert, the attorney general, to oversee the writing of an immigration bill, and the administration sent it to Congress in the summer of 1963. It would admit immigrants from around the world on a first-come, first-served basis, putting a priority on two categories: people with job skills that could benefit the economy and people wanting to reunite with family members already in the United States. The national origins quotas would be abolished, to be replaced by a single worldwide quota.

In the months immediately before and after John Kennedy's 1963 assassination, the restrictionists still had enough power in Congress to block the bill. By 1965, they no longer did. Lyndon Johnson had just won a resounding victory that swept dozens of liberals into Congress. The new majority saw immigration reform as another part of the 1960s movement to ensure that the United States lived up to its stated ideals of equality and opportunity. Even before Johnson's landslide, Congress managed to pass the 1964 Civil Rights Act, which banned job discrimination based on "race, color or national origin." Eliminating the immigration system's focus on national origin was a natural follow-up. The bill that Edward Kennedy would guide through the Senate closely resembled the bill that Robert Kennedy's Justice Department had written two years earlier. In addition to abolishing the country-specific quotas, it would repeal a ban on the entry of children with intellectual disabilities, which was also a personal subject for the Kennedys because of the disabilities of Rosemary, a sister of John, Robert, and Edward.

In treating would-be immigrants equally, the law could help restore a crucial part of the original definition of the American dream. As you may recall from the introduction of this book, the historian James Truslow Adams coined the phrase "American dream." In doing so, his signature example was Mary Antin, an immigrant who had escaped Russian pogroms with her family and moved to Boston as a teenager. In the United States, the Antins found far more opportunities than at home. Mary went on to write a celebrated memoir about the immigration experience, which ended with her proclaiming, "Mine is the shining future."

Not long after the publication of Antin's book, the 1924 law closed the country's door on families like hers. Four decades later, Edward Kennedy, Lyndon Johnson, and their allies set out to undo that injustice.

YET WHEN EDWARD KENNEDY opened the Senate immigration hearings on the morning of February 10, 1965, he did not start by making soaring arguments about equality and justice. Instead, he explained that he wanted to begin his remarks by correcting some misperceptions about the bill.

"Out of deference to the critics," Kennedy said, "I want to comment on the other side of the coin—what the bill will not do." In the two years since President Kennedy had made his original proposal, critics had argued that it would lead to a surge in the number of immigrants coming to the country. That claim was false, Edward Kennedy said, and Americans needed to know that it was false. The bill would make the rules fairer with respect to *who* could be admitted; it would not make major changes in *how many* people would be admitted. "Our cities will not be flooded with a million immigrants annually," he said. "Under the proposed bill, the present level of immigration remains substantially the same." The bill would set a global quota of 265,000 immigrants a year, little different from the combined national quotas in place at the time.

Kennedy added that he welcomed legitimate criticism of the bill. But the idea that it would lead to a large increase in immigration was unfounded. It was as unreasonable as some other accusations made against the bill, he said—like the claims that the bill would alter the country's ethnic makeup, aggravate unemployment, and permit the entry of criminals and political subversives.

"The charges I have mentioned are highly emotional, irrational, and with little foundation in fact," Kennedy continued. "They are out of line with the obligations of responsible citizenship. They breed hate of our heritage, and fear of a vitality, which helped to build America."

During the months of hearings that followed, the bill's supporters repeatedly returned to this point, arguing that the new system would not meaningfully change the amount of immigration. The 1960s were a less partisan time than today, and the supporters included both Democrats and Republicans. "The numbers are very, very small," Nicholas Katzenbach, the attorney general at the time, said, referring to the existing level of immigration, "and this bill does not really substantially increase it." Philip Hart, a Michigan Democrat known as "the conscience of the Senate," said the bill "makes no substantial change in the authorized level of people who will get into this country." Hugh Scott of Pennsylvania, soon to become the Republicans' Senate leader, also said there would be no serious increase. Senator Hiram Fong, a Hawaii Republican, explained, "We are actually not doing anything radically different from what we have done." To prove the point, Paul Douglas, the economist and senator from Illinois, turned to statistics and said that the population increase caused by the bill would be "only three-one-hundredths of one percent." In the House, Celler asked and answered his own question: "Do we appreciably increase our population, as it were, by the passage of this bill? The answer is emphatically no."

In addition to insisting that the overall numbers would not change much, the bill's advocates specifically promised that it would not lead to an increase in immigrants who would compete for blue-collar jobs. Any new immigrants would come from the two groups that the bill prioritized: family members of people who were already in the country and workers with high-level professional skills. The family members would not expand the pool of available workers because they would generally be outside the labor force—wives who stayed home, children too young to work, and elderly parents who were retired—according to the bill's advocates. The highly skilled workers would be coming to take jobs that were then going unfilled. Robert Kennedy, who had become a senator by 1965, liked to cite real-world examples of the people the existing laws had kept out of the country: a Korean radiologist, a Japanese microbiologist, a Greek chemist, a Turkish urologist, and a Filipina teacher of deaf children. The new bill would welcome experts like these, whom the economy needed, not ordinary workers.

In one testy exchange during the hearings, Sam Ervin, a North Carolina senator and immigration skeptic, asked Robert Kennedy whether the bill would also allow ditchdiggers to immigrate. Kennedy explained that it would not, because there was no shortage of them and thus they would not qualify for entry. "There are lots of ditchdiggers in the United States," Kennedy said. "So we would not be bringing ditchdiggers in here." Willard Wirtz, Johnson's labor secretary, went so far as to state that the bill offered "complete protection" against increased labor competition. The Labor Department would have the authority to decide which workers could enter the country, and it would admit only those with skills that the economy needed, Wirtz said in his congressional testimony.

These promises were crucial to the selling of the bill. Its advocates were political progressives, a mix of Democrats and liberal Republicans, and progressives had long worried about the damage that high levels of immigration could do to the country's most vulnerable citizens. The economic dynamic was straightforward: When the supply of an item rises, its price tends to fall. In the case of the labor supply, the price is the wage that a worker receives. By increasing the supply of workers, especially low-wage workers, immigration can allow employers to reduce wages and still attract workers.

There was a long history of this dynamic in the real world. Robert Fogel, a Nobel laureate in economics (and the son of immigrants), concluded that the mid-1800s immigration surge had caused "one of the most severe and protracted economic and social catastrophes of American history," affecting manual workers in major northern cities. Claudia Goldin, another Nobel laureate, studied the next immigration wave, around the turn of the twentieth century, by comparing cities with more and fewer new arrivals. She concluded that immigration had "substantial negative effects" on wages.

For similar reasons, the sharp decline in immigration during the middle decades of the twentieth century had the opposite effect: It contributed to the surge in working-class incomes. The supply of labor was restricted, and the price of labor rose. As the economists Peter Lindert and Jeffrey Williamson wrote, inequality during these years tended to decline the most in countries where the labor force grew the least. The benefits of low immigration were largest for low-wage workers, including many Black workers, who often competed with immigrants for jobs. One study found that Pittsburgh's steel mills became more willing to hire Black workers in the 1920s, after immigrant workers were no longer moving to the city in large numbers.

One factor was that high levels of immigration undermined labor unions' ability to organize workers. In the late 1800s and early 1900s, employers faced with a union-organizing drive could recruit nonunionized immigrants to replace the workers threatening to strike. After immigration plummeted in the 1920s, labor markets tightened, giving workers and their unions more leverage. "Immigration restriction, by making unskilled labor more scarce, tended to shore up wage rates," the labor historian Irving Bernstein wrote.

FOR THESE REASONS, leaders of labor unions and civil rights groups had historically been wary of high rates of immigration. They often praised immigrants themselves, but emphasized the problematic consequences of large-scale immigration. Samuel Gompers, the longtime head of the AFL, celebrated "the daring, the genius, the idealism of those who left homes and kindred to settle in the new land." He also worried that immigration surges "undermined standards and labor organizations." Booker T. Washington, in his 1895 Atlanta Exposition speech, urged White business owners to "cast down your bucket where you are"—meaning, to hire Black workers rather than recruit immigrants. Frederick Douglass lamented that "every hour sees us elbowed out of some employment to make room perhaps for some newly arrived emigrants."

A. Philip Randolph, whose labor activism helped transform Black America, likewise recognized the distinction between the questions of *who* and *how many* in the immigration debate. When Congress was updating the discriminatory national origins quotas in the 1950s, Randolph described them as "a sinister blow at civil rights and the doctrine of racial democracy and racial equality." But a just system, Randolph believed, was not necessarily one that permitted a large volume of immigration. As a union leader, he supported immigration restrictions for everyone—Germans, Italians, Chinese, Hindus, and "even the Negroes from the West Indies," as he put it. The country was suffering from "immigration indigestion," he argued in the 1920s. "Excessive immigration is against the masses of all races and nationalities in the country."

If anything, the push for higher levels of immigration had traditionally come more from the political right than the left. Even as some conservatives, like Senators Eastland and Ervin, had opposed immigration on xenophobic grounds, others favored higher levels of immigration on economic grounds. Business executives and lobbyists wanted to expand the country's labor supply for the same reason that unions opposed doing so: It could hold down wage costs and hamper labor organizing. During the debate over the 1924 law, the leaders of the National Association of Manufacturers and the chairman of U.S. Steel had both tried to prevent immigration restrictions from passing. They failed, but business interests did succeed in establishing an exception. The law did not place any limits on immigration from the Western Hemisphere, allowing farms to continue hiring many Mexican workers. Into the 1960s, the national origins quota system did not apply to Latin America or Canada.

High levels of immigration also appealed to the intellectuals of the rising free-market movement based at the University of Chicago. Immigration was a form of freedom, they argued. If somebody wanted to move to a new country and a business wanted to hire him or her, no government should block a voluntary agreement that could make both the worker and the employer better off. Milton Friedman celebrated the situation before the 1920s, when the country had both open borders and almost no welfare state. "Everybody benefitted," Friedman said. Immigrants could enter the country freely and were responsible for supporting themselves, rather than relying on welfare payments. These immigrants expanded the labor pool, allowing businesses to produce goods more cheaply and reduce prices for native-born families. Like free trade and deregulation, an open immigration system was a tenet of classical economic liberalism and of the neoliberalism that came later.

Edward Kennedy opened the 1965 hearings in the defensive way that he did to make clear that his bill was consistent with the progressive side of both major questions in the immigration debate. The bill would bring racial equality to the immigration system, and it would avoid the immigration surge that labor and civil rights leaders had traditionally feared. This combination had helped win the AFL-CIO's backing for the bill. A top lobbyist for the group told the Senate subcommittee that organized labor was not worried about the bill's effect on wages because it would not substantially increase immigration—and any increase would occur among professionals.

These arguments were consistent with broader public opinion. By the 1960s, most Americans favored a less racist system but one that kept the level of immigration roughly where it was, as Edward Kennedy and the Johnson White House understood. When Kennedy's bill was wending its way through Congress in the spring of 1965, a national poll created a brief crisis for its supporters. The poll, which received prominent newspaper coverage, had been conducted by Louis Harris, who ran one of the country's leading polling firms and had advised John Kennedy's 1960 presidential campaign. Harris's poll informed respondents that Johnson had proposed "letting more people come to the United States as immigrants." The survey then asked people's opinion of that idea. The response was extremely negative, with 58 percent of respondents saying they opposed the change and only 24 percent supporting it. The poll seemed to suggest that Congress was on the verge of passing a bill that a large majority of Americans opposed.

Seeing the results as a threat, Johnson administration officials set about discrediting them. Katzenbach, the attorney general, delivered a speech in New Jersey a few days after the poll's release praising Harris's firm but saying that this poll included a "misinformed" and "loaded" question. The question wrongly suggested that immigration levels would rise, the bill's supporters said. To dilute the poll's impact, a White House aide reached out to the Gallup Organization to encourage it to conduct its own poll, with different questions. Conveniently, Kennedy's Senate staff had drafted a few questions, which the White House made sure that Gallup received. Gallup agreed to do the poll.

As an independent firm known for rigorous polls, Gallup did not pose only the questions that the White House proposed. Gallup also asked a general question about what people believed should happen to immigration levels, and the results showed even stronger opposition to an increase than the Harris poll had. Only 7 percent of respondents said they favored more immigration; 40 percent supported keeping immigration at its current level, while 32 percent favored a reduction. But when Gallup asked the questions that Kennedy had suggested—about who should be admitted, which was the real substance of the bill, according to the White House—the results were more encouraging. Only 33 percent of respondents said that they supported quotas based on a person's country of origin, while 50 percent said they supported changing the system to make decisions based on job skills. "This is much better than the earlier Harris results," a White House aide wrote in an internal memo.

Americans grasped that immigration policy revolved around two distinct questions: Who? And how many? Many people supported the end of the discriminatory quotas for individual countries, but only if the total number of people coming into the country did not significantly increase.

THE SCARE FROM the Harris poll proved temporary, and Congress passed a bill in September 1965 that closely resembled President Kennedy's original proposal. It eliminated the national origins

Senator Edward Kennedy, center, shakes hands with President Lyndon B. Johnson after the signing of the immigration bill at the Statue of Liberty, 1965.

quotas and set an annual cap for worldwide admissions of 265,000. For the location of the signing ceremony, the White House chose the Statue of Liberty, making Johnson the first president to visit it since Franklin Roosevelt had gone to celebrate the statue's fiftieth birthday in 1936. Dozens of dignitaries, including nearly every member of Congress who had worked on the bill, took ferries from Lower Manhattan to Liberty Island on the Sunday afternoon of the ceremony. Johnson landed there by helicopter once the crowd had gathered. At the start of his remarks, with New York Harbor and the skyline behind him, he struck the same theme that Edward Kennedy had used to start the Senate hearings. Johnson emphasized what the new law would not do.

"This bill that we will sign today is not a revolutionary bill," Johnson said. "It does not affect the lives of millions. It will not reshape the structure of our daily lives, or really add importantly to either our wealth or our power." All that the bill would do, he explained, was repair the flawed national origins criteria for deciding who could enter the country. "This bill says simply that from this day forth those wishing to immigrate to America shall be admitted on the basis of their skills and their close relationship to those already here," he said.

The historical evidence suggests that Johnson, the Kennedy brothers, and the bill's other advocates genuinely believed the promises they were making. In their private exchanges, as well as their public comments, they insisted that the new law would not transform the flow of immigration.

But they turned out to be entirely wrong about that.

The 1965 bill changed both the *who* and the *how many* of the immigration system. The law sparked a decades-long immigration wave that continues today. As a percentage of the United States population, this modern wave has been similar in size to the immigration wave of the late 1800s and early 1900s. In terms of the sheer number of people moving to a single country, the modern American immigration wave may be the largest in history. During the year that Johnson signed the immigration bill, 297,000 immigrants legally entered the United States. Two years later, the number reached 362,000. It continued rising in subsequent decades and by 2001 exceeded 1 million.

How could the law's advocates have been so wrong about the effects of their own policy? One explanation is that they engaged in motivated reasoning. They believed, justly, that they were righting a historical wrong by eliminating the country-specific quotas and making the United States a fairer, more equal society. In their eagerness to achieve that victory, the reformers dismissed almost any criticism of the bill and failed to think carefully about its details. As Kennedy had done when opening the hearing, the bill's advocates painted almost any criticism of it as emotional, unreasonable, even hateful.

In part, they were reacting to the identity of the bill's critics: Many, like Eastland and Ervin, were opponents of the civil rights movement who indeed made racist arguments against the immigration bill. When Ervin spoke about countries that would benefit, he usually ignored southern and eastern Europe and instead named places where the residents had dark skin, like Cameroon, Ethiopia, Afghanistan, and India. He would ask what their cultures had contributed to American history and why the United States should be admitting more people from these countries.

Another critic was Michael Feighan, a conservative Democratic congressman from Ohio who chaired the House's hearings on the bill. By the mid-1960s, Feighan had been in Congress for more than twenty years, and many of his colleagues considered him to be something of a crank. He once sued a Howard Johnson's restaurant in a Washington suburb after he had broken his finger on a seat there. He also tried to block the actor Richard Burton from receiving a visa to enter the United States because Burton was having an extramarital affair with the actress Elizabeth Taylor. That unsuccessful effort reflected Feighan's general conservatism on immigration. Once he recognized that the reformers had the votes to change the law in 1965, Feighan focused on making sure the changes prioritized the admission of family members. Doing so, he believed, would benefit the Irish and Slavic families in his district, on the west side of Cleveland. More broadly, Feighan thought that such a policy would help ensure that future immigration resembled the European-centric immigration of the past. Like Eastland and Ervin, Feighan had racist motivations.

Yet these skeptics also raised legitimate questions about the bill. While the bill's supporters wishfully dismissed the possibility that the law might have unintended consequences, the skeptics were happy to point out the potential loopholes. The biggest loophole can seem blatant in retrospect, but the supporters insisted at the time that it did not matter: The bill's annual worldwide quota—265,000 people a year—did not apply to many immigrants. They were considered "nonquota" entries, allowed to enter the country without being counted. The most consequential of these nonquota entries proved to be family members. The law declared that immigrants who were coming to join relatives already in the United States would not count toward the 265,000. These relatives could enter the country without limit. Only the original immigrant in a family would count toward the cap. That loophole was not wholly new. But it had not mattered much before 1965, because the overall system was so restrictive. The new law opened the doors to the entire world without solving the nonquota problem.

Feighan focused on this loophole during the debate over the bill. He and his staff wrote a report in early 1965 about the gaps in the system and sent a copy to the White House. When Johnson administration officials mentioned the bill's annual 265,000 cap during House hearings, Feighan needled them by asking if they were referring to all immigration or only the kind that counted toward the cap. Most significantly, he proposed a true annual ceiling of 325,000 immigrants. Everybody—skilled workers, refugees, family members of immigrants—would count toward his ceiling. The bill's supporters never seriously considered the idea. They said it was unnecessary. They insisted that immigration would remain around 350,000 per year.

That is not what happened. The critics' predictions—that annual immigration might soon triple, as one conservative congressman forecast, and eventually surpass one million, as another anticipated—ended up being much more accurate. Nonquota immigration, especially family immigration, came to dominate the system. It did so partly because the world's population was growing so quickly in the 1960s. The world was also becoming richer and, paradoxical as it may sound, rising prosperity can lead more people to leave their native country. The process of migration—choosing to leave family behind, traveling to a departure city, paying for travel—can be beyond the reach of the very poor.

Within a year of the bill's passage, immigration officials admitted they had not expected the large number of people applying to enter the country as relatives of previous immigrants. "The extent of the change has surprised even those who fought hardest for it," a front-page *New York Times* story reported in 1968. Once these relatives arrived, the cycle repeated, with their own relatives eligible to follow. Because the law lacked the annual limit that Feighan had suggested, the loophole kept expanding, and immigration kept rising, far beyond the level that the law's authors had intended. In the late 1960s, the foreign-born share of the United States population was below 5 percent. It has since risen to almost 14 percent and in the years ahead is likely to exceed the 1890 peak of 14.8 percent. The advocates of the 1965 law were also incorrect about who would come. Many of the arrivals have been blue-collar workers, admitted as extended family, rather than specialists coming to fill specific job shortages.

I realize that some readers may be feeling a little uncomfortable about the history described here. The celebration of immigration has become core to the political beliefs of many Americans, on both the political left and right. Immigrants are underdogs, heroes, and—for most of us—ancestors. Opponents of immigration, by contrast, are often xenophobes like Feighan. In the twenty-first century, the contours of the immigration debate often seem binary: Somebody is either in favor of immigration or opposed to it. Historically, however, the debate was more nuanced. It included many people who were comfortable separating the questions of *who* and *how many*. They honored immigrants and decried bigotry without believing that more immigration was always better. The people who wrote the 1965 law claimed to hold precisely these beliefs.

That law deserves to be remembered as a monumental civil rights achievement. It ended decades of discrimination against Asians, Africans, eastern Europeans, southern Europeans, and disabled people. In other respects, though, the law represents a failure of democracy: It was sold to the American public with repeated promises that it would not do what, in fact, it did. In particular, it was sold with the false claim that there would be no increase in the number of immigrants who would be seeking blue-collar and low-wage jobs. Given this history, I think it is important to examine the law's legacy with an open mind and to ask whether the immigration surge has benefited everybody.

In 1965, the United States already had a more open immigration system than many other countries, with a higher percentage of foreign-born residents than most of Europe, and a far higher share than Japan. The 1965 law went further and created what the journalist Margaret Sands Orchowski has called arguably the world's most liberal immigration system. Theodore White, the chronicler of 1960s political history, described the law as "noble, revolutionary—and probably the most thoughtless of the many acts of the Great Society." More recently, Jay Caspian Kang, a journalist and child of immigrants, described the 1965 immigration law as the most important driver of contemporary politics that people rarely discuss. "The base narrative of American politics—especially as told by progressive lawmakers and the media machine that supports them—has not really acknowledged the profound demographic change in the country," Kang wrote.

The rest of this chapter is organized around three questions. The first focuses on immigrants: Have the millions of people who have arrived in this country since 1965 been able to achieve the American dream as successfully as earlier arrivals did? The second question addresses immigration's economic effects on people who were already in the United States: How has the immigration wave affected their wages and employment? The third question is less obviously economic yet also has major economic consequences: How has the post-1965 immigration wave altered American politics?

Along the way, I will introduce you to a modern version of A. Philip Randolph—an anti-racist voice for fairness and justice and a civil rights icon who became uncomfortable with the high levels of immigration in the United States. "Immigration is central to our American identity," she said. But she added, "There are costs. Good things are rarely free."

My goal is not to persuade you that any specific view of immigration policy is correct. You may decide that the United States has had the appropriate level of immigration over the past several decades or even that the level should rise further in the years ahead. But I hope to demonstrate that every piece of evidence does not line up neatly to support the conclusion that more immigration is always good or always bad. The advocates of the 1965 law did such a poor job anticipating its effects partly because they tried to ignore facts that they found inconvenient. They wanted to remake immigration law, for excellent reasons, and they chose to wave away evidence that did not neatly fit their argument. The rest of us do not need to repeat their mistakes.

. . .

MARY ANTIN, THE original immigrant to be associated with the phrase "American dream," thanks to Adams's book, landed in Boston as a thirteen-year-old in 1894. She came from Russia, where she was known as Mashke. Once in the United States, Antin quickly learned English and published poems in local newspapers while still a teenager. When she was in her twenties, her friend Josephine Lazarus—a sister of Emma, whose poem about immigration appears at the base of the Statue of Liberty—encouraged Antin to write a memoir. Antin titled the book *The Promised Land,* and it extolled the immigrant experience. Published in 1912, it became a bestseller. "My father had come to America to make a living," Antin wrote. "I thought it miracle enough that I, Mashke, the granddaughter of Raphael the Russian, born to a humble destiny, should be at home in an American metropolis, be free to fashion my own life, and should dream my dream in English phrases."

The Antins' experience was not typical, given Mary's literary success, but it did have broad similarities with most immigrants' lives. For one thing, her family did not enjoy immediate prosperity. The Antins remained mired in poverty after arriving in Boston. Mary's parents and their six children lived in a three-room tenement apartment without a bath. Mary's sister started working in a factory when she was fifteen. The institution that transformed the family was the Boston public school system, propelling the children into jobs that allowed them to escape poverty. In the decades that followed, Antin descendants lived middle-class lives in different parts of the United States, as nurses, members of the military, and more.

In recent years, two economists—Leah Boustan of Princeton and Ran Abramitzky of Stanford—have set out to compile an authoritative historical database tracking immigrant families. They have used ship manifests and census records dating to the 1800s and, for more recent years, the tax records assembled by Raj Chetty's research team at Harvard. The project is an example of how large amounts of digitized information, sometimes called "big data," can offer new insights into people's lives. These records have allowed Boustan and Abramitzky to compare the trajectories of immigrants from more than a century ago, such as the Antins, with the trajectories of more recent arrivals.

The earliest immigrants in the database are the millions who came in the late 1800s, predominantly from eastern and southern Europe, and who were subjected to intense bigotry. They tended to be poor and not to speak English. Many were Catholic or Jewish, rather than Protestant. Some had dark complexions. Because of these differences, native-born Americans often considered the new immigrants not to be White. These factors led to widespread worries that the immigrants would remain impoverished for decades, fomenting crime, alcoholism, and socialism. A journalist for *The Saturday Evening Post* wrote in the 1920s that an ostrich had a better chance of assimilating a croquet ball than the new immigrants had of assimilating into American life.

But of course they did assimilate. While typical immigrants remained poor for the duration of their own lives, their children made striking progress, no matter which country they had come from. Immigrants from Scandinavia tended to be the poorest when they arrived, and even their children quickly climbed the economic ladder, earning incomes close to the national average as adults, according to Abramitzky and Boustan. The children of poor Italian and Portuguese immigrants did better still, making more as adults on average than native-born children. The picture that Antin had drawn—of a shining future for new Americans—was much closer to reality than anything involving an ostrich and a croquet ball.

These success stories were easy to see in the second half of the twentieth century. Senator Jacob Javits of New York, a key supporter of the 1965 immigration bill, was a child of immigrants. So was Jack Valenti, an aide to President Johnson. In the business world, Walt Disney and Ray Kroc, who built McDonald's into a global chain, were both children of immigrants. In politics and law, Geraldine Ferraro, Antonin Scalia, and Ruth Bader Ginsburg were as well. In entertainment and sports, the list included Frank Sinatra, Lauren Bacall, Sid Caesar, Maria Callas, Rocky Marciano, Hank Greenberg, and Joe DiMaggio.

By the 1960s, the immigrants of eastern and southern Europe had done so well that they no longer seemed so different from their western European predecessors. Instead, concerns about assimilation during the debate over the 1965 bill focused on the next potential group of arrivals: those from Africa and Asia. "They don't look like we do," said Francis Walter, a Pennsylvania congressman and leading immigration opponent during the 1950s and 1960s. Walter was expressing a bigotry that has remained part of the debate. But bigots are not the only ones who wonder whether new immigrants can possibly fare as well as those from the past; many Americans, across the political spectrum, have shared this concern.

The post-1965 arrivals have been poorer on average when they arrive, relative to native-born Americans, than immigrants were in the late 1800s. Many recent arrivals lack education beyond high school, and they are trying to succeed in a technologically complex economy where good-paying blue-collar work is hard to find. A significant share of recent immigrants also enter the country without legal permission to do so, meaning that they lack access to basic resources and opportunities. The idea that recent immigrant families are less likely than earlier immigrants to climb the country's ladder is close to conventional wisdom.

It is also inaccurate.

Children of immigrants during the last several decades have ascended at a pace strikingly similar to that of earlier generations, Abramitzky and Boustan concluded. As in the past, immigrants themselves tend to remain poor if they arrive poor. And as in the past, the children tend to make up ground rapidly, regardless of what country their parents came from. Like Scandinavian families of the earlier era, recent immigrants from Mexico, Vietnam, and El Salvador tend to arrive poor, but their children still grow up to earn almost as much as native-born Americans. Like Italian families of the past, the children of immigrants from Colombia, Ecuador, China, and South Korea earn even more than the national average. Overall, most children of the recent immigration wave have grown up to earn at least a middle-class income. There is no permanent underclass of American immigrants.

Finding famous children of the post-1965 immigration wave is not as easy as it is for past waves, because most are still in their thirties or forties, if not younger. Many have yet to reach the peak of their careers. Yet some examples already exist: Mindy Kaling, the comedian; Pitbull, the singer; Chrissy Teigen, the television star; Nathan Chen, the gold-medal-winning figure skater; Nikki Haley, the former ambassador to the United Nations. More meaningful, perhaps, is the list of Americans whose parents came to the United States shortly before 1965. Even though immigration was low during these years, this small pool of families has produced an outsize share of success stories, including Barack Obama, Kamala Harris, Marco Rubio, Ted Cruz, the lawyer Preet Bharara and the surgeon and author Atul Gawande. Another member of this group is Raj Chetty, whose parents moved to the United States from India in 1962 and raised him in Milwaukee. One of the reasons that Chetty studies economic mobility, he has said, is that he appreciates the opportunities he has had and wants to understand how more Americans might have similar chances to build better lives.

There are certainly caveats to the encouraging findings by Abramitzky and Boustan. In a country as large as the United States, averages hide a lot of variation, and some immigrant families do struggle for decades. They suffer discrimination and remain in poverty for multiple generations, much as some native-born American families do. It is also worth pointing out that intergenerational research necessarily comes with a lag. There is not much earnings data on the children of immigrant families who arrived after 2000, because most of these children have not yet grown up. Many recent immigrants have indeed been quite poor, and many have made only modest economic progress since arriving—less on average than in the past, some data suggests. Perhaps their children will struggle more than earlier generations. The children of undocumented immigrants face particular hardships. In the past, undocumented immigrants benefited from amnesty provisions, like those in a 1986 law signed by Reagan that allowed many people to become citizens. During the 2020s, the prospects for any similar law seem dim.

In the big picture, however, the most likely scenario is that the past patterns will continue: Immigrants themselves will often remain poor, but their children will do considerably better. This may also be true for most children of undocumented immigrants, given that anybody born in the United States automatically becomes a citizen. Unlike their parents, they will be able to vote and receive government benefits including federal financial aid. (The so-called Dreamers, undocumented immigrants who came as young children, are in a more difficult situation.) In their research, Abramitzky and Boustan examine not only income but also other measures of assimilation, such as where immigrants live, whom they marry, and whether they speak English. On these metrics, today's immigrants look similar to those from past generations. By some measures, like intermarriage, the current wave is assimilating more rapidly than previous generations. Overall, the similarities between today's immigrants and the immigrant families of the past who fared so well appear greater than the differences.

WHY HAVE IMMIGRANTS done so well? Why are they a marvelous exception to the decline of the American dream over the past half century?

Some of their success stems from what scientists call the selection effect. Immigrants are not a random subset of the population. People who are willing to uproot their lives for better opportunities have more ambition and grit than an average person, and these qualities help them succeed after they have arrived in their new country. Some of them have also accumulated more skills and knowledge—"human capital," in the language of economics— than most native-born Americans of a similar social class. Think of a Russian doctor who works as a physician's assistant in the United States or a Bangladeshi scientist who drives a taxi. These immigrants had to take a step backward to find work in a new country, but their human capital can nonetheless help launch their children into better-paying jobs. The daughter of that taxi driver who was a scientist in his home country is more likely to become a scientist herself than the daughter of the taxi driver who never graduated from college.

One factor especially important to immigrants' success is their willingness to move, Abramitzky and Boustan discovered. Native-born Americans often feel tied to the place where they live because of family, friends, or other local ties. Immigrants more frequently pull up roots to move from one American city to another for better job opportunities or more affordable housing.

The city of Houston is a case study. Houston began its history in the 1800s as a railroad hub and later became a port, connected to the Gulf of Mexico by a canal. In 1900, when a hurricane destroyed much of Galveston, the original economic capital of southeast Texas, Houston suddenly looked like an appealing alternative. Unlike Galveston, Houston was far enough inland to be more protected from the storms that came off the Gulf. Not long after, the discovery of oil brought a new industry to the region. Next came the space industry and its offshoots, a result of President Johnson placing NASA's headquarters in Houston as a favor to his native state. Healthcare and higher education followed, with the MD Anderson Cancer Center, Rice University, and other research institutions. These industries created thousands of jobs and booming markets for retail and construction.

Houston's economy has benefited from some of the best parts of both the progressive and free-market economic traditions. Progressives, including Republicans like Eisenhower, recognized that economic growth depended on investments that the private sector would never make on its own. In Houston, government money was behind the rise of every major industry, through the financing of railroad tracks, the ship channel, oil infrastructure, and space and medical research. At the same time, Houston's skepticism of government regulation spared it the strict zoning laws that have hampered the building of new homes in much of the Northeast and California. Houston does not suffer so much from NIMBYism (an acronym that stands for "not in my backyard" and describes opposition to construction). As a result, housing is less expensive than in some other large urban areas.

Immigrants have responded to the combination of plentiful jobs and affordable housing by moving to Houston in droves. "New York is not really a good place to raise kids," Melody Mei-Ching Lo Shu, who emigrated from Taiwan in 1972 as a teenager, told an interviewer for an Asian American oral history project based at Rice University. Her brother had visited Houston, and it seemed more open and less crowded than New York. It also had weather like Taiwan's. Shu and her husband decided to give it a chance. "We just sold everything," she said, and went to Houston to "start with nothing." She graduated from a community college and worked at a bank, while one of her two children became an engineer and the other worked for a software company. There are thousands of similar stories among Houston's Asian and Latino immigrants.

In 1960, the city was almost entirely White or Black—74 percent non-Hispanic White (or Anglo, as many Texans say) and 20 percent Black. Since the 1960s, immigrant families have flocked to Houston, nearly quadrupling the population and turning the metropolitan area into the country's fifth largest. In 2021, it was only 33 percent Anglo and 17 percent Black. It was 39 percent Latino and 8 percent Asian. Houston has become a mosaic of post-1965 America—and a social mobility machine. According to the tax returns analyzed by Chetty and his colleagues, Latino and Asian immigrants have experienced more rapid upward mobility in Houston than in almost any other American city.

Immigrants have not been immune from the other forces described in this book, like shrinking labor unions, rising imports, and growing corporate concentration. The wages of immigrants and their children have grown more slowly than they would have absent these forces. But most immigrant families have made enormous progress over the past half century relative to where they started. As Abramitzky and Boustan write, "The American Dream is just as real for immigrants from Asia and Latin America now as it was for immigrants from Italy and Russia one hundred years ago."

By now, this story should feel familiar. Over the course of American history, each new cohort of immigrants has faced assumptions that it was less likely to succeed because it was somehow different from previous cohorts—poorer, darker, less educated, less able to assimilate. And each new cohort has proved the doubters wrong.

. . .

THE SECOND BIG question about immigration is how it has affected the living standards of people who were already in the United States. On the surface, the facts look damning.

The decades when the American masses enjoyed their fastest income gains—in the middle of the twentieth century—were also the decades when immigration was near historical lows. The 1965 law ended this era and caused a sharp rise in the number of immigrants entering the workforce. Shortly afterward, incomes for poor and working-class Americans began to stagnate. The 1940s, 1950s, and 1960s were a time of low immigration and rapidly rising mass living standards. The period since the 1970s has been neither.

Correlation and causation, obviously, are not the same thing. To distinguish between the two, economists have devoted extensive effort in recent years to figuring out how much immigration has affected the living standards of native-born Americans. The task is not easy. Immigration changes an economy in myriad ways, including some that increase the incomes of native-born workers. When an immigrant starts a business—as has been the case with Google, Moderna, Instagram, eBay, Chobani yogurt, and many other companies—it creates jobs. The presence of immigrants also increases demand for goods and services and creates other jobs. In many communities, immigrants enable parents to enter the workforce by providing affordable childcare. These factors need to be balanced against the costs of immigration, including immigrants' use of government benefits and their role in holding down wages by expanding the labor supply.

To make sense of all this, researchers have tried to break down the economy into smaller pieces and analyze those pieces. Some of the research has compared industries with many immigrant workers to industries with relatively few. Other research has compared geographic areas that have received different amounts of immigration. The Mariel boatlift of 1980, when about 125,000 Cubans moved to south Florida in a short period of time, has been studied extensively because it resembled a natural experiment. Social scientists were able to contrast economic outcomes in south Florida with outcomes in otherwise similar places that did not receive a sudden influx of new residents.

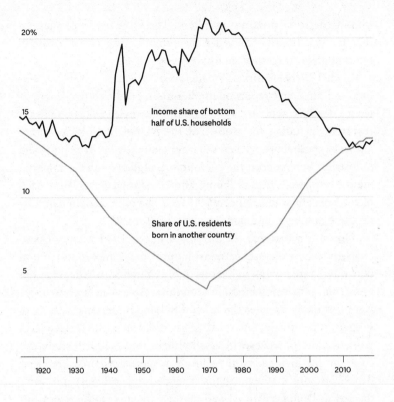

One finding from these studies is that immigration has not been the dominant cause of post-1970s wage stagnation, despite the suspicious timing. You do not need to be able to read peer-reviewed articles in an academic journal to grasp this conclusion (although those articles support it). You simply need to notice that the regions attracting the largest number of immigrants are not the ones suffering the worst wage stagnation. Houston, Chicago, New York, Boston, Washington, San Francisco, and Los Angeles are all immigrant magnets, and all have regional economies that have performed relatively well in recent decades. Income growth in these places, including for natives, has been faster than in many places where few immigrants have moved, like Indiana, Ohio, Mississippi, and Oklahoma. If competition from immigrant workers were the main cause of income stagnation, the states with less competition should have been relatively spared. They have not been.

But the story does not end here. The same evidence suggests that immigration has played a meaningful, if secondary, role in holding down wages for many workers.

In 2017, the National Academy of Sciences released a six-hundred-plus-page report on immigration, produced by a committee of leading scholars. The committee reviewed the relevant research, including the studies of the Mariel boatlift and other natural experiments, as well as larger comparisons of regions and industries. In its report, the committee included a table summarizing the estimated effect of immigration on native wages, from each of the relevant studies since the 1990s. The table is dominated by negative numbers. Immigration does have costs.

One study analyzed the aftermath of the 1994 Mexican peso crisis, which was another quasi-natural experiment, and found that wages fared worse in regions of the United States that received more migrants. Another study found that American-born workers were less likely to enter the field of nursing in regions with more foreign-born nurses. A third study concluded that teenagers worked more in places with less immigration. A fourth study, focused on the high end of the education spectrum, discovered that American-born mathematicians struggled to get faculty jobs after the Soviet Union collapsed and mathematicians from eastern Europe moved to the United States.

Logic and history point to the same conclusion as the economic data. That is why labor leaders opposed high levels of immigration for so long—and why the architects of the 1965 law vowed that it would not allow more ditchdiggers and other manual workers to enter the country. When immigration surges, employers often have the upper hand. When immigration is low, explained the economist Sumner Slichter, employers are forced "to adapt jobs to men rather than men to jobs." People sometimes claim that immigrants work in jobs that native-born Americans do not want. But Christopher Jencks of Harvard University has pointed out that this statement is incomplete: Immigrants typically work in jobs that native-born Americans do not want *at the wages that employers are offering.* One reason that employers can offer such wages, Jencks adds, is the availability of so many immigrant workers.

The precise answer to how much immigration has affected native-born workers will never be known. The subject is too complicated, too dependent on estimates and assumptions. But the bulk of evidence does not support the claim that some immigration advocates make—that immigration is virtually without costs. Instead, the post-1965 wave has had both benefits and costs.

On the plus side, it has probably accelerated economic growth, mostly by expanding the size of the labor force. With a larger population, the United States has been able to produce more goods and services. Immigration also appears to have benefited many high-earning, native-born professionals. The costs of immigration for these workers have been fairly low because they face relatively little competition from immigrant workers. The highly educated immigrants who come to the United States tend to be concentrated in certain fields, such as mathematics and information technology. Fewer are lawyers or doctors partly because some professions have created barriers that restrict entry. In medicine, for example, foreign doctors are required to complete a multiyear residency program in the United States, regardless of their prior experience. That rule, and similar licensing requirements in other professions, reduces competition from immigrants. Evidently, professionals who have enough political influence to shape labor-market rules, like doctors, understand that a larger labor pool can reduce incomes.

For many lower-earning workers, there are no such protections. In retail, construction, childcare, and many other service industries, more immigrants have been able to compete for jobs. Their entry has had two separate effects that have increased inequality. For the lower end of the income distribution, the expansion of the labor pool has held down wages. For the higher end of the income distribution, these lower wages have held down the prices of frequently used services like childcare, restaurant meals, and landscaping. For white-collar professionals, the economic benefits of immigration have been larger, while the costs have been smaller. Canada is a useful point of comparison. It also rewrote its immigration law in the 1960s but took a different approach. It created a system that prioritized the admission of educated workers rather than family members. As a result, Canada's immigration patterns have tempered rising income inequality by creating more high-wage labor competition.

Just how much immigration has held down wages in the United States is a matter of intense dispute among economists. Two giants of the field—George Borjas and David Card—have spent decades debating the question. Sometimes, they have come to dueling conclusions about the same evidence. After analyzing the Mariel boatlift, Card concluded that it had only a very small effect on native-born wages. Borjas concluded that it erased about a decade's worth of wage increases for Miami's least educated workers. The disagreement highlights the difficulty of teasing out the precise effects. So many other factors influence a region's economy that economists have a difficult time answering the hypothetical question of how reality would have been different if everything other than immigration levels had remained the same. Overall, Borjas's research has suggested that immigration between 1980 and 2010 might have reduced the wages of high school dropouts by more than 10 percent, with smaller declines for other groups.

Regardless, several other forces, like the decline of labor unions, have almost certainly had a larger impact. If the United States wanted to keep immigration high and ameliorate the effects on inequality, it could surely do so—say, by cutting taxes for low-earning workers and raising taxes on high-earning professionals. The problem is that the country has not used government policy to reverse the growth of inequality; the tax system has instead exacerbated inequality. For all the benefits of the post-1965 immigration wave, American workers are not delusional to think that it has had costs—and that they, rather than more affluent Americans, have borne those costs.

So far, I have focused on immigration's direct economic effects. But it has also had major political effects, and many Americans, both liberal and conservative, have misunderstood them. It was not until I dug into the research from another field—psychology—that the politics of immigration made sense.

. . .

IN THE 1990S, an American psychologist named Jonathan Haidt was thinking about how notions of morality differed from one culture to another. During that time, Haidt attended a conference in Brazil and met several Brazilian psychologists who were mulling over similar issues. They decided to collaborate.

They designed a survey based on very short stories in which somebody violated what Haidt called a "harmless taboo." In each anecdote, a fictional person took an action that did not hurt anybody else but that might nonetheless feel wrong to some people. The survey's respondents had to judge whether the behavior was immoral or simply a matter of individual choice. In one story, a boy refused to wear a required school uniform. In another, a woman cut up a national flag that she no longer needed and used the pieces as cleaning rags. In still another, a family's dog was killed by a passing car and the family decided to cook and eat the dog. The researchers conducted the survey in two Brazilian cities, and Haidt repeated it in Philadelphia, where he was a professor at the University of Pennsylvania. In all three cities, the psychologists surveyed people in two different social classes, one higher and one lower.

As Haidt expected, the answers varied by city. In Philadelphia, people were less likely to judge the violation of a social convention—like refusing to wear a uniform, cutting up a flag, or eating a dead pet—as immoral. Philadelphians were more individualistic: If nobody was harmed, what was the problem? In Porto Alegre, a relatively affluent, European-influenced city in southern Brazil, the responses fell somewhere in the middle. In Recife, a poorer Brazilian city in the north, respondents were most likely to judge violations of social convention as wrong: Society has rules and traditions, and defying those norms is immoral, many said.

But the data also contained a surprise. The class differences within each country were larger than the differences between Brazilians and Americans. In all three cities, lower-income people were much more likely than upper-class people to judge the violation of social conventions as wrong. The working-class respondents emphasized communal standards and traditions. The professionals emphasized individual notions of freedom. "I had flown five thousand miles south to search for moral variation when in fact there was more to be found a few blocks west of campus, in the poor neighborhood surrounding my university," Haidt later wrote.

In the years that followed, Haidt and his colleagues created a broader version of the survey, known as the Moral Foundations Questionnaire, and hundreds of thousands of people around the world have taken it. It asks how people feel about chaos and respect for authority, as well as whether they are proud of their country, whether somebody should be loyal to a family member who has done something wrong, and whether a soldier can justifiably defy a commanding officer's order. In one country after another, the patterns were similar. Educated professionals emphasize two values above all: care for others, especially the vulnerable, and fairness. Working-class people put significant weight on those values too, but not quite as much. And working-class respondents emphasize a set of values that are of little import to college graduates, like respect for authority, appreciation of tradition, and loyalty to family and community. Other researchers have come to use the terms "universal" and "communal" to describe the two belief sets.

Both universalism and communalism have important advantages, scholars emphasize. The universalist passion for fairness and harm prevention has undergirded every great social justice movement of the past century. While some communalists defended racial segregation as a cultural tradition, universalists refused to accept it. The same held true for sexism, homophobia, and religious discrimination. The universalist beliefs in fairness and care were also behind the pushes for Social Security, Medicare, Obamacare, and tax credits for the poor. In foreign policy, universalism helped lead to the Marshall Plan to rebuild Europe after World War II. Universalism has made the world both freer and more equal.

Communalism can claim its own accomplishments, though. Without loyalty, tradition, and respect, human beings would not have been able to form groups that allowed them to survive. Communalism helped city-states and nations to embark on grand building projects and repel enemies. In modern times, communalism has inspired Americans to enlist in the military and become teachers at local elementary schools. The same outlook helps explain why working-class households tend to give a greater percentage of their income to charity (often their churches) than upper-income households. Communalism also played a central role in social justice movements: Religious groups, and the loyalty they inspire, were crucial to both abolitionism and civil rights activism. Today, communalism continues to promote equality of opportunity: According to Chetty's research, children are more likely to escape poverty if they grow up in a place where people have strong social connections to one another.

The philosopher Michael Sandel has developed a set of thought experiments to help people consider the benefits and drawbacks of the two worldviews. Sandel is a Harvard professor who lectures at conferences around the world—settings where universalism is the dominant outlook—and he tries to persuade his audiences to grapple with the limits of their views. At one televised gathering with a group of young adults in the Netherlands, Sandel asked them whether a hypothetical food bank should prioritize feeding citizens over foreigners who were not citizens, and most of the attendees confidently said no. Other questions were thornier, however. If you lived in a city where food was scarce, would it be reasonable to feed your own child before another? What about feeding a child next door before a child farther away? How much responsibility does the Netherlands have to send its tax dollars to poorer countries?

A similar hypothetical is to imagine that somebody gave you $1,000 to split between an impoverished child who lived in your community and an even more impoverished child who lived in another country. Does one deserve more than the other? All these questions pose a dilemma about when people should prioritize those closest to them and when doing so is immoral. Communalists feel comfortable being loyal to their family, neighborhood, community, and nation. Universalists focus on who has the greatest need.

Immigration policy presents a distillation of the tensions between the two worldviews. To communalists, a government should limit arrivals and prioritize its own citizens. To universalists, national loyalties can be dangerous, and immigration can lift global living standards by allowing more people to share in a rich country's prosperity. In recent decades, this debate has become part of the growing political polarization in many Western countries, including the United States. Surveys show that liberals tend to be universalists who support higher levels of immigration, while conservatives tend to be communalists who favor less immigration.

This polarization is relatively recent. Across American history, communalism has not been simply a synonym for conservatism. Many communalists were progressives who emphasized fairness and equality within a community. When they had to choose between protecting neighbors who were vulnerable and others who were vulnerable, they were comfortable focusing on the needs of their vulnerable neighbors. These progressive communalists included A. Philip Randolph, Booker T. Washington, and Samuel Gompers. They also included the civil rights icon whom I promised you would meet in this chapter.

GROWING UP, Barbara Charline Jordan faced more discrimination than many Americans can fathom. She was a Black child living in segregated Houston during the 1940s. She was a girl whose father told her that the only reasonable career aspirations for girls involved music or teaching. She was a tall, powerful girl whose size did not conform to standard ideas about femininity. She also had dark skin, darker than her parents and siblings did. "The world had decided that we were all Negro, but that some of us were more Negro than others," Jordan said later. "You achieved more, you went further, you had a better chance, you got the awards, if you were not black-black with kinky hair."

Nonetheless, Barbara Jordan went very far. That she did was a testament to her talent and resilience. Jordan believed it was also a result of the strong communities in her life.

Jordan's first community was Good Hope Baptist Church, where her grandfather, a truck driver, had been a lay leader. Good

Hope was "a warm cocoon of love" and "a safe haven of activity, meetings, music, fellowship, friends, and support," as Jordan's biographer, Mary Beth Rogers, wrote. At Texas Southern University, a historically Black college in Houston, Jordan's community was the debate team. It won so many events that it became nationally renowned, inspiring Harvard's debate team to travel to Houston to compete against it. Jordan and her partner tied a duo from Harvard. Jordan always said it felt like a win.

After attending law school at Boston University, Jordan found another community in Houston's Democratic Party, where liberals and labor organizers who were trying to move the party beyond its segregated past recognized Jordan as a future star. In 1960, party officials had been impressed by her campaign work on behalf of the Kennedy-Johnson ticket. When she later decided to run for the state legislature, the officials repaid her dedication by backing her over more experienced candidates. It took her a few tries, but she eventually became the first Black member of the Texas Senate since Reconstruction. Every other senator in the chamber at the time was both White and male. In 1972, with encouragement from Lyndon Johnson, Jordan ran for Congress and won.

These experiences helped turn Jordan into a classic communalist. She believed that loyalty, tradition, and social connection were crucial to the struggle for a fairer world. She knew that human beings had a natural urge to be part of a group and feel pride in that group. It was true about a family and a church. It was true about a college debating team and a political party.

In the modern world, the most powerful organizing unit is a nation. The globe is divided into nations that govern, tax, and protect their citizens. Jordan thought that making the world a better place required an acceptance of this reality. She made the case for justice and equality by arguing that they were distinctly American values. She believed that her efforts would be more effective if she could tie them to traditions that Americans already embraced.

It was the same strategy that civil rights leaders had repeatedly used. Randolph cast his 1941 campaign to integrate the defense industry as a patriotic effort to strengthen American democracy against fascism. During the 1965 voting rights march from Selma to Montgomery, the marchers carried American flags. (Counter-protesters along the route did the marchers a political favor by holding up Confederate flags.) When Martin Luther King introduced the key metaphor in his speech at the March on Washington, he did so this way: "And so even though we face the difficulties of today and tomorrow, I still have a dream. It is a dream deeply rooted in the American dream."

Jordan, for her part, liked to talk about the United States as a community. "The real bottom line is community—the community," she told a group of schoolchildren. "We are all in this little village called America together." In the Texas Legislature, she used this idea to justify the state's first minimum wage and an increase in disability payments for workers who were injured on the job. In Congress, she successfully pushed for an expansion of the Voting Rights Act to require areas with a significant number of Latino residents to print election materials in Spanish. The goal of all these measures was to treat every American as a full member of the community.

The event that made Jordan famous likewise relied on a call to patriotic communalism. In her first term in Congress, she secured a seat on the House Judiciary Committee, which was holding hearings to consider impeaching Nixon. On the evening of July 25, 1974, near the end of a long day of testimony, Jordan delivered a rousing speech denouncing Nixon's cover-up of the Watergate break-in. The Constitution was a powerful document, she said in her booming voice. True, the Constitution had originally excluded Jordan from its definition of "we the people," she said, but the country had since amended it. The definition now included her and every other citizen. As an elected representative of the people, she explained, she had a duty to ensure that the president obeyed the Constitution.

"My faith in the Constitution is whole. It is complete. It is total," Jordan told the hearing. "I am not going to sit here and be an idle spectator to the diminution, the subversion, the destruction of the Constitution." Journalists described the speech as Churchillian. For many Americans, it was the first time they had heard a major speech from either a female or a Black member of

Congresswoman Barbara Jordan during a hearing to investigate
President Richard Nixon, 1974.

Congress. Nixon resigned two weeks after the hearing. Jordan became known for carrying a copy of the Constitution in her pocket.

Two decades later, after multiple sclerosis had led her to retire
from Congress and teach at the University of Texas, President Bill
Clinton asked for her help. He needed to find somebody to chair a
federal commission on immigration when the issue was roiling national politics. In 1986, Reagan had signed a bill that was meant
to be a grand bargain both reducing future illegal immigration and
allowing many undocumented immigrants who were already in
the country to become citizens. But the law lived up to only one
part of that bargain. The measures to reduce illegal immigration
proved to be relatively weak. The fines for employers that hired
undocumented workers were small, and the government did little
to enforce them. By the early 1990s, illegal immigration was rising
again, and the economy was struggling, leading to a surge of anti-
immigrant sentiment. California passed a ballot initiative, Proposition 187, denying some benefits to noncitizens. Immigrant
advocates were worried that people would lose access to education
and medical care. Clinton hoped the federal commission could
find more humane solutions, and he turned to Jordan because she
remained one of the country's most admired figures.

Jordan initially said no. She was too busy teaching, she explained, and she had little background in the subject. But Susan

Martin, an immigration expert who oversaw the commission's staff, persevered. Martin told Jordan that few other people in the country had the credibility to take on such a divisive subject. The commission's best hope for designing a better immigration policy depended on having a leader Americans already trusted. In the end, Jordan agreed to take the job.

AS JORDAN STUDIED the issue, she came to believe that being strongly pro-immigrant and strongly pro-immigration were not the same thing. At times, those two principles could be in conflict. When the citizens of a country grew unhappy about its immigration system, they could support policies that hurt immigrants who were already in the country. Proposition 187 was an example. In Jordan's view, there was sometimes a trade-off between immigrant rights and immigrant numbers. Higher immigration levels could lead to the persecution of immigrants. That was political reality.

Jordan considered herself resolutely pro-immigrant. She said that her main qualification for running the commission was that she, too, had endured discrimination and been made to feel alien. "The history of American immigration policy is full of racism and ethnic prejudice," she said during one speech while she chaired the commission. "There are always those who despise newcomers." She cited the Chinese Exclusion Act of 1882, the anti-Irish Know-Nothings of the 1850s, and Ben Franklin's eighteenth century doubts about the ability of German immigrants to assimilate. This immigration bashing had continued into present times, she said, and it had to stop. Borrowing Kennedy's phrase, she described the United States as a nation of immigrants.

Yet she believed that both parts of the phrase—"immigrants" and "nation"—were vital. The United States had been such a successful society, where millions of people aspired to move, because it was a distinct nation. It was not merely a place where people happened to live. It was a community, with traditions and bonds that fostered trust among citizens and investments in their shared future. Immigrants had become a part of this community, first by choosing to leave their homes for a new land and then by embracing that new land.

Jordan's preferred word for this process was Americanization. "That word earned a bad reputation when it was stolen by racists and xenophobes in the 1920s," Jordan said, "but it's our word, and we're taking it back." Americanization, she explained, depended on a common set of values. "E pluribus unum," she said in the final lines of one speech. "Out of many, one. One! One people. The American people."

If Americans were going to be one people, they had to make decisions about whom they would and would not admit, as every other nation did. They had to decide what forms of immigration were in the national interest and what forms were not. "Immigration is not a right, guaranteed by the U.S. Constitution to everyone anywhere in the world who thinks they want to come to the United States," Jordan said. "Immigration is a privilege. It is a privilege granted, granted by the people of the United States to those we choose to admit."

The drafters of the 1965 law had claimed to be prioritizing the national interest, but the law's loopholes had come to dominate the immigration system. As a result, that system did not maximize the well-being of Americans, immigrant and native-born alike. The country had an immigration system that almost nobody had meant to create.

To create a better one, Jordan's commission made separate recommendations for legal and illegal immigration. At the time, unlike during the 1960s, the political debate revolved mostly around illegal immigration. Between 1990 and 1995, the number of unauthorized immigrants living in the country had increased more than 60 percent, to almost six million. Jordan believed that the increase was undermining societal stability by creating an impression that rules did not matter, and she described unlawful immigration as unacceptable. "Any nation worth its salt must control its borders," she said. "What we are dealing with here is nothing less than the definition of America."

The United States might never be able to seal its borders, but there was no mystery about how to reduce unlawful immigration. The government could hold employers responsible for verifying the status of their workers and levy substantial fines on lawbreaking employers, rather than the minimal fines that the 1986 law imposed. Critics of the Jordan recommendations, which included the use of Social Security numbers and driver's licenses to verify citizenship, described them as a Big Brother system. Jordan thought they were common-sense law enforcement measures. The United States, she said, should be "a nation of immigrants dedicated to the rule of law." With fewer job opportunities for undocumented immigrants, fewer would attempt to enter the country. Companies would instead need to hire more native workers, increasing the demand for them and their pay.

Legal immigration was a different matter, Jordan and her colleagues thought. Many forms of legal immigration clearly were in the national interest. The commission cited three categories: highly skilled workers, political refugees, and people who wanted to be reunited with members of their nuclear family. In some cases, the country admitted too few of these would-be immigrants, the commission concluded. It called for a temporary increase in the admission of immediate family members, to reunite families, as well as an annual floor on refugee admissions so that no future anti-immigrant president or Congress could cut off such entrants. The United States needed to remain a haven for many people repressed by their own governments.

Overall, though, Jordan came to believe that the country was admitting too many immigrants to serve the national interest, not too few. The 1965 law had led to the entrance of millions of workers who were not reuniting with their nuclear family, had no specific skills, and were not political refugees. They had been admitted through the loophole that kept extended family members from being counted toward the annual cap set by Congress. Jordan thought this loophole, like the surge in illegal immigration, hurt American workers.

By the mid-1990s, wages for most workers had been growing slowly for two decades. In Houston, Jordan's hometown, wages for Black residents had barely kept pace with inflation; the median income for Black households was lower than for any other major racial group. Immigration may not have been the main reason, but it was not helping. "The commission finds no national interest in continuing to import lesser skilled and unskilled workers to compete with the most vulnerable parts of our labor force," Jordan said. "Many American workers do not now have adequate job prospects, and they are not improving. . . . We should not make that task harder with unskilled foreign labor."

On net, the commission called for a large reduction—by roughly one-third—in legal immigration, to about 550,000 annual entrants, down from about 800,000. Media coverage of the recommendations treated them as a potential turning point for immigration policy. Nobody seemed to notice it at the time, but there was a historical echo to the commission's preferred level of immigration. It happened to be similar to the level that the advocates of the 1965 law said they favored (adjusted for the growth of the population in the three decades since). Jordan was effectively calling for an immigration system that was true to the stated principles of the earlier reformers.

During an Oval Office meeting in 1995 to explain the recommendations to Clinton, Jordan told him that less immigration would help those Americans who most needed it. As an example, she cited the people who were trying to leave the welfare rolls and enter the job market. After their meeting, Clinton told reporters that he supported the commission's main recommendations.

CLINTON'S SUPPORT WAS fleeting.

By the 1990s, a powerful, bipartisan coalition had come to support the status quo on immigration, and the recommendations of Jordan's commission quickly came under attack. Business lobbyists and Republican leaders in Congress favored high immigration partly because it restrained wage growth. They also worried that reducing immigration would keep out future entrepreneurs. Liberal groups saw immigration as a human rights and civil rights issue and pointed out that any reductions would mostly affect Latin American and Asian immigrants, given that those regions accounted for most immigration. Many of Clinton's aides were also dubious of any policy that seemed to be trying to slow down globalization. Clinton claimed to be in favor of globalization. It was part of his administration's neoliberal instincts.

By the summer of 1996, Clinton had quietly backed away from Jordan's recommendations. Congress instead passed several provisions to reduce illegal immigration, though they were less aggressive than the commission's proposals. The laws governing legal immigration remained largely the same. The few members of Congress who complained tended to be conservative Republicans.

To many Democrats, support for immigration had come to feel like a moral imperative. Immigration lifted people out of poverty. It enhanced the country's cultural diversity. It reflected a universalist belief in human equality, regardless of a person's country of origin. Democrats cherished the legacy of the 1965 law, accidental though it may have been. In the years after Jordan's death—in 1996, from leukemia complications—progressives who otherwise venerated her rarely mentioned her position on immigration. A few quoted her with questionable selectivity, emphasizing her support for reuniting nuclear families and ignoring her overall views, including her call for less immigration. In Washington, the National Portrait Gallery hung a photograph of Jordan alongside a label that summarized her career. It mentioned only one minor recommendation from her immigration commission: that all people born in the United States continue to receive automatic citizenship. The label left out Jordan's call for a more orderly system with lower levels of immigration.

In the 2000s, the Democratic Party has moved even further toward a universalist position on immigration. Democrats now speak more positively about immigration than any party has in the country's history, according to an analysis of the *Congressional Record*. Many liberals have grown uncomfortable talking about restrictions and criticize both Bill Clinton and Barack Obama for their moderation on the issue. Obama combined full-throated support for immigrants, including legalization for many who were undocumented, with support for border security and the deportation of people who had committed crimes. In his 2008 speech at the Democratic National Convention, he said that when "an employer undercuts American wages by hiring illegal workers," it violated America's promise. Top Democrats would not make such an argument today. They are also unlikely to revere assimilation, and Americanization, as Jordan did. To universalists, glorifying American culture can be akin to suggesting it is superior to other countries' cultures.

Bernie Sanders's shifting positions on immigration are notable. For most of his career in Congress, Sanders sketched out a position consistent with the history of the American left. Like Jordan, he tried to be pro-immigrant without always being pro-immigration. Sanders favored pathways to citizenship for undocumented immigrants already living in the United States as well as the admission of LGBTQ partners before same-sex marriage was legal. He opposed long detentions for immigrants arrested at the border. At the same time, he tried to protect the wages of American workers by opposing increases in immigration that centrist Democrats supported.

"There is a reason why Wall Street and all of corporate America likes immigration reform, and it is not, in my view, that they're staying up nights worrying about undocumented workers in this country," Sanders said. "What I think they are interested in is seeing a process by which we can bring low-wage labor of all levels into this country to depress wages for Americans, and I strongly disagree with that." But by the time Sanders ran for president in 2016 and 2020, no Democrat could emphasize the downsides of immigration and expect to become a party leader. Sanders stopped talking so much about the effects on low-wage Americans and announced that he favored the abolition of the federal agency that managed border crossings.

There is a problem with the new Democratic approach, however. It is not popular with most Americans.

The polls in the mid-1960s—showing that public opinion opposed a large increase in immigration—were not a fluke. After 1965, Gallup continued to ask some of the same poll questions it had first asked in response to the Johnson White House's request. The share of Americans favoring a reduction in immigration has almost always exceeded the share favoring an increase. The gap was huge while Jordan's commission did its work in the mid-1990s: More than 60 percent of Americans favored a reduction in immigration, and only 7 percent favored an increase. Nonetheless, an increase is what happened. The number of undocumented immigrants living in the United States doubled in the decade after 1995. Annual legal immigration rose by roughly one-third, rather than the one-third reduction that Jordan had proposed. Americans, to be clear, are not opposed to immigration. Polls show that a large majority believe that it has strengthened the country, but they favor it in moderation. If immigration policy reflected public opinion, it would have been very different over the past half century.

The new Democratic consensus on immigration is part of the rise of the Brahmin left—the shift by progressive parties in both the United States and western Europe toward the views of highly educated professionals, as the economist Thomas Piketty has explained. For much of the twentieth century, left-leaning parties attracted the bulk of their support from working-class voters. Today, these parties increasingly represent college graduates. The parties have become more progressive on social issues than they once were, without becoming much more progressive on economic issues. In the late twentieth and early twenty-first centuries, the Democratic Party instead moved to the right on economic issues, as it adopted neoliberal positions on global trade, deregulation, and some tax rates. Over the past several years, the party has tacked back to the left on economics, especially through a more skeptical view of trade, but the Democratic economic agenda is not significantly more progressive than it was in the postwar decades. On taxes and regulation, for example, it remains less progressive than it once was.

Immigration is a fascinating part of this story. If you think about immigration as a social issue—a question of human rights—you might say that Democrats have moved to the left by favoring more immigration. If you think about it as a domestic economic issue—one that affects the power dynamic between American employers and workers—you would instead say that a policy of more immigration is a right-wing position. Either way, the party's shift on immigration policy is consistent with Brahminism, in which the party has become more progressive on social issues than economic ones.

As the party moved away from most forms of neoliberalism, immigration remains an exception. It is the one issue on which even the left flank of the Democratic Party continues to support the neoliberal position. Democrats have grown more skeptical of deregulation and the free flow of trade than they were during the Clinton years. But they have grown even more supportive of the deregulated flow of people across borders. Many liberals are passionately universalist on the subject.

Most voters take a more communalist view, which makes sense when you consider that most are not highly educated professionals. The American majority is a working-class, communalist majority. Most people without a four-year degree say that the United States is the greatest country in the world; most college graduates (and most Democrats) do not. Most Americans also believe that the country should prioritize its own citizens while welcoming a limited number of immigrants each year and taking steps to reduce unlawful immigration. The universalists may have won the struggle over government policy, but their victory has come with a political cost. The high level of immigration since the 1960s helped move the working class to the political right.

A rich stream of social science research has documented the phenomenon, and not only in the United States. After 2000, immigration also rose sharply in western Europe. In a study of polls and party positions in twenty-one democracies, Piketty and two colleagues, Amory Gethin and Clara Martínez-Toledano, found that immigration had contributed to alienation from left-leaning parties of people without bachelor's degrees. In Britain, unhappiness with rising immigration helped the Brexit campaign, other research has found. In Germany, France, Italy, Sweden, and Austria, immigration fueled the rise of far-right parties. In the United States, where two parties still dominate, immigration helped Donald Trump win the presidency in 2016 and helps explain why many working-class voters distrust Democrats.

Racism, of course, is part of this story. In both the United States and Europe, right-wing politicians like Trump have tried to raise fears of immigrants by using xenophobic stereotypes that echo the ugly, false claims of earlier times. These politicians accuse the newest generation of immigrants of bringing social ills from their home countries and of being incapable of assimilation. This racism can be anti-Latino, anti-Asian, anti-Black, or anti-Muslim, depending on the time and place. Social media has spread these lies, as have right-wing television channels like Fox News and its European imitators. The tactic has proved distressingly effective at winning working-class voters.

But the distinction between communalism and universalism is important partly because it highlights the fact that immigration is not only about race. There are good reasons why every country in the modern world maintains borders. If a prosperous country were simply to open its borders, especially if no other country did so, it would invite an influx of people and almost certain political chaos. Once a country has established borders, it must confront the unavoidably thorny issue of which outsiders it should admit and which it should not. In the United States—a nation of immigrants, where most of us, me included, live here only because of previous immigration—the question raises poignant tensions. "For those who believe in a multicultural America, this question can be uncomfortable to confront, because any system short of open borders invariably requires drawing distinctions that declare some people worthy of entry and others unworthy," wrote Jia Lynn Yang, a journalist, in her history of immigration law. Because of this discomfort, the modern Democratic Party has struggled to articulate an immigration policy beyond what might be summarized as: *More is better, and less is racist*. The party has cast aside the legacies of Jordan, Randolph, and other progressives who made finer distinctions.

In response, many working-class voters have decided that the Democratic Party does not share their values. Notably, some of these voters are not White and are themselves the descendants of recent immigrants. In the 2020 and 2022 elections, the Republican

Party made gains among Latino voters, especially in Texas and Florida, as well as Asian American voters. Polls showed that a sizable chunk of both Latino and Black voters who otherwise leaned toward the Democratic Party preferred the Republican position on illegal immigration. "Immigration," says Haidt, the psychologist, "is one of the top few blind spots of the left, which causes right-wing parties to win all over the Western world."

Several economists, including Alberto Alesina, Stefanie Stantcheva, and Marco Tabellini, have offered a useful framework for understanding why high levels of immigration have helped the political right. When immigration is a salient issue, it serves to remind many working-class voters that they agree with conservative parties on questions of patriotism, nationhood, and security. When immigration fades as an issue, voters think less about these questions and more about a society's economic divisions. Those class divisions, in turn, remind workers that they generally agree with progressive parties on economic policies, such as tax rates and government benefits.

Alesina also did pioneering research showing how immigration can undermine support for a generous welfare state. Societies are more likely to sustain such a welfare state, and the high taxes to fund it, when people view their fellow citizens as similar to themselves. Large amounts of immigration make a society feel more turbulent and less like a tight-knit community, at least in the short term. The contemporary United States fits this pattern. About one of every six workers is an immigrant, up from fewer than one in twenty in 1970, and roughly one-quarter of the population is either an immigrant or the descendant of a recent immigrant. The modern immigration wave has transformed the country in myriad ways, and communalists are often uncomfortable with rapid change, even when it has no economic downsides. They value tradition and stability. This is another reason that high levels of immigration tend to make a country more conservative.

Historically, the countries with the most progressive economic policies have tended to be those with low levels of recent migration. Scandinavia was the canonical example, at least until its twenty-first-century immigration wave began altering its politics. Sweden and Denmark were known for both cohesion and democratic socialism.

The United States of the mid-twentieth century is also telling. Immigration was so low during these decades that it disappeared as a major political issue. Polls found that Americans' view of immigrants became more positive. Many native-born Americans saw immigrants primarily as fellow citizens, rather than outsiders or recent arrivals. Americanization, in other words, described more than just the assimilation of immigrants; it described a national process of binding. A slowdown in the diversification of the country made Americans more comfortable with their newfound diversity. This cohesion fostered a progressive economic consensus, making possible high taxes on the affluent, large government investments in infrastructure and science, and modern welfare state programs like Social Security, Medicare, and Medicaid.

It was the flip side of Jordan's belief that high immigration numbers could damage immigrant rights. Low immigration numbers in the mid-1900s improved the lives of recent immigrants by fostering a stronger safety net for everybody.

One peculiar aspect of immigration politics is that many Republicans have misunderstood how post-1965 policies helped their party. They believe that the modern immigration wave has been a godsend for Democrats by expanding the number of Latino and Asian voters, who tend to lean left. It is true that many of these voters lean left. But not all of them do, and this notion misses the ways that immigration can nudge other voters to the right, including some recent descendants of immigrants such as the Latino voters in Texas and Florida who have drifted toward the Republican Party. After all, the modern era of high immigration levels has hardly been a golden age for progressive politics in either the United States or Europe.

PERHAPS THE MOST important point about immigration is that it involves trade-offs. For centuries, xenophobic opponents of immigration have portrayed it as inherently bad, and their claims have been disproved again and again. More recently, universalists have portrayed immigration as inevitably positive, an argument that depends partly on wishful thinking. Immigration can be wonderful, but good things are rarely free, as Jordan said.

The post-1965 immigration wave has had large benefits. Most important, it has helped lift millions of people out of poverty and allowed them to experience the American dream. When the Antins moved from Russia to Boston, they forever changed their family's trajectory. The same is true for the millions of people who have more recently moved to Houston and other American cities from Mexico, China, India, El Salvador, Vietnam, Nigeria, Ukraine, and elsewhere. Most immigrant families have both assimilated into their new country and changed it for the better. They have contributed to scientific breakthroughs, started businesses and community organizations, and enriched American culture, in literature, film, music, sports, and food.

By expanding the population, immigrants have also made the United States a more powerful nation than it otherwise would be. A country's international standing depends to a large degree on its total economic output, and economic output in turn depends heavily on the size of the population. Because of this immutable fact, the United States may struggle to compete globally with China without welcoming many more arrivals in the years to come, as the writer Matthew Yglesias has argued. Immigration is a way for the world's most powerful democracy to fend off the world's most powerful authoritarian state.

On both universalist and diplomatic grounds, a relatively open immigration system is easy to support. But the other side of the ledger matters, as well.

Immigration tends to impose costs on lower-wage workers and to alter the political atmosphere in ways that make government policy less generous to those same workers. Could a political party break this cycle and win elections with an agenda that was both heavily pro-immigration and pro–working class? Theoretically, yes. But it has not happened. Some affluent countries, like Japan and South Korea, admit few immigrants. In most others, politics have fractured between a Brahmin left that favors high levels of immigration and a nativist right. The past century suggests that there are trade-offs between immigration levels and progressive policy goals. For anybody who believes in reducing economic inequality in the United States, reducing immigration would probably make the task easier. Lower levels could also make Americans more amenable to policies that would benefit immigrants who are already here, such as a pathway to citizenship for the undocumented.

What might an ideal system look like? That is a difficult question, but Jordan's basic principles still seem relevant. The United States should treat immigrants with decency. This decency includes the admission of immediate family members—but only immediate family members, such as spouses and young children. The country should embrace its role as a beacon of political freedom and prioritize the admission of refugees fleeing persecution, a group that in recent years has included Iranians, Cubans, Sudanese, Ukrainians, and Uyghurs from China. The United States should also make clear that it is a nation of laws, as Jordan said, and do more to reduce illegal immigration than it has in the past. If citizens of other countries believe that they will be allowed to remain in the United States so long as they manage to enter it, the country's laws have little meaning. And high levels of undocumented immigration are a political gift for right-wing parties.

There is another theme from Jordan's recommendations, one that was also part of the promises that the authors of the 1965 law made. Both called for a system focused on the admission of people with specific job skills that the American economy needed. Both argued against the widescale admission of workers who could compete for most jobs. Canada did adopt such a system in the 1960s, and the politics of immigration there are more muted partly for that reason. This approach tends to reduce economic inequality. It expands the labor pool for professionals, making them less scarce and holding down their future wage increases, rather than focusing the wage effect on lower-income workers. Professionals also tend to pay more in taxes, which suggests that the admission of more high-earning immigrants can improve the country's fiscal situation as the population ages and more Americans retire.

The United States immigration system is always going to be complex, full of difficult decisions and tradeoffs. But the system we have today is not the only option, nor is it the one that political leaders promised us. It has instead become one more way that the economy and political system have drifted from the interests and values of many working people.

CHAPTER 10

Whence Shall Come Our Experts?

T HE CATHER FAMILY FARM IN SOUTHERN NEBRASKA WAS TOO remote for the children to attend school regularly. So after the oldest child, Willa, turned ten, her parents decided to move to the nearest town, called Red Cloud, in 1884. They bought a house a block from the town's small business district, and nine members of the extended family crowded into it. Willa's father stopped farming and became a broker who handled real estate loans.

At Red Cloud's grammar school and then its high school, Willa flourished. She took Latin classes and read *Paradise Lost*. She learned about ancient Rome. She studied with an inspiring teacher, Miss Eva King, who became a friend into adulthood. For Cather's high school graduation ceremony at the town's opera house in June 1890, every member of the senior class—all three of them— delivered a speech. Cather used her remarks to defend the pursuit of knowledge against the forces of superstition and ignorance. She described scientific investigation as the hope of their time and truth as the precursor to all of humanity's progress. She made the case for educating the masses: "If we bar our novices from advance- ment," she asked, "whence shall come our experts?" Red Cloud's weekly newspaper was impressed enough to publish a transcript of the speech. At the time, Willa was only sixteen years old.

In most of the world, her trajectory would have been impossi- ble. Children from humble backgrounds did not attend high school in the 1800s. They went to work. Even in relatively affluent Eu- rope, high school was generally reserved for the children of the elite. To educate the masses, many Europeans believed, was a waste of society's resources: Why did manual workers need to learn about Rome and read *Paradise Lost*?

The United States had long taken a more inclusive approach to education. Several of the country's founders believed that the success of their new democracy depended on an educated citizenry. Benjamin Rush, the only doctor who signed the Declaration of Independence, argued that education should cover practical subjects like agriculture and commerce as well as literature and the arts. Thomas Jefferson wrote that "the preservation of freedom and happiness" depended on the diffusion of knowledge. The Massachusetts Constitution, which John Adams drafted, called for "spreading the opportunities and advantages of education."

The country did not come close to achieving these ideals. It generally denied formal education to Black Americans. Many schools excluded girls. White boys from modest backgrounds often began working at young ages. But the early United States was nonetheless ahead of many other countries in the breadth of its education system. In the 1830s, a Massachusetts state official named Horace Mann advocated for government-financed elementary schools, known as common schools. Mann's political party, the Whigs, took up the cause in other states, and the United States population had soon surpassed Germany's as the world's most widely educated.

When parts of Europe began to catch up, the United States raced ahead again, opening high schools where teenagers could continue their studies. In Europe, a national or regional government tended to make centralized decisions about education, and officials continued to think that high schools for the masses were wasteful. Much of Europe restricted access by a family's economic background or by a student's scores on an entrance exam. In the United States, by contrast, local communities decided whether to build and finance schools, and some communities came to believe that universal education was worth the cost. Schools could teach students to become better citizens and more productive workers. The push became part of the Progressive movement of the late 1800s and early 1900s.

Rural towns in New England and the Upper Midwest were among the first to endorse this vision. They had the money to do so, thanks to the income from their farms. The places that pioneered high school tended to have low levels of economic inequality, high levels of community stability, and relatively homogeneous populations dominated by native-born Protestants, according to an analysis by the economists Claudia Goldin and Lawrence Katz. This pattern was an example of tribalism and communalism: Older residents were more willing to pay school taxes in places where people felt close connections to one another. The number of churches per capita helped predict how early a town built its high school.

Washington School, which Willa Cather attended, in Red Cloud, Nebraska, circa 1905.

Over time, a high school became a competitive advantage for a community. Farms could become more efficient when run by educated farmers, much as Benjamin Rush had foreseen. High school graduates could be hired by one of the growing number of corporations, be it in a white-collar job like secretary or bookkeeper or a more advanced blue-collar job. Companies like John Deere, General Electric, and National Cash Register started requiring a high school diploma for some jobs. Communities with high schools, in turn, attracted and launched thriving businesses, making young people less likely to leave for a big city. When they stayed, they could help care for their elderly relatives and neighbors, effectively repaying the investment that the older residents had made in the local high school. In the 1910s, education advocates in Iowa were already trying to persuade voters with the idea that a good local school would increase real estate values. Over the next two decades, the so-called high school movement spread. In *Middletown: A Study in Modern American Culture*, their much-cited 1929 sociological examination of life in Indiana, Robert and Helen Lynd reported that education evoked "the fervor of a religion, a means of salvation, among a large section of the population."

Public education became an exception to the laissez-faire American economy of the early twentieth century. Even as the federal government was investing relatively little in science and infrastructure and helping employers hold down workers' wages, local governments were planting the seeds for something different. They were educating the workforce of the future. Attending high school became the norm across much of the Great Plains, as well as in California, Indiana, Ohio, and New England. (The South lagged, with high school attendance rates very low among Black southerners and lower for White southerners than for White Americans in other regions.) By the start of World War II, more than 70 percent of Americans between the ages of fourteen and seventeen were enrolled in high school.

The beneficiaries of public education included Willa Cather, who earned a bachelor's degree from the University of Nebraska in 1895, was hired as an editor at *McClure's*, a crusading magazine in New York, and eventually became one of the country's great novelists. Another graduate was Mary Antin—she of the shining future—the Russian immigrant whose life had been transformed by the public schools in Boston. The graduates later included many Americans who contributed to the war effort in the 1940s: the young women who solved mathematical equations for the military as "computers" and the men and women who built vehicles, arms, and equipment in factories. The country's skilled workforce fueled its unmatched productive might.

As the war wound down, the rise of high schools made possible the next education wave—the surge in college attendance. Other countries were decades behind. Britain did not enact a law making it possible for many low-income students to attend high school until 1944. That same year, the United States Congress passed the GI Bill, vastly expanding college access. Education was the rare area of investment in which the United States was already ahead of the rest of the world when the war began, and the country's lead widened during the postwar decades.

Americans born in the late 1800s, like Cather, were part of the most educated generation in the world. The same was true of Americans born during the early twentieth century, and it remained true for decades. Nearly one out of every three Americans born in the early 1960s would earn a four-year college degree, a higher share than in Britain, Germany, Canada, Sweden, or any other country, even tiny Luxembourg.

But the country was changing by the time those Americans born in the 1960s graduated from college in the 1980s. By then, the United States was about to lose its status as the world's most educated nation.

EDUCATION IS THE investment that can turbocharge every other investment a society makes. It can help people live better by allowing them to learn from past mistakes and make new discoveries. It can help companies and workers accomplish tasks more effectively and produce goods that other people want to buy. By doing so, it can lift living standards and create good jobs. When a society is also investing in other areas, education is a force multiplier.

From the 1940s through the 1970s, the United States benefited from this dynamic. The long boom in American investment began with Vannevar Bush's crash science program during World War II and accelerated under Eisenhower. The effort stemmed from a combination of optimism about the country's potential and a fear of overseas threats, first from Germany and Japan, then from the Soviet Union. In response, this country built the modern computer industry, a national network of highways, the world's best air traffic system, and so much more. All the while, the federal government increased its commitment to education by helping local communities build K–12 schools and by financing much of higher education. And state and local governments were spending many times more than the federal government to operate K–12 schools and subsidize public colleges. By the mid-1970s, education spending by all levels of government accounted for almost as large a share of national income as military spending and a much higher share than government spending on healthcare. Education was central to the country's economic and national security strategies.

Education has always had its skeptics, of course. In the United States today, many people still believe that only an elite subset of the population benefits from college—that its benefits are overrated and that most Americans would be better off pursuing immediate employment or more practical knowledge. It is surely true that not all teenagers need to study Latin, as Cather did. Different people will be best served by different kinds of education, and education is not a cure-all for the American economy. Tax rates, workers' bargaining power, the quality of healthcare, and many other areas matter enormously.

But it is a mistake to downplay the importance of education, a mistake that the United States avoided during much of its rise to prosperity and global preeminence. The evidence is everywhere. Today, high school graduates earn more, and are less likely to be out of work, than people without a high school diploma, as has been the case for more than a century. College graduates earn more yet. Regions with highly educated populations, like Boston, Minneapolis, San Francisco, and Washington, D.C., have become the most affluent in the country. The countries with the fastest-growing economies in recent decades, like South Korea, Singapore, and Poland, have based their growth strategies in large part on education.

Not only does mass education increase the size of the economic pie, but it also evens out the distribution. The spread of American high schools and then colleges meant that graduates were no longer an elite group. The wage premium that they earned was spread among a larger group of workers. Relative to its economic rivals, the country could call on more college graduates to fill its professional ranks and more high school graduates to fill its blue-collar ranks. These educated workers made their companies more successful and received higher wages. As Goldin and Katz argued in their definitive history of the subject, the 2008 book *The Race Between Education and Technology,* the twentieth century was the American century in large part because it was the human capital century.

The benefits extend far beyond economic measures. While life expectancy was falling for Americans without a college degree in the early twenty-first century, it continued rising for college graduates. The Covid pandemic caused life expectancy to fall for both groups but substantially more for nongraduates. In 2021, the average American with a bachelor's degree could expect to live eight years longer than somebody without one. Many other measures of well-being also show stark gaps. More educated Americans report being more satisfied with their lives. They are less likely to suffer from chronic pain or to abuse alcohol and drugs. They are more likely to be married and to live with their young children.

The relationship between education and well-being is partly coincidental. Talented, hardworking people are more likely to finish school partly because of those characteristics. Attending high school and college does not confer magical powers, and some graduates would prosper even if they did not finish school. Bill Gates, Steve Jobs, Steven Spielberg, and Oprah Winfrey were all college dropouts. Still, much of the relationship is indeed causal. Gates himself has urged people not to confuse a few high-profile exceptions with a much larger pattern. A college degree, he has said, is "the surest path to a healthy, rewarding life and career."

A pair of clever academic studies highlighted the causal role by taking advantage of natural experiments in college admissions. Many public colleges, too large to spend hours individually reviewing each application, set admissions standards based on grades and standardized test scores. A student who just misses the benchmarks at a highly selective college, like the University of Michigan or University of Texas, will still be admitted to many others. But students who miss the cutoff at the least selective college in a state-wide system may not be admitted to any four-year college. They may instead decide not to attend college or to attend a two-year community college; two-year colleges tend to be starved for resources and have high dropout rates. The admissions cutoff for less selective four-year colleges can hover around a C+ grade average in high school or an 850 SAT score, and students on either side of the cutoff are very similar to each other academically. Nonetheless, they enroll in four-year colleges at very different rates because only those just above the cutoff are admitted. This situation creates the natural experiment.

The research found that college mattered a great deal. Students admitted to a four-year college earned more money by their late twenties, and the effect was especially large for those from lower-income backgrounds. Carlos Escanilla, a resident of Florida, was typical of the admitted students, and I interviewed him several years ago while reporting on this research. By his own account, Escanilla had been an unfocused high school student who spent much of his time hanging out with friends and dreamed about becoming a rock star. When that did not seem to be working out, he enrolled at Florida International University, a sprawling campus on the west side of Miami. It was one of the least selective four-year colleges in the state, which explained how he could get in.

Once he started taking classes, Escanilla discovered that he enjoyed coursework more than he had in high school and learned more. His experience also highlighted the benefits of education that are less obvious than the acquisition of concrete knowledge—namely, the development of independence and resilience. "What I learned in college was kind of how to have this, 'Yes, but how' attitude," he said. "You fall, dust yourself off and keep going." College is akin to adulthood's first obstacle course. Completing it teaches people how to overcome other obstacles and gives them confidence that they can do so. After graduating from Florida International, Escanilla became a psychotherapist. For fun, he still sings and plays guitar.

In addition to the social science research, there is another set of evidence that highlights the benefits of education: the choices that Americans make in their own lives. Parents—rich, middle-class, and poor—devote intense energy and resources to finding the right school district for their children and helping them get admitted to college. On a gut level, they understand how much education matters. Michael McPherson, an economist and former president of Macalester College in Minnesota, has a deft way of making this point: The next time you read an article in which the author describes college as overrated, find out whether that person's own children will be avoiding this allegedly overrated investment. Like the European critics of mass education from previous centuries, the modern skeptics usually believe in the value of school for the people closest to them.

ALTHOUGH IT WAS slow to do so, much of the rest of the world eventually came to copy the American approach to mass education. Between the 1970s and the early 2000s, the share of young adults receiving bachelor's degrees (or the equivalent) more than tripled in South Korea. It more than doubled in Belgium, Ireland, Poland, and Spain and roughly doubled in France and Japan. It rose more than 50 percent in Britain, Denmark, Norway, and Sweden and more than 30 percent in Canada. The share earning a vocational degree (similar to a community college degree) also rose sharply in several of these countries. Political leaders effectively acknowledged that their old, elitist approach to education had been wrong.

They recognized that the amount of education that people need to thrive tends to rise over the course of history. The economy becomes more complex, thanks to technological change, and citizens need new knowledge and skills to take advantage of that technology, rather than having their labor replaced by it. A grade school education was not enough to keep up with industrialization and the rise of global trade during the nineteenth and twentieth centuries. The new economic reality during those years often demanded a high school education. In the twenty-first century, likewise, a high school education is usually insufficient preparation for a well-paying job, but a college education, including from some community colleges, often is. When you think about education and technological change in these terms, you start to realize that the appropriate amount of schooling for a typical citizen changes over time. If thirteen years—kindergarten through twelfth grade—made sense a century ago, it almost certainly is not enough today.

While other countries accepted this idea in recent decades, the United States lost faith in its own strategy. The share of people receiving a bachelor's degree rose only slightly between the 1970s and the early 2000s. The same was true for the share with community college and vocational degrees. Among people under age fifty, the United States is no longer the most educated country in the world. A higher share of Canadians, Australians, Japanese, South Koreans, Dutch, Irish, and British now graduate from at least a two-year college. The lack of progress among American men has been especially stark. Men's wages, not coincidentally, have risen extremely slowly since the 1970s.

The rise of higher education in California in the middle of the 1900s, followed by its stagnation in recent decades, highlights these trends. As the state grew rapidly after World War II, it built a system of higher education with few peers. It featured both some of the world's finest research institutions, like the University of California's campuses in Berkeley, Los Angeles, and Davis, as well as a system of California State University campuses and community colleges that educated many first-generation students. Between 1945 and 1965, California went on a higher education building spree, opening almost forty new community colleges, eleven campuses in the Cal State system, and four new outposts of the University of California. "What the railroads did for the second half of the last century and the automobile for the first half of this century may be done for the second half of this century by the knowledge industry," Clark Kerr, the president of the University of California system, said. Kerr was the central figure in the development of the state's 1960 Master Plan for Higher Education, which sought to balance the competing demands of excellence and access.

Then the expansion largely stopped. Even as the state's population grew, only four new university campuses opened since the 1980s, three of them among the system's smallest. The existing campuses have not increased their enrollments to keep up with population growth. The schools also became much more expensive for students to attend, and the state's housing crunch has exacerbated the problem. The University of California lacks enough space to house all students and denies dormitory rooms to thousands of students each year. They are forced to find housing off campus, where rents can be high. Some must commute long distances to attend classes. In Santa Cruz, one of the country's most expensive real estate markets, students have slept in tents or vehicles. "It does definitely contribute to a decline in academic performance," Matthew Chin, who was sleeping in a trailer during the fall semester in 2022, said. "Socially, you feel estranged." The message from California seems clear enough: The state is no longer willing to invest in its young people.

A shortage of resources is not the only problem in American education. Both higher education and the K–12 system also suffer from uneven performance and a lack of accountability. Schools that serve similar student populations often perform very differently, and the laggards face few consequences. The Obama administration did crack down on some of the worst offenders— for-profit colleges that left students with significant amounts of debt and no degree or other marketable skills. Similarly, some states have rewarded high-performing colleges with additional funding, and some cities have allowed successful charter schools to expand while closing struggling schools. For the most part, however, poor-performing schools can continue doing what they are doing for years on end. Hundreds of public colleges also have high dropout rates, and no United States president has cracked down on them.

Political conservatives sometimes point to these issues and suggest that schools have all the money they need. But that diagnosis confuses a real but secondary problem with the core issue. It is worth remembering that the previous expansions of education—of high schools in the early twentieth century and colleges in the mid-twentieth century—did not depend on intricate systems of accountability. They depended on a combination of growing resources and relatively crude forms of accountability that still exist today. Better colleges drew more students than weaker colleges. Better K–12 schools attracted more people to their towns, and worse schools faced pressure to improve from the parents and students in their communities. The great American public schools of the first half of the 1900s were often local monopolies.

The bigger difference between the past and the present involves money. Into the 1960s, educational attainment rose, and so did government spending on education, across the federal, state, and local levels. Since the 1970s, the share of national income devoted to government spending on education has remained flat. Adjusted for inflation and population growth, spending on many community colleges and less selective four-year colleges—the places where working-class students typically enroll—has declined. The financial crisis that began in 2007 led to sharp cuts in state spending on higher education, and many of these declines persisted. All the while, the need for education has continued to increase along with the economy's technological sophistication.

While the portion of the economy devoted to education has stagnated, two other categories of government spending have surged: healthcare and income support. Together, those categories—which include Medicare and Social Security—accounted for only about 5 percent of the American economy in 1960. In recent years, their share has exceeded 15 percent. Their growth has more than cancelled out a decline in military spending that occurred after the end of the Cold War. Programs for healthcare and retirement are obviously important. They reduce poverty, provide needed medical care, and allow people to retire. But retirement programs are not an investment that will pay for itself through future economic growth, as education typically does. A society that allows spend-

Government spending, 1959-2019
As a percentage of G.D.P.

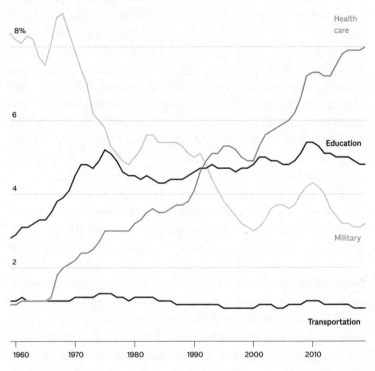

ing on old age to crowd out spending on schools will eventually have less money to spend on both.

The United States could ensure a decent retirement for its elderly without allowing Medicare and Social Security to overwhelm the federal budget. To do so, though, the country would need to address two issues with the programs. First, the American healthcare system is unusually wasteful. The United States today spends about $13,000 per person annually on healthcare, a far higher total than any other country. Canada spends about $8,000 per person, while France, Germany, and Japan spend closer to $6,000. Some of the American spending has ancillary benefits—high drug prices effectively subsidize drug development for the rest of the world—but much of the spending does not. It instead pays for inefficient bureaucracy and care that does not make people healthier.

Second, Medicare, Social Security, and other programs that purport to be part of the safety net devote a significant portion of their budgets to helping well-off Americans. (Housing subsidies are another example.) The universality of the programs was a deliberate part of their design and increased their popularity. But as the country has aged and the programs have grown, universality comes with a big downside: Increasingly, the federal government is prioritizing older adults over children. Even the affluent elderly can receive more government help than impoverished children.

In the early 2000s, this country spent almost two and a half times as much per capita on government programs for the elderly as on government programs for children, according to research by Julia Isaacs, a former official at the Congressional Budget Office. Given this discrepancy, nobody should be surprised that the child poverty rate far exceeds the elderly poverty rate. Other countries, despite having aging populations, have managed this challenge differently. They spend less on questionable medical care, and they tax their affluent citizens at higher rates. As a result, the countries can and do spend more on children. In recent decades, Sweden, Norway, and Denmark have devoted about twice as much of their national income as the United States has to programs for children. Britain, Canada, and Germany have also dedicated a substantially higher share.

One other area of government spending that has soared in recent decades is criminal justice. Spending on police, courts, and prisons, although much smaller than healthcare and retirement spending, has more than doubled as a share of national income, to between 1.5 percent and 2 percent. Clearly, a well-functioning society depends on having a manageable crime rate and a sense of public order. But the United States spends much more on criminal justice than is necessary to maintain public order. There is little reason to believe that the large-scale imprisonment of people for nonviolent offenses, like drug possession, is necessary. Mass incarceration damages public order in some ways by separating people—who are disproportionately Black, Latino, and Native American men—from their families and undermining their ability to find decent-paying work after their release. The prison construction boom of recent decades has been a negative investment in the future.

The full picture is of a country that devotes an increasing share of its resources to programs that will not improve life for our children, grandchildren, and beyond. By contrast, investments in education generally create a better future, as do investments in scientific research and a country's productive capacity. The United States has instead shifted money toward the world's most bloated healthcare sector, its largest prison network, and a safety net that often benefits the affluent.

As Eugene Steuerle, a former Treasury Department official, has said, "We have a budget for a declining nation."

EVERY MORNING IN twenty-first-century America, thousands of people wake up and prepare to take a cross-country trip. Some are traveling for business. Others are visiting family or going on vacations. Whether they are leaving from New York or Los Angeles, Atlanta or Seattle, their trips have a lot in common.

They leave their homes several hours before their plane is scheduled to depart. Many sit in rush-hour traffic on their way to the airport. Once they arrive, they park their cars and make their way through the airport, waiting in a security line, taking off their shoes, removing laptops and liquids from their bags. When they finally get to the gate, they often wait again because their flight is delayed. The flight itself typically lasts about six hours, and the travelers then need to find ground transportation to their destination. Door to door, cross-country journeys often last ten or even twelve hours.

In the sweep of human history, these trips remain a marvel of ingenuity. For centuries, long-distance travel required weeks or months and could be dangerous. Today, somebody can eat breakfast in almost any part of the United States and dinner in another. If you narrow the focus to recent decades, however, you will notice another striking fact about these trips: Almost none of the progress has occurred in the past half century, at least in the United States. A cross-country trip today typically takes *more* time than it did in the 1970s. The same is true of many trips within a region or a metropolitan area.

Compare this stagnation with the progress of the previous century. The first transcontinental railroad was completed in 1869, and passenger trains were running on its route five days later, revolutionizing travel. People could cross the country in less than a week. By the early 1900s, the time had been reduced to a few days. Next came commercial flight. In the 1930s, an airplane could beat a train across the country by hopscotching from city to city. One-stop transcontinental flights eventually reduced coast-to-coast travel time to less than twelve hours. Finally, the jet age arrived: The first regularly scheduled nonstop transcontinental flight took place on January 25, 1959, from Los Angeles to New York, on a new Boeing jet—the 707—with a longer range than its predecessors.

The poet Carl Sandburg was among the passengers on that inaugural American Airlines flight. "You look out of the window at the waves of dark and light clouds looking like ocean shorelines, and you feel as if you are floating away in this pleasantly moving room, like the basket hanging from the balloon you saw with a visiting circus when you were a boy," he wrote about the trip. "You move through rain and come out of it into a clear blue sky with a cloudland below you, and you say to yourself, 'My, that's purty to look at.'" Sandburg had been born in 1878, when crossing the country took almost a week. His cross-country flight had taken five and a half hours.

In the more than sixty years since then, there has been no progress. Instead, the flight time from Los Angeles to New York has become about an hour longer. Aviation technology has not advanced in ways that speed the trip, and the skies have become so crowded that planes slow down to accommodate traffic. Nearly every other part of a cross-country trip has also become longer. In previous decades, people could arrive at the airport only a few minutes before their departure time, and they could often be inside a taxi minutes after landing. All told, a trip across the United States can take several hours longer today than in the 1960s.

There have still been some advances. Airline travel has become less expensive and far safer. But the declines in both airfares and accident rates were even faster in the middle of the twentieth century, when travel times were also falling. The economist Robert Gordon argues that there was a connection between declining travel times and declining prices: A faster trip means that a passenger has to pay for less labor by the crew, and the airline can pack more flights into each day. Since the 1980s, prices have fallen only marginally. The promise of airline deregulation—that it would usher in an era of rapid progress—has gone largely unfulfilled. Instead, the concentration of the industry has reduced competition and kept prices higher than they otherwise might be. The country has also failed to invest enough money in its airports and air traffic network to prevent delays.

The speed at which people can get from one place to another is one of the most basic measures of a society's sophistication. It affects economic productivity and human happiness; academic research has found that commuting makes people more dissatisfied than almost any other daily activity. Yet the deterioration of American airline travel is part of a pattern. In one area of travel after another, progress has largely stopped over the past half century.

In 1969, Metroliner trains made two-and-a-half-hour nonstop trips between Washington and New York. Today, there are no nonstop trains on that route, and the fastest trip, on Acela trains, takes about twenty minutes longer than the Metroliner once did. Commuter railroads and subway lines in many places have also failed to become faster. A trip on many parts of the New York subway takes no less time than when my grandmother Esther took it in the 1950s. In some cities, the Covid pandemic led to schedule reductions that have not been reversed as of 2023. For drivers—the majority of American travelers—trip times have increased because traffic has worsened. In the metropolitan area that includes Silicon Valley and San Jose, California, a typical rush-hour drive that would have taken forty-five minutes in the early 1980s took nearly sixty minutes by 2019. In Atlanta, Denver, Miami, Minneapolis, New York, Seattle, and Washington, rush-hour drives became almost ten minutes longer during that same timespan; in

Boston, Charlotte, Chicago, and Philadelphia, the increase was more than five minutes.

The lack of recent progress is not the result of any physical or technological limits. In other parts of the world, travel has continued to speed up. As part of its planning for the 1964 Summer Olympics in Tokyo, Japan built a high-speed rail line called the Shinkansen. Bullet-nosed trains on elevated tracks traveled between Tokyo and Osaka more rapidly than any passenger train previously had. The line was so popular that Japan developed what residents called "Shinkansen fever," with cities competing to attract new lines and young people from rural areas viewing the trains as a way to expand their cultural horizons. France opened the world's next high-speed rail network in 1981, and other parts of western Europe and China followed. These rail networks have tangibly improved daily life, allowing people to attend family events and business meetings that they otherwise could not, and they have served as a sign of continuing human progress.

For American visitors, overseas rail networks can feel like something out of another world. When I first visited England, in the late 1990s, I was planning a trip to the countryside and trying to decide whether to drive or take a train from London. Looking at maps and train schedules, I became confused: How could a trip that took two and a half hours by car take less than an hour by train? What I did not immediately understand is that this gap is normal in many countries. Trains can travel much faster than cars and, for short trips, more efficiently than planes. If the United States had a similar rail network, you would be able to travel between Los Angeles and San Francisco—or Boston and Washington—in an hour and a half, downtown to downtown. High-speed trains have indirectly sped airline travel, as well. To get from downtown Shanghai to the city's main airport, almost twenty miles away, you can take an eight-minute ride on a train that reaches a speed of more than 250 miles an hour. When you return to the United States, you will often need nearly an hour to make the trip from an airport to a city center.

Because the United States is less densely populated than China,

Japan, or Europe, high-speed rail would not work in many parts of this country. But it could transform travel in California, the Northeast, and a few other regions. And it is not as if this country has been improving its highways and airline network instead of its rail system. All have languished.

Transportation is an example of what happens when the government stops making basic investments: Nobody makes them. In earlier decades, the government helped build the country's rails, its highways, and its air traffic system. Only after those initial government investments could private companies create valuable products and services. Boeing, for example, got its start during World War I selling planes to the navy. Later, the government paid for research that made possible jet airline technology and, by extension, the Boeing 707, the plane that launched the jet age. Since the 1970s, the share of national income flowing to government investments in transportation has stagnated. So has our ability to move from one place to another.

An American born in the early twentieth century witnessed transformational changes not only in transportation and schooling but also in cooking, house cleaning, and many other areas of daily life. The changes of recent decades have been considerably smaller, even with the creation of the internet and the potential of artificial intelligence. As Gordon, the economist, explained in his book *The Rise and Fall of American Growth*, recent advances have been concentrated in a few areas of human endeavor, mostly involving communication, entertainment, and information. "For the rest of what humans care about—food, clothing, shelter, transportation, health and working conditions both inside and outside the home—progress slowed down after 1970," Gordon wrote. That has been especially true in the United States.

MANCUR OLSON, AN American economist, was traveling in Europe as a young man when he became fascinated by an apparent paradox. Britain had defeated Germany in World War II, yet West Germany was faring better economically. In Asia, Japan, another defeated country, was booming. Were the differences merely a coincidence, Olson wondered, or had Britain's earlier successes somehow led to its later struggles?

Olson came to believe that there was a connection, and he wrote an influential book in the 1980s trying to explain it. He argued that stable, affluent societies created the circumstances for their own decline by giving rise to interest groups that accumulated more influence over time. The groups became powerful enough to win government favors, in the form of subsidies or friendly regulations, that benefited them at the expense of everyone else. Not only did the groups end up with a larger piece of the economy's pie, but they did so in a way that kept the pie from growing as much as it otherwise would have.

Britain, as a victor in World War II and an economic leviathan for more than two centuries prior, had accumulated one of history's great collections of interest groups. These interest groups—financial traders, farmers, miners, and others—had caused sclerosis in Britain's economy. Germany and Japan, by contrast, had been devastated during the war. "We wiped the institutional slate clean for them," Olson said. As they rebuilt their economies and political systems, they could prioritize the national interest over special interests because their special interests were so weak. Germany and Japan did not rise in spite of their defeat. They rose in part because of it.

The parallels between Britain and the United States, though not exact, are plain enough. This country's postwar period of preeminence produced a set of interest groups that were strong enough to block change. Farmers lobbied for policies that kept food prices high, as Olson had witnessed while growing up in North Dakota. Large corporations and Wall Street firms pushed for tax breaks. Some labor unions negotiated contracts that maximized wages even at the expense of a company's long-term success. Teachers' unions and university administrators opposed policies to hold schools accountable for poor performance. Neighborhood groups practiced NIMBYism, opposing new construction and keeping housing prices high. Community groups also blocked the building of high-speed rail lines and other improvements to the transportation network.

The biggest contemporary case study of Olson's theory is healthcare. Hospitals, health insurers, pharmaceutical companies, and doctors' groups have persuaded the country to create a medical system far more expensive than any other in the world. Two decades ago, a group of health scholars set out to explain why, and they titled their journal article, "It's the Prices, Stupid." Almost everything in the American system is more expensive, including doctor visits, hospital stays, medical procedures, and prescription drugs. These higher costs yield extra income for people who work or invest in healthcare, at the expense of everybody who does not.

Olson's theory is an important addition to my earlier discussion of political power. A central reason that America's future-oriented investment has stagnated is the working class's loss of political power. In the absence of such power, the post-1980 neo-liberal revolution has increased skepticism about government and reduced its role in the economy. Without the government making initial investments that are too expensive or risky for any one company to make, some of these investments no longer happen. But Olson's work highlights a second reason why investment has atrophied. In an economy as mature and affluent as ours, special interest groups of all types—not only those representing the wealthy—can prevent changes that would benefit society. The deterioration of the nation's transportation network and the shortage of housing in many metropolitan areas are both at least as much a story of old triumphing over new as rich triumphing over poor. The same applies to the growth of Medicare and Social Security at the expense of funding for schools.

Olson's work helps explain why the country's investment shortfalls are evident in both red America, where people tend to be hostile to taxes, and blue America, where government spending is more popular. California has starved its colleges of resources. The Northeast Corridor has failed to build high-speed rail or improve public transit. Housing tends to be more expensive, and homelessness higher, in liberal cities than conservative ones. Some families have responded by leaving the Northeast and West Coast for less expensive regions. The high cost of housing in New York City is the main reason that the city's Black population declined by almost 10 percent during the first two decades of the 2000s.

In part, these problems are another reflection of the modern left's slide toward Brahminism, with a greater focus on the interests of college-educated professionals than those of the working class. And in part, they are a reflection of what happens in a prosperous society over time: Entrenched interests, across political ideologies and economic classes, can prevail over the national interest.

Olson gave a sweeping title to the book that explained his ideas: *The Rise and Decline of Nations*. Societies that do not figure out how to change with the times—how to prioritize the many over the few and the future over the past—are doomed to decay.

SOME OF THE ways in which the investment slowdown has aggravated inequality are intuitive. Underfunded state universities and community colleges hurt middle-income and lower-income Americans, while the well-off can send their children to private colleges with large endowments. Creaking public transit systems create inconveniences for the working class, while the very wealthy increasingly avoid the unpleasantries of modern airline travel by flying private.

Another way in which the investment slump has increased inequality is less obvious. It involves gender: Women have often been left to bear the burden of the shortage of resources that the United States devotes to children.

Throughout most of modern history, education expanded upward, to include older children, teenagers, and young adults. The United States was first a pioneer in elementary education, enrolling children from all backgrounds in school into their adolescence, and other countries eventually caught up. The pattern repeated with the high school movement and, later, the growth of college attendance. Still, these expansions left a gap at the beginning of children's lives. Until the 1970s, few societies offered public education before a child turned five.

The successful effort to expand education and daycare to the youngest children began in Sweden. Olof Palme, a Social Democrat who became prime minister in 1969 when he was forty-two, was inspired by the ongoing global movements for equality, including the second wave of feminism. Palme believed the unequal responsibilities of childcare might be the biggest barrier for women's economic prospects. "We want to remove the obstacles that have always existed and still exist for women's equal rights and equal opportunities," he said.

As part of Palme's persuasion campaign, he framed the problem as one that was hurting both women and men. Industrialization had widened the differences between men's and women's life experiences by causing men to work far from home and women to concentrate on family life, Palme explained. A typical man became more distant from his family and faced social pressure "to assert himself, fight his way in life, to be aggressive," as Palme said in a speech titled "The Emancipation of Man," which he delivered during a trip to Washington in 1970. These forces caused men to have higher rates of stress and suicide and shorter life expectancies than women. Modern women, meanwhile, faced the absurd double burden of taking care of their families and trying to compete with men in the labor market. Gender inequality, Palme concluded, was not a women's problem. It was "a sex-role problem."

The central policy change in his equality agenda was an expansion of affordable daycare and preschool. The system started small, focused on six-year-olds, many of whom did not yet attend elementary school in Sweden, and grew over the next several decades. From the beginning, it was flexible and inclusive, attempting to appeal both to parents who wanted to work full-time and to those who did not. Some students attended preschool for the entire day, others for only a few hours. If parents wanted, they could attend school with their children for some activities. Disabled children were included in the classes. By the early twenty-first century, the system started at age one. The cost was low, especially for families with modest incomes. Swedish law also gave parents up to sixteen months of paid leave, with couples receiving more total leave if fathers took a significant portion of it.

The policies influenced dozens of countries around the world. Denmark, Norway, and others expanded early education and paid leave soon after Sweden did. In the United States, Palme's equality agenda influenced Ruth Bader Ginsburg, who was a researcher at Columbia University in the 1960s and then a law professor at Rutgers University. As part of her research on comparative international law, Ginsburg happened to focus on Sweden, learning some of the language to study its legal system. She lived there for several months, with her young daughter, and was struck by the country's progressive attitudes toward gender. In a 1974 textbook that Ginsburg cowrote, she printed the full text of Palme's "Emancipation of Man" speech. In some of the pathbreaking civil rights lawsuits that Ginsburg helped bring, she used a tactic that borrowed from Palme's notion of the "sex-role problem." Ginsburg chose male plaintiffs to challenge laws that treated the sexes differently—like higher drinking ages for men—as a way of demonstrating that gender inequality was not exclusively a women's issue.

Despite Ginsburg's legal victories, the United States did less to implement Palme's vision than almost any other high-income country. Having been a pioneer with elementary school, high school, and college, this country has remained a laggard with preschool. Only about half of three- and four-year-old children attend pre-K programs, compared with more than 95 percent in western Europe, Japan, South Korea, and Israel. Because the American system is mostly private and often expensive, children from higher-income families are more likely to attend, which exacerbates inequality in school readiness. The patchwork preschool system also restricts job options for women from every economic group.

In the past, the biggest cause of gender inequality was outright sexism that restricted women to certain jobs and tolerated workplace harassment. Today, the biggest cause is the unequal demands that men and women face outside of work, research has shown. "True pay and employment discrimination, while they matter, are relatively small," concluded the economist Claudia Goldin, whose work on the subject helped her win a Nobel Prize in 2023. "Are women actually receiving *lower pay* for *equal work*? By and large, not so much anymore." In one study, Goldin and two colleagues analyzed men and women coming out of business school and discovered that their careers followed similar trajectories in the years immediately after graduation, only to diverge sharply and permanently after marriage. Many women took time off or moved into more flexible jobs, putting them on a track with lower pay and reduced odds of big promotions. To this day, nearly 90 percent of large American companies have men as chief executives.

The United States also makes life difficult for parents who prefer to stay home full-time when their children are young. This country is one of only seven to have no national program of paid parental leave. The other six are all small and impoverished: the Marshall Islands, Micronesia, Nauru, Palau, Papua New Guinea, and Tonga. The message to new parents is the same as the message given to those California college students who cannot find housing: You are not a priority in our society.

Government investments cannot magically eliminate sexism or change the reality that only half the population can give birth. Full gender equality would require a revolution in attitudes toward fatherhood and motherhood. For now, even Sweden remains a long way from equality. But a lack of investment in children aggravates gender inequities. The trends in the United States over the past few decades makes this point. In the 1980s, the share of American women participating in the labor force was typical for a rich country. Since then, other countries have invested much more in early education and parental leave, and the share of women in the workforce has generally surged. Today, the United States has fallen nearly to the bottom of that ranking.

THE NOTION OF American exceptionalism dates to Alexis de Tocqueville. In 1840, writing in his book Democracy in America, de Tocqueville described Americans as "quite exceptional" because of their practical, earthbound focus. Almost a century later, Josef Stalin seems to have coined the actual phrase "American exceptionalism" to describe the country's imperviousness to Marxism. American intellectuals, especially on the political right, later used the phrase to describe the nation's unique strengths. For much of the twentieth century, that description was accurate. The United States turned the tide in two world wars, developed the polio vaccine, built the automobile industry, created the modern computer, launched the jet age, landed astronauts on the moon, pioneered mass high school and college education, and forged the world's largest middle class.

The accomplishments of the past half century have been much less exceptional. There are occasional successes, like the stunningly rapid development of Covid vaccines by American companies, building on government-financed research. For the most part, though, the glowing American successes of the twenty-first century do not translate into better lives for most citizens. The stars of American capitalism today include Amazon, Apple, and Google, as well as Visa, UnitedHealth (the health insurance company), and Berkshire Hathaway (Warren Buffett's investment company). All were among the ten companies with the highest market capitalization in the world at the end of 2022. Do they improve life for most Americans? In some ways, yes. The internet allows people to read any book, listen to any song, or order almost any product to their door. But this list underscores the reality that life has not improved much in many other dimensions. None of those companies has created huge numbers of jobs that vault people into the middle class. The companies also contribute to some of the country's biggest problems. The financialization of the economy increases inequality. The health insurance industry often leaves ordinary people confused and enraged without making them much healthier. Since smartphones and social media became ubiquitous, childhood mental health has deteriorated, and political polarization has increased.

The great successes of the postwar economy—the rapid increase in living standards, with the fastest progress for less advantaged groups—depended on the interaction of the forces that I have described in this book. Investments made possible a better future. A shift in political power enabled more Americans to claim their fair share of the economy's gains. A change in the culture allowed the country to retain some of the best parts of its individualist ethos, like a willingness to take risks, while also avoiding the excesses of the Gilded Age and the Roaring Twenties.

As the economist John Maynard Keynes wrote, "The political problem of mankind is to combine three things: economic efficiency, social justice, and individual liberty." In the middle years of the twentieth century, the United States moved closer to a happy medium among these competing objectives. It discovered a system that avoided both the inefficiencies of socialism and the excesses of rough-and-tumble capitalism. The country was still terribly flawed and unjust during these decades, but it was moving in the right direction. No other country was doing a better job of providing decent living standards to its citizens and raising those living standards over time.

Today, these forces have reversed. Our investments in the future have stagnated. Our workers have strikingly little influence over the economy and the political system. Our culture is individualist and angry rather than community oriented and hopeful. As a result, American exceptionalism often has a bleak meaning.

We live in the only high-income country that does not provide parents with paid leave. We live in one of the stingiest countries for daycare, preschool, and the resources devoted to children. A typical thirty-year-old American man is not much more educated than his parents were. The United States remains the only rich country without universal health insurance. American women are more likely to die in childbirth than women in many other countries. American babies are more likely to die, too. Income inequality is higher than in western Europe, Canada, Japan, South Korea, or Australia. Almost two million Americans wake up each day in a prison or jail. Our children consider it normal to spend time at school preparing for a mass shooting. Our opioid death rate leads the world. Our roads are more dangerous than the roads in other affluent countries, which was not true only a few decades ago. In 1980, life expectancy in the United States was similar to that in other high-income countries. We have since become a grim outlier.

This litany is certainly cause for frustration. But it is not cause for apathy. The United States retains tremendous advantages. It remains a wealthy country with broad political freedoms, a place where many millions of people around the world would live if they could choose any country.

Imagine how successful the country could be if we stopped pursuing strategies that have been failing for so long.

Conclusion

I WROTE MUCH OF THIS BOOK WHEN AMERICAN DEMOCRACY seemed to be in retreat. Throughout Donald Trump's presidency, he rejected democratic traditions that predecessors from both parties had accepted. He used the White House for personal profit and told hundreds of lies that he believed served his interest. When he lost the 2020 election, he tried to overturn the result and praised a violent mob that attacked the Capitol in his name. Although his effort to remain in office failed, some of the larger threats to American democracy linger. Trump may be president again by the time you read this sentence, and other Republicans have shown autocratic tendencies, too. American democracy today seems more vulnerable than many people imagined it ever could.

But it would be a grave mistake to give up on the American system of government. The levers of democracy—grassroots movements, public opinion, elections, and governance—remain the most powerful means for changing society. Indeed, those levers have already weakened Trump's anti-democracy movement before. In 2022, every major candidate who echoed his false claims of voter fraud and ran for an office overseeing elections in a swing state—signaling a willingness to overturn a future election—lost. The outcome was a reminder that the best response to an anti-democracy movement is often more democracy.

The longer-term record of American democracy is better yet. The levers of democracy do not always make the United States a better place, but they have an impressive record of success over the past century. Consider the stories you have read in the previous chapters. The labor movement arose during the 1930s and transformed American politics. It helped make possible the economy that lifted wages, extended life expectancy, narrowed racial inequality, created the modern social safety net, and helped change the self-interested culture of corporate America. Franklin Roosevelt understood the centrality of this movement and privately thanked labor leaders for enabling him to win reelection. Next came the civil rights movement, which grew in part out of the Black labor movement. It amassed enough grassroots power that A. Philip Randolph was able to face down Roosevelt in the Oval Office and insist on the integration of wartime factories. Inspired by the push for civil rights, the New Left became the next movement to alter American life. It energized young baby boomers and helped to end the Vietnam War, expand opportunities for women, reduce pollution, and pass a raft of consumer and workplace laws that saved lives. When the New Left set out to accomplish a specific goal, it often succeeded.

The conservative backlash that followed likewise used democracy to achieve its biggest victories. Richard Nixon and Ronald Reagan won elections by wooing a decisive group of voters from Roosevelt's majority coalition. From 1932 to 1964, the Democrats won seven of nine presidential elections, losing only to the moderate Dwight Eisenhower. From 1968 to 1988, Republicans won five of six elections, and the lone Democratic victory occurred in the aftermath of the Watergate scandal. With the power they had amassed, Reagan and his allies rewrote the country's economic rules.

The evidence for democracy's potency is not limited to the main thrusts of history, either. It is clear in narrower movements, too. After the Supreme Court established a constitutional right to abortion in its 1973 *Roe v. Wade* decision, opponents of abortion responded by creating a grassroots movement. Most Americans did not share its most radical aims, but the movement persuaded the Republican Party to adopt those aims—and many Americans were willing to vote for Republican politicians who promised to outlaw abortion. These politicians won power in many states, and Republican presidents appointed Supreme Court justices who ultimately reversed *Roe* and allowed those states to ban abortion. At the same time, abortion remains legal in many states where most voters support broad access to it. True, abortion policy is not a perfect reflection of public opinion. Access tends to be more restricted than most voters favor in red states, and somewhat less restricted than most voters favor in blue states. But the anti-abortion movement has nonetheless used the tools of democracy to achieve its victories. Since the demise of *Roe* in 2022, the movement in favor of abortion access has also turned democratic, passing ballot initiatives even in conservative states.

Arguably the greatest recent triumph of the political left also reflects a successful democratic movement. Advocates for same-sex marriage conducted a savvy campaign to change public opinion and change laws, and they did so more swiftly than almost anybody would have predicted. In the 1990s, less than 30 percent of Americans favored same-sex marriage. Today, more than 70 percent do, and same-sex marriage is the law nationwide. The campaigns for same-sex marriage and abortion restrictions did not give up on the political system as corrupt or hopeless. Nor did other successful movements, like those for disability rights and marijuana legalization. They developed plans to accomplish their goals, and they succeeded.

If there is a central reason for the decline of the American dream over the past half century, it has been the lack of a strong political movement dedicated to protecting that dream. Without such a movement, our country has abandoned democratic capitalism, the most successful strategy for lifting mass living standards.

THE POLITICAL RIGHT has pushed for this abandonment. It has attempted to create a modern version of the rough-and-tumble economy of the 1920s, in which tax rates on the wealthy are low and corporations are often free to behave as they want. Some Republican voters, especially affluent ones, are genuinely attracted to this laissez-faire model. Others agree with the party on social and cultural issues and have chosen to prioritize them over economic issues. The political left, for its part, has focused on those same social and cultural issues rather than economic ones. There are large progressive groups, filled with talented leaders and idealistic young activists, devoted to gun safety, environmentalism, abortion rights, immigrant rights, LGBTQ rights, and, during Trump's presidency, resistance specifically to him. There is no similarly strong movement that tries to increase workers' wages, raise taxes on the wealthy, or reduce corporate concentration. Labor unions are the closest approximation, but many focus more narrowly on the interests of their members, and they have been shrinking for decades.

In recent decades, progressives have instead relied on a top-down approach to lifting living standards. They focused their attention on Washington and passed laws to expand government benefits and tax credits for poor and middle-class families. This approach has a historical precedent. During the Progressive Era of the late 1800s and early 1900s, well-meaning activists and politicians tried to create a broadly prosperous economy with a top-down approach that minimized the importance of political power among workers themselves and instead emphasized actions by experts and regulators. The Progressives achieved some major victories. Yet they did not end the era of soaring inequality that began in the Gilded Age and survived into the Roaring Twenties. Their victories were more modest and less enduring than the victories of the New Deal era.

The experience of the early twenty-first century has been similar. Barack Obama's presidency was the most substantial of any Democrat's in decades. Whereas Bill Clinton failed to pass a major expansion of health insurance, as had presidents stretching back to Harry Truman, Obama and his congressional allies, led by Nancy Pelosi and Harry Reid, succeeded. Millions of Americans receive affordable medical care today as a result. Obama also had other achievements, including progress against climate change through investments in clean energy. But like the Progressives who came a century earlier, Obama and his allies did not end the country's extreme inequality, as had been his ambition. "The project of the next president," Obama told me in an interview during his 2008 presidential campaign, "is figuring out how do you create bottom-up economic growth, as opposed to the trickle-down economic growth that George Bush has been so enamored with." For all of

Obama's accomplishments, he did not set the economy on a lasting new trajectory or realign American politics to create a new progressive majority.

The central explanation for this limited success was the lack of a grassroots movement dedicated to forging that majority and altering the economy. There was no network of organizations playing the roles that labor unions had from the 1930s through the 1960s, helping workers win higher wages and explaining to them how American politics shaped their daily lives and finances. The political left was more focused on social issues that appealed primarily to professionals. The political right did dedicate enormous resources to influencing the working class (through cable television, talk radio, and evangelical churches), but not in the service of creating mass prosperity.

In this book, I have focused on three forces that have shaped the American economy over the past century: power, culture, and investment. Of them, power is the most important. It is the one that can drive changes in the other two forces and in much more. Power affects parts of the economy that top-down regulation often cannot reach, like the balance among wages, profits, and executive pay inside a company. Power also allows top-down policies to endure and expand, as happened in the decades after the New Deal.

Power is the central reason our economy became more broadly prosperous and less unequal in the middle of the twentieth century, and power is the central reason those trends have reversed over the past fifty years. Our modern Gilded Age is unlikely to end until there is a political movement dedicated to ending it.

THE POLITICAL RIGHT can play an important role in such a movement, as surprising as that may sound to some people. Throughout history, and in much of the world today, conservatism has not necessarily involved an embrace of laissez-faire economics. It can instead combine social conservativism with a belief that government has a responsibility to create a prosperous economy that strengthens communities and families.

William Jennings Bryan, although a Democrat, fit this mold in the late 1800s and early 1900s. He was a populist, a creationist, and an advocate of Prohibition. Much of Southeast Asia today is run by governments that are right-wing in many respects, but also consider it their responsibility to deliver rising living standards through economic interventions. In the contemporary United States, this kind of conservative populism has been mainly rhetorical: Trump talked about protecting American workers but ran an administration that loosened corporate regulations, reduced taxes on the wealthy, and tried to take health insurance from lower-income families. Yet there are more genuine versions of populist conservatism percolating inside the Republican Party and the American right.

Trump's success at winning over Republican voters has been the catalyst for these efforts. He rejected the neoliberal consensus that had long dominated the party's economic agenda and promised to cancel free-trade agreements, protect American industries, reduce immigration, and leave Social Security alone. Instead of hurting him in the 2016 and 2024 Republican primaries, this populism seemed to help him. Trump's 2016 victory had multiple causes, including his fame stemming from reality television and his White nationalism. Still, his success demonstrated that many Republican voters were no longer excited about the neoliberal agenda; they were merely willing to tolerate it when it was packaged with social conservatism. Reagan had appealed to many middle- and lower-income Americans because he promised to solve the economic problems of the 1970s. Instead, his agenda created new and larger problems, and its failure left many voters looking for an alternative.

A candidate who combined social conservatism with economic populism might, if anything, be electorally stronger than a laissez-faire Republican. That candidate would be appealing to the heart of American public opinion in the 2000s: progressive on many economic issues, but to the right of the Democratic Party on social issues. This combination explains why Republicans keep winning elections in places like Missouri and Nebraska while those same red states are among those that have passed ballot initiatives to raise the minimum wage and expand Medicaid.

In response, some Republicans have begun to talk about the

economy in decidedly un-Reaganesque ways. Senator Josh Hawley of Missouri has urged more aggressive enforcement of antitrust policy, especially in the technology sector. Senator Marco Rubio of Florida has called for a capitalism of the "common good" and said that labor unions are important to that vision. Senator Mitt Romney has proposed a new government program to reduce child poverty. A think tank, American Compass, founded by a former Romney aide, is pushing these ideas and similar ones. "For the past generation, American conservatives have outsourced their economic thinking to libertarians," proclaims one of the organization's manifestos. "Conservatives rightly value free markets, but we also recognize that markets require rules and institutions to work well, that they are a means to the end of human flourishing and exist to serve us (not the other way around)." Among American Compass's signature proposals is a reimagined and expanded version of organized labor.

It is true that these proposals often contain conservative ideas—which is part of the point. Conservative populism is not liberal populism. It is intended to appeal to voters who hold conservative views. Republican anti-poverty proposals, for example, typically provide larger benefits to people who work because conservatives worry that no-strings-attached welfare payments can create bad incentives. Likewise, some of the conservative criticism of large companies is aimed at the social liberalism that corporate America has adopted. On some of these issues, Democrats and Republicans will not find common ground. On others, such as whether a small number of technology companies have too much control over Americans' lives and should be broken up, it is easier to imagine a consensus that leads to policy changes. Politics often involves compromises that focus on limited areas of agreement and leave disagreements to be resolved another day.

The emergence of a genuine conservative populism could be an important development. It could persuade people who distrust the Democratic Party to join grassroots groups fighting for democratic capitalism. It could make possible bipartisan coalitions in Washington that pass bills to strengthen antitrust enforcement, collective bargaining, and anti-poverty programs.

But I do not want to exaggerate the significance of conservative populism. The primary energy behind a movement to reassert democratic capitalism will probably still need to come from the left. The influence of big business and the wealthy on the Republican Party remains too strong to believe that conservative populists are likely to take over the party anytime soon. Republican politicians rely on campaign donations from laissez-faire billionaires like the Koch family and from corporate lobbying groups like the Chamber of Commerce. The Supreme Court is dominated by allies of corporate America and may remain so for decades. Much of the Republican Party is comfortable with a hard-line stance that evokes that of the Citizens Alliance and the National Association of Manufacturers from the early 1900s. For these reasons, the most plausible coalition for economic reform would include both progressives and conservatives, but more of the first group than the second.

WHAT MIGHT A new progressive movement dedicated to the American dream look like?

As with any successful movement, it will need to tell a persuasive story. In the 1930s, Roosevelt helped build a broadly prosperous economy by telling a story about freedom and power. He connected that story to the country's origins. The founders had rebelled against British royalists who oppressed Americans through special privileges granted by the Crown. In Roosevelt's own time, he explained, "economic royalists carved new dynasties" through their concentrated control over material resources. "These economic royalists complain that we seek to overthrow the institutions of America," Roosevelt said in 1936, accepting the Democratic nomination during his first reelection campaign. "What they really complain of is that we seek to take away their power. Our allegiance to American institutions requires the overthrow of this kind of power." The economic royalists wrapped themselves in the flag and the Constitution, Roosevelt said, but the flag and the Constitution in fact stood for democracy and freedom over tyranny and subjugation. Reasserting the country's true values, he explained, could repair the economy.

Decades later, the intellectuals and politicians who created the Reagan revolution told a different story, also based on enduring American ideals. Government had failed, they argued. It had failed to halt the disorder of the 1960s and the economic malaise of the 1970s. The answer, Reagan said, was to shrink government and trust the creativity of American workers and businesses. "Freedom and the dignity of the individual have been more available and assured here than in any other place on Earth," Reagan said in his first inaugural address. "If we look to the answer as to why for so many years we achieved so much, prospered as no other people on Earth, it was because here in this land we unleashed the energy and individual genius of man to a greater extent than has ever been done before." Doing so again, Reagan vowed, would create opportunity and prosperity for every group of Americans.

Reagan was wrong about the effects of his policies, but it is notable that both these politically successful stories revolved around freedom. Freedom is America's national creed, the idea that has helped justify most major political changes—the American Revolution, the abolition of slavery, trust-busting, women's suffrage, the rise of organized labor, civil rights laws, same-sex marriage, and more. Yes, freedom can be an effective message for advocates of the status quo and a laissez-faire economy, but the promise of freedom can also inspire Americans to create a fairer economy and a more equal society. The philosopher Michael Sandel describes this notion as "the civic republican idea that freedom means sharing in self-rule, having a voice in shaping the forces that govern our lives." As was the case in Roosevelt's time, today's extreme inequality is hampering Americans' freedom in ways large and small.

Most children who grow up in poverty are not free to escape it, as Raj Chetty's research has demonstrated. Many children are not free to achieve their potential because they attend inadequate schools. Workers are not free to earn wages that reflect their economic contributions. Consumers are not free to avoid surprise medical bills and sneaky mobile phone fees. Americans are not free to travel around the country as rapidly or easily as the citizens of other affluent countries move around theirs. Nor do we live as long as they do. In each of these cases, the main culprit is our highly unequal economy, in which corporations have grown larger, most workers have little power, and the wealthy can bequeath millions of dollars from one generation to the next with only light taxation.

I do not pretend to know exactly what the next persuasive story about the American economy should sound like. It will probably involve a celebration of freedom, along with patriotism, justice, and the common good, and it may require a politician with skills on the order of Roosevelt's and Reagan's. It may also require a national crisis. But it would be a mistake to wait for a political genius or a singular crisis. The historian Jefferson Cowie has pointed out that the New Deal depended on an outrageously unlikely series of events—a depression that gripped the country for more than three years before a reform-minded president took office; an unsustainable coalition of northern liberals and southern segregationists; a reactionary Supreme Court that yielded only after the president won a landslide reelection; and, finally, a world war that unified the country and solidified the creation of mass prosperity. In his book *The Great Exception*, Cowie argued that modern progressives have wrongly imagined they could repeat the New Deal's big bang of policy making. His argument helps make sense of the fact that the tumultuous events of recent decades, including the September 11 attacks, the housing crisis, and the Covid pandemic, were insufficient to reorder the economy.

A more plausible scenario for doing so involves a series of policy victories won over several decades. A future crisis may lead to some of these victories, but they could also come when the economy was growing. Benjamin Friedman, an economic historian, has pointed out that the New Deal is an exception in another way: Many periods of social and economic progress in the United States and other countries have occurred during good times that made citizens feel generous and optimistic. The Industrial Revolution's role in fostering the Enlightenment and the American Revolution is one example. Friedman's book on this subject is called *The Moral Consequences of Economic Growth*. A crucial lesson is that political reform can occur during periods of either prosperity or stagnation.

The missing ingredient in the United States over recent decades has been a strong grassroots movement focused on achieving these economic changes. Our political energy has been focused elsewhere, sometimes for good reason, but our extreme inequality will not end until there is a movement devoted to ending it. The lack of such a movement is the biggest shortcoming of the modern American left.

Labor unions still have a vital role to play in the creation of this movement. The share of American workers who belong to a union has fallen to 10 percent, from more than 30 percent in the 1960s, but polls in recent years have found rising interest in unions. According to Gallup, the approval rating for unions reached its highest level in a half century in 2022. Paradoxically, the repeated failure of modern Democratic presidents—Lyndon Johnson, Jimmy Carter, Bill Clinton, Barack Obama, and Joe Biden—to pass laws making it easier for workers to form unions provides reason to believe that federal policy can make a meaningful difference for the labor movement. The problem has not been that laws protecting unions have failed in their intended effect; the problem has been that the government has not passed these laws.

The key feature of any such policy is an overhaul of the protracted, burdensome process that workers must endure to win union recognition. Today, employers can require workers to attend meetings at which they are urged to vote against a union, and employers face only superficial penalties for violating the labor laws that do exist. Another reason for optimism about the potential impact of a new labor policy is the growth of the service sector in recent decades. A factory can respond to a workers' organizing drive by moving to another state or country. A hospital, a retailer, or a warehouse supplying nearby stores has a harder time. Its business is inherently local.

Still, some union organizers and labor experts believe that new protections for individual organizing drives are insufficient. Even if workers can join unions more easily, a basic problem will remain. When one company is unionized and another is not, the nonunionized company will have some competitive advantages. It can earn higher profits because its wages will be on the lower end of the range of indeterminacy, and these higher profits will help it attract more investment. With this investment, a nonunionized company may be able to grab market share from a unionized rival. A better approach might be to change federal law so that workers across an entire sector—such as all warehouse workers—could belong to the same union and bargain collectively. Germany uses this model of sectoral bargaining to considerable success. Blue-collar wages tend to be higher there than in the United States, and the manufacturing sector is stronger, in part because sectoral unions and company management often have cooperative relationships that empower workers to share ideas that can increase productivity. The German system is also flexibile, with companies able to override sector-wide agreements when workers and management agree to do so. Countries with more rigid sectoral systems, like France, have not fared so well. Germany's success suggests that the best approach may be a middle ground between the anti-union economy of the United States and the union-dominant sectors of some other countries.

Whatever the details would be in the United States, a reanimated labor movement has the potential to benefit more than just its own members. Labor unions have long provided political support that makes possible the passage of safety net programs that benefit all workers. Unions remind people of the economic stakes when they vote. In the 1960s, unions persuaded many voters not to support George Wallace by highlighting his anti-worker record in Alabama. A stronger labor movement in recent years might have been able to do the same to Trump. Instead, many of the messages that working-class Americans heard from outside groups were pro-Trump, coming from evangelical groups and Fox News.

There has been one recent demonstration of unions' ability to shape a national debate. In 2012, a group of workers at McDonald's, Burger King, and other fast-food restaurants in New York began to hold demonstrations demanding higher wages. The protests soon spread, with support from several unions, and they became the basis for a movement to increase the minimum wage, known as the Fight for $15. Bernie Sanders announced his support for the effort, and it eventually became a standard part of the Democratic Party's agenda. With polls showing that the idea was popular even among many Republican voters, activists saw an opportunity to raise statewide minimum wages through ballot initiatives, and labor groups like the Service Employees International Union again provided financial and logistical support. Almost twenty-five states, including red states like Arkansas, Florida, Missouri, and Ohio, have since raised their minimum wage. These increases are one reason that wages for low-income workers rose during and immediately after the Covid pandemic. Other recent recessions, by contrast, tended to cause the most damage to low-wage workers. The increases have also played a role in the modest shrinking of the White-Black wage gap since the mid-2010s.

The Fight for $15 campaign has been an exception that helps prove the rule: When a political movement can attract dedicated organizers and win over public opinion—when it can tell a persuasive story—it can often change society. Think about how different American society might be if there were also strong movements to reduce corporate concentration, raise taxes on the wealthy, lower medical costs, create universal pre-K education, and increase middle-class pay.

FOR PROGRESSIVES INTERESTED in building these kinds of movements, there is one important step that is also hard. It involves listening more to the views of working-class Americans. It requires making the left less upscale than it now is and more inclusive of people who are not white-collar professionals.

Democrats today frequently fail to do so. They adopt the approach that Eugene McCarthy and George McGovern did decades ago rather than the one that Robert F. Kennedy did. They effectively ask working-class Americans to ignore the party's positions on social issues and insist that people base their votes on economic issues. When voters choose not to, progressives ask how anybody could vote against their own interests. But this question lacks self-awareness. Many progressives also base their votes on issues other than economics. The country's most affluent places—neighborhoods in Manhattan and San Francisco, vacation spots like Aspen and Martha's Vineyard, and well-to-do suburbs across the country—often vote Democratic. The residents of these places are voting to raise their own taxes. They are doing so because they believe that politics is about more than their personal finances.

Poor, working-class, and middle-class voters feel the same way. And they recognize that the Brahmin left has stopped engaging with them on many major issues, much as McCarthy refused to say the words "law and order" during the 1968 campaign despite the country's concerns about a crime wave that had lasted more than five years by that point. Today, many well-off progressives have decided that their views are the only acceptable ones on a long list of subjects, including guns, immigration, Covid, abortion, affirmative action, and gender issues. Opposing views are not merely different; they are some combination of ignorant and bigoted.

There was a telling example in the weeks after Trump's shocking victory in 2016. Media organizations, feeling guilty and somewhat ashamed that they had not foreseen the outcome, dispatched reporters to Trump-friendly communities to ask about his appeal. Some of these stories were set in diners, and a meme soon arose in progressive corners of social media, deriding the media's obsession with Trump voters in diners. No doubt, some of the diner stories were flawed. Journalism often is. But the meme was symbolic of the upscale left's attitude toward much of the country: We are tired of listening to you.

Robert Kennedy remains a pertinent figure because of both his willingness to listen and his refusal to compromise on certain core issues. Kennedy did not just use the words "law and order"; he made them a theme of his campaign. He understood that racists like Wallace and race-baiters like Richard Nixon used those same words as dog whistles. Kennedy also recognized that the phrase spoke to legitimate concerns from people of all races about personal safety and societal chaos. If he did not address these concerns and tried to change the subject to, say, tax policy, voters would tune him out and might vote for a racist instead. At the same time, Kennedy drew a few hard lines that he knew would alienate some voters. He stood forthrightly for civil rights. Whenever he mentioned law and order in a speech, he made sure to mention racial equality as well. Kennedy was proud to be the most popular White politician in Black America.

I understand why liberals today have chosen to draw so many hard lines. American society has deep problems: Guns are killing children. Police officers are killing innocent people. Covid is killing Americans who could easily be spared by a vaccine. Abortion restrictions deny women control over their bodies. Desperate immigrants want to find a better life in the United States. The White-Black wage gap is almost as wide as it was seventy years ago. But some of the underlying explanations for these problems are legitimately complex, and it should be possible to understand why another person might have a different view of them. Progressives cannot hope to build a majority coalition if they shut out everybody who disagrees with any of the core planks of Brahmin liberalism. There are tens of millions of vaccine skeptics, hunting enthusiasts, supporters of tighter border security, and people who support abortion restrictions after the first trimester, including many women. When the political left tells them that all their views are irredeemable, these voters naturally drift to the right. It is already happening. Every Democratic president from Truman to Obama won voters without a college degree. The party no longer does.

I have my own example. It is a progressive policy that I strongly support and yet have come to understand why many working-class people oppose it. I think that a soda tax—a dedicated tax on sweetened beverages—is an effective way to reduce obesity and the health problems associated with it. Real-world evidence supports this conclusion, and the public relations campaigns that claim otherwise are financed by soda companies that care more about their profits than their customers' well-being. But I also know that many Americans who make less money than I do disagree about the wisdom of a soda tax. They see it as an unnecessary and paternalistic burden that interferes with a small daily pleasure. I hope that people will eventually change their minds, as they did about tobacco taxes, but I respect the opposing view. For that reason, I write about soda taxes less often and with more nuance than I once did. The United States can become a better country—and can reanimate the American dream—without immediately fixing its soda addiction. Public opinion deserves some deference.

Specific policy positions are not even the main point. The basic human desire for respect is. Much of the Brahmin left genuinely does not respect the views that many working-class Americans hold. Today's liberalism can be harshly judgmental about the political positions people have, the language they use, the vehicles they drive, and the food they eat. Yes, as liberals point out, many conservatives also treat opposing ideas with scorn. If anything, conservative scorn tends to be nastier, as cable television, talk radio, and social media demonstrate every day. But the problem for liberals is that their own views on some of these contentious issues are less popular than their opponents' ideas.

Patriotism is a good example. Many upscale progressives have become uncomfortable with long-standing American symbols and traditions: the flag, the Pledge of Allegiance, the national anthem, the Thanksgiving holiday, and presidents long seen as national heroes. The most intense version of these views is concentrated among a small slice of liberals, like the members of the San Francisco school board who voted to remove Abraham Lincoln's name from a high school, only to reverse themselves after being criticized. This faction of the left tends to have access to modern megaphones. It is overrepresented in academia, Hollywood, the national media, and activist groups, all of which shape perceptions of the Democratic Party. Those perceptions have a basis in truth: Patriotism really is passé on today's left. In a recent poll, only about one-quarter of Democratic voters with a bachelor's degree described the United States as the greatest country in the world.

The underlying reasons for liberalism's discomfort with mainstream American culture are often legitimate. Past American injustices have too often been ignored if not glamorized. But a political ideology that derides its own country's symbols cannot expect to win power in that country. Both the labor leaders of the 1930s and the civil rights leaders of the 1950s and early 1960s understood this and embraced patriotic symbols. They cast themselves as more faithful to American ideals than their opponents, as Roosevelt did when talking about freedom, the flag, and the Constitution. You may recall a quotation by the historian Nelson Lichtenstein from an earlier chapter: "All of America's great reform movements, from the crusade against slavery onward, have defined themselves as champions of a moral and patriotic nationalism, which they counterpoised to the parochial and selfish elites who stood athwart their vision of a virtuous society."

A contemporary version of these reform movements would, as Robert Kennedy did, choose a few issues on which compromise was unacceptable—and treat opposing views respectfully on most issues. To take one example, fundamental civil rights for transgender people, including the ability to use the name and pronoun that they want, strikes me as a line worth drawing. To do otherwise is to deny a fellow human being the dignity that everybody deserves. The age at which a child or teenager is old enough to have a gender-related medical procedure with permanent effects, by contrast, seems like an issue on which well-meaning people might disagree. Or consider voting rights: Closing polling stations in Black neighborhoods and not White ones deserves condemnation; requiring everybody to bring a photo identification to the polls—which is the law in many countries—seems like a policy worthy of respectful engagement even if you do not support it.

It is possible to disagree with others without believing that their views are hateful and unacceptable. It should also be possible for citizens with differing views on some important subjects nonetheless to belong to the same political coalition. Any coalition that rejects this idea is unlikely to be very large.

Some contemporary progressive politicians have figured out how to manage these tensions. They treat working-class voters with respect, and they have often been rewarded for it. Before Vermont became as liberal as it is now, Bernie Sanders needed to woo more swing voters, and he won elections partly by taking moderate positions on gun policy and immigration. Today, Sanders remains at least somewhat skeptical of high levels of immigration even if he no longer emphasizes this skepticism. Several other Democratic members of Congress also manage to win a large number of votes in conservative areas. Some are on the left flank of the party (like Sherrod Brown of Ohio), while others are more moderate (like Amy Klobuchar of Minnesota, Joe Manchin of West Virginia, and Jon Tester of Montana). The latest examples are John Fetterman, Pennsylvania's junior senator, and Marie Gluesenkamp Perez, who co-owns an auto repair shop in Washington State and was elected to Congress in 2022. All use a populist approach that avoids condescension.

The two most recent Democratic presidents are also examples. Obama fared far better among Midwestern working-class voters than either the Democratic nominee before him (John Kerry) or after him (Hillary Clinton) partly by projecting an unabashed patriotism and speaking respectfully about moderate social views. Central to his image, and somewhat lost to the partisan battles that followed, was the idea that he enjoyed talking to and working with conservatives.

Biden, meanwhile, owes his political career to avoiding the elitism of modern liberalism. He originally won election to the Senate in 1972, defeating a Republican incumbent during the same election in which Nixon was trouncing McGovern. While McGovern allied himself with the New Left, Biden distanced himself from it. On economic issues, Biden ran as a populist, complaining about "millionaires who don't pay any taxes at all" and "billion-dollar corporations who want a ride on the public's back." On other issues, including the Vietnam War and marijuana, he signaled that he was more moderate. More recently, as president, Biden has tried to downplay issues that alienate working-class voters, including immigration, and focused on broadly popular economic policies. This approach helped him pass a surprisingly long list of bills in his first two years, some with only Democratic votes in Congress and others with bipartisan support.

Building a less upscale coalition may require uncomfortable compromises for progressives, but the upsides are enormous. It would make possible not only a resurgence of democratic capitalism but also progress on many social policies that matter dearly to liberals. Today's version of the Democratic Party is so unpopular in more than twenty states that it loses almost every statewide election. And demographic change may not save Democrats in these states, now that a growing number of Latino and Asian voters are dissatisfied with the party's social liberalism. Imagine how many more elections the party might win—in states like Florida, North Carolina, Ohio, and Texas—if it could attract more working-class support. Then imagine how many more women might have access to abortion in these states. Imagine the gun safety measures that might be able to pass. Imagine how different the Senate—and eventually the federal judiciary—might be.

Trump and the radicalized Republican Party have created an opportunity for Democrats. Republican positions are more extreme on many issues, both economic and social, than public opinion. A more open-minded and patriotic Democratic Party, a less purist and judgmental one, would have a chance to win over enough of these voters to decide elections. For more than fifty years, Democrats have moved their party ever closer to the Brahmin values of professionals and college graduates, but the original arithmetic problem that undermined the New Left has never disappeared. Most Americans do not have a bachelor's degree. They tend to be socially moderate and economically progressive. They are a crucial part of any political coalition that hopes to fix our broken economy.

CREATING A MORE inclusive progressivism is necessary to build a successful movement for democratic capitalism. But it is not sufficient. Successful grassroots movements also need intellectual leadership. They need people who develop and refine the ideas that a governing coalition can one day implement.

A. Philip Randolph helped play this role for the civil rights movement, recognizing that wartime production offered an opportunity to integrate the nation's factories and pushing for a specific solution, in the form of an executive order whose language he shaped. Robert Bork, Milton Friedman, and other Chicago School economists played this role for the Reagan revolution, spending decades sharpening their ideas on taxes, deregulation, and anti-trust. Their job, as Friedman said, was to develop alternatives that might seem politically impossible in the moment but could eventually triumph.

The past decade has seen the stirrings of an intellectual movement devoted to democratic capitalism. Both Democratic and Republican politicians have turned against the trade liberalization agenda that dominated American politics for decades. In antitrust policy, Lina Khan, Tim Wu, and other legal scholars have questioned the old Bork-forged consensus. Academics like Nicholas Bagley and journalists like Ezra Klein are advocating a "supply-side progressivism" that would remove the bureaucratic barriers that prevent the construction of new homes, schools, and transportation systems. Young workers are showing new interest in forming labor unions in both blue-collar and white-collar settings.

The past decade of electoral politics has demonstrated the interest in a new economic approach. Obama was less of a neoliberal than Clinton or Carter and pushed for substantially higher taxes on the rich as well as more income support for the middle class and poor. After Obama came Trump, who was overwhelmingly a destructive force, but he did puncture the myth that most Republican voters favor free trade and Social Security cuts. Trump's successor, Biden, represented the sharpest break with the neoliberal era. He continued Trump's skepticism of trade and enacted legislation that prioritizes American companies and workers. Biden appointed prominent critics of corporate concentration, including Khan and Wu, to positions in which they could shape antitrust policy. Biden also oversaw the largest increase in federal investment since the Eisenhower era (albeit still much smaller in scale than Eisenhower's, relative to the size of the economy). During the first two years of the Biden administration, Congress passed bills with billions of dollars of spending on roads, semiconductor factories, clean energy development, and basic scientific research. These are classic examples of investments that benefit an economy but that the private sector often does not make because they do not bring reliable profits to any one company.

Intriguingly, there are tentative signs that the economic approach of the past decade is making a difference. Since the mid-2010s, average wages for lower-income workers have risen somewhat more rapidly than wages for higher-income workers. Economists are still trying to understand the full explanation, but government policy has surely played a role. The minimum wage has risen by at least 50 percent in nearly twenty states since 2013. Even Trump, in 2017, appointed a Federal Reserve chair who, at least until recently, prioritized the creation of a tight labor market through low interest rates, and tight labor markets particularly benefit lower-income workers. Another factor contributing to that tightness has been a shrinking of the number of people in the labor force in recent years; the reasons include the aging of the population, a wave of early retirements after Covid shutdowns, and a slowing of immigration during the pandemic. All else equal, a labor force that grows more slowly lifts the wages of the people in that labor force. The recent rise in educational attainment, with both the high school and college graduation rates having increased somewhat, helps too. Workers with more education earn a lot more money on average.

Even with all this energy, the movement for a new democratic capitalism remains in its early stages. For one thing, the recent low-end wage increases may turn out to be fleeting. That was the case during the other significant spurt in workers' wages over the past half century, during the late 1990s. It did not last and did not alter the economy's fundamental trajectory toward higher inequality. The movement's agenda also remains vague in crucial areas. On antitrust, for example, the new would-be trustbusters have not developed a standard to replace Bork's clear, though deeply flawed, standard. He argued that any merger that could not be proved to raise consumer prices would benefit the economy and should be allowed to proceed. In reality, rising corporate concentration has led to more long-term price increases than Bork-style analysis suggested; one reason Americans pay more for mobile telephone and internet service is because our economy has fewer providers than much of Europe. Bork's analysis also underplayed the ability of large companies to hold down wages and influence the political system. The new trustbusters have made all these arguments persuasively. They have not yet developed a clear technical definition of when a company is too large. Their argument is more general, and the specifics are important. They will make it possible for judges, legislators, and regulators to enact a new agenda, much as Bork's disciples did.

There are similarly important questions in other policy areas. How might the United States develop its own version of sectoral-level bargaining for workers? How can the federal government effectively tax not only top incomes but also the accumulated wealth that has created a modern aristocracy? How should the country build a pre-K and childcare system that can reduce childhood and gender inequities? How can the country reduce mass incarceration and police violence while also holding down crime levels? What would it take to create an immigration system that did not increase economic inequality? Why is medical care uniquely expensive in the United States? How can colleges and employers create a version of class-based affirmative action that is legally protected and more popular than the old race-based affirmative action but that also fosters racial diversity?

Many of these questions involve the technocratic tools of economics and other social sciences. But politics is also a vital part of the background work. One reason that government intervention has lost public support in recent decades is that progressives have often created benefits that are hidden from view. Tax credits are the leading example: They help Americans pay for college, housing, and medical care, and they have become a major way that Washington fights poverty. But many people do not think of these benefits as being government programs. They are often camouflaged in their tax returns. The political scientist Suzanne Mettler has referred to these programs as being part of "the submerged state," and she argues that their lack of salience has contributed to skepticism of government. Many Americans distrust government partly because they do not realize that it is helping to pay for their home and their child's college tuition.

The programs enacted by Franklin Roosevelt and Lyndon Johnson tended to be more obvious: Social Security, protection of bank deposits, jobless benefits, Medicare, and huge infrastructure projects. In January 1937, near the end of Roosevelt's first term as president, *Life* magazine published a map of the United States spread over two full pages. The headline read: "What President Roosevelt Did to the Map of the U.S. in Four Years with $6,500,000,000." Scattered around the map were dozens of small drawings, each showing a project funded by Roosevelt's stimulus program. They included tunnels and the Triborough Bridge in New York, schools in South Carolina, dorms at Texas Tech University, the Kansas City Civic Auditorium, the Los Angeles Aqueduct, and the Grand Coulee Dam. Roosevelt understood that he needed both to rescue the country from the Depression and to make sure that people knew he had done so. His projects changed how Americans thought about government. There is a lesson here for today's reformers. Universal pre-K and other worthy goals may be more attainable and enduring if they are not tucked away in the federal tax code.

Politics matters in a second way, as well. The structure of American government makes it harder to pass reforms than to protect the status quo. The founders, rebelling against King George's centralized power, deliberately created a system in which passing laws was complicated. In many other democracies today, a party that wins an election can swiftly enact its agenda through parliament. In the United States, it is not so easy. The president is elected separately from the legislature, and the legislature has two chambers, one of which—the Senate—is designed to slow lawmaking. The Supreme Court is also more powerful than the top court in most countries. Elsewhere, the courts typically make modest, technical changes to policies rather than act as a super-legislature that can overturn laws enacted by democratically elected officials elsewhere in government.

The founders did not create all these features for the purpose of protecting wealth and privilege, but they often serve that function. As the economist Thomas Piketty has explained, inequality naturally tends to increase over time in a capitalist economy, absent a crisis or legislation that pushes in the opposite direction. Because American government is biased toward the status quo, it is biased toward economic inequality. This dynamic has been exacerbated in recent years by two additional factors: The Supreme Court is dominated by laissez-faire justices who are generally hostile to regulation, while the Senate gives outsize power to rural regions that tend to vote for laissez-faire politicians.

All of which suggests that future economic reform will probably depend on changes to the structure of government. Such changes would be consistent with American history. The Constitution includes mechanisms for Congress and the president to check the power of the Supreme Court because the court is supposed to be a coequal branch of government, not the dominant one. The Constitution also includes ways to reform the country's governing structure to keep up with the times, such as amendments to the Constitution itself or the admission of new states. Yet the United States government is now in the midst of its longest period of structural sclerosis.

The number of federal appeals court judges increased under both George H. W. Bush and Ronald Reagan but not since then. No constitutional amendment has been ratified in three decades, the longest period without one in more than a century. No new state has joined the union in six decades, by far the longest such stretch in the country's history. There are two obvious candidates for new states now: Puerto Rico and Washington, D.C., places where American citizens lack representation in their own government. Adding them would both make the country more democratic and probably aid the cause of democratic capitalism, given the views of the people who live there.

Limiting the authority of the Supreme Court is a more difficult task, but it may ultimately be necessary to create a more broadly prosperous economy. Roosevelt's showdown with the court in the 1930s is often remembered, mistakenly, as an outright defeat for him. In truth, his threat to add justices to the court probably contributed to their sudden willingness not to overturn New Deal programs and to protect labor unions' right to organize. A future president and Congress may need to confront the court again. The Constitution, in addition to giving Congress and the president the power to expand the number of justices (which would be an extreme step), also allows them to deem certain subjects beyond the authority of Supreme Court review. The court is a political institution and has increasingly acted like one in recent decades. The rest of the federal government has the constitutional right to treat it as such.

With all these issues, both political and economic, the details matter. Carefully designed policies, refined over years of work, are more likely to become law and change people's lives than hastily designed policies. For progressives, an inspiring recent case study should be Obamacare. Universal access to health insurance was the canonical liberal policy failure of the late twentieth century. Truman could not pass it. Edward Kennedy long regretted not taking Nixon up on his offer of a bipartisan bill. Carter could not pass a bill despite solid Democratic majorities in Congress. Clinton's first two years as president were defined by his inability to pass a plan. In response to these failures, health reformers—congressional aides, state officials, community activists, think tank experts, academic researchers—did not give up. They tried to learn from their failures and spent years designing a plan that could pass. Finally, in 2010, they succeeded. Obama's law sharply reduced the number of uninsured and expanded access to medical care for millions of low- and middle-income families. It improved their lives.

The ensuing battle over Obamacare became one more sign of the power of grassroots movements. When Trump and congressional Republicans tried to repeal it in 2017, progressive activists responded. They filled town hall meetings and staged protests on Capitol Hill, highlighting the stories of people who would be hurt if the law was eliminated. Some of the most effective advocates came from the disability rights community, which had been strengthened by its own long political struggle. This activism helped increase popular support for the law. Even though Republicans controlled Congress, just enough Republican senators defected from their party and voted to save Obamacare.

American democracy has always been deeply flawed, and it has major problems today. More often than not, though, it works. The mechanisms of democracy remain the most viable means for improving living standards in the United States.

. . .

THE STORY OF healthcare is instructive for another reason, too. Before the eventual victory, there were years of disappointments and setbacks.

That theme runs through the history of social and economic reform in the United States. Before the labor movement forged a high-wage economy in the 1940s, it endured decades of often violent defeats. The railroad porters' union led by Randolph was in such dire shape at one point that it was evicted from its Harlem headquarters. When Carl Skoglund set out to organize the truck drivers of Minneapolis in 1933, he was a forty-nine-year-old who had lost almost every previous union campaign in which he had participated. The histories of the movements for civil rights, women's rights, disability rights, and gay rights are similarly fraught. In hindsight, we remember them as victorious. For the leaders and members of the movement, the day-to-day and year-to-year experience often felt more like defeat. Yet people did not give up. They kept fighting.

The same is true of the most influential conservative movements of modern times. Friedman was bitterly disappointed when mainstream publications did not even review his book about capitalism in 1962, while abortion opponents spent years seething about Republican-appointed justices who failed to overturn *Roe v. Wade*. Less partisan campaigns, neither purely conservative nor liberal, also fit the pattern. Dwight Eisenhower drove across the country with hundreds of fellow soldiers to promote the Good Roads movement in 1919. He did not sign a law creating a national highway system until almost forty years later.

None of these movements, to be clear, were destined to succeed. Some political movements never do. Other times, injustice can prevail for so long that it lasts for people's entire lives, as was the case in the post-Reconstruction Jim Crow South. A naïve faith in the inevitability of progress can make progress less likely. Irrational optimism, however, is not America's main problem in the early twenty-first century. Cynicism and negativity are bigger obstacles. Many Americans have come to believe that the system is rigged and change is impossible. Their lack of faith helps the status quo endure.

I understand why so many people feel frustrated. We live in a country where most people's incomes and wealth have grown slowly, where inequality has soared, and where life expectancy has stopped increasing for most of the population. The story that I have told in this book is cause for outrage. Yet it is also cause for hope, for resilience, and for confidence that Americans have the power to create a better economy than the one we now have.

After all, the notion of an American dream was invented not during good times. It was invented during the Great Depression. The future can be different from the past.

ACKNOWLEDGMENTS

THE BEST EDITORS MANAGE TO COMBINE OPTIMISM WITH honesty. They imbue writers with a confidence that the writers themselves often lack, a belief that ambitious projects can be accomplished. Then, as the writer gets to work on a specific project, the editor offers blunt criticism about its weaknesses—combined with an unwavering belief that the writer will fix those weaknesses and all will be well in the end. It is quite the balancing act.

Laura Bissell Auwers Leonhardt, my wife, played that role for this book. She told me that I could obviously write this book when it was not obvious to me. She told me that my rough drafts were very good except for a few minor issues (which was a kind way of saying they were not good enough), and she encouraged me to focus on my favorite form of nonfiction writing: human storytelling interwoven with plainspoken analysis. When I doubted that I would make a deadline, she told me that there was nothing to do but continue writing, and she predicted that I would indeed make the deadline.

What made this expert editing remarkable is that Laura is neither an editor nor a writer. She is a onetime lawyer, a teacher, and an obsessive reader. Over the course of this project, she made me understand the common strands between editing and many other realms of life. In everything Laura does, she makes people believe that they can accomplish ambitious goals of which they are less certain, and she has devoted her life to helping them accomplish them. Along the way, she happens to be constitutionally incapable of hiding her honest criticism, as she herself likes to joke. I am spectacularly fortunate to be her partner. This book, like everything else in our lives, is a joint project.

Random House bought this book twelve years ago and remained invested in it as it became a larger project that took much more time than I initially envisioned. I am grateful to Andy Ward for his steadfast enthusiasm and to the entire Random House team, including Tom Perry, Ben Greenberg, Michelle Jasmine, Windy Dorrestyn, Amy Schroeder, Dennis Ambrose, Rebecca Berlant, Benjamin Dreyer, Elizabeth Rendfleisch, and Robbin Schiff. I am most grateful to Marie Pantojan, the book's lead editor, who devoted many hours over multiple years to shaping and improving it. By the latter stages of the process, I stopped worrying about solving every writing problem before sending draft chapters to Marie because I knew she would find solutions that had not occurred to me.

Christy Fletcher, my agent, is a wise and fierce advocate. Kevin Quealy, a friend and collaborator for more than a decade, created the charts for this book. Carol Poticny found the photographs that brought the historical figures to life. Hilary McClellan caught errors and suggested smart changes during fact checking. Steve Alexander offered design advice.

This book has depended on the expertise of research librarians around the country: at the Library of Congress; the presidential museums of Franklin Roosevelt, Harry Truman, Dwight Eisenhower, John F. Kennedy, Lyndon Johnson, Richard Nixon, and Ronald Reagan; the Minneapolis Historical Society; Columbia University; Texas Southern University; the Hoover Institution at Stanford University; the University of Chicago; and the University of Iowa. Research librarians are the quiet heroes of history and journalism.

Several other researchers and scholars helped me locate material that I would not have located without them, including Jefferson Cowie, Randy Furst, Howard Kling, Peter Rachleff, Richard Rosenfeld, and Paul Spickard.

I am deeply grateful to the writers, historians, economists, and others who took time to read parts of this manuscript and offer feedback. Every reader improved the project. Thank you to Binyamin Appelbaum, Emily Bazelon, Barry Bienstock, Sheldon Danziger, Drew Gilpin Faust, Claudia Goldin, Michael Kazin, German Lopez, Daniel Okrent, Paul Sabin, Michael Sandel, Richard Thaler, and Jia Lynn Yang. A special thank you to those who offered thoughts on the entire manuscript: Linda Auwers, Andrew Graybill, James H. Jones, and Lawrence Katz.

I have worked at *The New York Times* since 1999 and been able to learn from the world's finest journalists. *The Times* does not exist by happenstance. It exists because of generations of commitment from the extended Ochs-Sulzberger family to aspiring toward journalism without fear or favor. Over the years, I have been given wonderful opportunities by Arthur Sulzberger, Bill Keller, Jill Abramson, Dean Baquet, Andy Rosenthal, James Bennet, and, most recently, A. G. Sulzberger, Meredith Kopit Levien, Katie Kingsbury, Sam Dolnick, and Joe Kahn. My editors and mentors have included Carl Hulse, Larry Ingrassia, Trish Hall, Tom Redburn, Winnie O'Kelley, Jim Schachter, Phyllis Messenger, Dick Stevenson, Gerry Marzorati, Aaron Retica, and Vera Titunik. I appreciate the chance to work with Steve Duenes, Matt Ericson, Marc Lacey, Carolyn Ryan, Sam Sifton, Kitty Bennett, Ian Prasad Philbrick, and many others. I will always be grateful to Glenn Kramon and Alison Leigh Cowan for hiring me. My colleagues on "The Morning," led by Amy Fiscus and Tom Wright-Piersanti, enabled me to take time off by being so good at what they do.

During the years of writing the book, I have benefited from a loving group of friends who encouraged me about the project and, even better, distracted me from it. They include Angela and Jacob Buchdahl, Ariela Dubler and Jesse Furman, Richard Ford, Erin and Josh Galper, Kolo and Susannah Kerest, Greg Raskin and Jackie Weiss, David Rousseau, and Brett and Lori Zbar, as well as the members of the Regis Philbin National League and Seven Locks Pickleball. I wrote much of this book at Compass Coffee, and it is an excellent place to put words to paper, especially when Franklin Foer is doing so a few tables away and available for coffee breaks.

I am lucky to be going through life with my rock-steady sister, Robin Peterson, and with a close extended family. In addition to those I have already mentioned, thank you to Rich and Suzie Bissell, the Alexanders, Lawlers, Nashes, Petersons, Korzenik-Posners, Lippmanns, O'Neill-Bissells, Castle-Joneses, Dholakia-Joneses, and Harbesons. R. B. and T. T. Alexander are my grandparents who did not figure in this book, and they were a central part of my life for four decades.

Laura's and my three children were small when this project began. They are not anymore. Jonah, Felix, and Eva: The bad news is that you can no longer make fun of me for not having finished my book; the good news is that you'll no doubt find other material. Mom and I are immensely proud of the people you have become. We are never happier than we are with you.

I want to end by thanking my teachers over the decades. Decades later, I still think frequently about the people who have taught me to write and to think about history, numbers, and evidence. They include classroom teachers like Priscilla Sandler, David Schiller, Joan Bowen, Susan Kornstein, and Steven Gillon, as well as editors like Simon Lipskar, Jodi Rudoren, Mary Kuntz, and John A. Byrne.

The best teachers I have had are my parents, Bob and Joan Leonhardt. When I think back on my childhood, I see one of them reading a newspaper or book at the dining room table. They made ideas seem exciting by presiding over dinner conversations in which children were full participants, and they edited the first draft of nearly everything I wrote as I was discovering that I wanted to be a writer. They somehow knew how to laugh about my malapropisms and long sentences without making me feel insecure. They turned clear expression into an exciting game that anybody could learn and nobody ever mastered. Their dedication to creating a better society, starting with their involvement in Students for a Democratic Society, remains an inspiration.

My mom is, as recognized by her friends and family, one of the world's sweetest souls. Her curiosity and her delight at listening to other people tell their stories showed me about how to be a reporter. Her unconditional support encourages her children and grandchildren to follow their passions.

My dad died in the early stages of this project, and I miss him every day. He is very much a part of this book, not only because I listened to Oscar Peterson while writing it. My dad and I spent decades debating many of the ideas in these pages. He would have agreed with some parts of my argument and disagreed with others. Still, he would have been the book's most enthusiastic promoter.

Among my mom's and dad's many lessons was that children can embody their parents' values while developing their own ideas. I hope I have done so.

NOTES

Introduction

ix **The Met branded** "Opera Clears Out 20 Enemy Aliens," *The New York Times,* April 27, 1918, 10.

ix **Not long afterward** "Robert Leonhardt, Opera Baritone," *The New York Times,* February 3, 1923, 13.

ix **He wore round-frame eyeglasses** Personal correspondence and photos in author's collection.

ix **"the hated target"** Robert Lazner [Rudolf Leonhard], "Frankreich," cited in Melanie Krob, "Imprisoned in Paradise: Antifascist Germans in the French Wartime Internment Camps, 1939–1940," *Journal of European Studies* 38, no. 1 (March 2008): 63.

x **René felt so** Esther Leonhardt's personal correspondence in author's collection.

x **In and around Paris** Vicki Caron, "The Missed Opportunity: French Refugee Policy in Wartime, 1939–1940," *Historical Reflections* 22, no. 1 (Winter 1996): 117–57; Regina M. Delacor, "From Potential Friends to Potential Enemies: The Internment of 'Hostile Foreigners' in France at the Beginning of the Second World War," *Journal of Contemporary History* 35, no. 3 (July 2000): 361–68; Krob, "Imprisoned in Paradise."

x **The writer Arthur Koestler** Arthur Koestler, *Scum of the Earth* (New York: Eland, 1941), 57–69.

x **"France is supposed"** "France Copies Hitler," *The New Republic,* January 15, 1940, cited in Caron, "Missed Opportunity," 132.

xi **Jewish relief organizations** "French Speed Aid for Enemy Aliens," *The New York Times,* December 17, 1939, 37.

xi **After a two-week** "States Immigrant Inspector at Port of Arrival," February 26, 1940, Family History Library, Salt Lake City, Utah.

xi **There, American authorities detained René** "Record of Aliens Held for Special Inquiry," February 26, 1940, Family History Library.

xi **He probably obtained** Elizabeth Burnes (National Archives and Records Administration), email correspondence with author.

xi **The two were married** Marriage record of René Leonhardt and Esther Messing, June 3, 1940, Virginia Department of Health, Richmond, Va.

xii **They are also stories** I chose to capitalize the names of all racial groups, including Black and White. Kwame Anthony Appiah, a philosopher, made a persuasive case for capitalizing both Black and White in a June 2020 essay in *The Atlantic* magazine, "The Case for Capitalizing the B in Black." Neither term is a literal description of skin color, Appiah noted, and both are social constructs. To capitalize only Black and not White is to risk treating Whiteness as a neutral state and Blackness as something different. "Racial identities were not discovered but created," Appiah wrote, "and we must all take responsibility for them. Don't let them disguise themselves as common nouns and adjectives. Call them out by their names." I made exceptions for quotations of written language, in which I deferred to the capitalization style that the writer used.

xii **that American dream** James Trunslow Adams, *The Epic of America* (Boston: Little, Brown, 1931), v–vi.

xiii **Two Broadway plays** Brooks Atkinson, "Fate of the Idealist," *The New York Times,* March 5, 1933, 122; Sam Zolotow, "Drama by Albee Will Open Feb. 28," *The New York Times,* February 9, 1961, 37.

xiii **"I still have a dream"** Martin Luther King, Jr., speech at the March on Washington, Washington, D.C., August 28, 1963.

xiv **"Mine is the shining future"** Adams, *Epic of America,* 327.

xiv **"That is the story"** Michelle Obama, speech at the Democratic National Convention, Philadelphia, Pa., July 25, 2016.

xv **Measures of public health** Elizabeth Arias and Jiaquan Xu, "United States Life Tables, 2019," *National Vital Statistics Reports* 70, no. 19 (March 22, 2022).

xv **In very few other countries** "Life Expectancy at Birth, Total (Years)," World Bank.

xvi **Life Expectancy at Birth [chart]** "Life Expectancy," World Bank.

xviii **The first Up film** The first film in the series, *Seven Up!,* was directed by Paul Almond; all others were directed by Michael Apted. The first film aired May 5, 1964, on ITV; the latest, *63 Up,* aired June 4–6, 2019, on BBC One.

xviii **"iPod government"** David Leonhardt, "Closing Income Gap Tops Obama's Agenda for Economic Change," *The New York Times,* February 2, 2008; Barack Obama, interview with author, January 29, 2008.

xix **One researcher** Raj Chetty (Harvard University), interview with author.

xix **After writing about his work** David Leonhardt, "The American Dream, Quantified at Last," *The New York Times,* December 8, 2016.

xxi **"At first I was"** Martin Tolchin, "Taking Over Business Helped Widows Adjust," *The New York Times,* September 23, 1963, 24.

xxii **Well before the great victories** Patrick Bayer and Kerwin Kofi Charles, "Divergent Paths: A New Perspective on Earnings Differences Between Black and White Men Since 1940," *The Quarterly Journal of Economics* 133, no. 3 (August 2018): figure 5.

xxii **Black life expectancy** Elizabeth Arias and Jiaquan Xu, "United States Life Tables, 2017," *National Vital Statistics Reports* 68, no. 7 (June 24, 2019).

xxii **The large gains** Jim Tankersley, *The Riches of This Land: The Untold, True Story of America's Middle Class* (New York: PublicAffairs, 2020).

xxii **"achieving the American dream"** Chetty, interview with author.

xxii **Chetty and five colleagues** Raj Chetty, David Grusky, Maximilian Hell, Nathaniel Hendren, Robert Manduca, and Jimmy Narang, "The Fading American Dream: Trends in Absolute Income Mobility Since 1940," *Science* 356, no. 6336 (April 24, 2017): 398–406; Gareth Cook, "The Economist Who Would Fix the American Dream," *The Atlantic,* August 2019; Christiane Amanpour, "Raj Chetty Discusses the Fading of the American Dream," PBS website, October 14, 2019; Ezra Klein, "You Have a Better Chance of Achieving 'the American Dream' in Canada Than in America," *Vox,* August 15, 2019.

xxiii **First, the economy** U.S. Bureau of Economic Analysis, "Real Gross Domestic Product," FRED, Federal Reserve Bank of St. Louis.

xxiii **Change in Household Income [chart]** Thomas Piketty, Emmanuel Saez, and Gabriel Zucman, "Distributional National Accounts: Methods and Estimates for the United States," *The Quarterly Journal of Economics* 133, no. 2 (2018): 553–609, updated in Thomas Blanchet, Emmanuel Saez, and Gabriel Zucman, "Real-Time Inequality" (working paper 30229, National Bureau of Economic Research, November 2022); Gabriel Zucman, data provided to author, January 9, 2023.

xxiv **The White-Black wage gap** Bayer and Charles, "Divergent Paths," cited in David Leonhardt, "The Black-White Wage Gap Is as Big as It Was in 1950," *The New York Times,* June 25, 2020.

xxiv **A typical family** Board of Governors of the Federal Reserve System, "Survey of Consumer Finances, 1989–2019"; World Inequality Database.

xxiv **The number of children** "National Single Parent Day: March 21, 2022," U.S. Census Bureau website, March 21, 2022, table CH-1.

xxiv **The obesity rate** "Obesity Rate Nearly Triples in the United States over the Last 50 Years," USAFacts, September 4, 2019.

xxiv **The number of Americans** David Leonhardt, "A Great Fight of Our Times," *The New York Times,* October 11, 2016.

xxiv **Measures of childhood mental health** Matt Richtel, " 'It's Life or Death': The Mental Health Crisis Among U.S. Teens," *The New York Times,* April 23, 2022.

xxiv **"deaths of despair"** Anne Case and Angus Deaton, *Deaths of Despair and the Future of Capitalism* (Princeton, N.J.: Princeton University Press, 2020).

xxiv **Progress against heart disease** Nilay S. Shah, Donald M. Lloyd-Jones, and Martin O'Flaherty, "Trends in Cardiometabolic Mortality in the United States, 1999–2017," *Journal of the American Medical Association* 322, no. 8 (2019), 780–82.

xxiv **These trends have hit** Anne Case and Angus Deaton, based on data provided to author, December 23, 2022. The life expectancy data by education level measures additional years of expected life for people who are twenty-five years old.

xxv **At no point since 2005** "Satisfaction with the United States," Gallup.

xxv **After all, many** Ruy Teixeira, "Democrats' Long Goodbye to the Working Class," *The Atlantic,* November 6, 2022.

xxvii **China's communist economy** Ezra F. Vogel, *Deng Xiaoping and the Transformation of China* (Cambridge, Mass.: Belknap Press of Harvard University Press, 2011).

xxvii **"democratic capitalism"** Michael Kazin, *What It Took to Win: A History of the Democratic Party* (New York: Farrar, Straus and Giroux, 2022), x–xiii; Steve Lohr, "Clinton Proposals Seek Political Middle Ground," *The New York Times,* April 18, 1992, 7; Steven Pearlstein, *Moral Capitalism: Why Fairness Won't Make Us Poor* (New York: Macmillan Publishers, 2020); Martin Wolf, *The Crisis of Democratic Capitalism* (New York: Penguin Press, 2023). *The New York Times* described Bill Clinton's economic agenda during his 1992 presidential campaign as "managed capitalism." The historian Michael Kazin has used the phrase "moral capitalism." The financial commentator Martin Wolf is among those who have used "democratic capitalism."

xxviii **One way to see** David Leonhardt, "Why Are Republican Presidents So Bad for the Economy?," *The New York Times,* February 2, 2021.

xxix **"economic history"** Zachary D. Carter, *The Price of Peace: Money, Democracy, and the Life of John Maynard Keynes* (New York: Random House, 2020), 189.

xxx **The contemporary economist Thomas Piketty** Thomas Piketty, *Capital and Ideology,* trans. Arthur Goldhammer (Cambridge, Mass.: Belknap Press of Harvard University Press, 2020); see also Amory Gethin, Clara Martínez-Toledano, and Thomas Piketty, "Brahmin Left Versus Merchant Right: Changing Political Cleavages in 21 Western Democracies, 1948–2020," *The Quarterly Journal of Economics* 137, no. 1 (February 2022): 1–48.

xxx **Instead, the Brahmin left** David Leonhardt, "What's the Matter with Scarsdale?," *The New York Times,* November 4, 2021.

xxx **From World War II** Nate Cohn, "How Educational Differences Are Widening America's Political Rift," *The New York Times,* September 8, 2021; updated data provided to author, February 26, 2023.

xxxi **Most Latino and Asian** David Leonhardt, "A Shrinking Margin," *The New York Times,* September 21, 2022; David Leonhardt, "Asian Americans, Shifting Right," *The New York Times,* March 6, 2023.

xxxi **The flip side** "Beyond Red vs. Blue: The Political Typology," Pew Research Center, November 9, 2021.

xxxi **A few right-leaning** Oren Cass, "The 2023 Cost-of-Thriving Index: Tracking the Catastrophic Erosion of Middle-Class Life in America," American Compass, February 2023.

Chapter 1: A Union Town

3 **The drivers spent** Farrell Dobbs, *Teamster Rebellion* (New York: Pathfinder Press, 1972), 70–71.

3 **Coal work was also seasonal** Dobbs, *Teamster Rebellion,* 31.

3 **Minneapolis had sprung up** Charles Rumford Walker, *American City: A Rank and File History of Minneapolis* (Minneapolis: University of Minnesota Press, 2005).

4 **The executives had formalized** William Millikan, *A Union Against Unions: The Minneapolis Citizens Alliance and Its Fight Against Organized Labor, 1903–1947* (St. Paul: Minnesota Historical Society Press, 2001).

4 **"failed utterly"** Deborah Neubeck, "Citizens Alliance of Minneapolis. Records, Updated and 1903–1953: Historical Sketch," May 1984, in Minnesota Historical Society Archives, St. Paul, Minn.

4 **It resembled cities** U.S. Department of Labor, *Monthly Labor Review* 31, no. 3 (September 1930).

5 **A Swedish immigrant** Oral history of Carl Skoglund, January 24, 1955, and other documents in Minnesota Historical Society Archives, St. Paul, Minn.

5 **"a little brick shit-house"** Marvel Scholl Dobbs, Letter in Minnesota Historical Society Archives, 5.

5 **"on the Q.T."** Philip A. Korth, *The Minneapolis Teamsters Strike of 1934* (East Lansing: Michigan State University Press, 1995), 30.

6 **"America is an employer's paradise"** Irving Bernstein, *The Lean Years: A History of the American Worker, 1920–1933* (Chicago: Haymarket Books, 2010), 144.

6 **The share of income** Peter H. Lindert and Jeffrey G. Williamson, *Unequal Gains: American Growth and Inequality Since 1700* (Princeton, N.J.: Princeton University Press, 2016), 173.

6 **"range of indeterminacy"** Richard A. Lester, "A Range Theory of Wage Differentials," *ILR Review* 5, no. 4 (July 1952): 483–500.

7 **"Masters are always"** Adam Smith, *The Wealth of Nations* (New York: Cosimo, 2007), 70.

8 **"The labourer in an isolated"** John Stuart Mill, *Dissertations and Discussions* (London: Longmans, Green, Reader, and Dyer, 1875), 67.

9 **The United States economy** Lindert and Williamson, *Unequal Gains,* 119.

9 **"The average American colonist"** Lindert and Williamson, *Unequal Gains,* 43.

9 **Franklin invested** Walter Isaacson, *Benjamin Franklin: An American Life* (New York: Simon & Schuster, 2003), 126.

9 **"Fellows who would have"** Robert A. Gross, ed., *In Debt to Shays: The Bicentennial of an Agrarian Rebellion* (Charlottesville: University of Virginia Press, 1993), 309.

10 **On the eve** Lindert and Williamson, *Unequal Gains,* 115.

10 **The main explanation** Thomas Piketty, *Capital in the Twenty-First Century,* trans. Arthur Goldhammer (Cambridge, Mass.: Belknap Press of Harvard University Press, 2014).

10 **In the decades after** Jefferson Cowie, *The Great Exception: The New Deal and the Limits of American Politics* (Princeton, N.J.: Princeton University Press, 2016), 36–37.

11 **"Middle-class progressive"** Cowie, *Great Exception,* 73–74.

12 **"After all, the chief business"** "President Warns Editors to Avoid Propaganda Evil," *Washington Evening Star,* January 18, 1925, 5; see also Ellen Terrell, "When a Quote Is Not (Exactly) a Quote: The Business of America Is Business Edition," *Inside Adams Blog* (January 17, 2019), Library of Congress.

13 **"composed of the People"** Millikan, *Union Against Unions,* 167.

13 **"every man to work out"** Melvyn Dubofsky and Foster Rhea Dulles, *Labor in America: A History* (Germany: Wiley, 2014), 225.

13 **The organization was** Millikan, *Union Against Unions.*

13 **Many politicians were** "Minnesota: Electoral College Vote," 270toWin website.

14 **After taking office** Millikan, *Union Against Unions,* 55–56.

14 **"Our men have been efficient"** "Henry Ford Explains Why He Gives Away $10,000,000," *The New York Times,* January 11, 1914, 47.

14 **As vehicle sales** "Ford Raise Helps Men at Bottom," *Detroit Free Press,* December 4, 1929, 3.

14 **At the start of the 1920s** Henry S. Farber, Daniel Herbst, Ilyana Kuziemko, and Suresh Naidu, "Unions and Inequality over the Twentieth Century: New Evidence from Survey Data," *The Quarterly Journal of Economics* 136, no. 3 (April 9, 2021): 1382–85; union density data from Farber et al., "Unions and Inequality," provided to author, January 4, 2023.

15 **National magazines** Louis Adamic, "The Collapse of Organized Labor," *Harper's Monthly Magazine,* January 1932, 167–78; Bernstein, *Lean Years,* 83.

15 **"That faction"** Robert Zieger, *Republicans and Labor, 1919–1929* (Lexington: University of Kentucky Press, 1969), 261.

15 **The share of income** Lindert and Williamson, *Unequal Gains,* 173, 197.

15 **The historian Alexander Field** Alexander J. Field, *A Great Leap Forward: 1930s Depression and U.S. Economic Growth* (New Haven, Conn.: Yale University Press, 2012).

16 **Six-foot-two with swept-back** Walker, *American City,* 199–205; oral history and other documents in Minnesota Historical Society Archives.

16 **"I knew what"** *American Illustrated Magazine* 120 (1935): 107.

16 **"special privilege"** Floyd Olson, "Farm Labor Association Program," document in Minnesota Historical Society Archives, 3.

17 **The administration's first** Cowie, *Great Exception,* 103; Stephen Greene, "Emergency Banking Act of 1933," Federal Reserve Historywebsite, November 22, 2013.

18 **"Labor can never"** Kirstin Downey, *The Woman Behind the New Deal: The Life and Legacy of Frances Perkins—Social Security, Unemployment Insurance and the Minimum Wage* (New York: Anchor Books, 2009), 126.

18 **Fannie Perkins** Jonathan Alter, *The Defining Moment: FDR's Hundred Days and the Triumph of Hope* (New York: Simon & Schuster, 2006); Penny Colman, *A Woman Unafraid: The Achievements of Frances Perkins* (New York: Atheneum, 1993); Downey, *Woman;* George Martin, *Madam Secretary Frances Perkins* (Boston: Houghton Mifflin, 1983); Lillian Holmen Mohr, *Frances Perkins: "That Woman in FDR's Cabinet!"* (Great Barrington, Mass.: North River Press, 1979); Frances Perkins, *The Roosevelt I Knew* (New York: Penguin Books, 1946).

18 **She often wore** Adam Cohen, *Nothing to Fear: FDR's Inner Circle and the Hundred Days That Created Modern America* (New York: Penguin Press, 2009), 162.

19 **"I'd much rather"** Cohen, *Nothing to Fear,* 168.

19 **"lunatics and grafters"** Downey, *Woman,* 176.

23 **"employees shall have"** "National Industrial Recovery Act, June 16, 1933," National Archives website.

23 **"No 7(a), no bill"** John Brooks, "Profiles: Simon Hirsch Rifkind," *The New Yorker,* May 23, 1983, 59.

23 **"No business"** Franklin D. Roosevelt, "Statement on N.I.R.A.," June 16, 1933, American Presidency Project website.

23 **"The President wants you"** Irving Bernstein, *The Turbulent Years: A History of the American Worker, 1933–1940* (Chicago: Haymarket Books, 1969), 41.

24 **On June 17** Bernstein, *Turbulent Years,* 41–42.

25 **The parade** "1,500,000 Cheer Vast NRA Parade: March of 250,000 City's Greatest; Demonstration Lasts Till Midnight," *The New York Times,* September 14, 1933, 1.

25 **"All of America's great"** Nelson Lichtenstein, *State of the Union: A Century of American Labor* (Princeton, N.J.: Princeton University Press, 2002), 34–35.

25 **"The United States"** "Olson Urges Job Insurance, Easing of Farm Mortgage," *Minneapolis Star Tribune,* January 5, 1933, 6.

25 **In rural parts** Walker, *American City,* 65–66.

25 **In Minneapolis's coal yards** Oral history and other documents in Minnesota Historical Society Archives; Walker, *American City,* 88–111.

26 **"to enter into trouble"** Dobbs, *Teamster Rebellion,* 57.

26 **"They're uninformed"** Harry DeBoer, *"How to Win Strikes: Lessons from the 1934 Minneapolis Truckers Strike,"* pamphlet in Minnesota Historical Society Archives, 7.

27 **Several organizers, including Skoglund** "Carl Skoglund," *International Socialist Review* 22, no. 1 (Winter 1961), 2.

27 **From the beginning** Michael Kazin, *What It Took to Win: A History of the Democratic Party* (New York: Farrar, Straus and Giroux, 2022), 185.

29 **As part of** Christiane Diehl-Taylor, "Partners in the Struggle: The Role of Women's Auxiliaries and Brigades in the 1934 Minneapolis Truck Drivers Strike and the 1936/37 Flint General Motors Sit-Down Strike" (directed research project, University of Minnesota, November 19, 1990), Minnesota Historical Society Archives.

30 **"Strikes were lost"** Dobbs, Letter, 1–2.

30 **"How Do You Like"** *The Minneapolis Star,* July 20, 1934, 6.

31 **"The motor manufacturers"** Bernstein, *Turbulent Years,* 96.

32 **In a 1919 essay** Max Weber, "Politics as a Vocation," 1919.

32 **"The United States"** Philip Taft and Philip Ross, "American Labor Violence: Its Causes, Character, and Outcome," in *The History of Violence in America: A Report to the National Commission on the Causes and Prevention of Violence,* 1969.

33 **"Employers and unions"** Taft and Ross, "American Labor Violence."

33 **"Though it is a bloody business"** William Letwin, *Law and Economic Policy: The Evolution of the Sherman Antitrust Act* (Chicago: University of Chicago Press, 1981), 127.

34 **"You have shotguns"** Korth, *Minneapolis Teamsters,* 147.

34 **Many of the victims** Eric Sevareid, *Not So Wild a Dream* (Columbia: University of Missouri Press, 1946), 57–59.

34 **Forty thousand people** Dobbs, *Teamster Rebellion,* 144; Korth, *Minneapolis Teamsters,* 152.

35 **"You should follow"** Dobbs, *Teamster Rebellion,* 91.

35 **"You're crazy"** Floyd Olson, interview in Minnesota Historical Archives, 5.

37 **They exchanged** Documents in Minnesota Historical Society Archives.

38 **"Glad to report"** Jesse S. Jones to Franklin Roosevelt, telegram, August 22, 1934, National Archives; Korth, *Minneapolis Teamsters,* 162.

38 **A banner headline** "VICTORY! Settlement Goes Through," *The Northwest Organizer,* August 22, 1934, 1.

38 **Historically, politicians had** Kazin, *What It Took,* 187.

39 **"He who hates"** Eric Schickler, *Racial Realignment: The Transformation of American Liberalism, 1932–1965* (Princeton, N.J.: Princeton University Press, 2016), 88.

39 **"Negro workers ought"** Schickler, *Racial Realignment,* 63.

40 **More than 30 percent** Union density data from Farber et al., "Unions and Inequality."

41 **That project** Farber et al., "Unions and Inequality."

43 **Income and Unionization [chart]** Union density data from Farber et al., "Unions and Inequality"; World Inequality Database website.

43 **In 2021, Minnesota** U.S. Bureau of Economic Analysis, "Real Median Household Income by State, Annual," FRED, Federal Reserve Bank of St. Louis; U.S. Bureau of Economic Analysis, "Per Capita Personal Income by State, Annual," FRED, Federal Reserve Bank of St. Louis.

45 **"For the first time"** Taft and Ross, "American Labor Violence."

45 **"best thing"** Cowie, *Great Exception,* 57.

45 **"It is very possible"** Lizabeth Cohen, *Making a New Deal: Industrial Workers in Chicago, 1919–1939* (Cambridge: Cambridge University Press, 1990), 289.

Chapter 2: Trustees of the Common Welfare

47 **Paul Hoffman** Paul G. Hoffman Papers, Harry S. Truman Presidential Library and Museum, Independence, Mo.; Paul F. Douglass, *Six upon the World: Toward an American Culture for an Industrial Age* (Boston: Little, Brown, 1954).

47 **"The surest way"** "Forecast," *Yo-Mag* 6, no. 2 (May 1938): 32, Hoffman Papers.

47 **"grease boy"** F. Edw. Hebert, "Auto Magnate, Once Grease Boy, Is Here," *New Orleans States,* January 13, 1937, 1.

48 **"upset all tradition"** "Studebaker Picks High Executive from Local Field," *Los Angeles Times,* April 12, 1925, 2.

49 **"The N.R.A. was a thoroughly"** Paul Hoffman, "Free Enterprise or Feudalism," address to the National Institute, Northwestern University, August 18, 1939, Hoffman Papers.

49 **"scathing attacks"** Paul Hoffman, "The Collective Responsibility of Business for Free Enterprise," address to University of Chicago's School of Business, May 26, 1938, p. 2, Hoffman Papers.

49 **"unanimous in their hate"** Franklin D. Roosevelt, speech at Madison Square Garden, New York, October 31, 1936, American Presidency Project website.

51 **In *The Wealth*** David Leonhardt, "Theory and Morality in the New Economy," *The New York Times,* August 19, 2009.

51 **"Culture is a set"** Joel Mokyr, *A Culture of Growth: The Origins of the Modern Economy* (Princeton, N.J.: Princeton University Press, 2016), 8.

51 **In the 1980s** Ann Swidler, "Culture in Action: Symbols and Strategies," *American Sociological Review* 51, no. 2 (April 1986): 273–86.

52 **Swidler pointed out** Ann Swidler (University of California, Berkeley), interview with author, March 6, 2020.

53 **Only 41 percent** "What Business Thinks," *Fortune,* October 1939, 52.

54 **"severe depression"** Jacob L. Mosak, "National Budgets and National Policy," *The American Economic Review* 36, no. 1 (March 1946): 20, 40.

54 **"more people might be"** "Unemployment Storm Warning," *The New Republic,* July 23, 1945, 94.

54 **A poll by *Fortune*** "Fortune Survey," *Fortune,* July 1944, 86.

54 **A cartoon** "A New Landing Coming," *The Stars and Stripes,* October 5, 1944.

55 **"Business men who believe"** Paul Hoffman, manuscript submitted to *The Saturday Evening Post,* July 8, 1939, Hoffman Papers.

55 **"The best way"** Douglass, *Six upon the World,* 27.

55 **"a spirit of futility"** Paul G. Hoffman, commencement address, June 6, 1940, Hoffman Papers.

56 **"I think the time"** William Benton, "Speech Before Citizens Board of the University of Chicago," October 26, 1943, p. 1, Hoffman Papers.

56 **"The system which best"** Douglass, *Six upon the World,* 33.

57 **Crashes were killing** "Mortality Statistics, 1935," U.S. Department of Commerce, Table G.

57 **"I have changed my mind"** Paul Hoffman, "Making the Highways Safe for the Motorists," speech, 1936, Hoffman Papers.

57 **"Our selfish interests"** Paul G. Hoffman, "The Safety Program of the Automobile Manufacturers," *Proceedings of the Annual Convention of the Association of Highway Officials of the North Atlantic States* (February 12–14, 1936): 50.

58 **This approach has** Theda Skocpol, Marshall Ganz, and Ziad Munson, "A Nation of Organizers: The Institutional Origins of Civic Voluntarism in the

United States," *American Political Science Review* 94, no. 3 (September 2000): 527–46.

58 **The death rate per mile** "Motor Vehicle Traffic Fatalities and Fatality Rates, 1899–2020," U.S. Department of Transportation, National Highway Traffic Safety Administration website.

60 **"a dual date with destiny"** Paul G. Hoffman, address to the Tulsa Chamber of Commerce, January 14, 1942, Hoffman Papers; Paul G. Hoffman, "Jobs—the Key to the Maintenance of Freedom," speech, Hoffman Papers.

61 **"evangelistic fervor"** "C.E.D. Speaks Up," *Business Week*, July 1944, 21.

62 **"After it"** Robert Henry Brand, address to the American Bankers Association, New York, September 15, 1943, William Benton Papers, University of Chicago Library.

62 **"The challenge is coming"** Charles Wilson, keynote address, cited in *Looking Ahead: A Digest of Fact and Opinion on Post-war Preparation* (New York: Batten, Barton, Durstine & Osborne, August 31, 1942), 2, Benton Papers.

63 **"THERE'S STILL AN AMERICAN DREAM"** William B. Benton, "The Economics of a Free Society: A Declaration of American Economic Policy," *Fortune,* October 1944, 163.

63 **"intellectual Neanderthals"** Karl Schriftgiesser, *Business Comes of Age: The Story of the Committee for Economic Development and Its Impact upon the Economic Policies of the United States, 1942–1960* (New York: Harper & Brothers, 1960), 7.

63 **"old guard"** Jay Hormel to William B. Benton, February 2, 1943, Benton Papers.

63 **"I had forgotten"** William Benton to Jay C. Hormel, February 4, 1943, Benton Papers.

63 **To win them** Letters in Benton Papers.

64 **"You are too much concerned"** Jay C. Hormel to Howard Myers, August 28, 1945, Benton Papers.

64 **In September 1943** "Businessman Hoffman," *Time,* September 6, 1943.

65 **"There are few lovable"** Robert A. Brady, "The Committee for Whose Economic Development?," speech, p. 22, Benton Papers.

65 **"a rich man's tax program"** Oscar Gass, "A Rich Man's Tax Program," *The New Republic,* October 16, 1944, 481.

65 **"Look Who's Planning!"** Helen Fuller, *The New Republic,* July 26, 1943, 104–5.

65 **In later decades** Mark S. Mizruchi, *The Fracturing of the American Corporate Elite,* (Cambridge, Mass.: Harvard University Press, 2013), 94, describing the debate, citing Elizabeth A. Fones-Wolf, *Selling Free Enterprise: The Business Assault on Labor and Liberalism, 1945–60* (Urbana, Il.: University of Illinois Press, 1994); James A. Gross, *Broken Promise: The Subversion of U.S. Labor Relations Policy* (Philadelphia: Temple University Press, 1995); Thomas A. Kochan, Harry C. Katz, and Robert B. McKersie, *The Transformation of American Industrial Relations* (Ithaca, N.Y.: Cornell University Press, 1994).

66 **"By the end of"** Mizruchi, *American Corporate Elite,* 43.

66 **The unemployment rate** U.S. Bureau of Economic Analysis, "Unemployment Rate for United States," FRED, Federal Reserve Bank of St. Louis.

67 **"First by far"** "Sweet and Low . . . a Melody in Metal," *Baltimore Sun,* July 7, 1946, 114.

67 **The share of income** Peter H. Lindert and Jeffrey G. Williamson, *Unequal Gains: American Growth and Inequality Since 1700* (Princeton, N.J.: Princeton University Press, 2016), 197.

67 **In 1950, General Motors** Frank Levy and Peter Temin, "Inequality and Institutions in 20th Century America," (working paper 13106, National Bureau of Economic Research, May 2007).

67 **At some companies** Richard Freeman and James Medoff, *What Do Unions Do?* (New York: Basic Books, 1984).

68 **"put the labor movement"** John B. Judis, *The Paradox of American Democracy: Elites, Special Interests, and the Betrayal of Public Trust* (New York: Routledge, 2001), 69; see also Jefferson Cowie, *Stayin' Alive: The 1970s and the Last Days of the Working Class* (New York: New Press, 2010), 160.

68 **They favored measures** Mizruchi, *American Corporate Elite,* 58.

68 **Into the 1960s** Henry S. Farber, Daniel Herbst, Ilyana Kuziemko, and Suresh Naidu, "Unions and Inequality over the Twentieth Century: New Evidence from Survey Data" (working paper 24587, National Bureau of Economic Research, April 2021); union density data from Farber et al., "Unions and Inequality," provided to author, January 4, 2023.

68 **When he finished** Jean Edward Smith, *Eisenhower in War and Peace* (New York: Random House, 2013), 469–70. Augusta National's roots are more corporate—and less southern—than many people realize: Of the club's eighty founding members, sixty were from New York.

69 **"the privileged few"** Harry S. Truman, speech at the Democratic Convention, July 15, 1948.

69 **"For more than twenty years"** Dwight David Eisenhower, *The White House Years: Mandate for Change, 1953–1956* (New York: Doubleday, 1963), 304.

70 **He and Eisenhower** Viola K. Pedersen to Robert R. Mullen, November 13, 1952, Hoffman Papers.

70 **In 1951 and** Paul Hoffman to Dwight D. Eisenhower, September 26, 1951, and October 29, 1951, Hoffman Papers.

70 **"If *you* would only"** Dwight D. Eisenhower to Paul Hoffman, October 4, 1951, Hoffman Papers.

70 **"Whether you like it"** Paul Hoffman to Dwight D. Eisenhower, December 5, 1951, Hoffman Papers.

70 **The morning after** William I. Hitchcock, *The Age of Eisenhower and America in the World in the 1950s* (New York: Simon & Schuster, 2018), 87.

70 **"nine millionaires"** Doris Fleeson, "Weeks Faces Trip to Woodshed," *Evening Star,* April 14, 1953, 11.

70 **"I thought what"** Associated Press, "Post Says Wilson 'Victim of Words,'" *The Manhattan Mercury,* January 23, 1953, 1.

71 **Sustaining that model** Gary Gerstle, *The Rise and Fall of the Neoliberal*

Order: America and the World in the Free Market Era (New York: Oxford University Press, 2022), 38.

71 **Before Eisenhower's presidency** Mizruchi, *American Corporate Elite,* 58; Schriftgiesser, *Business Comes of Age,* 127.

72 **Once Eisenhower** Ira Katznelson, interview with author, September 16, 2020.

72 **"By conserving and enlarging"** Mizruchi, *American Corporate Elite,* 62.

72 **Under Eisenhower** "Historical Highest Marginal Income Tax Rates," Tax Policy Center website, February 9, 2022.

72 **Labor unions grew** Union density data from Farber et al., "Unions and Inequality."

72 **"We cannot see"** Hitchcock, *Age of Eisenhower,* 266.

73 **One executive who** T. George Harris, *Romney's Way: A Man and an Idea* (Englewood Cliffs, N.J.: Prentice Hall, 1967); Tom Mahoney, *The Story of George Romney: Builder, Salesman, Crusader* (New York: Harper & Brothers, 1960).

73 **"Is your car"** "Is Your Car a Dinosaur to Park?," *Nashville Banner,* July 22, 1958, 7.

73 **Sales of the Rambler** Because of a merger, the company was known as the American Motors Corporation in the late 1950s.

74 **"the temptations of success"** Harris, *Romney's Way,* 186.

74 **Over a five-year period** Associated Press, "American Motors Chief Snubs $100,000 Bonus," *The Enid Morning News,* January 6, 1960, 3; Ed Kandlik, "Here's Way to Make Five Million Dollars," *The Miami Herald,* January 10, 1960, 79.

75 **"far exceeds my needs"** "John O. Ekblom, 71, of Hupp Corp. Dies," *The New York Times,* March 24, 1966; see also Associated Press, "Boss Turns Back Bonus," *The Virginian-Pilot,* June 26, 1959, 54.

75 **The pay of the typical CEO** Frydman and Saks [Molloy], "Executive Compensation."

76 **CEO Pay [chart]** Carola Frydman and Raven E. Saks [Molloy], "Executive Compensation: A New View from a Long-Term Perspective" (working paper 14145, National Bureau of Economic Research, June 2008), updated data provided to author, January 6, 2023; U.S. Bureau of Economic Analysis, "Real Gross Domestic Product per Capita," FRED, Federal Reserve Bank of St. Louis; U.S. Census Bureau, "Historical Income Tables: Families."

77 **The younger Romney** David Leonhardt, "Two Candidates, Two Fortunes, Two Distinct Views of Wealth," *The New York Times,* December 23, 2007; David Leonhardt, "When the Rich Said No to Getting Richer," *The New York Times,* September 5, 2017.

77 **The firm had** Michael Barbaro, "After a Romney Deal, Profits and then Layoffs," *The New York Times,* November 12, 2011; Greg Sargent, "Mitt Romney's new antagonists: His layoff victims," *The New York Times,* January 2, 2012.

78 **"the avenues"** Jefferson Cowie, *The Great Exception: The New Deal and the Limits of American Politics* (Princeton, N.J.: Princeton University Press, 2016), 220.

78 **In the late twentieth** David Leonhardt, "A C.E.O. Who's Scared for America," *The New York Times,* March 31, 2019.

Chapter 3: Sacrifice for the Long Term

81 **"in a meaningless chair-bound"** Jean Edward Smith, *Eisenhower in War and Peace* (New York: Random House, 2013), 49.

81 **When word began** John E. Wickman, "Ike and 'the Great Truck Train'—1919," *Kansas History* 13, no. 3 (August 1990): 139–48.

82 **"resulted in excessive speeding"** "Report on Trans-Continental Trip," November 3, 1919, Eisenhower Presidential Library website.

83 **"the longest trip"** "Army Convoy to Cross Iowa," *Evening Times-Republican,* June 23, 1919, 5.

84 **The next two** Dwight David Eisenhower, *Mandate for Change, 1953–1956: The White House Years* (Garden City, N.Y.: Doubleday, 1963); Dwight David Eisenhower, *Waging Peace, 1956–1961* (Garden City, N.Y.: Doubleday, 1965); William I. Hitchcock, *The Age of Eisenhower: America and the World in the 1950s* (New York: Simon & Schuster, 2018); Smith, *Eisenhower in War and Peace.*

85 **"We were never able"** Smith, *Eisenhower in War and Peace,* 265.

85 **"The battle is fought"** Smith, *Eisenhower in War and Peace,* 265.

87 **Europe dominated** Jonathan Gruber and Simon Johnson, *Jump-Starting America: How Breakthrough Science Can Revive Economic Growth and the American Dream* (New York: Hachette, 2019), 20.

87 **Once the United States** "U-Boat Attacks of World War II: 6 Months of Secret Terror in the Atlantic," New England Historical Society website; Gruber and Johnson, *Jump-Starting America,* 28.

88 **"What was needed"** Gruber and Johnson, *Jump-Starting America,* 25.

88 **In the 1600s, the French mathematician** "Pascal Adding Machine Section (Replica)," National Museum of American History website.

88 **By the 1900s** Jennifer Light, "When Computers Were Women," *Technology and Culture* 40, no. 3 (July 1999): 455–83; "Admiral Grace Murray Hopper: When Women Were Computers," National WWII Museum website, March 25, 2022.

89 **Grace Hopper** "Oral History of Captain Grace Hopper," interview by Angeline Pantages, December 1980, Computer History Museum; Kurt W. Beyer, *Grace Hopper and the Invention of the Information Age* (Cambridge, Mass.: MIT Press, 2009); Kathleen Broome Williams, *Grace Hopper: Admiral of the Cyber Sea* (Annapolis, Md.: Naval Institute Press, 2012).

89 **"They disapproved"** Beyer, *Grace Hopper,* 28.

90 **"Where in the Hell"** Grace Hopper, "Commander Aiken and My Favorite Computer," in I. Bernard Cohen and Gregory W. Welch, Editors, *Makin' Numbers: Howard Aiken and the Computer* (Cambridge, Mass.: The MIT Press, 1999), 185; see also Grace Murray Hopper, interview by Uta C. Merzbach, July 1968, p. 29, Computer Oral History Collection, National Museum of American History.

90 **"Algebra Machine"** "Algebra Machine Spurs Research Calling for Long Calculations," *The New York Times,* August 7, 1944, 17.

90 **"Robot Brain"** Paul Stevens, "Fabulous Robot Brain Now Works for Navy," *Boston Herald,* August 7, 1944.

90 **"a lazy man's dream"** Williams, *Grace Hopper,* 28.

90 **"land-based ship"** Beyer, *Grace Hopper,* 38.

91 **"We used to shake"** Grace Murray Hopper, interview by Beth Luebbert and Henry Tropp, July 5, 1972, p. 15, Computer Oral History Collection, National Museum of American History.

91 **One day, Hopper** Beyer, *Grace Hopper,* 74.

93 **"That was the first mention"** Luebbert and Tropp, 29.

94 **"It didn't move me"** H. W. Brands, *Masters of Enterprise: Giants of American Business from John Jacob Astor and J. P. Morgan to Bill Gates and Oprah Winfrey* (New York: Free Press, 2012), 130.

95 **"The military"** Gruber and Johnson, *Jump-Starting America,* 52.

95 **"People sort of"** "Oral History of Captain Grace Hopper," 35.

96 **"saw the need"** "Oral History of Captain Grace Hopper," comments by Phil Vincent, 53.

96 **"a trim, attractive blonde"** Beyer, *Grace Hopper,* 311–13.

97 **She chose the** The company was later known as both Remington Rand and Sperry Rand because of mergers.

97 **"bring computers down"** Ira Chinoy, "Battle of the Brains: Election-Night Forecasting at the Dawn of the Computer Age" (dissertation, University of Maryland, 2010); Jill Lepore, *These Truths: A History of the United States* (New York: W. W. Norton & Company, 2018), 558.

98 **As the early returns** "November 4, 1952: Univac Gets Election Right, But CBS Balks," *Wired,* November 4, 2010. The Univac's basic statistical method for analyzing election returns is the same one that the *The New York Times'* "election needle" and television analysts like Steve Kornacki of MSNBC would use in later decades. Both compared returns in specific geographic areas to historical patterns in those areas rather than focusing on the overall vote count before it was close to being complete.

99 **"The principal contradiction"** Dwight David Eisenhower, Alfred Dupont Chandler, and Louis Galambos, *The Papers of Dwight David Eisenhower: The Presidency; The Middle Way* (Baltimore, Md.: Johns Hopkins University Press, 1996), 360.

99 **He was the president** Travis Jacobs, *Eisenhower at Columbia* (New Brunswick, N.J.: Transaction Publishers, 2001), 327.

100 **"Although he typically"** Robert Griffith, "Dwight D. Eisenhower and the Corporate Commonwealth," *The American Historical Review* 87, no. 1 (February 1982): 88.

100 **As a share** "National Income and Product Accounts," U.S. Bureau of Economic Analysis website, tables 1.1.5 and 3.9.5.

101 **Government Investment [chart]** "National Income and Product Accounts," U.S. Bureau of Economic Analysis website, tables 1.1.5 and 3.9.5.

101 **"wave of near-hysteria"** Robert A. Divine, *The* Sputnik *Challenge: Eisenhower's Response to the Soviet Satellite* (Oxford: Oxford University Press, 1993), 15.

102 **"We have been complacent"** Gruber and Johnson, *Jump-Starting America*, 44.

102 **When Eisenhower left office** "National Income and Product Accounts."

104 **Government funding** Gruber and Johnson, *Jump-Starting America*, 29–31, 41–45.

Chapter 4: Enforcing Racial Democracy

106 **When the steel mill** Earl E. Buie, "Steel Plant Begins Production," *The San Bernardino County Sun*, December 31, 1942, 9.

106 **Its owner was** Mark S. Foster, *Henry J. Kaiser: Builder in the Modern American West* (Austin: University of Texas Press, 1989), 31, 53.

106 **Kaiser was also** Foster, *Henry J. Kaiser*, 62.

106 **The federal government** Foster, *Henry J. Kaiser*, 97; "Big Forty Million Dollar South Fontana Steel Mill Assured Thru U.S. Help," *The Pomona Progress Bulletin*, March 6, 1942, 9.

106 **"surveyors, designers"** "Engineers Wanted," *Los Angeles Times*, March 29, 1942, 35.

106 **He and his wife** 1940 United States Federal Census records, Population Schedule, Los Angeles, Calif., U.S. Department of Commerce, Bureau of the Census.

107 **A few days after** Mike Davis, *City of Quartz: Excavating the Future in Los Angeles* (London: Verso, 1990), 373–440; Rebecca Onion, "Roller Skating Socials and a Black Rosie the Riveter," *Slate*, March 8, 2016; Paul R. Spickard, "Fire in the Night: A 1945 Southern California Hate Crime and Historical Memory," *Southern California Quarterly* 82, no. 3 (Fall 2000): 291–304.

107 **"They're just trying"** Matthew F. Delmont, "February 14, 1946," Black Quotidian website.

108 **"That family is burning"** Spickard, "Fire in the Night," 293.

108 **By the next morning** "Child, 7, Burns to Death in Fontana Blaze," *The Pomona Progress Bulletin*, December 17, 1945, 18; "Fontana Girl Fatally Burned," *The San Bernardino County Sun*, December 17, 1945, 1; "Mother, Son, 7, Die of Burns Suffered in Lamp Explosion," *The San Bernardino County Sun*, December 18, 1945, 9; "Father Burned in Blast May Die," *The San Bernardino County Sun*, December 19, 1945, 9.

108 **The National Association** Spickard, "Fire in the Night," 302–3; "Origin of Fatal Fire Listed as Unknown," *The Pomona Progress Bulletin*, December 28, 1945, 14; "On . . . the Sidewalk," *California Eagle*, March 21, 1946, 1.

109 **On the night** Cyril Briggs, "O'Day Short Dies, Grand Jury Fails to Act in Fire Deaths of Family," *California Eagle*, January 24, 1946, 1.

110 **"raise the same kind"** Ira Katznelson, *Fear Itself: The New Deal and the Origins of Our Time* (New York: Liveright, 2013), 85.

110 **"paradoxical combination"** Katznelson, *Fear Itself*, 127.

110 **At the time** 1940 United States Federal Census records, Population: Volume II, U.S. Department of Commerce, Bureau of the Census, 9.

110 **"a sieve"** Genna Rae McNeil, *Groundwork: Charles Hamilton Houston and the Struggle for Civil Rights* (Philadelphia: University of Pennsylvania Press, 1983), 119.

110 **The Civilian Conservation Corps** Richard Rothstein, *The Color of Law: A Forgotten History of How Our Government Segregated America* (New York: Liveright, 2017), 19–20.

110 **Once World War II** Ira Katznelson, *When Affirmative Action Was White: An Untold History of Racial Inequality in Twentieth-Century America* (New York: W. W. Norton, 2005), 105–12.

111 **The GI Bill did help** Sarah E. Turner and John Bound, "Closing the Gap or Widening the Divide: The Effects of the G.I. Bill and World War II on the Educational Outcomes of Black Americans" (working paper 9044, National Bureau of Economic Research, July 2002).

111 **Across the country** Rothstein, *Color of Law,* 73, 106.

111 **Among the residents** Karol Stonger, "No More Suspense," *Chicago Tribune,* October 8, 2000; "Stuy-Town Disaster," *The Brian Lehrer Show,* NPR website, April 4, 2013; David Axelrod, *Believer: My Forty Years in Politics* (New York: Penguin Books, 2015), 1; Paul Reiser, "Paul Reiser on Growing Up in New York's Stuyvesant Town," *The Wall Street Journal,* April 26, 2016.

112 **"We are 100 percent"** Rothstein, *Color of Law,* 72.

112 **The contracts** Bruce Lambert, "At 50, Levittown Contends With Its Legacy of Bias," *The New York Times,* December 28, 1997.

112 **Those maps** Rothstein, *Color of Law,* 64.

112 **The combination** Rothstein, *Color of Law,* 140–45.

113 **In the Los Angeles area** "Bombs Rip Homes in W Adams Area," *Los Angeles Times,* March 17, 1952, 1; "Protect Citizens in L.A., Veteran Group Demands," *Los Angeles Times,* March 17, 1952, 2; "Protests Mount in Terror Bombings of L.A. Homes," *Daily News,* March 18, 1952, 2; "Cross Burned in L.A. Man's Yard," *San Pedro News-Pilot,* June 18, 1952, 17.

114 **Black Male Earnings [chart]** Patrick Bayer and Kerwin Kofi Charles, "Divergent Paths: A New Perspective on Earnings Differences Between Black and White Men Since 1940," *The Quarterly Journal of Economics* 133, no. 3 (August 2018); David Leonhardt, "The Black-White Wage Gap Is as Big as It Was in 1950," *The New York Times,* June 25, 2020.

114 **Despite the government's** Kerwin Kofi Charles (Yale University), interview with author, June 2, 2020.

114 **The gap in life expectancy** Elizabeth Arias and Jiaquan Xu, "United States Life Tables, 2017," *National Vital Statistics Reports* 68, no. 7 (June 24, 2019), table 19.

115 **One of the largest** Jervis Anderson, *A. Philip Randolph: A Biographical Portrait* (Berkeley: University of California Press, 1972), 157–59; Andrew E. Kersten, *A. Philip Randolph: A Life in the Vanguard* (Lanham, Md.: Rowman & Littlefield, 2007), 28.

115 **"Everybody listened"** Anderson, *A. Philip Randolph,* 160.

116 **"The work was hard"** Anderson, *A. Philip Randolph,* 158.

116 The practice Anderson, *A. Philip Randolph*, 163–64.

116 In the 1920s "Reminiscences of Asa Philip Randolph," interview by Wendell Wray, July 18, 1972, p. 107, Columbia Center for Oral History, Columbia University.

116 One of the budding "Reminiscences," 154; Anderson, *A. Philip Randolph*, 5, 77.

117 "His only vanity" Anderson, *A. Philip Randolph*, 13.

118 After Asa read Anderson, *A. Philip Randolph*, 52.

118 "There is no hope" "Reminiscences," 223.

118 He also had no interest Anderson, *A. Philip Randolph*, 63, 126–27.

119 "The Republicans" Anderson, *A. Philip Randolph*, 76.

119 "a journal of scientific socialism" "Reminiscences," 168.

119 His wife, Lucille Anderson, *A. Philip Randolph*, 70–82.

119 "by long odds" Anderson, *A. Philip Randolph*, 82.

119 Pullman was a Anderson, *A. Philip Randolph*, 220.

119 "The history" "Reminiscences," 235.

120 "a Bolshevik hustler" Anderson, *A. Philip Randolph*, 179, 185.

120 "Any Sunday you went" Anderson, *A. Philip Randolph*, 184.

120 Lucille Randolph's hair salon Anderson, *A. Philip Randolph*, 214.

121 It included Associated Press, "Rail Unions Set Sept. 6 for Walkout," *Nashville Banner*, August 26, 1937, 11; "Victory for Negro Labor," *Time*, cited in *The Morning Post*, September 22, 1937, 10.

121 "No labor leadership" Elmer Anderson Carter, *Opportunity: Journal of Negro Life* 13 (1935): 231.

121 Only about 1 percent Cheryl Greenberg, *"Or Does It Explode?": Black Harlem in the Great Depression* (New York: Oxford University Press, 1991), 279.

121 Samuel Gompers Bernard Mandel, "Samuel Gompers and the Negro Worker: 1886–1914," *The Journal of Negro History* 40, no. 1 (January 1955): 48.

122 The CIO Eric Schickler, *Racial Realignment: The Transformation of American Liberalism, 1932–1965* (Princeton, N.J.: Princeton University Press, 2016), 60.

122 At labor conventions Anderson, *A. Philip Randolph*, 294.

122 The United Auto Workers Beth Tompkins Bates, *The Making of Black Detroit in the Age of Henry Ford* (Chapel Hill: University of North Carolina Press, 2012), 233–234.

122 "the most racially integrated" Katznelson, *Fear Itself*, 175.

122 "live in different sections" Katznelson, *Fear Itself*, 393.

122 "Probably the greatest" Michael Goldfield, "Race and the CIO: The Possibilities for Racial Egalitarianism During the 1930s and 1940s," *International Labor and Working-Class History*, no. 44 (Fall 1993): 2.

123 By the 1960s Henry S. Farber, Daniel Herbst, Ilyana Kuziemko, and Suresh Naidu, "Unions and Inequality over the Twentieth Century: New Evidence from Survey Data," *The Quarterly Journal of Economics* 136, no. 3,

1382–85; Suresh Naidu, email correspondence with author, January 24, 2023.

124 **"the most popular"** Anderson, *A. Philip Randolph*, 225.

124 **"His home is everywhere"** Anderson, *A. Philip Randolph*, 168.

125 **"For whites only"** Lucy Grace Barber, *Marching on Washington: The Forging of an American Political Tradition* (Berkeley: University of California Press, 2002), 113.

125 **"I think we ought"** Anderson, *A. Philip Randolph*, 247–48.

125 **"We loyal Negro American"** Anderson, *A. Philip Randolph*, 249; J. Cullen Fentress, "Gab Stuff," *California Eagle,* January 23, 1941, 9.

125 **The NAACP** Anderson, *A. Philip Randolph*, 249–50.

126 **"It scared everybody"** Anderson, *A. Philip Randolph*, 248.

126 **"We cannot inscribe"** Schickler, *Racial Realignment*, 86.

126 **One Washington columnist** Ray S. Tucker, Burton Heath, and Gabriel Vogliotti, "News Behind the News," *The York Dispatch,* June 28, 1941, 4.

126 **"a very grave mistake"** Anderson, *A. Philip Randolph*, 252–56; "First Lady Advises Randolph Against March on Washington," *California Eagle,* June 19, 1941, 6.

127 **When Randolph entered** Anderson, *A. Philip Randolph*, 256–58.

128 **"Who the hell"** Anderson, *A. Philip Randolph,* 258–59.

128 **On June 25** "Executive Order 8802: Prohibition of Discrimination in the Defense Industry," June 25, 1941, National Archives website.

128 **Roosevelt himself had suggested** Doris Kearns Goodwin, *No Ordinary Time: Franklin and Eleanor Roosevelt; The Home Front in World War II* (New York: Simon & Schuster, 2013), 252.

128 **"most astonishing"** Anderson, *A. Philip Randolph*, 262.

129 **"a lamentable specie"** Kersten, *Life in the Vanguard*, 146.

129 *The New York Times* "President Orders an Even Break for Minorities in Defense Jobs," *The New York Times,* June 26, 1941, 12.

129 **"There is manifest confusion"** Emmett J. Scott, "President Called Upon to Issue Order Discontinuing Segregation and Discrimination in Government," *The New York Age,* August 2, 1941, 2.

129 **Some workers staged** Paul Frymer, *Black and Blue: African Americans, the Labor Movement, and the Decline of the Democratic Party* (Princeton, N.J.: Princeton University Press, 2008), 53; James Wolfinger, "World War II Hate Strikes," in Aaron Brenner, Benjamin Day, and Immanuel Ness, eds., *The Encyclopedia of Strikes in American History* (London: Routledge, 2015), 118.

129 **Some companies retained** Jennifer Delton, *Racial Integration in Corporate America, 1940–1990* (New York: Cambridge University Press, 2009).

130 **"the leading edge"** Schickler, *Racial Realignment*, 272.

130 **In response** Schickler, *Racial Realignment*, 143.

131 **Bayer and Charles** Patrick Bayer and Kerwin Kofi Charles, "Divergent Paths: A New Perspective on Earnings Differences Between Black and White Men Since 1940," *The Quarterly Journal of Economics* 133, no. 3 (August 2018): 1459–501.

132 **The civil rights movement** John J. Donohue III and James Heckman, "Continuous Versus Episodic Change: The Impact of Civil Rights Policy on the Economic Status of Blacks," *Journal of Economic Literature* 29, no. 4 (December 1991): 1603–43.

132 **To be sure** Ellora Derenoncourt and Claire Montialoux, "Minimum Wages and Racial Inequality," *The Quarterly Journal of Economics* 136, no. 1, 169–228.

133 **"Negroes are almost"** Martin Luther King, Jr., speech at the AFL-CIO's Fourth Constitutional Convention, Miami, Fla., December 11, 1961.

133 **"The great movements"** "Reminiscences," 201.

134 **"Prison is better"** Anderson, *A. Philip Randolph,* 280.

134 **The local Brotherhood** Taylor Branch, *Parting the Waters: America in the King Years, 1954–1963* (New York: Touchstone, 1988), 128–36.

136 **"Those who deplore"** A. Philip Randolph, speech at the March on Washington, Washington, D.C., August 28, 1963.

136 **It was the only time** Anderson, *A. Philip Randolph,* 332.

Chapter 5: The Young Intelligentsia

141 **"There are so many"** John Judis, "Grist for Mills," *Texas Monthly,* March 2001.

141 **To better understand it** Joseph A. Loftus, "Labor Leaders and Trade Unions—Two Studies," *The New York Times,* October 3, 1948, 77; C. Wright Mills, *The New Men of Power: America's Labor Leaders* (Urbana: University of Illinois Press, 1948), 301.

141 **"lead the only organizations"** Mills, *New Men of Power,* 3.

142 **He ended the book** Mills, *New Men of Power,* 291.

142 **"countervailing power"** John Kenneth Galbraith, *American Capitalism: The Concept of Countervailing Power* (New Brunswick, N.J.: Transaction Publishers, 1993); Richard Flacks and Nelson Lichtenstein, eds., *The Port Huron Statement: Sources and Legacies of the New Left's Founding Manifesto* (Philadelphia: University of Pennsylvania Press, 2015), 5.

143 **He was not a typical** "C. Wright Mills, a Sociologist, 46," *The New York Times,* March 21, 1962, 39; Kathryn Mills, ed., *C. Wright Mills: Letters and Autobiographical Writings* (Berkeley: University of California Press, 2000), 11; Daniel Geary, *Radical Ambition: C. Wright Mills, the Left, and American Social Thought* (Berkeley: University of California Press, 2009), 1–13.

143 **"Take it big"** Mills, *C. Wright Mills,* 8.

143 **He believed** Geary, *Radical Ambition,* 6–7.

144 **On February 1, 1960** Joseph McNeil, interview by William Chafe, 1978, William Henry Chafe Oral History Collection, Duke University.

144 **Something about their bravery** Taylor Branch, *Parting the Waters: America in the King Years, 1954–1963* (New York: Touchstone, 1988), 272–75.

144 **"cling so mightily"** Charles Wright Mills, "Letter to the New Left," in *The Politics of Truth: Selected Writings of C. Wright Mills* (New York: Oxford University Press, 2008), 263–64.

144 "The Age of Complacency" Mills, "Letter," 266.

147 "Making us feel" Tom Hayden, *Reunion: A Memoir* (New York: Random House, 1988), 26–27.

147 "boring and prearranged" Hayden, *Reunion,* 14.

148 "get the nation moving" Maurice Isserman and Michael Kazin, *America Divided: The Civil War of the 1960s* (New York: Oxford University Press, 2008), 60.

148 "We thought that" Hayden, *Reunion,* 76.

148 "Here were four students" Flacks and Lichtenstein, *Port Huron Statement,* 5.

149 SDS had only three Kirkpatrick Sale, *SDS: The Rise and Development of the Students for a Democratic Society* (New York: Random House, 1973), 7.

149 The group Richard Flacks, "Philosophical and Political Roots of the American New Left," in Flacks and Lichtenstein, *Port Huron Statement,* 224; Sale, *SDS,* 21.

149 He soon moved Hayden, *Reunion,* 64–67.

149 A newspaper photographer "Hayden Beaten in McComb, Mississippi," *Resistance and Revolution: The Anti-Vietnam War Movement at the University of Michigan, 1965–1972,* Michigan in the World website.

150 Their aim Todd Gitlin, *The Sixties: Years of Hope, Days of Rage* (New York: Bantam Books, 1987), 124.

150 "He seemed to be" Mills, *C. Wright Mills,* 4.

150 The final version Sale, *SDS,* 45.

150 "We are people" "The Port Huron Statement," in Flacks and Lichtenstein, *Port Huron Statement,* 239.

150 The tone Alan Adelson, *SDS* (New York: Charles Scribner's Sons, 1972), 206.

151 "was unabashedly middle class" Sale, *SDS,* 50.

151 Hayden, reflecting his Hayden, *Reunion,* 123–150; Sale, *SDS,* 222.

151 Mills rejected Stanley Aronowitz, *Taking It Big: C. Wright Mills and the Making of Political Intellectuals* (New York: Columbia University Press, 2012), 2.

152 Like Mills, Betty Goldstein Betty Friedan, *Life So Far: A Memoir* (New York: Simon & Schuster, 2000), 30–32; Judith Hennessee, *Betty Friedan: Her Life* (New York: Random House, 1999), 6–7.

152 "I no longer" Friedan, *Life So Far,* 118.

152 "an existential guilt" Friedan, *Life So Far,* 97.

153 She filled Friedan, *Life So Far,* 97–99.

153 Two years later Hennessee, *Betty Friedan,* 97–108.

153 "The problem" Betty Friedan, *The Feminine Mystique* (New York: W. W. Norton, 2013), 302.

155 "suburban wife" Friedan, *Feminine Mystique,* 9.

155 The book had "Notable Alums," Smith College website.

155 At the time Thomas D. Snyder, Editor, "120 Years of American Education: A Statistical Portrait," Center for Education Statistics, 1993.

155 "I was, admittedly" Friedan, *Life So Far,* 108.

155 **"She must learn"** Friedan, *Feminine Mystique,* 310.

155 **She was critical** Rebecca Jo Plant, *Mom: The Transformation of Mother-hood in Modern America* (Chicago: University of Chicago Press, 2010), 161–67; Rebecca Jo Plant, interview with author, November 4, 2021.

155 **"comfortable concentration camp"** Friedan, *Feminine Mystique,* 234, 256; Friedan, *Life So Far,* 132.

155 **In 1960** Leah Platt Boustan and William J. Collins, "The Origins and Persistence of Black-White Differences in Women's Labor Force Participation" (working paper 19040, National Bureau of Economic Research, May 2013), 31.

156 *McCall's,* **one of** Plant, *Mom,* 232.

156 **"is something we simply"** Daniel Horowitz, "Rethinking Betty Friedan and *The Feminine Mystique:* Labor Union Radicalism and Feminism in Cold War America," *American Quarterly* 48, no. 1 (March 1996): 1–42.

156 **"She did not discuss"** Ashley Fetters, "4 Big Problems with *The Feminine Mystique,*" *The Atlantic,* February 12, 2013.

156 **In the founding** "Statement of Purpose," National Organization for Women website, 1966; Megan Rosenfeld, "A Woman's Work: Forget Sexual Politics, Betty Friedan Says. Economic Empowerment Is the Real Issue," *The Washington Post,* June 21, 1995.

156 **The welfare-rights movement** "Johnnie Tillmon Blackston, Welfare Reformer, Dies at 69," *The New York Times,* November 27, 1995, 26.

156 **"For a lot of middle-class women"** Johnnie Tillmon, "Welfare Is a Women's Issue," *Ms.,* Spring 1972.

157 **Abortion was another** Friedan, *Life So Far,* 200–1; Hennessee, *Betty Friedan,* 106.

157 **It would try** Hennessee, *Betty Friedan,* 103.

157 **"She has been portrayed"** Tony Mazzochi, quoted in Jefferson Cowie, *Stayin' Alive: The 1970s and the Last Days of the Working Class* (New York: New Press, 2010), 67.

158 **"the usual kinds"** Hennessee, *Betty Friedan,* 83–84.

158 **The auto safety campaign** "Car Crash Deaths and Rates," National Safety Council website.

159 **Nader went to work** Justin Martin, *Nader: Crusader, Spoiler, Icon* (New York: Basic Books, 2002), 40.

159 **But it spooked** Craig R. Whitney, "G.M. Settles Nader Suit on Privacy for $425,000," *The New York Times,* August 14, 1970, 1.

159 **After the detective's hiring** Paul Sabin, *Public Citizens: The Attack on Big Government and the Remaking of American Liberalism* (New York: W. W. Norton, 2021), 29.

159 **To create this** Sabin, *Public Citizens,* 38, 87–88.

160 **Nader vilthed** Michael Kazin, *What It Took to Win: A History of the Democratic Party* (New York: Farrar, Straus and Giroux, 2022), 258.

160 **That nominee received** "1980 Presidential General Election Results," Atlas of U.S. Elections website.

160 **"Few Black activists"** Sabin, *Public Citizens,* 89.

161 **In 1966** Mark Whitaker, *Saying It Loud: 1966—The Year Black Power Challenged the Civil Rights Movement* (New York: Simon & Schuster, 2023), 121, 257.

161 **This disdain** Sabin, *Public Citizens*, 193.

161 **"We believe that"** "Port Huron Statement," in Flacks and Lichtenstein, *Port Huron Statement*, 282.

161 **But less than** "Census Bureau Releases New Educational Attainment Data," U.S. Census Bureau website, February 24, 2022.

162 **The Pew Research Center** "Beyond Red vs. Blue: The Political Typology," Pew Research Center, November 9, 2021.

162 **College Split [chart]** Nate Cohn, "How Educational Differences Are Widening America's Political Rift," *The New York Times,* September 8, 2021; Nate Cohn, updated data provided to author, February 26, 2023.

163 **During the 2021** David Leonhardt, "The Bronx vs. Manhattan," *The New York Times,* December 7, 2020.

163 **"limousine liberals"** David Leonhardt, "How Biden Thinks," *The New York Times,* February 20, 2023.

163 **Sabin, the historian** Sabin, *Public Citizens,* xvii; see also Louis Menand, "The Making of the New Left," *The New Yorker,* March 22, 2021.

163 **There was an irony** Irving Bernstein, *The Lean Years: A History of the American Worker, 1920–1933* (Chicago: Haymarket Books, 2010), 771–72; Nelson Lichtenstein, *State of the Union: A Century of American Labor* (Princeton, N.J.: Princeton University Press, 2002), 134.

164 **William George Meany** Joseph C. Goulden, *Meany* (New York: Atheneum, 1972), 4–18; Nelson Lichtenstein, *The Most Dangerous Man in Detroit: Walter Reuther and the Fate of American Labor* (New York: Basic Books, 1995), 333; A. H. Raskin, "The New Labor Leaders—a Dual Portrait," *The New York Times,* December 21, 1952, 130.

164 **"They could drop dead"** Lichtenstein, *State of the Union,* 66.

165 **"an immense neck"** A. H. Raskin, "Meany and Reuther: Uneasy Togetherness," *The New York Times Magazine,* April 5, 1959, 14.

165 **He put a high priority** Raskin, "Meany and Reuther," 14.

165 **At one point** Goulden, *Meany,* 118.

165 **"Never beg, never threaten"** A. H. Raskin, "At 81, George Meany Is Still Mr. Labor," *The New York Times,* October 5, 1975, 201.

165 **"Ideology is baloney"** Lichtenstein, *State of the Union,* 187.

166 **"Who the hell"** Michael Williams, *Commonweal* 75, University of Michigan Commonweal Publishing, 1961, p. 140.

166 **He was also** Raskin, "Meany and Reuther," 14.

166 **"I must say"** Goulden, *Meany,* 267.

166 **Each year** Goulden, *Meany,* 201; Lichtenstein, *Most Dangerous Man,* 333.

166 **The AFL's narrower focus** Isserman and Kazin, *America Divided,* 52.

167 **Meany and other labor leaders** Charles Mohr, "Johnson to Back Labor Act Change," *The New York Times,* December 18, 1964, 20.

167 **The push** John D. Pomfret, "Labor Lobby vs. 14(B)," *The New York Times,* June 13, 1965, 156; David R. Jones, "Labor Bill Faces Defeat in Senate,"

The New York Times, October 1, 1965, 6; David Jones, "14(b) a Tough Target for Labor," *The New York Times,* January 23, 1966, 172.

167 **"Somebody might drop over"** Marjorie Hunter, "Filibuster Opens over Union Shop," *The New York Times,* January 25, 1966, 1.

168 **At the time** Henry S. Farber, Daniel Herbst, Ilyana Kuziemko, and Suresh Naidu, "Unions and Inequality over the Twentieth Century: New Evidence from Survey Data," *The Quarterly Journal of Economics* 136, no. 3, 1382–1385; union density data from Farber et al., "Unions and Inequality," provided to author, January 4, 2023.

168 **When a journalist** Miles McMillen, "Hello, Wisconsin," *Capital Times,* February 24, 1972, 1; Goulden, *Meany,* 466.

168 **"In my opinion"** Cowie, *Stayin' Alive,* 37. Rauh was one of the White House aides who negotiated the text of Executive Order 8802 with Randolph and was astonished by Randolph's toughness in the face of presidential pressure.

168 **One economist described** Michael C. Burda, "Membership, Seniority and Wage-Setting in Democratic Labour Unions," *Economica* 57, no. 228 (November 1990), 455–66. The economist was the late Lloyd Ulman of the University of California, Berkeley.

169 **When Carter had** Kazin, *What It Took,* 262.

169 **"the most pro-union"** Noam Scheiber, "'Most Pro-Union President' Runs into Doubts in Labor Ranks," *The New York Times,* December 27, 2022.

170 **In the service sector** "Annual Earnings and Employment Patterns of Private Nonagricultural Employees—1965," U.S. Department of Labor, FRASER, Federal Reserve Bank of St. Louis.

171 **They started not** David Harris, "The Battle of Coachella Valley: Cesar Chavez and UFW vs. Teamsters," *Rolling Stone,* September 13, 1973; Matt Garcia, *From the Jaws of Victory: The Triumph and Tragedy of Cesar Chavez and the Farm Worker Movement* (Berkeley: University of California Press, 2012), 33.

171 **In exchange for monthly dues** Art Berman, "Chavez a Modern Zapata to Grape Strikers," *Los Angeles Times,* May 6, 1966, 1.

171 **Eventually, the organization** "Rent Raise Protest," *Tulare Advance-Register,* May 22, 1965, 1; "Strikers Side Told," *Tulare Advance-Register,* August 26, 1965, 11.

171 **"They began seeing us"** Berman, "Chavez," 3.

171 **"The rich get richer"** "Rent Raise Protest," 1.

172 **To achieve lasting improvements** Berman, "Chavez," 1.

172 **Established labor unions helped** Harry Bernstein, "Teamsters Boycott Di Giorgio Goods," *Los Angeles Times,* May 6, 1966, 3.

172 **"You are leading history"** Lichtenstein, *Most Dangerous Man,* 410.

173 **"I don't think"** Ron Taylor, "Hoffa Okays NFWA DiGiorgio Free Hand," *The Fresno Bee,* June 9, 1966, 44; see also Gene Kuhn, "Teamsters May Demand DiGiorgio Recognition," *The Fresno Bee,* June 5, 1966, 30.

173 **Above all** Ron Taylor, "Chavez: Delano Will Be Organizing Battleground," *The Fresno Bee,* April 9, 1966, 16; Harry Bernstein, "AFL-CIO Snubs Peace Talks on Farm Labor," *Los Angeles Times,* May 25, 1966, 24.

174 **"highly sophisticated people"** Harry Bernstein, "Teamsters' Farm Workers Leader Quits Brown Drive," *Los Angeles Times,* August 31, 1966, 3.

174 **"An N.F.W.A. organizer"** Ray Christiansen, "'Mexican Power' Charge in Farm Vote," *San Francisco Examiner,* August 23, 1966, 2.

174 **"to build"** Associated Press, "AFL-CIO Man Quits over Farm Worker Merger," *The Sacramento Bee,* August 3, 1966, 28.

174 **When workers were voting** Bernstein, "Teamsters' Farm Workers Leader," 3; Harry Bernstein, "Union Battle Believed Near in Grape Fields," *Los Angeles Times,* May 17, 1966, 7; Associated Press, "Chavez: 'Teamsters Are Company Union,'" *The Fresno Bee,* August 15, 1966, 20.

175 **Another person** "Three Bishops Lead Service for Slain UFW Member," *The Modesto Bee and News-Herald,* August 21, 1973, 2.

176 **The family's leftist** Eric Schickler, *Racial Realignment: The Transformation of American Liberalism, 1932–1965* (Princeton, N.J.: Princeton University Press, 2016), 53.

176 **"the most dangerous man"** Lichtenstein, *Most Dangerous Man,* 230.

177 **He called for** Goulden, *Meany,* 206.

177 **"This is an unparalleled"** "Eisenhower's Talk, Excerpts from Meany and Reuther Speeches," *The New York Times,* December 6, 1955, 22.

178 **"We don't have"** Lichtenstein, *Most Dangerous Man,* 353.

178 **"sunny beaches"** Lichtenstein, *Most Dangerous Man,* 352–53.

178 **The other prominent** Joseph C. Goulden, *Jerry Wurf: Labor's Last Angry Man* (New York: Atheneum, 1982), 5–17.

179 **President John Kennedy** William Serrin, "A Leader for the Little Guy," *The New York Times,* September 12, 1982, 14.

179 **Wurf, in a decision** Goulden, *Jerry Wurf,* 143, 159, 174.

180 **The sanitation strike** Goulden, *Jerry Wurf,* 182.

180 **"exuberant atmosphere"** Cowie, *Stayin' Alive,* 70–71.

180 **"fertile beyond belief"** Goulden, *Jerry Wurf,* 120.

180 **"There is nothing wrong"** Lichtenstein, *Most Dangerous Man,* 346.

181 **"petty, mean-spirited"** Serrin, "Leader," 51.

181 **Reuther was the most effective** Lichtenstein, *Most Dangerous Man,* 322, 334, 357, 366. Archie Robinson, *George Meany and His Times: A Biography* (New York: Simon & Schuster, 1981), 252–54, 273.

181 **"What Reuther wants"** Lichtenstein, *Most Dangerous Man,* 334.

181 **Sometimes, as *Time*** Cowie, *Stayin' Alive,* 72–73.

182 **"The intellectuals"** Michael Vester, "Port Huron and the New Left Movements in Federal Germany," in Flacks and Lichtenstein, *Port Huron Statement,* 163.

183 **"For us, the role"** Vester, "Port Huron," 177.

183 **"The left could only"** Vester, "Port Huron," 180.

183 **In Scandinavia** Tony Judt, *Postwar: A History of Europe Since 1945* (New York: Penguin Press, 2005), 364–65.

184 **It was enough** Myrna Oliver, "David Riesman Jr., 92: Sociologist Coauthored 'The Lonely Crowd,'" *Los Angeles Times,* May 12, 2002, 102.

184 **"Among members"** Daniel Geary, "The New Left and Liberalism Reconsidered: The Committee of Correspondence and the Port Huron Statement," in Flacks and Lichtenstein, *Port Huron Statement,* 92.

185 **"I have always felt"** David Riesman, "With Such Friends," *The Correspondent* 30 (January–February 1964): 92, in University of Iowa Library.

185 **"uncivil disobedience"** Oliver, "David Riesman Jr.," 102.

185 **They might help elect** Geary, "New Left," 92.

Chapter 6: The Problem of Crime

187 **The crime** "Glory Enough for All," *The Boston Globe,* August 22, 1962, 18.

187 **"Open the door"** Jerome Sullivan, "Witness Places Mrs. Diaferio Near Mail Robbery Site," *The Boston Globe,* November 8, 1967, 14.

187 **By the next day** "Hijackers Get $1.5 Million," *Fort Lauderdale News,* August 15, 1962, 1; Associated Press, "Armed Band Robs Mass. Mail Truck," *The Times-Argus,* August 15, 1962, 1; Associated Press, "4 Gunmen Vanish with Heavy Cash from Mail Truck," *Chattanooga Daily Times,* August 15, 1962, 1; Associated Press, "Bandits Net $1.5 Million," *Spokane Daily Chronicle,* August 15, 1962, 1; Sandy Smith, "Huge Mail Truck Robbery!," *Chicago Tribune,* August 15, 1962, 1.

187 **To save money** Associated Press, "U.S. Mail Truck Robbed by Gang," *Fitchburg Sentinel,* August 15, 1962, 1.

187 **The prosecutors' case** Robert S. Anglin, "Mail Trial Verdict: Not Guilty," *The Boston Globe,* November 18, 1967, 1.

188 **To this date** "Ernest R. Tidyman, Screen Writer, Dies at 56," *The New York Times,* July 16, 1984, 35.

188 **Based on his reporting** Ernest Tidyman, *Big Bucks: The True, Outrageous Story of the Plymouth Mail Robbery . . . and How They Got Away with It* (New York: W. W. Norton, 1982).

188 **By the early 1960s** "United States Crime Rates, 1960–2019," Disaster Center website.

188 **On May 22** United Press International, "Possibility of Murder, Suicide Pact," *Ames Daily Tribune,* May 28, 1962, 1.

188 **On the night** "3 Bank Robbers Escape Alcatraz," *Oakland Tribune,* June 12, 1962, 1.

188 **Three days later** "Hub Woman Strangled," *Newport Daily News,* June 15, 1962, 18; Jess Bidgood, "50 Years Later, a Break in a Boston Strangler Case," *The New York Times,* July 11, 2013, A8.

188 **In Chicago, an alderman** "Crime, Return of the Rub-Out," *Time,* March 8, 1963, 28.

188 **In New Jersey** "Crime Goes On and Gets Worse," *U.S. News & World Report,* September 9, 1963, 76.

188 **In Queens** David W. Dunlap, "1964. How Many Witnessed the Murder of Kitty Genovese?," *The New York Times,* April 6, 2016. A later review of the case suggested that the bystanders might not have been able to save her and that *Life* magazine and *The New York Times* sensationalized details of the case, shaping national perceptions of it.

188 **"Crime is"** "Crime in the U.S.—Is It Getting Out of Hand?," *U.S. News & World Report,* August 26, 1963, 40.

188 **By 1976, crime** Rick Perlstein, *Reaganland: America's Right Turn, 1976–1980* (New York: Simon & Schuster, 2020), 6.

189 **Nationally, the murder rate** "United States Crime Rates, 1960–2019," Disaster Center website.

189 **Homicide Rates [chart]** Douglas Lee Eckberg, "Estimates of Early Twentieth-Century U.S. Homicide Rates: An Econometric Forecasting Approach," *Demography* 32, no. 1 (February 1995): 1–16; Roth, American Homicide, 4; data provided to author by Randolph Roth, March 7, 2023.

189 **People often assume** "The Extent of Poverty in the United States, 1959 to 1966," *Current Population Reports,* U.S. Department of Commerce, May 31, 1968.

189 **The trend** Randolph Roth, *American Homicide* (Cambridge, Mass.: Belknap Press of Harvard University Press, 2009), 4.

190 **"Here was an explosion"** Gary LaFree, *Losing Legitimacy: Street Crime and the Decline of Social Institutions in America* (Boulder, Colo.: Westview Press, 1998), 6.

190 **"crime amidst plenty"** LaFree, *Losing Legitimacy,* 122.

191 **When Gurr studied** LaFree, *Losing Legitimacy,* 96.

192 **Another scholar** Roth, *American Homicide,* 436–37.

192 **"People responded violently"** Roth, *American Homicide,* 301.

192 **During periods of** Roth, *American Homicide,* 22–23, 149, 301–2.

192 **Officials in New Jersey** "Ocean County Timeline," Ocean County, New Jersey website; "History," Gordon County Government website.

192 **In the 1930s** LaFree, *Losing Legitimacy,* 108.

193 **Once citizens** Elijah Anderson, *Code of the Street: Decency, Violence, and the Moral Life of the Inner City* (New York: W. W. Norton, 1999); Elijah Anderson, "The Code of the Streets," *The Atlantic,* May 1994.

193 **Male teenagers** "Estimated Number of Arrests by Offense and Age Group, 2019," Office of Juvenile Justice and Delinquency Protection, U.S. Department of Justice website; National Research Council and Institute of Medicine, *Juvenile Crime, Juvenile Justice,* ed. Joan McCord, Cathy Spatz Widom, and Nancy A. Crowell (Washington, D.C.: National Academies Press, 2001), 320.

193 **This combination** Robert A. Caro, *The Power Broker: Robert Moses and the Fall of New York* (New York: Vintage Books, 1975); Thomas J. Sugrue, *The Origins of the Urban Crisis: Race and Inequality in Postwar Detroit* (Princeton, N.J.: Princeton University Press, 1996); William Julius Wilson, *The Truly Disadvantaged: The Inner City, the Underclass, and Public Policy* (Chicago: The University of Chicago Press, 1987).

194 **"Nothing increases homicide"** Roth, *American Homicide,* 469.

195 **"the school 'crime wave'"** "The School 'Crime Wave,'" *The Nation,* March 30, 1964, 310.

195 **"the problem of 'crime'"** "The High Cost of Imprisonment," *The Nation,* December 26, 1966, 693.

195 **One** *Nation* **writer** George Shadoan, "Behind the Crime Scare," *The Nation,* May 10, 1965, 495.

195 **The increases** "The History of Homicide in the U.S.," National Academies website.

195 ***The New Republic*** James Ridgeway, "Barry Fights Crime," *The New Republic,* October 3, 1964, 9–11.

195 **President Johnson** J. Skelly Wright, "Crime in the Streets and The New McCarthyism," *The New Republic,* October 9, 1965, 10–11.

195 **"A steep, decade-long"** Edward K. Faltermayer, "Some Here-and-Now Steps to Cut Crime," *Fortune,* July 1970, 94.

196 **Divorce became** LaFree, *Losing Legitimacy,* 143.

196 **The share of Americans** "Public Trust in Government: 1958–2022," Pew Research Center, June 6, 2022.

196 **"In the public perception"** Thomas Byrne Edsall, *Chain Reaction: The Impact of Race, Rights, and Taxes on American Politics* (New York: W. W. Norton, 1992), 71.

196 **"The main crisis"** James Reston, "Washington: The Paradox of America," *The New York Times,* March 6, 1968, 46, cited in Jill Lepore, *These Truths: A History of the United States* (New York: W. W. Norton, 2018), 629.

196 **The experts at Gallup** "Gallup Calls Public Disillusioned and Cynical," *The New York Times,* February 10, 1968, 12.

196 **On the night** Tom Wicker, "Johnson Says He Won't Run," *The New York Times,* April 1, 1968, 1.

196 **When Johnson made** U.S. Bureau of Labor Statistics, "Unemployment Rate," FRED, Federal Reserve Bank of St. Louis; "US Business Cycle Expansions and Contractions," National Bureau of Economic Research website, July 19, 2021.

197 **"You know who lit"** Spiro T. Agnew, "Opening Statement," Conference with Civil Rights and Community Leaders, April 11, 1968.

197 **Most of the leaders** "Agnew Angers Negroes," *The New York Times,* April 12, 1968, 20.

197 **Until then** "The Candidate from Maryland," *The New York Times,* August 9, 1968, 18.

198 **Wallace had grown up** Theodore H. White, *The Making of the President, 1968* (New York: Harper Perennial, 1969), 400–1.

199 **"Segregation now"** White, *Making of the President,* 401.

200 **"I'm not running on segregation"** United Press International, " 'I'm Not Running on Segregation'—Wallace," *The Delta Democrat-Times,* October 1, 1967, 1.

200 **"bearded professors"** Ben A. Franklin, "Wallace Weighs 3d Party Convention," *The New York Times,* September 30, 1967, 17.

200 **"You young people"** Garry Wills, *Nixon Agonistes: The Crisis of the Self-Made Man* (New York: New American Library, 1969), 57.

200 **"the glassworker, the steelworker"** Richard M. Scammon and Ben J. Wattenberg, *The Real Majority* (New York: Coward-McCann, 1970), 62.

201 "This new-found respectability" Gene Roberts, "Says George Wallace in Awe: 'They Like Me!,'" *The New York Times,* November 12, 1967, 211.

201 One poll found Louis H. Bean, *How to Predict the 1972 Election* (New York: Quadrangle Books, 1972), 182.

201 "Forget the Goldwater South" John A. Farrell, *Richard Nixon: The Life* (New York: Doubleday, 2017), 329.

201 Sure enough, Wallace won "Statistics, 1968," American Presidency Project website.

201 "It is time" "The Living Room Candidate: Presidential Campaign Commercials, 1952–2020; 1968 Nixon vs. Humphrey vs. Wallace," Museum of the Moving Image website.

201 At the Republican Richard Nixon, "Address Accepting the Presidential Nomination at the Republican National Convention in Miami Beach, Florida," August 8, 1968, American Presidency Project website.

202 During college Farrell, *Richard Nixon,* 61–62.

202 "The lives of American presidents" Farrell, *Richard Nixon,* 7.

202 Once he entered politics Farrell, *Richard Nixon,* 23, 39, 130, 150; Richard Pearson, "Ex-Rep. Jerry Voorhis Dies," *The Washington Post,* September 12, 1984.

202 "Every campaign" Wills, *Nixon Agonistes,* 89.

202 Once Eisenhower Wills, *Nixon Agonistes,* 100–4.

202 The accusations Farrell, *Richard Nixon,* 181.

203 "It's essential" Richard Nixon, televised address, September 23, 1952.

203 Many media commentators Farrell, *Richard Nixon,* 195.

203 "The sophisticates" Robert C. Ruark, "Nixon Adds Common Touch to GOP," *The Dispatch,* September 29, 1952, 6.

203 Farmers and laborers Lee Huebner, "The Checkers Speech After 60 Years," *The Atlantic,* September 22, 2012.

203 "the highbrow and the heretical" Farrell, *Richard Nixon,* 199.

204 "You can see" Nixon, "Address Accepting the Presidential Nomination."

204 As a New York senator "Kennedy Denounces Apartheid as Evil," *The New York Times,* June 7, 1966, 1.

204 In a national poll Richard D. Kahlenberg, "The Inclusive Populism of Robert F. Kennedy," Century Foundation, March 16, 2018; Larry Tye, "The Most Trusted White Man in Black America," *Politico Magazine,* July 7, 2016.

204 Behind the scenes William vanden Heuvel and Milton Gwirtzman, *On His Own: Robert F. Kennedy, 1964–1968* (Garden City, N.Y.: Doubleday & Company, 1970), 337.

204 The head Arthur M. Schlesinger, Jr., *Robert Kennedy and His Times* (Boston: Houghton Mifflin, 1978), 899.

205 When Kennedy traveled Larry Tye, *Bobby Kennedy: The Making of a Liberal Icon* (New York: Random House, 2016), 411.

205 "He had the capacity" John R. Lewis, interview by Vicki Daitch, March 19, 2004, 6, John F. Kennedy Oral History Collection, John F. Kennedy Presidential Library and Museum, Boston, Mass.

205 **Only 9 percent** Jules Witcover, *85 Days: The Last Campaign of Robert Kennedy* (New York: G. P. Putnam's Sons, 1969), 151.

206 **At Kennedy rallies** White, *Making of the President,* 208.

206 **The singers** John Herbers, "Indiana Seeing a New Kennedy With Shorter Hair, Calm Manner and Pleas for Local Rule," *The New York Times,* May 3, 1968, 28; Ralph Kramer, "David vs. Goliath: 4 Pave Way For McCarthy 'Army,'" *The Indianapolis News,* April 6, 1968, 32.

206 **At a meeting** Thurston Clarke, *The Last Campaign: Robert F. Kennedy and 82 Days That Inspired America* (New York: Henry Holt and Company, 2008), 140.

206 **"I think"** Jefferson Cowie, *Stayin' Alive: The 1970s and the Last Days of the Working Class* (New York: New Press, 2010), 95.

207 **Branigin, the governor** vanden Heuvel and Gwirtzman, *On His Own,* 341.

207 **In the 1920s** Clarke, *Last Campaign,* 80.

207 **McCarthy avoided** Kahlenberg, "Inclusive Populism."

207 **He decided** White, *Making of the President,* 206.

208 **"violence of institutions"** Robert S. Boyd, "Kennedy Cancels Tours, Calls for End to Violence," *The Miami Herald,* April 6, 1968, 58.

208 **Kennedy was also careful** Tye, *Bobby Kennedy,* 415; vanden Heuvel and Gwirtzman, *On His Own,* 345.

208 **"We can't tolerate"** Clarke, *Last Campaign,* 176–77.

208 **"favor civil rights"** Clarke, *Last Campaign,* 82; Schlesinger, *Robert Kennedy,* 880.

208 **"I promise"** White, *Making of the President,* 199.

208 **To emphasize his commitment** Clarke, *Last Campaign,* 65.

208 **"the only man seeking"** *Anderson Daily Bulletin,* May 3, 1968, 3.

209 **"a good Republican"** Mary McGrory, "The New Kennedy: Hair Trimmed, Voice Lowered and Less of JFK—He Even Sounds Like Republican on Stump," *The Boston Globe,* May 1, 1968, 20.

209 **"the euphemisms"** Clarke, *Last Campaign,* 176.

209 **"the illusion of change"** Tye, *Bobby Kennedy,* 408.

209 **"Kennedy: Meet"** "Kennedy: Meet the Conservative," *The New York Times,* April 28, 1968.

209 **"We're going to talk"** Witcover, *85 Days,* 154; see also Evan Thomas, *Robert Kennedy: His Life* (New York: Simon & Schuster, 2000), 370.

209 **"Law-and-order?"** White, *Making of the President,* 206.

209 **During a speech** White, *Making of the President,* 199–201.

209 **He also tried stylistic appeals** Herbers, "Indiana Seeing a New Kennedy"; "'It Is Much Better to Win,'" *Newsweek,* May 20, 1968, 34; Tye, *Bobby Kennedy,* 414

210 **To all these political messages** "Kennedy: Meet the Conservative"; Clarke, *Last Campaign,* 141; Herbers, "Indiana Seeing a New Kennedy"; Schlesinger, *Robert Kennedy,* 890; Witcover, *85 Days,* 155.

210 **He began** Clarke, *Last Campaign,* 84–85; Schlesinger, *Robert Kennedy,* 883; Tye, *Bobby Kennedy,* 406.

210 **"American children"** Clarke, *Last Campaign,* 57; Tye, *Bobby Kennedy,* 415.

210 **"From you"** Witcover, *85 Days,* 165.

210 **"It's unjust and unreasonable"** "Excerpts from the Kennedy-McCarthy Televised Discussion of Campaign Issues," *The New York Times,* June 2, 1968, 64.

210 **"We must reform"** "Robert F. Kennedy 1968 for President Campaign Brochure," 4President.org.

210 **The largest newspapers** Tye, *Bobby Kennedy,* 413; Witcover, *85 Days,* 160–64.

211 **Fortune magazine published** Kahlenberg, "Inclusive Populism."

211 **"have-not coalition"** Witcover, *85 Days,* 173.

211 **"inclusive populism"** Kahlenberg, "Inclusive Populism."

211 **"He believed"** Clarke, *Last Campaign,* 178.

211 **"The very qualities"** Kahlenberg, "Inclusive Populism."

212 **He finished** Louis Harris, "Part Way With RFK—The Price He Paid," *Newsweek,* May 20, 1968, 35.

212 **"In a painful era"** " 'It Is Much Better to Win,' " *Newsweek,* May 20, 1968, 34.

212 **"the last liberal"** Schlesinger, *Robert Kennedy,* 891.

212 **He had even won** "Vote County by Counties Announced," *The Indianapolis News,* May 9, 1968, 56; Associated Press, "Breakdown of Voting Released," *The Hammond Times,* May 7, 1964, 16; Witcover, *85 Days,* 181.

213 **"The poor people"** Derek Pogson, "Chavez Makes No Glib Pledges in Aiding RFK," *The Sacramento Bee,* May 29, 1968, 13.

213 **"He was walking"** Schlesinger, *Robert Kennedy,* 908.

214 **Kennedy's relationship** Tom Wicker, "In the Nation: Labor's Love Lost," *The New York Times,* April 25, 1968, 46.

214 **"that jitterbug"** Thomas, *Robert Kennedy,* 362; see J. E. Lighter, ed., *Random House Historical Dictionary of American Slang* vol. 2 (New York: Random House, 1997), 285.

214 **When it was time** Schlesinger, *Robert Kennedy,* 914.

214 **"What I think"** "June 5, 1968: Robert F. Kennedy's Last Speech," *ABC News,* June 1, 2018.

216 **Even though Madison** Scammon and Wattenberg, *Real Majority,* 108.

216 **"silent center"** James Ott, "Nunn Turns Out to Be Phrase-Maker," *The Cincinnati Enquirer,* August 18, 1968, 85.

216 **"Who needs Manhattan?"** Wills, *Nixon Agonistes,* 248.

217 **"the secret"** Wills, *Nixon Agonistes,* 247.

217 **Phillips recognized** Wills, *Nixon Agonistes,* 250.

217 **"In his gut"** Farrell, *Richard Nixon,* 334.

217 **"He could reach"** Farrell, *Richard Nixon,* 335.

218 **The AFL-CIO also** White, *Making of the President,* 418.

218 **One problem** Scammon and Wattenberg, *Real Majority,* 56.

218 **"the end of the New Deal"** Kevin P. Phillips, *The Emerging Republican Majority* (New Rochelle, N.Y.: Arlington House, 1969), 25.

218 **Democrats mistakenly** Scammon and Wattenberg, *Real Majority*, 46.

218 **Hollywood celebrities** Michael Kazin, *What It Took to Win: A History of the Democratic Party* (New York: Farrar, Straus and Giroux, 2022), 233–54.

Chapter 7: A New Way of Looking at the World

220 **His name was Pete Hamill** Pete Hamill, *A Drinking Life: A Memoir* (New York: Back Bay Books, 1994); Robert D. McFadden, "Pete Hamill, Quintessential New York Journalist, Dies at 85," *The New York Times,* August 5, 2020.

220 **"they believed America"** Pete Hamill, "The Revolt of the White Lower Middle Class," *New York,* April 14, 1969.

220 **He also informed** Hamill, "Revolt."

220 **"a dumping ground"** Hamill, "Revolt."

221 **"A large reason"** Hamill, "Revolt."

221 **Hamill's article** Jefferson Cowie, *Stayin' Alive: The 1970s and the Last Days of the Working Class* (New York: New Press, 2010), 132; Rick Perlstein, *Nixonland: The Rise of a President and the Fracturing of America* (New York: Scribner, 2008), 367.

221 **"Iron Butt"** Rick Perlstein, *Nixonland: The Rise of a President and the Fracturing of America* (New York: Scribner, 2008), 23.

222 **After Nixon read** Jefferson Cowie, "Nixon's Class Struggle: Romancing the New Right Worker, 1969–1973," *Labor History* 43, no. 3 (2002): 257–83; Bruce J. Schulman and Julian Zelizer, *Rightward Bound: Making America Conservative in the 1970s* (Cambridge, Mass.: Harvard University Press, 2008), 188.

223 **"I was a registered"** Jerome Rosow, interview by Morris Weisz, April 15, 1993, p. 4, Foreign Affairs Oral History Program, Association for Diplomatic Studies and Training.

223 **The result** Jerome M. Rosow, "The Problem of the Blue-Collar Worker," memo for the Department of Labor, ERIC, Institute of Education Sciences, April 16, 1970.

223 **"shares the same concern"** Rosow, "Problem," 1.

223 **"To a considerable extent"** Rosow, "Problem," 7–9.

224 **The report was intended** Cowie, *Stayin' Alive,* 133–34; Jack Rosenthal, "U.S. Aide Asks Blue-Collar Gains," *The New York Times,* October 30, 1970, 69.

225 **Its adherents** Kim Phillips-Fein, *Invisible Hands: The Businessmen's Crusade Against the New Deal* (New York: W. W. Norton, 2009), 1–86.

225 **Charls Walker was** "Walker Discusses Purchasing Power," *Longview News-Journal,* April 29, 1958, 2; John McConal, "Washington Exec's a Long Way from Home," *Fort Worth Star-Telegram,* April 19, 1974, 5.

225 **"A tall, lean and balding Texan"** Jules Witcover, "The Lobbyist's Art: Charls Walker and the Washington Way to Influence," *The Washington Post,* March 16, 1975, 220.

226 **He belonged to Burning Tree** Bart Barnes, "Charls E. Walker, Tax Lobbyist for GOP and Big Business, Dies at 91," *The Washington Post,* June 29, 2015. A May 27, 1975, letter from Walker to Richard Cheney, the White

House chief of staff, mentioned that he ran into President Ford at "BT" the previous weekend. A sample of 1973 correspondence from Walker's papers includes personal letters from Vice President Spiro Agnew; Speaker of the House Carl Albert; Federal Reserve chairman Arthur Burns; Senators Lloyd Bentsen, Bob Dole, Adlai Stevenson, and Robert Taft; Henry Kissinger; Donald Rumsfeld; and future presidents Gerald Ford and George H. W. Bush.

226 **"Where I come from"** Rick Perlstein, *Reaganland: America's Right Turn, 1976–1980* (New York: Simon & Schuster, 2020), 278–79.

226 **In speeches representing** Charls E. Walker, "LBJ Start on Budget and Tax Cut Held 'Impressive,'" *The Austin American,* January 18, 1964, 4.

226 **At times, Walker** Harold Monroe, "Fight Joined on Control of Fed," *Fort Worth Star-Telegram,* February 7, 1965, 36.

226 **Walker, by contrast** "Business Called 'Goat' White Government, Labor Grow Bigger," *Philadelphia Inquirer,* January 5, 1962, 4.

226 **Tom Charles Huston** Cowie, *Stayin' Alive,* 133.

226 **Trying to bolster** Cowie, *Stayin' Alive,* 133–34.

226 **Walker channeled ideas** Charls Walker to Richard Nixon, memo, November 30, 1970, FF: President's Handwriting, President's Office Files, Contested Documents from Boxes 1–13, Folder 1 of 4, Richard Nixon Presidential Library and Museum, Yorba Linda, Calif.; Jefferson Cowie, email correspondence with author, September 6, 2022.

227 **"The legitimate question"** Walker, memo, 1–2.

227 **Schultz, before joining** David Greenberg, "How George Schultz Escaped Two Scandal-Plagued Administrations Unscathed," *Politico,* February 9, 2021.

228 **Nixon loved** David Paul Kuhn, *The Hardhat Riot: Nixon, New York City, and the Dawn of the White Working-Class Revolution* (New York: Oxford University Press, 2020), 253.

228 **"take the gloves off"** Charles Colson to Richard Nixon, memo, December 7, 1970, FF: President's Handwriting, President's Office Files, Contested Documents from Boxes 1–13, Richard Nixon Library; Jefferson Cowie, email correspondence with author, September 7, 2022.

228 **Nixon governed** Perlstein, *Reaganland,* 198.

229 **He made clear** Tom Wicker, *One of Us: Richard Nixon and the American Dream* (New York: Random House, 1991); see also John A. Farrell, *Richard Nixon: The Life* (New York: Doubleday, 2017), 390–91; Dean J. Kotlowski, *Nixon's Civil Rights: Politics, Principle, and Policy* (Cambridge, Mass.: Harvard University Press), 2002.

229 **"Probably more new regulation"** Steven F. Hayward, *The Age of Reagan: The Fall of the Old Liberal Order, 1964–1980* (New York: Three Rivers Press, 2001), 257.

229 **"I just want to say"** White House Tapes, Tape 719, May 4, 1972, 12:56 P.M.– 1:21 P.M.

230 **Among the researchers** Binyamin Appelbaum, *The Economists' Hour: False Prophets, Free Markets, and the Fracture of Society* (New York: Little, Brown, 2019), 25–27; Douglas Martin, "Aaron Director, Economist, Dies at 102," *The New York Times,* September 16, 2004; Sam Peltzman, "Aaron

Director's Influence on Antitrust Policy," *The Journal of Law and Economics* 48, no. 2 (October 2005): 313–30; Stephen M. Stigler, "Aaron Director Remembered," *The Journal of Law and Economics* 48, no. 2 (October 2005): 307–11.

230 **Rose recognized** Appelbaum, *Economists' Hour,* 29.

231 **"If an exchange"** Milton Friedman and Rose Friedman, *Free to Choose: A Personal Statement* (New York: Avon Books, 1980), 5.

231 **"Anything that prevents"** Friedman and Friedman, *Free to Choose,* 8.

232 **Their son, Robert Heron Bork** Dale Russakoff and Al Kamen, "A Trip Across the Political Spectrum," *The Washington Post,* July 26, 1987; Dale Russakoff and Al Kamen, "An Odyssey of Ideas from Yale to Watergate," *The Washington Post,* July 27, 1987; Dale Russakoff and Al Kamen, "Bork's Appetite Is Whetted for Place on Supreme Court," *The Washington Post,* July 28, 1987.

232 **"My mother and I"** Russakoff and Kamen, "Trip."

233 **Hutchins also encouraged** "Robert M. Hutchins, Long a Leader in Educational Change, Dies at 78," *The New York Times,* May 16, 1977, 1.

233 **The young Bork** Finding aid, p. 6, Robert H. Bork Papers, Manuscript Division, Library of Congress.

234 **"It was a new way"** Russakoff and Kamen, "Trip."

234 **"a little bit"** Stuart Taylor, Jr., "Bork on His Evolution: Far from the New Deal," *The New York Times,* July 8, 1987, 1.

234 **But the press** Stephen Stigler, email correspondence with author, September 11, 2022. They made so many postcards that in 2022, long after all the economists involved had died, Stigler's son Stephen, a statistics professor at the University of Chicago, still owned some and generously mailed me a set of the five.

234 **In subsequent years** Finding aid, Bork Papers.

234 **Big companies** Appelbaum, *Economists' Hour,* 141.

235 **"I cannot believe"** Edward Levi to Robert Bork, memo, June 30, 1954, Bork Papers.

235 **Antitrust came to dominate** Robert Bork, "Vertical Integration and the Sherman Act: The Legal History of an Economic Misconception," *The University of Chicago Law Review* 22, no. 1 (Autumn 1954): 157; Robert H. Bork, "Legislative Intent and the Policy of the Sherman Act," *Journal of Law and Economics* 9 (1966): 7–48; Robert H. Bork, "The Goals of Antitrust Policy," *The American Economic Review* 42, no. 2 (May 1967): 242.

235 **Levi wrote letters** Bork Papers.

235 **At Yale, Bork published** Robert H. Bork, *The Antitrust Paradox: A Policy at War with Itself* (New York: Basic Books, 1978).

236 **After Bork joined** Aaron Director to Robert Bork, December 13, 1962, Bork Papers.

236 **Subsequently, Bork** Robert Bork to Aaron Director, January 11, 1963, Bork Papers.

236 **"uncommon charm"** Russakoff and Kamen, "Trip."

236 **As a young lawyer** Russakoff and Kamen, "Trip."

236 **Although he also worried** Russakoff and Kamen, "Bork's Appetite."

236 **"The deformation"** Russakoff and Kamen, "Bork's Appetite."

236 **"Would it be accurate"** Steve Lohr (*The New York Times*), interview with author, October 11, 2022.

237 **"The president tells me"** Robert H. Bork to George Will, June 6, 1978, Bork Papers.

237 **"The avenues to wealth"** Richard Theodore Ely, "Report of the Organization of the American Economic Association," 1887, p. 16, cited in part in Sidney Blumenthal, *The Rise of the Counter-establishment: The Conservative Ascent to Political Power* (New York: Union Square Press, 1986), 80–81.

237 **In the United States** Appelbaum, *Economists' Hour,* 134.

237 **One example** Appelbaum, *Economists' Hour,* 131–32.

238 **A similar federal** Appelbaum, *Economists' Hour,* 132; Tim Wu, *The Curse of Bigness: Antitrust in the New Gilded Age* (New York: Columbia Global Reports, 2018), 112.

238 **Bork pointed out** Appelbaum, *Economists' Hour,* 150.

238 **Bork considered** Bork, *Antitrust Paradox,* 211–13.

239 **"A free economy"** Taylor, "Bork on His Evolution."

239 **"The title"** Aaron Director to Robert Bork, December 30, 1963, Bork Papers.

240 **Other historians** Appelbaum, *Economists' Hour,* 149–50, 380.

240 **"Perhaps the single most"** Lewis F. Powell, Jr., "Attack on American Free Enterprise System," August 23, 1971, Lewis F. Powell Jr. Papers, Washington and Lee University School of Law, Lexington, Va.

241 **"Business leaders"** John B. Judis, *The Paradox of American Democracy: Elites, Special Interests, and the Betrayal of Public Trust* (New York: Routledge, 2001), 121–22.

241 **It helped persuade** Jane Mayer, *Dark Money: The Hidden History of the Billionaires Behind the Rise of the Radical Right* (New York: Anchor Books, 2016), 88–106; Appelbaum, *Economists' Hour,* 102.

242 **The chairmen** Judis, *Paradox of American Democracy,* 121.

242 **The executives agreed** Sidney Blumenthal, "Defining 'Reaganomics,'" *The Boston Globe,* November 2, 1980, 51.

242 **Today, more than** "Factbox—How many lobbyists are there in Washington?," *Reuters,* September 13, 2009.

242 **"What we did"** Mayer, *Dark Money,* 90; see also Blumenthal, *Rise of the Counter-establishment,* 46.

243 **Deaths from vehicle crashes** "Historical Fatality Trends," National Safety Council website.

243 **The list** Milton Friedman, *Capitalism and Freedom* (Chicago: University of Chicago Press, 1982), vi.

243 **"primarily judge-made"** Robert H. Bork, "Will Capitalism Survive?," *Yale Alumni Magazine and Journal,* April 1978, 16.

244 **"gave way"** Bork, "Will Capitalism Survive?," 16.

244 **"Wreak yourself"** Russakoff and Kamen, "Bork's Appetite."

244 **One of Bork's friends** Russakoff and Kamen, "Bork's Appetite."

244 **At the time** Robert H. Bork, "Antitrust in Dubious Battle," *Fortune*, September 1969, 103; Robert H. Bork, "The Supreme Court Versus Corporate Efficiency," *Fortune*, August 1967, 92.

244 **After one ran** Warren Burger to Robert Bork, Bork Papers.

244 **In his thank-you note** Robert H. Bork to William Rehnquist, August 10, 1978, Bork Papers.

244 **"Capitalism is the name"** Bork, "Will Capitalism Survive?," 15.

245 **They launched** Perlstein, *Reaganland*, 285.

246 **"There is enormous inertia"** Friedman, *Capitalism and Freedom*, viii–ix.

Chapter 8: Clear the Track for Business

247 **The crisis began** "Saudis Cut Oil Output 10% to Put Pressure on U.S.," *The New York Times*, October 19, 1973, 1; "Saudis Cut Oil Production 10%," *Chicago Tribune*, October 19, 1973, 68; "Oil Flow to U.S. Halted by Saudis," *The New York Times*, October 21, 1973, 28; Associated Press, "Faisal Cuts Saudi's Oil Output 10%," *Hartford Courant*, October 19, 1973, 1; Richard Eder, "4 More Arab Governments Bar Oil Supplies for U.S.," *The New York Times*, October 22, 1973, 1; Leonard Silk, "Crisis on Two Fronts," *The New York Times*, October 24, 1973, 63; William D. Smith, "Rise in Oil Prices Seems a Record," *The New York Times*, October 19, 1973, 61; William D. Smith, "Cutoff in Oil to U.S. Ordered by Libya," *The New York Times*, October 20, 1973, 1; United Press International, "Saudi Arabia Puts Pressure on U.S.," *The Tampa Tribune*, October 19, 1973, 30; Daniel Yergin, *The Prize: The Epic Quest for Oil, Money, and Power* (New York: Simon & Schuster, 1991), 588–612.

247 **They called it** Clyde H. Farnsworth, "Oil as an Arab Weapon," *The New York Times*, October 18, 1973, 97; William D. Smith, "The Arab Oil Weapon Comes into Play," *The New York Times*, October 21, 1973, 185.

248 **"His majesty's government"** Associated Press, "Saudi Arabia's Faisal Orders 10% Oil Cutback," *Albany Democrat-Herald*, October 18, 1973, 1.

248 **Annual inflation** U.S. Bureau of Labor Statistics, "Consumer Price Index for All Urban Consumers: All Items in U.S. City Average," FRED, Federal Reserve Bank of St. Louis.

248 **After Iran's 1979 revolution** "Spot Crude Oil Price: West Texas Intermediate (WTI)," FRED, Federal Reserve Bank of St. Louis.

248 **Even with inflation** Organisation for Economic Co-operation and Development, "Consumer Opinion Surveys: Confidence Indicators: Composite Indicators: OECD Indicator for the United States," FRED, Federal Reserve Bank of St. Louis. A modest recession that began in late 1969 reduced consumer confidence from its lofty levels during most of the decade, but confidence had rebounded by 1972.

249 **The Republican Party's internal** Rick Perlstein, *Reaganland: America's Right Turn, 1976–1980* (New York: Simon & Schuster, 2020), 70.

249 **That same year** "Michigan Income Tax Limitation Amendment, Proposal C

(1976)," Ballotpedia website; Otis White, "Nobel Winner for Tax Plan," *Lansing State Journal,* October 15, 1976, 1; Otis White, "Proposals C&D," *Lansing State Journal,* October 17, 1976, 61.

249   **Reagan began to emphasize** Lou Cannon, *Governor Reagan: His Rise to Power* (New York: PublicAffairs, 2003), 157.

249   **A recession began** "Unemployment Rate and Recessions Since 1948," National Bureau of Economic Research website.

249   **Consumer confidence** University of Michigan, "University of Michigan: Consumer Sentiment," FRED, Federal Reserve Bank of St. Louis.

250   **"The notion"** Reis Thebault, "Long Lines, High Prices and Fistcuffs: The 1970s Gas Shortages Fueled Bedlam in America," *The Washington Post,* May 31, 2021.

251   **When the campaign began** Robert Lindsey, "Howard Jarvis, 83, Dies; Led Drive for Tax Limit," *The New York Times,* August 13, 1986; Perlstein, *Reaganland,* 236–38.

251   **"I'm as mad as hell"** Binyamin Appelbaum, *The Economists' Hour: False Prophets, Free Markets, and the Fracture of Society* (New York: Little, Brown, 2019), 107; Perlstein, *Reaganland,* 309.

251   **As in Michigan** United Press International, "Friedman Endorses Prop. 13," *Ukiah Daily Journal,* March 23, 1978, 2.

251   **This time, the measure passed** "California Proposition 13, Tax Limitations Initiative (June 1978)," Ballotpedia website.

251   **"refurbishing my estate"** Jeff Gerth, "A Power Broker's Many Roles," *The New York Times,* October 29, 1980, 89.

251   **He set up a lobbying** Sidney Blumenthal, *The Rise of the Counter-establishment: The Conservative Ascent to Political Power* (New York: Union Square Press, 1986); Sidney Blumenthal, "Defining 'Reaganomics,'" *The Boston Globe,* November 2, 1980, 10; John B. Judis, *The Paradox of American Democracy: Elites, Special Interests, and the Betrayal of Public Trust* (New York: Routledge, 2001); Jules Witcover, "The Lobbyist's Art: Charls Walker and the Washington Way to Influence," *The Washington Post,* March 16, 1975, 220; Mark Bloomfield (American Council for Capital Formation), interview with author, July 26, 2022.

252   **It passed** Appelbaum, *Economists' Hour,* 109; Perlstein, *Reaganland,* 260.

252   **A key advocate** Blumenthal, *Rise of the Counter-establishment,* 44, 168; Blumenthal, "Defining 'Reaganomics'"; Morton Kondracke and Fred Barnes, *Jack Kemp: The Bleeding-Heart Conservative Who Changed America* (New York: Sentinel, 2015); Perlstein, *Reaganland,* 287–90; Irwin Ross, "Jack Kemp Wants to Cut Your Taxes—a Lot," *Fortune,* April 10, 1978, Jack Kemp Papers, Manuscript Division, Library of Congress.

253   **Kemp dismissed** Ross, "Jack Kemp."

253   **Some conservatives** Irwin Ross, "Jack F. Kemp—The JFK of the 80s?," *Buffalo Evening News,* June 18, 1978, 41. By the late 1970s, Laffer had moved from the University of Chicago to the University of Southern California.

253   **Most experts found** Blumenthal, "Defining 'Reaganomics.'"

254   **"I really think"** Kondracke and Barnes, *Jack Kemp,* 88.

254 "Liberalism has not" Blumenthal, "Defining 'Reaganomics,'" 10.

254 "anti-women, anti-minority" Kondracke and Barnes, *Jack Kemp*, 46.

255 "If the Dow" Robert H. Bork, "The Danger of Great Nations," speech at the General Motors Economics Marketing Conference, November 1978, Robert H. Bork Papers, Manuscript Division, Library of Congress. The three widely-read conservative columns Bork mentioned were by George Will, James Kirkpatrick, and the team of Robert Evans and Rowland Novak.

256 Neither caricature Lou Cannon, *President Reagan: The Role of a Lifetime* (New York: PublicAffairs, 1991); Cannon, *Governor Reagan*.

257 "a calculating, imaginative mind" Martin Anderson, *Revolution: The Reagan Legacy* (Stanford, Calif.: Hoover Institution Press, 1988), xxvi.

257 "a warmly ruthless man" Cannon, *President Reagan*, 106–7.

257 "Would you laugh" Cannon, *President Reagan*, 92.

257 Reagan enjoyed Cannon, *Governor Reagan*, 123, 138–39; Kondracke and Barnes, *Jack Kemp*, 62.

257 But his supposed Lou Cannon, email correspondence with author, September 9, 2022 and March 20, 2023.

257 His favorite novel Blumenthal, *Rise of the Counter-establishment*, 223.

257 Some became close friends Blumenthal, *Rise of the Counter-establishment*, 55, 227–28.

258 Like his affluent friends Cannon, *President Reagan*, 68–69.

258 Boulware saw the issue Kim Phillips-Fein, *Invisible Hands: The Businessmen's Crusade Against the New Deal* (New York: W. W. Norton, 2009), 87–114.

258 As part of Cannon, *President Reagan*, 471.

258 "Reagan's appeal" Blumenthal, "Defining 'Reaganomics,'" 49.

258 "Well, I think" Ronald Reagan, "A Time for Choosing," televised address on behalf of Barry Goldwater, October 27, 1964.

259 In the summer of 1979 Anderson, *Revolution*, 113–21.

259 "bracket creep" Kondracke and Barnes, *Jack Kemp*, 48.

259 As Alan Greenspan Blumenthal, "Defining 'Reaganomics.'"

260 Yet Reagan believed Anderson, *Revolution*, 121.

260 "The Business Roundtable" Blumenthal, "Defining 'Reaganomics,'" 48; see also Peter Dworkin, "What Big Business Thinks of Him," *Fortune*, May 19, 1980; Donald D. Holt, "What He'd Be Like as President," *Fortune*, May 19, 1980.

260 "He was able to" Bloomfield, interview.

260 "I know we can" Ronald Reagan, "Remarks at the International Business Council in Chicago," September 9, 1980, American Presidency Project website.

261 "The events of the last" Blumenthal, *Rise of the Counter-establishment*, 46.

261 During Reagan's 1980 campaign Tax Policy Task Force, "Summary of Recommendations," October 27, 1980, Charls E. Walker Papers, Hoover Institution Library and Archives, Stanford University.

261 **Walker insisted** Gerth, "Power Broker's Many Roles," 89, 94.

262 **"The whole time"** Steve Lohr, "Antitrust: Big Business Breathes Easier," *The New York Times,* February 15, 1981, 179.

263 **To ensure Reagan** Thomas C. Hayes, "The Reagan Team's Chief Recruiter," *The New York Times,* June 30, 1981, D1; documents in Ronald Reagan Presidential Library and Museum, Simi Valley, Calif.

264 **"to agree completely"** Anderson, *Revolution,* 200.

264 **Among the most dynamic** Associated Press, "Colorado Campaign News Briefs," *Greeley Daily Tribune,* October 26, 1976, 11; Associated Press, "State House Results," *Fort Collins Coloradoan,* November 4, 1976, 7; Anne Burford, *Are You Tough Enough?* (New York: McGraw-Hill, 1986); Joanne Omang, "Denver Lawyer Reagan's Choice to Head EPA," *The Washington Post,* February 21, 1981; Joanne Omang, "New EPA Head Sought Job as Second Toughest in Town," *The Washington Post,* June 23, 1981; United Press International, "Election Bitter Demos Defeat," *Greeley Daily Tribune,* December 28, 1976, 9.

265 **"Whether you contact"** Omang, "Denver Lawyer."

265 **Schroeder argued** Associated Press, "Campaign Briefs," *Greeley Daily Tribune,* October 28, 1976, 15.

265 **"The government that"** Anne Gorsuch, interview by Lee Bahrych, Colorado Oral History Library, June 14, 1996.

265 **"She did that almost"** Omang, "Denver Lawyer."

265 **At the end** United Press International, "Freshmen Solons Get High Marks," *Greeley Daily Tribune,* June 3, 1977, 10.

267 **In the decade before** Caroline E. Mayer, "U.S. Relaxing Enforcement of Regulations," *The Washington Post,* November 15, 1981; see also Joanne Omang, "Internal Rifts, Huge Staff Cut Hint EPA Retreat on Programs," *The Washington Post,* September 30, 1981.

267 **In one Senate hearing** Tom Raum for the Associated Press, "Just the Gist of 1,500 Speeches," *The Marshall News Messenger,* May 4, 1982, 4.

267 **The Interior Department** Mayer, "U.S. Relaxing Enforcement."

268 **"Bigness in business"** Appelbaum, *Economists' Hour,* 151.

268 **His department ended** Matt Stoller, *Goliath: The 100-Year War Between Monopoly Power and Democracy* (New York: Simon & Schuster, 2019), 371–89.

268 **"followed directly"** Douglas H. Ginsburg, "Originalism and Economic Analysis: Two Case Studies of Consistency and Coherence in Supreme Court Decision Making," *Harvard Journal of Law and Public Policy* 33 (2010): 223.

268 **Over the course** "US Mergers & Acquisitions," data provided to author by Refinitiv Financial Solutions, October 14, 2022.

269 **"Judges make law"** Robert H. Bork, "Will Capitalism Survive?," *Yale Alumni Magazine and Journal,* April 1978, 16.

269 **"We must know"** Memo by Roger Clegg, Ronald Reagan Presidential Library and Museum.

269 **No previous president** Russell Wheeler (Brookings Institution), data pro-

vided to author, October 4, 2022. Reagan was able to appoint so many judges partly because of a 1984 law expanding the size of the judiciary.

270 **In the so-called** Tom Mathews"A Man for the Middle," *Newsweek* 86, 22. The Saturday Night Massacre occurred during the same chaotic weekend in October 1973 that Saudi Arabia cut off oil shipments to the United States.

270 **The second opening** Documents in Ronald Reagan Presidential Library and Museum.

270 **"a jurisprudence of original intent"** Edwin Meese, address to the American Bar Association, July 9, 1985.

271 **"Robert Bork has been"** Document in Ronald Reagan Presidential Library and Museum.

271 **Another memo** "Supreme Court—Robert Bork—Copy of Candidate Datebook, Calvahouse, Arthur Files, p. 3, Ronald Reagan Presidential Library and Museum.

271 **"He is 59 years old"** Document in Ronald Reagan Presidential Library and Museum.

271 **"He scares me"** "Antonin Scalia," *Almanac of the Federal Judiciary*, vol. 2 (Chicago: LawLetters, 1985), 15.

271 **When a third Supreme Court** Edward Walsh, "In the End, Bork Himself Was His Own Worst Enemy," *The Washington Post*, October 24, 1987.

272 **"If you nominate him"** Paul Simon, *Advice and Consent: Clarence Thomas, Robert Bork, and the Intriguing History of the Supreme Court's Nomination Battles* (Bethesda, Md.: National Press Books, 1992), 68; see also Walsh, "Bork Himself."

272 **Her EPA tenure** Burford, *Are You Tough Enough?*, 218.

272 **"You didn't do anything"** Adam Liptak, Peter Baker, Nicholas Fandos, and Julie Turkewitz, "In Fall of Gorsuch's Mother, a Painful Lesson in Politicking," *The New York Times*, February 4, 2017.

273 **"Ronald Reagan changed"** "Twisted Words?," *Los Angeles Times*, January 25, 2008, 24.

273 **"On nearly all issues"** Cannon, *President Reagan*, 153.

274 **"I'd rather get 80 percent"** Peter Baker and Susan Glasser, *The Man Who Ran Washington: The Life and Times of James A. Baker III* (New York: Anchor Books, 2020), 224.

274 **The top marginal income tax rate** "Historical Highest Marginal Income Tax Rates," Tax Policy Center website, February 9, 2022.

274 **In 1980** Gabriel Zucman, data provided to author, October 16, 2022.

274 **After endorsing Reagan** William A. Niskanen, *Reaganomics: An Insider's Account of the Policies and the People* (New York: Oxford University Press, 1988), 191.

274 **The share of total compensation** "Compensation of Employees by Industry," U.S. Bureau of Economic Analysis website, July 31, 2021.

275 **These intellectuals** Gerstle, *Rise and Fall of the Neoliberal Order*, 73–149.

276 **Democrats also came** J. Bradford DeLong, *Slouching Towards Utopia: An Economic History of the Twentieth Century* (New York: Basic Books, 2022), 447–49.

276 **In his 1992 presidential campaign** Ron Goldwyn, "A Biting Attack," *Philadelphia Daily News,* April 17, 1992, 7.

277 **"Where are all"** Michael J. Sandel, *Democracy's Discontent: A New Edition for our Perilous Times* (Cambridge, Mass.: The Belknap Press, 2022), 291.

278 **One example** Rothery Storage & Van Co., et al., Appellants v. Atlas Van Lines, Inc., 792 F.2d 210 (D.C. Cir. 1986).

279 **In the White House memo** Document in Ronald Reagan Presidential Library and Museum.

279 **In 1982** Steven M. Teles, *The Rise of the Conservative Legal Movement: The Battle for Control of the Law* (Princeton, N.J.: Princeton University Press, 2008), 137–42.

279 **"The court responds"** Associated Press, "US Judge Attacks High Court 'Trend,'" *Fort Worth Star-Telegram,* April 25, 1982, 41.

279 **"the stigma associated"** Amanda Hollis-Brusky, *Ideas with Consequences: The Federalist Society and the Conservative Counterrevolution* (New York: Oxford University Press, 2015), 159.

280 **By 2020** Peggy Quince and Lauren Rikleen, "Federalist Society's Influence on Courts is Bad for Democracy," *Bloomberg Law,* November 8, 2022.

281 **"a healthy, vigorous"** Ronald Reagan, "Inaugural Address," January 20, 1981, American Presidency Project.

281 **"We are creating"** Ronald Reagan, "Inaugural Address," January 21, 1985, American Presidency Project.

282 **"It's morning again"** "The Living Room Candidate: Presidential Campaign Commercials, 1952–2020; 1984 Reagan vs. Mondale," Museum of the Moving Image website.

282 **"the greatest economic expansion"** Anderson, *Revolution,* 74.

282 **Over the past century** David Leonhardt, "Why Are Republican Presidents So Bad for the Economy?," *The New York Times,* February 2, 2021. Starting a president's clock a year or two into his term, to avoid blaming him for the problems he inherited, and extending it until a year or two after his term would not change these conclusions.

283 **Starting in the 1980s** Thomas Piketty, Emmanuel Saez, and Gabriel Zucman, "Distributional National Accounts: Methods and Estimates for the United States," *The Quarterly Journal of Economics* 133, no. 2 (2018): 553–609, updated in Thomas Blanchet, Emmanuel Saez, and Gabriel Zucman, "Real-Time Inequality" (working paper 30229, National Bureau of Economic Research, November 2022); Gabriel Zucman, data provided to author, January 9, 2023.

283 **This can be seen** U.S. Bureau of Economic Analysis, "Real Median Household Income by State, Annual," FRED, Federal Reserve Bank of St. Louis; U.S. Bureau of Labor Statistics, "Average Hourly Earnings of Production and Nonsupervisory Employees, Total Private," FRED, Federal Reserve Bank of St. Louis; Piketty, Saez, and Zucman, "Distributional National Accounts"; Zucman, data; Raj Chetty, David Grusky, Maximilian Hell, Nathaniel Hendren, Robert Manduca, and Jimmy Narang, "The Fading American Dream: Trends in Absolute Income Mobility Since 1940," *Science* 356, no. 6336 (April 24, 2017): 398–406.

283 **Several years ago** David Leonhardt, "Our Broken Economy, in One Simple Chart," *The New York Times,* August 7, 2017.

284 **Some of the arguments** Phil Gramm, Robert Ekelund, and John Early, *The Myth of American Inequality: How Government Biases Policy Debate* (Lanham, Md.: Rowman & Littlefield, 2022).

284 **Nor does data** "Life Expectancy at Birth, Total (Years)," World Bank website.

284 **The post-1980** DeLong, *Slouching Towards Utopia,* 445–47.

285 **Life Expectancy by Education [chart]** Anne Case and Angus Deaton, *Deaths of Despair and the Future of Capitalism* (Princeton, N.J.: Princeton University Press, 2020); Case and Deaton, data provided to author, April 1, 2023.

286 **One of the ways** Milton Friedman and Rose Friedman, *Free to Choose: A Personal Statement* (New York: Avon Books, 1979), 224.

286 **But with the market power** David Leonhardt, "The Charts That Show How Big Business Is Winning," *The New York Times,* June 17, 2018; David Leonhardt, "Big Business Is Too Big, *The New York Times,* April 2, 2018.

286 **The merger** Zack Cooper and Martin Gaynor, "Addressing Hospital Concentration and Rising Consolidation in the United States," 1% Steps for Health Care Reform website.

286 **Americans have fewer choices** David Leonhardt, "Big Business Is Overcharging You $5,000 a Year," *The New York Times,* November 10, 2019.

286 **Rising corporate concentration** Alan B. Krueger and Eric Posner, "Corporate America Is Suppressing Wages for Many Workers," *The New York Times,* February 28, 2018.

287 **These ideas led** Zachary D. Carter, *The Price of Peace: Money, Democracy, and the Life of John Maynard Keynes* (New York: Random House, 2020), 493–504; Justin R. Pierce and Peter K. Schott, "The Surprisingly Swift Decline of US Manufacturing Employment," *The American Economic Review* 106, no. 7 (2016): 1632–62.

287 **"the China shock"** David H. Autor, David Dorn, and Gordon H. Hanson, "The China Shock: Learning from Labor-Market Adjustment to Large Changes in Trade," *Annual Review of Economics* 8 (2016): 205–40; David Autor, David Dorn, Gordon Hanson, and Kaveh Majlesi, "Importing Political Polarization? The Electoral Consequences of Rising Trade Exposure," *The American Economic Review* 110, no. 10 (2020): 3139–83.

287 **But Chinese society** John J. Mearsheimer, "The Inevitable Rivalry: America, China, and the Tragedy of Great-Power Politics," *Foreign Affairs,* October 19, 2021.

288 **By the early 2020s** U.S. Bureau of Economic Analysis, "Shares of Gross Domestic Income: Corporate Profits with Inventory Valuation and Capital Consumption Adjustments, Domestic Industries; Profits After Tax with Inventory Valuation and Capital Consumption Adjustments," FRED, Federal Reserve Bank of St. Louis.

288 **For a typical family** Estimate based on data from U.S. Bureau of Economic Analysis, "Gross Domestic Product, Third Quarter Data 2022 (Advance Estimate)," October 27, 2022, FRED, Federal Reserve Bank of St. Louis; "U.S.

Census Bureau, Total Households," November 21, 2022, FRED, Federal Reserve Bank of St. Louis.

288 **"The doctrine of non-interference"** Blumenthal, *Rise of the Counter-establishment,* 86.

Chapter 9: This Little Village Called America

290 **But when Senate hearings** U.S. Senate, *Hearings Before the Subcommittee on Immigration and Naturalization of the Committee on the Judiciary: First Session on S.500 to Amend the Immigration and Nationality Act* (Washington, D.C.: U.S. Government Printing Office, 1965).

291 **To reciprocate** John A. Farrell, *Ted Kennedy: A Life* (New York: Penguin Press, 2022), 123–25; Meg Greenfield, "The Senior Senator Kennedy," *The Reporter* 35, no. 10 (December 15, 1966): 22.

291 **"little noticed"** Dan Cordtz, "Immigration Reform," *The Wall Street Journal,* October 4, 1965, 16.

291 **"It is fashionable"** Jia Lynn Yang, *One Mighty and Irresistible Tide: The Epic Struggle over American Immigration, 1924–1965* (New York: W. W. Norton, 2020), 180.

291 **The annual quota** "Annual U.S. Immigration Quota Announced To-Day," *Victoria Daily Times,* July 28, 1924, 16.

291 **The law virtually banned** Yang, *Tide,* 162.

292 **"gratuitous condescension"** "Amending the Immigration and Nationality Act," *Congressional Record,* August 25, 1965, 21755.

292 **That same year** Fredrik Logevall, *JFK: Coming of Age in the American Century, 1917–1956* (New York: Random House, 2020); Stephen Thomas Wagner, "The Lingering Death of the National Origins Quota System: A Political History of United States Immigration Policy, 1952–1965," (dissertation, Harvard University, 1986); Yang, *Tide.*

292 **The book** John F. Kennedy, *A Nation of Immigrants* (New York: Harper Perennial, 1964); Wagner, "Lingering Death." Shortly after publication, Myer Feldman, Kennedy's aide, complained to the ADL that the book's cover did not include the word "Senator" before Kennedy's name. An ADL staff member replied: "We have every confidence that 'A Nation of Immigrants' is going to be a smashing success and will endure for years which is the reason why we didn't use the Senator's title. After all it could change."

293 **Even before** *Civil Rights Act of 1964, Title VI, U.S. Code* 42 (1964), §2000d. The wording of the 1964 Civil Rights Act echoed the wording of the 1941 executive order that A. Philip Randolph pushed Roosevelt to sign. That order banned wartime factories from discriminating based on "race, creed, color, or national origin."

293 **The bill** Wagner, "Lingering Death"; Yang, *Tide.*

294 **"Out of deference"** U.S. Senate, *Hearings,* 1.

294 **"Our cities"** U.S. Senate, *Hearings,* 1.

295 **"The charges"** U.S. Senate, *Hearings,* 3.

295 **"The numbers"** U.S. Senate, *Hearings,* 19.

295 **"makes no substantial change"** U.S. Senate, *Hearings,* 29.

295 **Hugh Scott** U.S. Senate, *Hearings,* 72.

295 **"We are actually"** U.S. Senate, *Hearings,* 72.

295 **"only three-one-hundredths"** U.S. Senate, *Hearings,* 164.

295 **"Do we appreciably"** "Amending the Immigration and Nationality Act."

296 **"There are lots"** U.S. Senate, *Hearings,* 233.

296 **"complete protection"** U.S. Senate, *Hearings,* 92.

296 **"one of the most"** Robert William Fogel, *Without Consent or Contract: The Rise and Fall of American Slavery* (New York: W. W. Norton, 1989), 356.

297 **"substantial negative effects"** Claudia Goldin, "The Political Economy of Immigration Restriction in the United States, 1890 to 1921" (working paper 4345, National Bureau of Economic Research, April 1993), 2.

297 **As the economists** Peter H. Lindert and Jeffrey G. Williamson, *Unequal Gains: American Growth and Inequality Since 1700* (Princeton, N.J.: Princeton University Press, 2016).

297 **One study** Otis Graham, Jr., *Unguarded Gates: A History of America's Immigration Crisis* (Lanham, Md.: Rowman & Littlefield, 2004), 60.

297 **"Immigration restriction"** Irving Bernstein, *The Lean Years: A History of the American Worker, 1920–1933* (Chicago: Haymarket Books, 2010), 52.

297 **"the daring"** Graham, *Unguarded Gates,* 16.

297 **"cast down your bucket"** Booker T. Washington, "Civil Rights Act of 1964: A Long Struggle for Freedom," speech at the Atlanta Exposition, September 18, 1895, Library of Congress website.

298 **"every hour sees"** Frederick Douglass, *My Bondage and My Freedom* (New York: Miller, Orton & Mulligan), 1855.

298 **"a sinister blow"** Yang, *Tide,* 171.

298 **"Excessive immigration"** Graham, *Unguarded Gates,* 47.

298 **During the debate** Yang, *Tide,* 40.

299 **"Everybody benefitted"** Milton Friedman, "What Is America," speech at the University of Chicago, October 3, 1977.

299 **A top lobbyist** Wagner, "Lingering Death"; Yang, *Tide,* 239–40.

299 **The poll** Louis Harris, "The Harris Survey: U.S. Public Is Strongly Opposed to Easing of Immigration Laws, *The Washington Post,* May 31, 1965.

299 **Harris's poll** Wagner, "Lingering Death," 421–23.

300 **Katzenbach, the attorney general** United Press International, "US Immigration Bill Defended by Katzenbach" *The News,* June 3, 1965, 13.

300 **"This is much better"** Wagner, "Lingering Death," 424.

301 **For the location** Associated Press, "President 'Opens Doors' to All Cuban Refugees," *The Tampa Tribune,* October 4, 1965, 25; Robert B. Semple, "U.S. to Admit Cubans Castro Frees," *The New York Times,* October 4, 1965, 1; "The White House President Lyndon B. Johnson Daily Diary," October 3, 1965.

301 **"This bill"** Lyndon B. Johnson, "Remarks at the Signing of the Immigration Bill, Liberty Island, New York," October 3, 1965.

302 **During the year** "Persons Obtaining Lawful Permanent Resident Status: Fiscal Years 1820 to 2021," DHS Office of Immigration Statistics; Julia Gelatt

(Migration Policy Institute), email correspondence with author, September 6, 2022.

302 **When Ervin spoke** U.S. Senate, *Hearings,* 272.

303 **He once sued** "Finger Hurt, Rep. Feighan Asks $50,000," *The Washington Post,* January 17, 1953, 9.

303 **He also tried** Robert Allen and Paul Scott, "President Concerned over Burton's Visa," *The Lima News,* February 17, 1964, 14.

303 **Once he recognized** Tom Gjelten, *A Nation of Nations: A Great American Immigration Story* (New York: Simon & Schuster, 2015), 105; Wagner, "Lingering Death," 393; David K. Willis, "Immigration Battle Shapes in Congress," *The Christian Science Monitor,* May 29, 1965, 1; Yang, *Tide,* 250.

303 **The biggest loophole** Yang, *Tide,* 265.

304 **Feighan focused on** Willis, "Immigration Battle."

304 **When Johnson administration** House of Representatives, *Hearings Before Subcommittee No. 1 of the Committee on the Judiciary* (Washington, D.C.: U.S. Government Printing Office, 1964), 419–52.

304 **Everybody—skilled workers** Willis, "Immigration Battle," 4.

304 **They insisted** Robert S. Allen and Paul Scott, "Feighan Committee Upsetting Plans to End Immigration Quotas," *Idaho Daily Statesman,* February 25, 1965, 4; Adam Clymer, "Immigration Action Seen," *Baltimore Sun,* July 11, 1965, 6; Robert McClory, "Your Congressman," *Marengo Republican-News,* July 8, 1965, 19; Cabell Philips, "House Judiciary Panel Expected to Reach Accord on Immigration Bill," *The New York Times,* June 30, 1965, 10.

304 **"The extent of the change"** John Corry, "Immigration Shows an Ethnic Change," *The New York Times,* March 18, 1968, 1.

304 **It has since** Julia Gelatt (Migration Policy Institute), email correspondence with author, November 22, 2022.

305 **The 1965 law** Margaret Sands Orchowski, *The Law That Changed the Face of America: The Immigration and Nationality Act of 1965* (Lanham, Md.: Rowman & Littlefield, 2015), vii.

305 **"noble, revolutionary"** Theodore H. White, *America in Search of Itself: The Making of the President, 1956–1980* (New York: Harper & Row, 1982), 363.

306 **"The base narrative"** Jay Caspian Kang, "A Farewell to Readers," *The New York Times,* September 1, 2022.

306 **"Immigration is central"** Barbara Jordan, speech at United We Stand America Conference, Dallas, Tex., 1995.

307 **"My father"** Mary Antin, *The Promised Land* (Boston: Houghton Mifflin, 1912), 197.

307 **For one thing** Ran Abramitzky and Leah Boustan, *Streets of Gold: America's Untold Story of Immigrant Success* (New York: PublicAffairs, 2022); Ran Abramitzky, Leah Boustan, Elisa Jácome, and Santiago Pérez, "Intergenerational Mobility of Immigrants in the United States over Two Centuries," *American Economic Review* 111, no. 2 (February 2021): 580–608.

307 **The Antins remained mired** "The Immigrant," *The New York Times,*

April 14, 1912, 28; Mary Antin, "How I Wrote 'The Promised Land,'" *The New York Times,* June 30, 1912, 23; Pamela S. Nadell, "Mary Antin," *The Shalvi/Hyman Encyclopedia of Jewish Women,* Jewish Women's Archive website, June 23, 2021; documents on Ancestry.com website.

308 **A journalist** Yang, *Tide,* 8–9.

308 **Immigrants from Scandinavia** Abramitzky et al., "Intergenerational Mobility," figures 1A–C.

309 **"They don't look"** Meg Greenfield, "The Melting Pot of Frances E. Walter," *The Reporter* 25, no. 7 (October 26, 1961): 25.

309 **Like Italian families** Abramitzky et al., "Intergenerational Mobility," figures 1A–C.

310 **One of the reasons** Raj Chetty (Harvard University), interview with author.

310 **Many recent immigrants** George J. Borjas, *We Wanted Workers: Unraveling the Immigration Narrative* (New York: W. W. Norton & Company, 2016), 88–109.

311 **By some measures** Abramitzky and Boustan, *Streets of Gold,* 126.

311 **"human capital"** Abramitzky and Boustan, *Streets of Gold;* Chetty, interview.

312 **In Houston** Stephen L. Klineberg, *Prophetic City: Houston on the Cusp of a Changing America* (New York: Avid Reader Press), 2020.

312 **As a result** Henry Gass, "No Zoning: Is Houston an Affordable Housing Model or Morass?," *The Christian Science Monitor,* November 17, 2022.

312 **"New York is not"** Melody Mei-Ching Lo Shu, interview by Susan Siyu Xie, March 30, 2013, p. 25, Houston Asian American Archive, Rice University.

313 **In 1960** Klineberg, *Prophetic City,* 189–90.

313 **In 2021** "Hispanic or Latino Origin by Race," American Community Survey, 2021, Table B03002.

313 **According to the tax returns** John Friedman (Brown University), email correspondence with author, October 30, 2022.

313 **"The American Dream"** Abramitzky and Boustan, *Streets of Gold,* 10–11.

315 **Comparing Income Inequality and Foreign-born Share of Population** [chart] U.S. Census Bureau, "U.S. Immigrant Population and Share over Time, 1850–Present," Migration Policy Institute; World Inequality Database.

315 **If competition** "Historical Income Tables: Households," U.S. Census Bureau website, August 18, 2022, table H-8.

316 **The table is dominated** National Academies of Sciences, Engineering, and Medicine, *The Economic and Fiscal Consequences of Immigration,* ed. Francine D. Blau and Christopher Mackie (Washington, D.C.: National Academies Press, 2017), 242–43.

316 **"to adapt jobs"** Sumner Slichter, "The Worker in the Modern Economic Society," *Journal of Political Economy* 34, no. 1 (February 1926): 105.

316 **But Christopher Jencks** Christopher Jencks, "Who Should Get In?," *The New York Review of Books,* November 29, 2001, and December 20, 2001.

317 **In medicine** "Practicing Medicine in the U.S. as an International Medical Graduate," American Medical Association website.

318 **Two giants** George Borjas, "The Wage Impact of the *Marielitos*," *Industrial and Labor Relations Review* 70, no. 5 (October 2017): 1077–110;

David Card, "The impact of the Mariel boatlift on the Miami labor market," *Industrial and Labor Relations Review* 43, no. 2 (January 1990): 245–57; National Academies, *Economic and Fiscal Consequences,* 223.

319 **In the 1990s** Jonathan Haidt, *The Righteous Mind: Why Good People Are Divided by Politics and Religion* (New York: Pantheon Books, 2012).

319 **"I had flown"** Haidt, *Righteous Mind,* 25.

320 **Other researchers** Benjamin Enke, "Moral Values and Voting," *Journal of Political Economy* 128, no. 10 (2020): 3679–729.

321 **The same outlook** "Key Elements of the U.S. Tax System: How Large Are Individual Income Tax Incentives for Charitable Giving?," Tax Policy Center Briefing Book, table 2.

321 **Other questions** "Nationalism, Cosmopolitism and the Common Good," *Change Your Mind,* episode 5, Human.nl website, September 4, 2018.

322 **Surveys show** Enke, "Moral Values and Voting."

322 **Growing up** Edward J. Boyer, "Ex-Rep. Barbara Jordan, Eloquent Orator, Dies at 59," *Los Angeles Times,* January 18, 1996, VCA1; Francis X. Clines, "Barbara Jordan Dies at 59; Her Voice Stirred the Nation," *The New York Times,* January 18, 1996, A1; Mary Beth Rogers, *Barbara Jordan: American Hero* (New York: Bantam Books, 1998).

322 **"The world had decided"** Rogers, *Barbara Jordan,* 3–4.

323 **"a warm cocoon of love"** Rogers, *Barbara Jordan,* 35.

323 **Jordan always said** Rogers, *Barbara Jordan,* 56.

323 **Randolph cast** A. Philip Randolph, "The Call to Negro America to March on Washington for Jobs and Equal Protection in National Defense," *Black Worker* 14 (May 1941).

323 **During the 1965** "Participants, some carrying American flags, marching in the civil rights march from Selma to Montgomery, Alabama in 1965," 1965, photograph, Library of Congress; "Composite of two photographs: lower photograph shows the Selma-Montgomery civil rights march, with Dr. Martin Luther King, Jr. (front/center), Coretta Scott King (behind Dr. King), and John Lewis (right of Mrs. King); upper photograph shows five white segregationists, two with Confederate flags," 1965, photograph, Library of Congress.

324 **"And so even though"** Martin Luther King, Jr., speech at the March on Washington, Washington, D.C., August 28, 1963.

324 **"The real bottom line"** Barbara Jordan, "Speaking Up," *Los Angeles Times,* December 15, 1993, VYB11.

324 **In the Texas Legislature** John Ford, "Voting Rights," *Austin American-Statesman,* July 16, 1975, 1; Margaret Gentry, "Discrimination at Polls Still Problem," *The Corpus Christi Caller,* April 13, 1975, 54.

324 **"My faith in the Constitution"** Rogers, *Barbara Jordan,* x.

325 **Jordan became known** Philip C. Bobbitt, "Barbara Jordan: Constitutional Conscience," *Texas Journal of Women and the Law* 5 (1995–96): 171.

326 **The commission's best hope** Susan Martin (Georgetown University), interview with author, December 1, 2022.

326 **In Jordan's view** Martin, interview.

326 **"The history of American"** Jordan, speech at United We Stand America Conference.

326 **Borrowing Kennedy's phrase** David Broder, "Immigration: 'Time for Reason and Logic,'" *The Washington Post,* October 4, 1994, A17.

327 **"That word earned"** Jordan, speech at United We Stand America Conference.

327 **"Immigration is not"** Jordan, speech at United We Stand America Conference.

327 **To create** Barbara Jordan, "Documenting Workers," *The Washington Post,* October 19, 1994, A22; Barbara Jordan, "The Americanization Ideal," *The New York Times,* September 11, 1995, A15; Roberto Suro, "New Voice in Immigration Debate," *The Washington Post,* April 13, 1994, A15; "The Jordan Immigration Report," *The Washington Post,* October 6, 1994.

327 **Between 1990 and 1995** Jeffrey Passel and D'Vera Cohn, "U.S. Unauthorized Immigrant Total Dips to Lowest Level in a Decade," Pew Research Center website, November 27, 2018.

327 **Jordan believed** Jordan, speech at United We Stand America Conference.

327 **"Any nation worth"** Broder, "Immigration."

328 **In Houston** IPUMS USA data.

329 **"The commission finds"** Jordan, speech at United We Stand America Conference.

329 **On net, the commission** Bill McAllister, "Commission to Propose Lowering Number of Immigrants Let into U.S.," *The Washington Post,* June 6, 1995, A4; Seth Mydans, "Narrowing the U.S. Immigration Gate," *The New York Times,* September 24, 1995, 18; "How Many Legal Immigrants?," *The Washington Post,* June 12, 1995, A18; "Immigrants with Skills," *The Washington Post,* September 16, 1995, A16.

329 **Media coverage** Robert Pear, "Change of Policy on U.S. Immigrants Is Urged by Panel," *The New York Times,* June 5, 1995, A1; Roberto Suro, "Fortress America? Suddenly, the Golden Door Is Closing," *The Washington Post,* November 6, 1994, C3.

329 **After their meeting** Joe Davidson, "Clinton Endorses Proposal for Cuts in Immigration," *The Wall Street Journal,* June 8, 1995, B8; John F. Harris and Barbara Vobejda, "Clinton Backs Call to Reduce Immigration," *The Washington Post,* June 8, 1995, A1; Robert Pear, "Clinton Embraces a Proposal to Cut Immigration by a Third," *The New York Times,* June 8, 1995, B10.

330 **Clinton claimed** Eric Schmitt, "Milestones and Missteps on Immigration," *The New York Times,* October 26, 1996, 1.

330 **A few quoted her** Paul Donnelly, "Immigration: Families First," *The Washington Post,* July 28, 1998, A18.

330 **Many liberals** Muzaffar Chisti, Sarah Pierce, and Jessica Bolter, "The Obama Record on Deportations: Deporter in Chief or Not?," Migration Policy Institute, January 26, 2017.

331 **"an employer undercuts"** Barack Obama, speech at the Democratic National Convention, Denver, Colo., August 28, 2008.

331 **"There is a reason"** Nicole Narea, "Bernie Sanders's Evolution on Immigration, Explained," *Vox,* February 25, 2020.

331 **But by the time Sanders** "Bernie Sanders, Senator from Vermont," *The New York Times,* January 13, 2020; Megan Apper, "Bernie Sanders on Immigration in 2007 Video: This is a Bad Bill for American Workers," *BuzzFeed News,* February 19, 2016; Sam Frizell, "Why Conservatives Praise Bernie Sanders on Immigration," *Time,* January 7, 2016.

331 **The share of Americans** "Immigration," Gallup News website; see also William Branigan, "High-Tech Firms Oppose Major Immigration Cuts," *The Washington Post,* September 13, 1995, A4; William Branigan, "Unusual Alliance Transformed Immigration Debate," *The Washington Post,* March 23, 1996, A8. The only exception occurred in 2020 and 2021, when Americans reacted to Trump's harsh anti-immigrant rhetoric and policies by moving their own views in the other direction. This is an example of the thermostatic theory of politics, as developed by Christopher Wlezien of the University of Texas, in which public opinion acts as a thermostat and moves in the opposite direction as the current president's views.

332 **The new Democratic** Amory Gethin, Clara Martínez-Toledano, and Thomas Piketty, "Brahmin Left Versus Merchant Right: Changing Political Cleavages in 21 Western Democracies, 1948–2020," *The Quarterly Journal of Economics* 137, no. 1 (February 2022): 1–48.

333 **Most people** *The New York Times*/Siena College National Survey, September 6–14, 2022.

333 **A rich stream** Alberto Alesina and Marco Tabellini, "The Political Effects of Immigration: Culture or Economics?" (working paper 30079, National Bureau of Economic Research, May 2022); see also Lee Drutman, "How Race and Identity Became the Central Dividing Line in American Politics," *Vox,* August 30, 2016.

334 **"For those who believe"** Yang, *Tide,* 267.

335 **Polls showed** *The New York Times*/Siena College National Survey.

335 **"Immigration is"** Jonathan Haidt (New York University), email correspondence with author, November 1, 2022.

335 **Several economists** Alesina and Tabellini, "Political Effects of Immigration"; Alberto Alesina, Armando Miano, and Stefanie Stantcheva, "Immigration and Redistribution," *Review of Economic Studies* (2022): 1–39.

335 **About one of every** Audrey Singer, "Immigrant Workers in the U.S. Labor Force," Brookings Report, March 15, 2012.

337 **Because of this immutable fact** Matthew Yglesias, *One Billion Americans: The Case for Thinking Bigger* (New York: Portfolio, 2020).

337 **Some affluent countries** "International Migrants by Country of Destination, 1960–2020," Migration Policy Institute.

Chapter 10: Whence Shall Come Our Experts?

340 **They bought a house** James Woodress, *Willa Cather: A Literary Life* (Lincoln: University of Nebraska Press, 1987); E. K. Brown, *Willa Cather: A Critical Biography* (Lincoln: University of Nebraska Press, 1953).

340 **For Cather's high school** Brown, *Willa Cather,* 43

340 **"If we bar our novices"** Woodress, *Willa Cather,* 62.

340 **Red Cloud's weekly newspaper** Woodress, *Willa Cather,* 60.

341 **The United States** Claudia Goldin and Lawrence F. Katz, *The Race Between Education and Technology* (Cambridge, Mass.: Belknap Press of Harvard University Press, 2008), 12, 24.

341 **Benjamin Rush** Goldin and Katz, *Race,* 135–36.

341 **"the preservation of freedom"** Thomas Jefferson to George Wythe, August 13, 1786, Monticello website.

341 **"spreading the opportunities"** Massachusetts Constitution, chapter V, section II.

341 **In the 1830s** Goldin and Katz, *Race,* 141–47.

341 **Mann's political party** Claudia Goldin and Lawrence F. Katz, "Why the United States Led in Education: Lessons from Secondary School Expansion, 1910 to 1940," revised version of a presentation at a Rochester Conference in honor of Stanley Engerman, December 2008, 1.

341 **The push** Goldin and Katz, *Race,* 194–284.

341 **The places** Goldin and Katz, *Race,* 208–45.

342 **Companies like** Goldin and Katz, *Race,* 176–77.

343 **In the 1910s** Claudia Goldin and Lawrence F. Katz, "Human Capital and Social Capital: The Rise of Secondary Schooling in America, 1910 to 1940" (working paper 6439, National Bureau of Economic Research, March 1998), 1.

343 **"the fervor of a religion"** Robert S. Lynd and Helen Merrell Lynd, *Middletown: A Study in Modern American Culture* (San Diego, Calif.: Harvest Book, 1929), 187.

343 **By the start** Goldin and Katz, *Race,* 196.

344 **As the war wound down** Goldin and Katz, *Race,* 248–51.

344 **Nearly one out of** Organisation for Economic Co-operation and Development, "Education at a Glance 2010: OECD Indicators," 2010, p. 36, table A1.3a.

345 **By the mid-1970s** "National Income and Product Accounts," tables 1.1.5 and 3.16.

345 **The countries with the fastest-growing** Amanda Ripley, *The Smartest Kids in the World and How They Got That Way* (New York: Simon & Schuster, 2013); "GDP per Capita, 1962 to 2018," Our World in Data website.

346 **In 2021, the** Anne Case and Angus Deaton, *Deaths of Despair and the Future of Capitalism* (Princeton, N.J.: Princeton University Press, 2020); Case and Deaton, data provided to author, December 23, 2022.

346 **Many other measures** David Leonhardt and Stuart A. Thompson, "How Working-Class Life Is Killing Americans, in Charts," *The New York Times,* March 6, 2020.

346 **"the surest path"** Bill Gates, Twitter, May 16, 2019.

347 **The research found** Jonathan Smith, Joshua Goodman, and Michael Hurwitz, "The Economic Impact of Access to Public Four-Year Colleges" (working paper 27177, National Bureau of Economic Research, May 2020); Seth D. Zimmerman, "The Returns of College Admission for Academically Marginal Students, *Journal of Labor Economics* 32, no. 4 (October 2014): 711–54.

347 **Carlos Escanilla** David Leonhardt, "College for the Masses," *The New York Times,* April 24, 2015.

348 **The next time** Michael McPherson, interview with author.

348 **Between the 1970s** Organisation for Economic Co-operation and Development, "Education at a Glance 2010," p. 36, table A1.3a; Organisation for Economic Co-operation and Development, "Education at a Glance 2022: OECD Indicators," 2022, p. 199, figure B5.1.

349 **A higher share** Organisation for Economic Co-operation and Development, "Education at a Glance 2022," p. 37, figure A1.1.

349 **"What the railroads"** Grace Hechinger, "Clark Kerr, Leading Public Educator and Former Head of California's Universities, Dies at 92," *The New York Times,* December 2, 2003.

350 **"It does definitely"** Teresa Watanabe, "College Housing Shortage Pushes Students into Crisis as Most UC Classes Start Up," *Los Angeles Times,* September 26, 2022.

350 **The Obama administration** Kevin Carey, "Programs That Are Predatory: It's Not Just at For-Profit Colleges," *The New York Times,* January 13, 2017.

350 **Similarly, some states** Amy Y. Li, "Lessons Learned: A Case Study of Performance Funding in Higher Education," Third Way website, October 29, 2018.

352 **Types of Government Spending [chart]** "National Income and Product Accounts," U.S. Bureau of Economic Analysis website, tables 1.1.5 and 3.16.

352 **The United States** "Health Care Spending per Capita: Selected Health and System Statistics," The Commonwealth Fund website; "NHE Fact Sheet," Centers for Medicare & Medicaid Services website.

353 **In the early 2000s** Julia B. Isaacs, "A Comparative Perspective on Public Spending on Children," Brookings Center on Children and Families, November 2009.

353 **Mass incarceration** Leah Wang, Wendy Sawyer, Tiana Herring, and Emily Widra, "Beyond the Count: A Deep Dive into State Prison Populations," Prison Policy Initiative, April 2022.

354 **"We have a budget"** David Leonhardt, "Generational Divide Colors Debate over Medicare's Future," *The New York Times,* April 5, 2011.

355 **People could cross** "The Fast Train to 'Frisco," *Evening Star,* June 3, 1876, 2.

355 **In the 1930s** "Official Airline Guide: Worldwide Airline Schedules, Fares, and Information," *American Aviation,* July 1950; "Official Airline Guide: Worldwide Airline Schedules, Fares, and Information," *American Aviation,* October 1950; "Official Airline Guide: World Wide Timetable Edition," *American Aviation,* March 1969.

355 **The first regularly** United Press International, "Breakfast in L.A., Lunch in New York," *Redlands Daily Facts,* January 26, 1959, 1.

355 **"You look out"** Andy Newman, "Lobster on the Menu and History in the Air," *The New York Times,* January 25, 2009.

355 **In previous decades** Robert J. Gordon, *The Rise and Fall of American Growth* (Princeton, N.J.: Princeton University Press, 2016), 396–97.

355 **Airline travel** Gordon, *Rise and Fall,* 401; U.S. Department of Transportation, "U.S. Air Carrier Safety Data," Bureau of Transportation Statistics.

356 **Since the 1980s** Gordon, *Rise and Fall,* 402.

356 **It affects economic** Daniel Kahneman and Alan B. Krueger, "Developments in the Measurement of Subjective Well-Being," *Journal of Economic Perspectives* 20, no. 1 (Winter 2006): 3–24.

356 **In 1969, Metroliner** Edward Hudson, "Metroliner Discontinues Nonstop Runs," *The New York Times,* March 23, 1970, 3.

356 **In the metropolitan** Bureau of Transportation Statistics, "Travel Time Index," table 1-70.

357 **"Shinkansen fever"** Agis Salpukas, "Hideo Shima, a Designer of Japan's Bullet Train, Is Dead at 96," *The New York Times,* March 20, 1998, 42.

358 **Boeing, for example** "Boeing History Chronology," Boeing website, 6.

358 **"For the rest of what"** Gordon, *Rise and Fall,* 2.

358 **Mancur Olson** "Mancur Olson, Obituary," *The Economist,* March 5, 1998.

359 **Not only did** David Leonhardt, "The Big Fix," *The New York Times Magazine,* February 1, 2009.

359 **"We wiped the institutional slate"** Bart Barnes, "Mancur Olson Dies at 66," *The Washington Post,* February 25, 1998.

360 **Two decades ago** Gerard F. Anderson, Uwe E. Reinhardt, Peter S. Hussey, and Varduhi Petrosyan, "It's The Prices, Stupid: Why The United States Is So Different From Other Countries," *Health Affairs* 22, no. 3 (May 2003): 89–105.

360 **Olson's work helps** Ezra Klein, "The Economic Mistake the Left Is Finally Confronting," *The New York Times,* September 19, 2021; Eric Levitz, "When Supply, Not Demand, Is the Problem," *New York,* January 2, 2023.

360 **The high cost of housing** Troy Closson and Nicole Hong, "Why Black Families Are Leaving New York, and What It Means for the City," *The New York Times,* January 31, 2023.

361 **Olson gave a sweeping** Mancur Olson, *The Rise and Decline of Nations: Economic Growth, Stagflation, and Social Rigidities* (New Haven, Conn.: Yale University Press, 1982).

362 **"We want to remove"** Rolf Torstendahl, ed., *State Policy and Gender System in the Two German States and Sweden, 1945–1989* (Uppsala, Sweden: Uppsala Universitet, 2001), 15.

362 **"to assert himself"** Heidi Dorudi, "Olof Palme on the Emancipation of Man," Dorudi.nl, February 22, 2016; Olof Palme, "The Emancipation of Man," address to the Women's National Democratic Club, Washington, D.C., June 8, 1970.

362 **The system started** "Sweden's 1975 National Preschool Reform," Centre for Public Impact, June 7, 2018; Juliana Herman, Sasha Post, and Scott O'Halloran, "The United States Is Far Behind Other Countries on Pre-K," Center for American Progress, May 2, 2013; Barbara Martin Korpi, "The Politics of Preschool—Intentions and Decisions Underlying the Emergence of Growth of the Swedish Preschool," Ministry of Education and Research.

363 **In the United States** Ruth Bader Ginsburg, "Gender and the Constitution," *University of Cincinnati Law Review* 44, no. 1 (1975).

363 **Only about half** National Center for Education Statistics, "Enrollment Rates for Young Children," U.S. Department of Education, May 2022; Organisation for Economic Co-operation and Development, "Enrollment Rate in Early Childhood Education."

363 **"True pay and employment"** Claudia Goldin, *Career and Family: Women's Century-Long Journey Toward Equity* (Princeton, N.J.: Princeton University Press), 4.

363 **In one study** David Leonhardt, "A Labor Market Punishing to Mothers," *The New York Times,* August 3, 2010.

364 **To this day** Emma Hinchliffe, "Women CEOs Run More Than 10% of Fortune 500 Companies for the First Time in History," *Fortune,* January 12, 2023.

364 **The other six** Claire Cain Miller, "The World 'Has Found a Way to Do This': The U.S. Lags on Paid Leave," *The New York Times,* October 25, 2021.

364 **Today, the United States** "Women's Progress Stalls," *The New York Times,* September 24, 2013. The only high-income country with a lower female labor participation rate is Italy. Organisation for Economic Co-operation and Development, "Employment: Labour Force Participation Rate, by Sex and Age Group," OECD.stat, February 3, 2023.

364 **The notion of American exceptionalism** Alexis de Tocqueville, *Democracy in America* (Cambridge, Mass.: Sever and Francis, 1863), 42.

364 **Almost a century later** Uri Friedman, " 'American Exceptionalism': A Short History," *Foreign Policy,* June 18, 2012.

366 **"The political problem"** Zachary D. Carter, *The Price of Peace: Money, Democracy, and the Life of John Maynard Keynes* (New York: Random House, 2020), 160.

366 **American women** Munira Gunja, Evan D. Gumas, and Reginald D. Williams II, "The U.S. Maternal Mortality Crisis Continues to Worsen: An International Comparison," Commonwealth Fund website, December 1, 2022.

366 **American babies** UnitedHealth Foundation, *America's Health Rankings 2019 Annual Report,* 6.

366 **Income inequality** "Gini Index, 1967–2021," World Bank.

366 **Our opioid death rate** Jesse C. Baumgartner, "Too Many Lives Lost: Comparing Overdose Mortality Rates and Policy Solutions Across High-Income Countries," Commonwealth Fund website, May 19, 2022.

366 **Our roads are more dangerous** David Leonhardt, "America Is Now an Outlier on Driving Deaths," *The New York Times,* November 19, 2017; David Zipper, "US Traffic Safety Is Getting Worse, While Other Countries Improve," *Bloomberg,* November 3, 2022.

366 **In 1980, life expectancy** "Life Expectancy at Birth, Total (Years)," World Bank website.

Conclusion

369 **Throughout Donald Trump's presidency** David Leonhardt and Stuart E. Thompson, "Trump's Lies," *The New York Times,* December 14, 2017; David Leonhardt and Ian Prasad Philbrick, "Trump's Corruption: The Definitive List," *The New York Times,* October 28, 2019.

369 **In 2022, every major** Amy Gardner, Reis Thebault, and Robert Klemko, "Election Deniers Lose Races for Key State Offices in Every 2020 Battleground," *The Washington Post,* November 13, 2022.

370 **Franklin Roosevelt understood** Michael Kazin, *What It Took to Win: A History of the Democratic Party* (New York: Farrar, Straus and Giroux, 2022), 196.

371 **Access tends to be** David Leonhardt, "How Abortion Views Are Different," *The New York Times,* May 19, 2021; David Leonhardt, "The Politics of Abortion," *The New York Times,* June 13, 2022.

371 **In the 1990s** Justin McCarthy, "Same-Sex Marriage Support Inches Up to New High of 71%," Gallup News website, June 1, 2022.

372 **Barack Obama's presidency** Jonathan Chait, *Audacity: How Barack Obama Defied His Critics and Created a Legacy That Will Prevail* (New York: HarperCollins, 2017).

372 **"The project"** David Leonhardt, "Closing Income Gap Tops Obama's Agenda for Economic Change," *The New York Times,* February 2, 2008.

374 **That candidate would be** David Leonhardt, "Americans Aren't Centrist on Economics," *The New York Times,* April 23, 2018.

374 **This combination** "Minimum Wage on the Ballot: Outcomes of Minimum Wage Measures, 1996–2021," Ballotpedia website; "Health Care on the Ballot: Notable Health Policy Measures," Ballotpedia website.

375 **Senator Josh Hawley** "A Trust-Busting Agenda for the 21st Century," Josh Hawley website.

375 **Senator Marco Rubio** David Leonhardt, "Conservatives for Labor," *The New York Times,* September 8, 2020; Marco Rubio, "The Case for Common-Good Capitalism," *National Review,* November 13, 2019.

375 **Senator Mitt Romney** Lois M. Collins, "Romney's Proposal for a Pro-family, Pro-work and Pro-birth America," *DeseretNews,* July 28, 2022.

375 **"For the past generation"** "Charting the Course," American Compass website.

375 **Republican anti-poverty** Matt Darling, "Work Requirements and Income Requirements, Explained," Niskanen Center website, November 8, 2022.

376 **Republican politicians rely** Luis Melgar, Chris Alcantara, Isaac Stanley-Becker, Anu Narayanswamy, and Chris Zubak-Skees, "Meet the Megadonors Pumping Millions into the 2022 Midterms," *The Washington Post,* October 24, 2022.

376 **"economic royalists"** Franklin D. Roosevelt, "Acceptance Speech for the Renomination for the Presidency, Philadelphia, Pa.," June 27, 1936, American Presidency Project website.

377 **"Freedom and the dignity"** Ronald Reagan, "Inaugural Address 1981," Ronald Reagan Presidential Library and Museum website.

377 **"the civic republican"** Michael J. Sandel, *Democracy's Discontent: A New Edition for our Perilous Times* (Cambridge, Mass.: The Belknap Press, 2022), 285.

378 **It will probably** Sandel, *Democracy's Discontent,* 286.

378 **In his book** Jefferson Cowie, *The Great Exception: The New Deal and the*

Limits of American Politics (Princeton, N.J.: Princeton University Press, 2016).

379 **Friedman's book** Benjamin M. Friedman, *The Moral Consequences of Economic Growth* (New York: Random House, 2005).

379 **The share of American workers** Henry S. Farber, Daniel Herbst, Ilyana Kuziemko, and Suresh Naidu, "Unions and Inequality over the Twentieth Century: New Evidence from Survey Data," *The Quarterly Journal of Economics* 136 no. 3, pp. 1382–1385; union density data from Farber et al., "Unions and Inequality," provided to author, January 4, 2023.

379 **According to Gallup** Justin McCarthy, "U.S. Approval of Labor Unions at Highest Point Since 1965," Gallup News website, August 30, 2022.

380 **A better approach** Isabelle Gius, "Thinking Sectorally," *The American Prospect,* July 27, 2022; David Madland and Malkie Wall, "What Is Sectoral Bargaining?," Center for American Progress Action Fund website, March 2, 2020.

380 **Germany's success suggests** Simon Jäger, Shakked Noy, and Benjamin Schoefer, "The German Model of Industrial Relations: Balancing Flexibility and Collective Action" (working paper 30377, National Bureau of Economic Research, August 2022).

381 **With polls showing** Steven Greenhouse, *Beaten Down, Worked Up: The Past, Present, and Future of American Labor* (New York: Alfred A. Knopf, 2019), 232–52.

381 **Almost twenty-five states** Ben Zipperer (Economic Policy Institute), email correspondence with author, February 23, 2023.

382 **The country's most affluent** David Leonhardt, "What's the Matter with Scarsdale?," *The New York Times,* November 4, 2021; Alice Park, Charlie Smart, Rumsey Taylor, and Miles Watkins, "An Extremely Detailed Map of the 2020 Election," *The New York Times,* updated March 30, 2022.

382 **But the meme** James Wolcott, "The 'Left Behind' Trump Voter Has Nothing More to Tell Us," *Vanity Fair,* September 7, 2018.

383 **I think that a soda tax** David Leonhardt, "Sodas a Tempting Tax Target," *The New York Times,* May 19, 2009; David Leonhardt, "The Battle over Taxing Soda," *The New York Times,* May 18, 2009.

383 **But I also know** Sarah Kliff, "A New Poll Shows Why It's So Hard to Pass a Soda Tax," *Vox,* May 6, 2016.

384 **The most intense version** Gregory Downs, "The S.F. School Board Renaming Attempt Was a Disaster. It Can Still Be Done Right," *San Francisco Chronicle,* February 25, 2022.

384 **In a recent poll** "September 2022 Times/Siena Poll: Cross-Tabs for Hispanic and Latino Respondents," *The New York Times,* September 18, 2022.

385 **"All of America's great"** Nelson Lichtenstein, *State of the Union: A Century of American Labor* (Princeton, N.J.: Princeton University Press, 2002), 34–35.

386 **"millionaires who don't pay"** David Leonhardt, "How Biden Thinks," *The New York Times,* February 20, 2023.

387 **Today's version** "NCSL State Elections 2022," National Conference of State Legislatures, December 15, 2022; Drew Desilver, "U.S. Senate Has Fewest

Split Delegations Since Direct Elections Began," Pew Research Center, February 11, 2021.

387 **And demographic change** David Leonhardt, "Asian Americans, Shifting Right," *The New York Times,* March 6, 2023.

387 **The past decade** Nicholas Bagley, "The Procedure Fetish," *Michigan Law Review* 118, no. 3 (2019): 345–401; Lina M. Khan, "Amazon's Antitrust Paradox," *The Yale Law Journal* 126, no. 3 (2017): 710–805; Ezra Klein, "The Economic Mistake the Left is Finally Confronting," *The New York Times,* September 19, 2021; Tim Wu, *The Curse of Bigness: Antitrust in the New Gilded Age* (New York: Columbia Global Reports, 2018).

390 **"the submerged state"** Suzanne Mettler, *The Submerged State: How Invisible Government Policies Undermine American Democracy* (Chicago: University of Chicago Press, 2011).

391 **The headline read** "What President Roosevelt Did to the Map of the U.S. in Four Years with $6,500,000,000," *Life,* January 4, 1937, 30–31.

391 **As the economist** Thomas Piketty, *Capital in the Twenty-First Century,* trans. Arthur Goldhammer (Cambridge, Mass.: Belknap Press of Harvard University Press, 2014).

392 **No constitutional amendment** Jill Lepore, "The United States' Unamendable Constitution," *The New Yorker,* October 26, 2022.

392 **No new state** David Leonhardt, "The Senate: Affirmative Action for White People," *The New York Times,* October 14, 2018.

392 **The Constitution, in addition to giving** David Leonhardt, "Defying the Supreme Court," *The New York Times,* August 4, 2022.

393 **Obama's law** Jonathan Cohn, *The Ten Year War: Obamacare and the Unfinished Crusade for Universal Coverage* (New York: Macmillan, 2021).

393 **Even though Republicans controlled** David Leonhardt, "The Americans Who Saved Health Insurance," *The New York Times,* August 1, 2017.

PHOTOGRAPH PERMISSIONS

INDEX

Page numbers of illustrations appear in italics.

© DOUG MILLS

David Leonhardt is a senior writer at *The New York Times,* where he writes its flagship newsletter, "The Morning." He has also been the newspaper's Washington bureau chief, an op-ed columnist, and a staff writer for the *Times Magazine.* He has won the Pulitzer Prize for commentary. This is his first book.